John Lewis-Stempel is the author of numerous anthologies and books on military history. He lives on a farm in Herefordshire with his wife and two children.

By John Lewis-Stempel

Fatherhood: An Anthology

England: The Autobiography

The Autobiography of the British Soldier

The Wild Life

Six Weeks: The Short and Gallant Life
of the British Officer in the First World War

SIX WEEKS

The Short and Gallant Life of the
British Officer in the First World War

John Lewis-Stempel

An Orion paperback

First published in Great Britain in 2010
by Weidenfeld & Nicolson
This paperback edition published in 2011
by Orion Books Ltd,
Orion House, 5 Upper St Martin's Lane,
London WC2H 9EA

An Hachette UK company

1 3 5 7 9 10 8 6 4 2

A CIP catalogue record for this book
is available from the British Library.

ISBN 978-1-4091-0214-4

Typeset by Input Data Services Ltd, Bridgwater, Somerset

Printed and bound in Great Britain by
CPI Group (UK) Ltd, Croydon, CRO 4YY

The Orion Publishing Group's policy is to use papers that
are natural, renewable and recyclable products and
made from wood grown in sustainable forests. The logging
and manufacturing processes are expected to conform to
the environmental regulations of the country of origin.

www.orionbooks.co.uk

Contents

List of Illustrations

Schoolboys at Eton College playing the Wall Game. (Mary Evans Picture Library)

An officer leads a contingent of the Officers' Training Corps on a march at Mytchett Camp, Surrey, 1910. (Mary Evans Picture Library)

Uppingham schoolboys Edward Brittain, Roland Leighton and Victor Richardson at OTC camp. (The Vera Brittain Estate and William Ready Division of Archives and Research Collections, McMaster University, Hamilton, Canada)

Anthony Eden at Aldershot, 1915, aged 18. (Getty Images)

Territorial Captain Lionel Crouch (Private collection)

Students from Cambridge University's Officer Training Corps have their rifles inspected at Mytchett Camp, Summer 1914. (Imperial War Museum)

Led by a sergeant instructor, officer cadets – distinguished by their white hat bands – take a riding lesson at Aldershot. (Imperial War Museum)

Officers finishing their leave say goodbye to their wives and family at Charing Cross. (Imperial War Museum)

British officers travelling by rail in France. (Mary Evans Picture Library)

Officers tossing a colleague in a blanket on board ship, 1915. (Getty Images)

Second Lieutenant F. Forrester Agar and his bride Majorie Laird Collins, June 1917. (Getty Images)

A pillow fight at the Guards Division Sports Day at Bavincourt, June 1918. (Imperial War Museum)

British troops receive hot stew in the trenches near Cambrai. (Mary Evans Picture Library)

Members of a wiring party set out to lay new wire. (Getty Images)

Officers of the 12/East Yorkshire Regiment wash and shave in a dug-out near Roclincourt. (Imperial War Museum)

An officer of the Royal Field Artillery feeds his pet duck outside a dug-out in Salonika. (Imperial War Museum)

British infantry officers observe and mark the enemy's movements on a map at Pilckem Ridge, Belgium, 1917. (Mary Evans Picture Library)

Officers wade through mud in a trench near St. Quentin, 1917. (Getty Images)

A doctor dresses the wounds of Lieutenant Guy Morgan, Irish Guards, at a Regimental Aid Post at Pilckem Ridge, 1917. (Imperial War Museum)

The Officers' Quarters at Rastatt prisoner of war camp, near Karlsruhe, Germany. (Imperial War Museum)

Officers of the 1st Royal West Kent Regiment pose for their picture a day before their attack on Hill 60, 1915. (Courtesy of The Princess of Wales Royal Regiment)

Cartoon from *The Wipers Times*: 'Am I Offensive Enough?' (Author's collection)

Officer POWs captured during the Dardenelles campaign. (Mary Evans Picture Library)

A wounded British soldier making his first attempt to walk with artificial legs. (Mary Evans Picture Library)

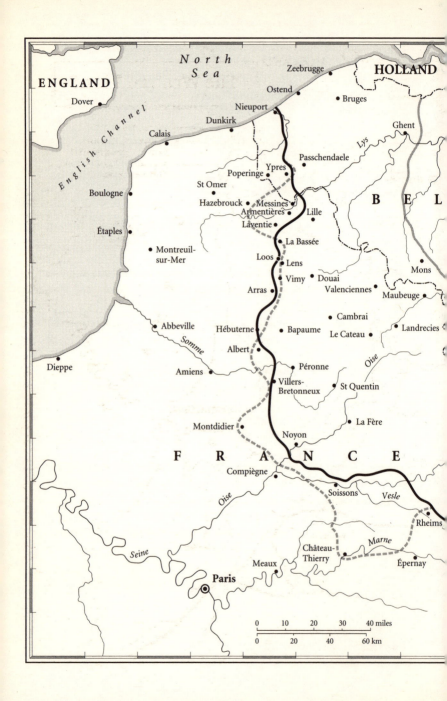

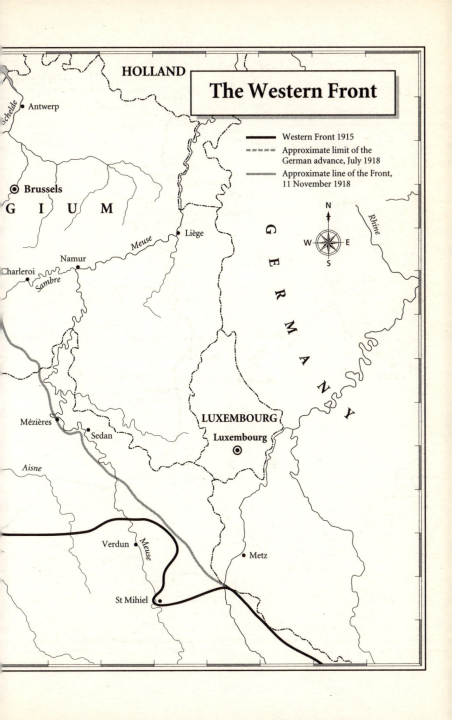

Note on Terminology in the Text

Where individuals are identified by rank, the rank stated is that held by the individual at the time. Where battalions are identified, I have generally rendered 2nd Battalion Royal Welch Fusiliers as 2/Royal Welch Fusiliers and so on.

Prologue: The Subaltern

It was odd, he thought, as he leant against the wet trench side, how the flecks of chalk lumined in the dark. Nearby one of his men coughed, and he was reminded of the cows in the winter-darkened sheds on his father's farm, the cattle's hacking expulsions as they chomped through the dusty hay. What would his father be doing at 5.54 on a November morning? Standing, he supposed, under the stable porch, much as he did every morning, telling Tomson the bailiff the jobs to be done by the men that day. He wished that he was there, in the untroubled English countryside.

Instead he faced the coming light in France. And the light was now definitely coming; he could see the first smear of grey in the eastern sky. He checked his watch for the umpteenth time. The minute hand had turned a full revolution; he could not linger any longer. A deep breath, and he began walking with leaden legs along the greasy duck-boards in the trench bottom; the men were standing sentinel-stiff along the fire-step, their bayonets fixed to their rifles. He had been tempted to make a speech but doubted whether he could, in the circumstances, emulate his performance as Henry V in the School's production of the Shakespeare history. Was it only six months ago that he had still been at School? No oratory then, but a quiet encouraging word to each white face of the platoon as it loomed out of the dark. A refrain of 'Good luck to you too, Sir', was whispered back. For young Haddon he had a joke: 'With that ugly mug, Haddon, you don't need a rifle – one look at you and the Germans will run for it.' Such bally bad jokes he told! But everyone laughed under their steaming breath, glad to have their mind taken off the duty of the morning. And for Manning, there was a reassuring adjustment of the helmet, Manning who was old enough to be his father.

At the far end of his section, he shook hands with Corporal Probert, and told him to make sure any malingerers came along with the rest. A clerk in a Monmouthshire colliery, Probert was the same age as himself, nineteen, but with creases of work already around his eyes. His conversations with Probert about the pit and its surrounding terraced houses, he realized, had opened up a country as foreign to him as France itself. A good chap Probert; they had been – were – a good team. Over the last weeks he had caught the corporal watching him like a hawk, not harshly, to criticize, but benignly, to learn. Front-line battalions used up public school subalterns by the score and very soon they would have to start commissioning men like Probert, even if they didn't have pukka manners; he'd suggested Probert for a commission to the CO only yesterday morning.

Making his skidding way back along the trench, he heard behind him one of the men murmur, 'That young Mr Lewes, he's a cool one. We could do with a few more officers like him.'

If only they knew how the fear was drying his mouth!

Someone lurched out in front of him: 'I can't do it, I'm ill, I'm ill.' Reeves.

'We've been over this Reeves. The MO says there's nothing wrong with you. You're going over with everyone else.' He kept his voice low; there was no sense in alerting the Germans a hundred yards away on the other side of the tangled wire forest of No-Man's Land.

Reeves came closer, his eyes wild and wide, and was about to blurt out something more when the officer interrupted, 'I'll shoot you myself if you don't pipe down and go over with the rest.'

Someone said: 'You tell him, Sir.'

Reeves backed away, cursing, into the shadow wall of the trench.

The subaltern finished his last walk up and down the platoon, and resumed his position in the centre. Another look at the watch. It was now 5.59 on the 13th November 1916 in the Somme Valley.

What time is it, Sir?

Obsessive asking about time, matched only by his obsessive watch-watching.

He surreptitiously took the flask out of his pocket; he had already given the men their tot of rum. The whisky obliterated the trench's stink of fear and damp, and comforted as it burned down to his gullet. Gosh it was cold, even with the whisky. Anxiously, he touched his tunic pocket, where he kept the photograph of his parents and sister inside Horace's *Odes*. He had left a letter to his family, 'Only to be Opened in the Event of My Death', with the Adjutant. Along with the letter were his sketches of birds on the Somme; last week he had seen a snow bunting in No-Man's Land.

Only seconds now ... At 6.05 exactly the guns opened up, and shell upon shell roared overhead onto the German front line. The earth moved and moaned. So awesome was the din that he found it, curiously, a suppressant of his anxiety and not an intensifier. He lit a Woodbine cigarette with exaggerated calm, the flaming match illuminating his face, aware of the eyes of the men upon him.

Oh God, he prayed inaudibly, please help me to be brave, for the men's sake, for my family's sake, for the School's sake.

At 6.10 on the dot, he blew hard on his whistle and shouted, 'Follow me!' Then he was scrambling up the pegs on the slick side of the trench, over the sandbags on top of the parapet and out onto the grey land above. It felt naked to be in the open; German bullets zipped around him, spurting up divots of earth. Crouching slightly, he started walking forwards, and as he did so euphoria washed over him – the bullets were not hitting him. Glancing left, he could see the men clambering over and coming on – oh, well done, you plucky boys. 'Keep steady!' His words were drowned in the steel rain, but it didn't matter – they could see him. He was setting the example. 'Come on, boys, forward!' It was quite like the lumbering charge of the rugby pack at school ...

We know what happened next, not from him but from the men he led, and the Regimental war diary. The officer was as cool as a cucumber, the men said, and just trotted towards the Hun, despite the mud and all that they were chucking at him (so much for the artillery barrage!), popping off his pistol. It was bedlam out there. But the men could do nothing but follow in his wake. It was infectious: one did it, then another ... till the whole platoon was going forward.

The officer reached the wire, and seeing a gap shouted, 'Through here, men!' Probably, there was a better gap to the left of the section's line, but sometimes any firm decision is all the decision required. He stood there, waving the men through – and that's when the Hun got him. He spun around like a top. Corporal Probert and another soldier got to him through the smoke and shells, and picking him up a shoulder apiece dragged him back to the trench.

Bundling him down, he was lain on the fire-step. Probert screamed, 'Get the stretcher bearers'. Someone tore the field dressing out of his tunic and tried to stem the frothing blood that was pumping out through his chest.

He was pale and, a funny thing for men to say, he looked quite beautiful lying there.

There was more shouting for the stretcher bearers, but everyone knew there was no chance. Not with froth from the chest. He was groaning very slightly, and then said, clear as a bell, 'You shouldn't have bothered about me ... Tell the men to stick at it.'

'It's okay Sir,' said Probert. 'Most of the men got through the wire and joined up with Mr Cadwallader's platoon.'

There was one more thing the officer said, and it was said very softly. Corporal Probert had to lean right over him to hear it. He told Probert to let Uppingham know that he did all right. The corporal supposed it was the village that the lieutenant came from.

It was only when Probert told the story to the captain later that he understood that Uppingham was Lewes' school.

Second Lieutenant Gerald Lewes, 10/ Royal Welch Fusiliers, was awarded a posthumous mention in dispatches for his gallantry on that dull Somme morning.

His platoon, together with the remnants of Mr Cadwallader's, took the enemy trench to their front. When they discovered that Mr Lewes was dead, some of his men cried. He'd been such a kind young gentleman, slipping them cigarettes, making them tea on night sentry duty, and always smiling. Once, he had crept out into No-Man's Land to take some boots off a dead German to give to Manning, whose own had sprung a split as wide as a cavern.

*

Second Lieutenant Lewes was a nearly perfect statistic. He had lasted six weeks and four days on the front line: the average time a British Army junior officer survived during the Western Front's bloodiest phases was six weeks.

Introduction

The trenches of the First World War are now almost impossible to reach. It is not just that those excavations on the plains of Flanders and the Somme are buried under the plough of the farmer and the grass of time, it is that they are surrounded by a moat deep with the pitying tears of the war poets. Across the lachrymose ditch though, some definite khaki figures loom: there is the heroic, cheerful Tommy and the sclerotic, incompetent general. Much less distinct is the junior officer, who seems to be either composing exquisite pacifist poems in the manner of Wilfred Salter Owen, or braying stupidly. When the historian (and bon viveur) Alan Clark conjured the phrase 'lions led by donkeys' in the 1960s to describe the relationship between the Rankers and Officers in the Great War, the Officers he had in mind were the red-tabbed generals in chateaux, but down the decades, the sentiment has come to cover the platoon and company commanders in the trenches. The proof positive came with the arrival on TV of the dismally dim – if side-splittingly funny – Lieutenant The Honourable George Colthurst St Barleigh in *Black Adder Goes Forth*, who wants to give 'Harry Hun a darn good British style thrashing, six of the best, trousers down'.

There is worse than caricature. There is extinction. Sometimes the junior officer cannot be glimpsed at all. It is quite possible to pick up a modern school textbook on the Great War and find that the frontline British officer merits not a mention.

Contrast all of the above with one single line from the Great War memoir of Private Burrage, no particular admirer of officers: ' ... I who was a private, and a bad one at that, freely own that it was the British subaltern who won the war'.[1]

Private Burrage hardly exaggerated. A subaltern or second lieutenant was the most junior commissioned officer, in charge of a platoon of about fifty men. Above him was the lieutenant and the captain. It was these three ranks that led at platoon and company level in the trenches. Together they were the single most important factor in Britain's victory on the Western Front. They led gallantly in battle, the first over the top, the last to retreat – and as a result suffered something like a holocaust. One young subaltern, J.R.R. Tolkien, found that 'By 1918 all but one of my close friends were dead'.[2] As Captain Robert Graves – another soldier who made a post-war literary reputation – noted: 'A soldier who had the honour to serve with one of the better divisions . . . could count on no more than three months' trench service before being wounded or killed; a junior officer, a mere six weeks'.[3]

In some months of the Great War, the casualty rate amongst junior officers was more than double that of 'Other Ranks.'[4] Usually, these junior officers were more than junior in rank; they were junior in age, as young as seventeen. Still, for all their callow years they had the responsibilities of command.

Junior officers came, initially at least, from a very thin stratum of British society. Almost all were volunteers from public schools, or occasionally a well-established grammar school. When August 1914 came the values of the public school were exactly what the country at war needed. After all, who could withstand the highly drilled militarism of the Kaiser's Army – except for a corps of young British men who believed in the qualities of courage, patriotism, selfless service, leadership and character? Wellington allegedly quipped that Waterloo was won on the playing fields of Eton. Indisputably the First World War was part won in the classrooms, fields, and Officers' Training Corps parade grounds of the public schools.

The martial and patriotic spirit of the Edwardian and Georgian public schools dismays contemporary historians and culturati; on feeling obliged to include Captain Julian Grenfell's warrior song 'Into Battle' in *Anthem for Doomed Youth*, his anthology of First World War poetry, John Stallworthy opined that the Old Etonian's poem was 'horrifying' and illustrated 'the hypnotic power of a long cultural tradition, the tragic outcome of educating a generation to face not the future but the past'.[5] Peter Parker made much the same claim about

Edwardian public school education in book length in *The Old Lie*,[6] a reference to Owen's lines, 'My friend you would not tell with such high zest/To children ardent for some desperate glory/The old lie; Dulce et decorum est/ Pro patria mori'. (The Latin tag, from Horace, means 'It is sweet and right to die for one's country.') All this is 180 degrees south of the magnetic truth; a generation educated to face the past would have been steeped in the solipsistic 'values' of Regency fops and not altruistically prepared to lay down their lives for others in an epochal crisis. And any teenage boy who thought it positively glorious to die for his country between 1914 and 1918 was a singular bird indeed, but tens of thousands, after holding the matter to the light and turning it around, thought it might be necessary and even honourable. In the words of Lieutenant H.E.L. Mellersh: 'I and my like entered the war expecting an heroic adventure and believing implicitly in the rightness of our cause; we ended greatly disillusioned as to the nature of the adventure, but still believing that our cause was right and we had not fought in vain.'[7]

'Our cause was right.' Mellersh wrote his memoir *Schoolboy into War* in 1978, by which time the popular view of the Great War as anything other than an unending tragedy was fifty years lost. Poor junior officers: not only duped, silly boys, lambs to the slaughter (runs the prevailing opinion), but oh!, what an unlovely war they fought in – a war that was a hopeless attritional conflict caused by a few great European men falling out, and so much less noble than the freewheeling struggle against fascism that was the Good War of 1939–45.

The First World War was a tragedy, because all wars are; only a man or woman with stone for a heart can fail to find tears welling when they stand at the little cemetery of the Devonshires by Mametz Wood. But, the age-influencing 'pity of war' poems of Owen and Sassoon aside, the First World War was no bigger a tragedy than the Second, which was just as much a war of attrition – however, conveniently for the British, the 'attriting' was done out of sight on the Eastern Front.

The parallels between the World Wars extend to their origins. In 1961, in a quiet ivory tower of German academia, an historian built an explosive mine which was detonated as *Griff nach der Weltmacht: Die*

8

Kriegzielspolitik der Kaiserlichen Deutschland 1914–1918.[8] With handfuls of documentary evidence, Dr Fritz Fischer showed persuasively that a reactionary German elite used the crisis caused by the assassination of Archduke Franz Ferdinand to carry out long-held plans for the creation of a German-dominated *Mitteleuropa* and *Mittelafrika*. In other words, Germany caused the First World War. It got worse; so similar were the 'Lebensraum' and racist designs of 1914 and 1939, that Fischer dubbed the Imperial German Chancellor, Dr Theobald von Bethmann Hollweg, 'The Hitler of 1914'. The Germany of the Kaiser and the Fuhrer were different only in degree; the Kaiser's troops committed war crimes – the deliberate shooting of 6,500 French and Belgian civilians, enslaving of conquered peoples – with a savagery their SS descendants would have appreciated. The Great War was just as much a moral crusade as the Second World War. The Germany of the Kaiser was a right-wing military dictatorship bent on the subjugation of Europe. In order to preserve her independence and the liberties of others, Britain was right to fight. All that we have, and all the freedoms we hold dear, are because of the sacrifice of the thin khaki line of 1914–18, led by their junior officers.

After spending two years in the ghosts of their company, I find it hard not to like and admire the young officers of the 1914–18 vintage. They were golden and rare. They pleasantly sabotage stereotypes. A quite extraordinary number of them were, indeed, poets, but the despairing, hand-wringing Sassoon and Owen were not typical of them. (Actually, whether Owen's and Sassoon's anti-war poems were representative of themselves is a fair query; after treatment for shell-shock at Craiglockhart Hospital both willingly returned to active service, Owen to win a Military Cross for machine-gunning Germans and Sassoon to positively enjoy 'a St Martin's summer' [his words] as a warrior, before going on to write pro-war poetry in 1939.) Meanwhile, some of the seemingly loudest and 'hearty' of officers proved to have unending hinterlands.

It is an almost unwritten rule of the Great War that it must have no heroes, because that would spoil the myth of the war as one of pitiable, conned victims. But young Second Lieutenant Robin Kestell-Cornish rallying his men, amid gas and a German attack, to hold the line at Ypres was a hero. So was Second Lieutenant Alfred Pollard who, with three men, led a desperate counter-attack into the German trenches at Gavrelle in 1917, a deed for which he won the VC. There were thousands like them. The sheer, smiling bravery of junior officers in the face of death, especially in the grinding, pivotal battle of the Somme, left an indelible memory for many of their fellow soldiers.[9] And yet, the inspirational bravery of junior officers and their intelligence in adversity, when they frequently found themselves cut off from HQ, are not the ultimate reasons for the claim that the British junior officer won the war. Long before the Beatles, British officers of the Great War realized that all you needed was love. As Second Lieutenant Adams was told by a fellow 'sub' in the Royal Welch Fusiliers as they sat around in their billets at Morlancourt on the Somme in 1916, 'You know as well as I do, Bill, the only way to run a company is by love'.[10] By looking after the men in the trenches, junior officers made the lives of the men in the trenches bearable. On his way to the Somme subaltern Max Plowman reminded himself: 'If I can mitigate the hardness of their – the men's – lot, that's my job.'[11] Thus was morale amongst the ranks maintained, even through the dog months of Passchendaele and the German Spring Offensive of 1918.

The chivalric values of the junior officers trickled down. When the army began commissioning men from the ranks, because a whole generation of public schoolboys had all but been wiped out by 1917, these promoted rankers took on the attitudes and attributes of the public school boys they replaced. They became caring gentlemen as well as plucky officers. Their time in the trenches too was valiant and short, curtailed by death or wounding.

But frontline officers lived as well as died, or went to a convalescent bed in a hospital. They had dreams and fears, they played practical jokes and listened to nightingales in No-Man's Land, they had dinner parties in their dug-outs and shot rats for sport, they read Palgrave's *Golden Treasury* and wrote staggeringly literate letters home, they customized their uniforms and they prayed and prayed that they might be brave. They lit up the darkness like flares.

This is the war the officers knew.

I

Hello To All This:
School and Joining Up

'I hope we're lucky and get a youngster straight from school. They're the kind that do best.'

R.C. Sherriff, ex-captain in the East Surrey Regiment
and author of *Journey's End*, 1928

July 14, 1914. Speech Day at Uppingham School: a day that would be preserved in literary autobiographical amber by Vera Brittain in *Testament of Youth*. Brittain, then twenty and about to go up to Oxford, attended Speech Day by invitation of her younger brother, Edward, but her reasons for going to Rutland on that glorious honey-suckled summer weekend were not confined to sisterly love. She had already begun the flirtation with Edward's friend Roland Leighton which would lead to their engagement.

Behind Roland Leighton's imposing broad forehead – and even the smitten Brittain described him as 'powerful looking rather than handsome' – was a colossal brain. Almost nineteen, with a scholarship to Merton College, Oxford, already under his belt, Leighton was departing Uppingham with seven school prizes: a record. Leighton himself was as proud of his other great distinction at Uppingham. He was Colour-Sergeant of the School's Officers' Training Corps. Colour-Sergeant was the highest rank a boy could obtain in the Uppingham OTC.

As a result of R.B. Haldane's Army Reforms of 1907, the Officers' Training Corps had been introduced into the universities, public schools and some grammar schools as a way of preparing for the war against Germany that many feared was coming. Haldane's OTCs, which reorganized the existing schools' corps (themselves the off-spring of the 1850s Rifle Volunteer movement), did what they said on the label: they trained public schoolboys to become army officers. Successful cadets in the junior, or school, division earned a Certificate A, a basic qualification in military know-how; in the senior division, university students could achieve a Certificate B, which fitted them for a Territorial commission as platoon leader. By 1911 there were 153 schools with OTCs, and in the majority of the schools 'the Corps' was compulsory.

There was always an air of 'playing soldiers' about school OTCs, and S.P.B. Mais at Sherborne considered the School's OTC as 'a piffling waste of time'.[1] Even so, many of the schools' OTCs trained their boys effectively and realistically. Monmouth School, a minor public school foundation in Wales, which had a cadet corps modelled on the OTC but affiliated to the county regiment, the Monmouthshires (under Army order 233), reported on its Field Day of October 1912:

> At 1.10 sharp the Corps paraded and ammunition was served out to each member to the extent of 25 rounds. Captain Pearson had previously explained the idea of the ensuing manoeuvres. A convoy, under the protection of a division consisting of the School House, County Boys and band, commanded by Lieut. Edwards, was to make its way from the Staunton Road to Hadnock Road. The remainder of the Corps, under the command of colour-sergeant Buchanan, was to seize the convoy by means of an ambush or otherwise ... For the ambush, Sergt. Buchanan made an excellent attempt, but was outflanked, and finally driven from his strong central point of opposition.[2]

Four years later as a lieutenant in the South Wales Borderers Angus Buchanan won the Victoria Cross. He had already sewn a Military Cross and Bar onto his uniform.

Monmouth School Cadet Corps placed great stress on marksmanship, which was practised almost daily. At Uppingham no one was allowed to take part in any inter-house athletic or sporting contest, or win a school prize, without first passing the OTC shooting test.

For every school OTC the highlight of the calendar was the Summer Camp, which was conducted on the same lines as the instruction classes for young officers. At a joint camp held between Cheltenham College and Sedbergh School OTCs:

The programme of work included drill, tactics, map-reading and sketching, semaphore, musketry and bayonet fighting.

Lectures were followed by practical work in the field. The party, which numbered forty-eight, was divided into four sections, and each section was in turn divided into two syndicates – each section and syndicate being under a commander or leader.

Reveille sounded at 6 a.m., early parade followed at 7–15, and most of us found forty-five minutes' drill an excellent appetiser for breakfast.

The morning (9 a.m.–1p.m.) was divided between lectures and practical work; the afternoon (2p.m.–5p.m.) was generally given to practical work, and was followed by an evening lecture (8–9) . . .

As the course progressed, each cadet was given opportunities of giving instruction and carrying out drill (with ropes).

In semaphore and map-reading there was a more advanced course for those who had some previous knowledge of the subjects.

The tactical schemes brought welcome freedom, and gave us fine opportunities of seeing a splendid country . . . At the place of assembly the general idea was propounded, and syndicates were then told off to various points to answer questions and deal with problems arising from the situation.

The subjects dealt with included occupation of a defensive position, outposts, advance-guards, advance in savage warfare, and an attack practice.[3]

Summer camps and field days were invariably successful in boosting *esprit de corps*; after a field day at Marlborough in 1913 Charles Sorley wrote, 'We go away thinking each of us personally is the smartest member of the smartest corps in the world.'

Haldane's OTC scheme was intended to attract boys of the 'intellectual and moral attainment likely to fit them for the rank of officers'. For Haldane and his biodeterministic age, public schoolboys had these attributes by virtue of their breeding. They were upper class: therefore they were born to lead. As Lieutenant-General Sir Frederick Hamilton had so pithily written in *Origins and History of the First or Grenadier Guards* in 1874:

The soldier in his hour of need and danger will ever be more ready to follow the officer and gentleman whom education, position in life, and accident of birth point out to be his natural leader ... than the man who, by dint of study and brain work, has raised himself (much to his own credit, certainly) from the plough or anvil.[4]

The programme of the OTC was, in a sense, merely gilding the lily. Such was Haldane's assumption. It was almost entirely wrong. Only in one respect did blood make the officer; fee-paying public schoolboys in Edwardian Britain were on average five inches taller than their state-educated fellows, and generally healthier; a pre-war survey of Cambridge undergraduates (who were almost exclusively former public schoolboys) found that 70 per cent of them were Grade I physical fitness; in Britain as a whole, only about 34 per cent of the male population was in that category.[5] The bread-and-margarine diet that damned the industrial workers to stunted growth damned them to disease; in Leeds in 1904, medical authorities recorded that 50 per cent of school children were suffering from rickets. Physical fitness, of course, was the indispensable condition for being a warrior leader.

In truth, the British public schools were not congregations of boys of good breeding. Outside of Eton, Harrow and Winchester, few of the 150 or so Edwardian schools in the Headmasters' Conference – membership of which constituted the definition of public school status – drew their intake from the aristocracy, or even the cream of the landed gentry. The prospective parents clamouring at the wrought iron gates or oaken door were the professional classes – doctors, army and navy officers – and successful businessmen. They were men like Vera and Edward Brittain's father, Thomas, the director of a paper mill, and Roland Leighton's father, Robert, the literary editor of the *Daily Mail*. Manufacturers like Thomas Brittain and savvy professionals like Robert Leighton understood almost instinctively that public schools engineered a product: in went boys from trade, out came gentlemen. Public schools had performed the same function for 600 years[6] and, in a sense, Great Britain was the very model of social mobility. All one needed was money. Many an Edwardian gent in a country house was only a generation or two away from the counting house via Charterhouse. Haldane was correct to identify the public schools and the grammar schools which imitated them as the key repository of potential army officers. But the material he liked wasn't raw; it was made.

Uppingham and the other public schools of Britain made gentlemen and officers rather well. Since the reforms of the educationalist Dr Thomas Arnold (1795–1842) at Rugby – whose reign was immortalized in *Tom Brown's Schooldays* – public schools no longer mechanically imparted knowledge by rote learning. Boys were to become true and thinking scholars. They were also to become Christian gentlemen, who felt responsible for others, were loyal to their side, were knightly fighters for right, were healthy in body and mind, and suffered hardships, like the Lord himself, without complaint. Edward Thring, the headmaster of Uppingham between 1853 and 1887, defined 'muscular Christianity' in a nutshell:

The learning to be responsible and independent, to bear pain, to drop rank and wealth and luxury is a priceless boon ... with all their faults the public schools are the cause of this manliness.[7]

The public schools had, in addition to the OTC, a triumvirate of means by which the warrior Christian gentleman was cultivated. Sport. Curriculum. Chapel.

At Uppingham, rigorous athleticism was the order of the day, every day. Some boys complained, most did not, but almost all became fit. The elders of Sparta would have understood the stress on cold showers and cross country runs. Sedbergh's school song even required boy athletes to 'laugh at pain'. When the public schoolboys of England – as Britain was universally called in those far-off days – went soldiering between 1914 and 1918, many found the army regime of Physical Training (PT) and route marches a relative breeze after school.[8] Stuart Graham, who attended Lancing, considered the regime there so harsh that war was actually preferable, adding, 'If it [public school] doesn't break them [the boys], it makes them. It only breaks the weaklings and the artists.'[9] Sport, however, was concerned with more than strength and stamina. Sport was, and is, the continuation of war and hunting by other means. The javelin, discus, archery, boxing, polo are all obvious in their bloody origins, yet every sport has residual DNA from its past purpose in training a man for war. Even cricket. After all, what is the bat but a shield? At their most elementary, ball games teach the hand-eye coordination necessary for the aiming of weapons. To play sports was to learn, in an attenuated manner, the skills of combat.

More, much more than all this, sport in the form of team games was widely assumed in the nineteenth and twentieth centuries to create the 'character' required for leadership. In March 1915, the *Eton College Chronicle* reminded its readers via the leader 'The School at War':

> it is not mere training in the principles of war which makes a really useful officer in the British Army, but something else is required which cannot be got from the closest study of military books alone, but which, it is said, is especially inculcated by an ordinary Eton education, so that critics who think that Eton, in these days, gives to athletics greater prominence than they deserve, must remember that the battle of Waterloo was won in the playing fields and not the parade grounds of Eton, and that while we seem most careless we are most preparing ourselves for the great duty which lies before us as soon as we leave the School.[10]

In all probability, Eton's most famous military son, the Duke of Wellington, did not claim that Waterloo was won on the lush water meadows alongside the Thames.[11] The *Eton College Chronicle* was correct, however, in matching sports with military victory. Team sports taught discipline, the sublimating of the individual to the needs of the group, confidence in companions. By enabling boys to take decisions on the sports field, it was understood that they would be able to make decisions on the battlefield. In sports, boys took risks and disregarded personal safety, all good lessons for when they grew up to be soldiers. (Team ball games also developed the subtle arts and senses of deployment, spatial awareness, momentum, each as useful on the warfield as on the rugger and soccer pitch.) Clearly, team captains learned to lead. No less than Field Marshal Douglas Haig stated in 1919 that team games needed 'decision and character on the part of the leaders, discipline and unselfishness among the led, and initiative and self-sacrifice on the part of all'.[12] Not quite the imprimatur of Wellington, but not so far off either.

Team games bred loyalty. House games in school birthed loyalty to the house; school games against other schools bred loyalty to the school. So intense was the loyalty of an Edwardian public schoolboy that, as a soldier, his school could be in his uppermost thoughts when death waited on the horizon. As a lieutenant in the Sherwood Foresters in March 1916, Edward Brittain wrote to his sister from France: 'Promise me one thing – that, should I die also, you will nevertheless go down to Uppingham . . . and see those chapel walls and the Lodge and the Upper VIth Class room where we all sat so often'.[13]

Uppingham was far from unique in creating such fidelity amongst its boys. Geoffrey Thurlow, a friend of Edward Brittain who attended Chigwell School in Essex, wrote in a final letter from France in April 1917 as he waited for the action at Monchy-le-Preux in which he would be killed by snipers: 'I only hope I don't fail at the critical moment as truly I am a horrible coward: wish I could do well especially for the School's sake'.[14] As a 'Town Major' in France, a sort of glorified billeting officer, Thurlow took to sentimentally re-naming streets after his school, to cheer up any Old Chigwellians passing through. If anything the devotion of Lionel Sotheby, killed in action in 1915, to Eton College was greater yet. In a letter to be opened in the event of his death, he wrote:

> To my Parents, School, dear Friends, and Brother:
> These few words are meant to embody a farewell . . . In bidding farewell, I feel no remorse, as indeed I have been resigned to the future paved out for me by One who knows best . . . Eton will be to the last the same as my Parents and dear Friends are to me . . . To die for one's school is an honour . . . [15]

Another Etonian, Henry Dundas, wrote that in his officers' mess in France in 1917: 'We talk pure Eton the whole time. Most of the Etonians here, John Dwyer, Budget, V.C., all left too young to know of its true greatness – which was like nothing else on earth.'[16] The war not withstanding, Etonians on the Western Front gathered every Glorious Fourth of June to celebrate Founders Day with a lively dinner; Etonians in the Rifle Brigade once topped off the celebration by launching 'anti-German fireworks.'

Noel Hodgson wrote 'Ave – Atque Vale' about Durham School:

From her full breast we drank of joy and mirth
And gave to her a boy's unreasoned heart. [17]

Heart-deep loyalty to a school was easiest to build at a boarding establishment, where a boy lived apart from his biological relatives. The *alma mater* became the boy's new family. Robert Graves, who attended Charterhouse, observed: 'School life becomes the reality, and home life the illusion. In England, parents of the governing classes virtually lose all intimate touch with their children from about the age of eight ... '.[18] Like a 'nourishing mother' indeed, a school admired and supported her children after they had departed the school gates. She would do so especially when her sons were at war. When the death of Lieutenant R. Courtenay Woodhouse was listed in the *Eton College Chronicle* the obituary concluded: 'He loved Eton and Oxford, and Eton and Oxford are beyond words proud of him.'[19] In the poem 'To the School at War' Eton's head, C.A. Alington, reassured his old boys, 'You know we don't forget ... / Be sure we don't forget ... / The school will not forget'. All ex-pupils of Rugby School who went on to serve in the war were sent a postcard which read: 'Each day at noon work stops while the Chapel Bell rings and we think of you and wish you well.'[20]

Loyalty is a quality that need not be constrained. Loyalty, like love, is elastic. As one can love more than one person, one can be loyal to more than one thing. Schoolboys had no problem in stretching their loyalty, from their house, through their school, to their country.

Off the sports field and into the classroom, the boys of Uppingham and the public schools were steeped in the Classics, spending as much as half their time at their desks with Greek or Roman books in front of them. (Athleticism was not in opposition to academicism; the ideal public schoolboy was Aristotelian-sharp in mind, Apollonean-toned in body.) Homer's *Iliad* and *Odyssey*, Caesar's *The Gallic Wars* and text after text portrayed war as a natural part of a leader's duty. More, the leaders were heroes who led the troops in person, rather than skulking and commanding from a tent on the dusty plain; they were sinewy men like Achilles, Hector, and Horatio on the bridge, warriors who excelled in close combat. Exposure to the Classics forged an heroic mental template in the minds of young boys and men; 19-year-old Edmund Blunden, formerly senior classical scholar at Christ's Hospital school, crossed over to France with Julius Caesar's *De Bello Gallico* stashed in his pack, while 29-year-old Patrick Shaw-Stewart, latterly Baring's youngest ever director, took, appropriately enough, *The Iliad* to Gallipoli.[21] While serving in the trenches, Douglas Gillespie, a Wykehamist (a pupil of Winchester School), heard the news of his brother Tom's death in action. Douglas wrote to his parents, consciously placing his brother in the company of the classical heroes:

> for the first few weeks after Tom was killed I found myself thinking perpetually of all the men who had been killed in battle – Hector and Achilles and all the heroes of long ago, who were at once so strong and active, and now so quiet.[22]

The heroic template did more than prepare boys to die for their country; in the trenches it turned to supportive scaffolding inside the head. Patrick Shaw-Stewart, stationed on Imbros, opposite the historic site of Troy, called on the ultimate Greek warrior:

> Was it so hard, Achilles,
> So very hard to die?
> Thou knowest, and I know not,
> So much happier am I.
>
> I will go back this morning
> From Imbros o'er the sea.
> Stand in the trench, Achilles,
> Flame-capped, and shout for me.[23]

But the sacred Ancient texts reminded the young soldier that the heroes of old endured, as well as died. The tales of the austere Ancient Greeks especially, led by Homer's *Odyssey* and Xenophon's *Anabasis* (which told of the march of the 10,000 to the sea), were stories of triumph over deprivation and disaster.

Along from the classroom, on the shelves of the school library, any boy running his finger across the bookcases could not but touch literary lionizations of the military leader in magazines and books, from the *Boy's Own Paper* to William Ernest Henley's verse anthology *Lyra Heroica*, from the adventure novels of G.A. Henty (all 25 million copies of them) to just about everything by Rudyard Kipling. Kipling did a particularly fine fictional line in boy subalterns, be they Parnesius and Pertinax on Hadrian's Wall in *Puck of Pook's Hill* or Bobby Wick in India in 'Only a Subaltern' from *Under the Deodars*. Charles Carrington, schoolboy turned Great War officer turned Kipling's biographer, considered that Bobby Wick

> moulded an entire generation of young Englishmen into that type. They rose up in their thousands in 1914, and sacrificed themselves in the image that Kipling had created. [24]

So devoted to his men was young Bobby Wick that he died nursing them through a cholera epidemic. Wick was, a Tommy in the story exclaimed, an 'Hangel! Bloomin' Hangel!' Bobby Wick's antecedents were indeed of the holiest variety; he was modelled on Christ himself. With all due nods to Carrington, the great purveyor of the ideal of self-sacrifice was not Kipling, but the church.

In most public schools, chapel was mandatory every morning and evening (and thrice on Sunday), and the religion propounded from the pulpit the milk-and-water Anglicanism that was the flavour of the Victorian and Edwardian era, being light on doctrine and ritual, heavy on ethics. As John Drewett, a Sheffield clergyman, noted of the public schools since the reforms of Thomas Arnold:

> [The] middle class Englishman has been trained [in] Christian-Humanist values. He has learnt from the sermons in his school chapel and in the general atmosphere of its community that he must shoulder the responsibilities of government as well as accept the privileges of a ruling class. The conception of the English gentleman is a product of

classical humanism and liberal Christianity. Its essence is a code of behaviour, an ethical system and not a religion of faith. [25]

During the Great War, Anglican army chaplains would moan constantly that public school-educated officers were 'frankly ignorant of most of the intellectual propositions of Christianity'; the willingness of the self-same officers to assume responsibility and lay down their lives was equally noted. The sermons of the school chaplain were emphasized by the Hymn Book, the most thumbed-pages being those that exhorted the pupils to go 'Onward Christian Soldiers'. The hymn in chapel was far from being the only source of musical inspiration, for nearly all schools had a rousing yet noble song. That of King Edward's School, Birmingham, where John Ronald Tolkien was a pupil, ran:

> Here's no place for fop or idler, they who made our city great
> Feared no hardship, shirked no labour, smiled at dust and conquered fate;
> They who gave our school its laurels laid on us a sacred trust,
> Forward therefore, live your hardest, die of service, not of rust. [26]

Of course, a chivalric conception of Christianity was aided by England's pleasing choice of patron saint, George, slayer of dragons, and abetted by chapels and school buildings that soared with spires and crenelles redolent of Camelot.

The so-called 'public school ethos' had still other aspects useful in the making of an officer. Schools were permeated by the culture of command. As Graham Greenwell (Winchester) stated:

> A boy of eighteen, public school, he's had two years as a fag and another two years going up. Then he either was or wasn't selected to be first a house prefect then a school prefect. He rightly or wrongly was given responsibilities at a very early age. [27]

By the age of twenty Graham Greenwell had heavy responsibilities indeed; he was a company commander of the 4/Ox and Bucks Light Infantry on the Western Front. Outside school, at home, boys from the upper and middle classes lived in the same culture of command, because their families employed servants. From the earliest age, boys of the public school background ordered, or saw their parents ordering, the boot boy, the scullery maid and the gardener. Giving orders was first nature. And home and school were politically seamless; as a young boy at bedtime, Roland Leighton's mother, Marie, read to him Sir Newbolt's ubiquitous verse *Vitai Lampada*, which combined the virtues of sport, war, patriotism and the Classics in one intoxicating poetic amalgam:

There's a breathless hush in the Close to-night
Ten to make and the match to win –
A bumping pitch and a blinding light,
An hour to play and the last man in.
And it's not for the sake of a ribboned coat,
Or the selfish hope of a season's fame,
But his Captain's hand on his shoulder smote –
'Play up! play up! and play the game!'

The sand of the desert is sodden red, –
Red with the wreck of a square that broke; –
The Gatling's jammed and the Colonel dead,
And the regiment blind with dust and smoke.
The river of death has brimmed his banks,
And England's far, and Honour a name,
But the voice of a schoolboy rallies the ranks:
'Play up! play up! and play the game!'

This is the word that year by year,
While in her place the School is set,
Every one of her sons must hear,
And none that hears it dare forget.
This they all with a joyful mind
Bear through life like a torch in flame,
And falling fling to the host behind –
'Play up! play up! and play the game!'[28]

Marie Leighton would come to wish, when 'The Boy of My Heart' was buried in a French field, that she had not read *Vitai Lampada* to him of an evening.

Donald Hankey, an ex-Rugbeian who would die with blood spilling over his khaki uniform on that bright first day of the Somme, wrote that 'the whole training, the traditions of his kind' prepared the public schoolboy for war.[29] Hankey's claim is impossible to gainsay. The ethos of the Edwardian and Georgian public schools might stick in the craw of modern sensibilities, particularly after ninety years of exposure to the 'pity of war' poetry of Wilfred Owen, but viewed dispassionately, as a Darwinian survival exercise, Britain's ability to create a waiting, willing reserve of young military leaders was the ultimate in self-preservation. An odd proof of this comes from a critic of the public schools, Richard Aldington. An old boy of Brighton College and an infantry officer in the Royal Sussex Regiment during the Great War, Aldington damned his fellow public schoolboy as 'amazingly ignorant', inhibited, prejudiced against foreigners, prejudiced against culture ('appeared to have read nothing but Kipling, Jeffrey Farnol, Elinor Glyn ... didn't like Shakespeare ... thought *Chu Chin Chow* was the greatest play ever produced'), prejudiced against the lower classes, with an unrealistic, elevated attitude to women ('had been taught to respect all women as if they were his mother') and yet:

> **he was honest, he was kindly, he was conscientious, he could obey orders and command obedience in others, he took pains to look after his men. He could be implicitly relied upon to lead a hopeless attack and to maintain a desperate defence to the very end. There were thousands and tens of thousands like him.[30]**

Presumably, Aldington – the author of *Death of a Hero* – excluded himself from the charges of contemporary stupidity and philistinism, along with Graves, Blunden, Siegfried Sassoon, Edward Thomas, Raymond Asquith (so able as a Classics student at Oxford that his professor doffed his cap to him every time they met in the street), the composer George Butterworth, J.R.R. Tolkien, Charles Sorley, and so on and on. R.C. Sherriff MC, a captain in the 9/East Surreys, concurred that the public schools produced the right stuff for leadership in war:

Without raising the public school boy officers onto a pedestal it can be said with certainty that it was they who played the vital part in keeping the men good-humoured and obedient in the face of their interminable ill-treatment, and well-nigh insufferable ordeals ... They [the public school boys] led them [the other ranks] not through military skill, for no military skill was needed. They led them from personal example, from the reserves of patience and good humour and endurance. They won the trust and respect of their men, not merely through their willingness to share the physical privations, but through an understanding of their spiritual loneliness ...

So the common soldier turned instinctively to his own company officers for the leadership that he required, to the young officers who lived with him and talked to him as a human being like themselves and helped him hold onto a shred of pride and self respect ... if the officer had it [that indefinable quality] the soldier instinctively recognized it, and that indefinable something was what was instilled into a boy at the public school ... The common soldier liked them because they were 'young swells', and with few exceptions the young swells delivered the goods.[31]

Sherriff, whose autobiographical play about the war, *Journey's End*, ran for 594 performances when staged at the Savoy in 1928, was right to highlight the spill-over of the ideals of Christian and chivalric care from school into the trenches; officers who had failed as Hercules on the Fives court or Hermes in the mile, made up for this by their unstinting care for their men. There were more ways than one in which the junior officer would win the war.

And so to Speech Day at Uppingham, 1914. The proceedings opened with a review of the Officers' Training Corps on Middle Field, during which 335 boys stood to attention, to be inspected under the azure morning sky. The inspection over, Colour-Sergeant Leighton led the boys to the Chapel for the service. There followed the giving of the prizes, after which R.A. Leighton reputedly needed a wheelbarrow to take away his haul of the Nettleship Prize for English Essay, the Holden Prize for Latin Prose, Greek Prose Composition, Latin Hexameters, Greek Epigram and Captain in Classics. Sitting and shuffling occasionally, few of the audience of boys and relatives had any inkling that war was only three weeks away. The be-gowned headmaster, the Reverend McKenzie, was either wiser or more attuned to the political weather, to the deluge which approached. His prize day speech, Vera Brittain recorded, had a deliberate solemnity, and ended with a paraphrase of an adage from the Japanese general Count Nogi: 'If a man cannot be useful to his country, he is better dead'.

His boys wanted to be useful to their country. Of the 335 cadets of the Uppingham OTC who stood to attention in their polished-buttoned uniforms on Speech Day July 1914, all but 18 served in the First World War. In a year and half from Speech Day Leighton would be dead. Within four years Edward Brittain and his and Leighton's mutual friend Victor 'Tah' Richardson were dead. (The trio had been dubbed 'The Three Musketeers' by Marie Leighton.) In all, 447 old boys of Uppingham would die in the First World War. Up and down the land, the scene of Uppingham's Speech Day was mirrored in the quads and on the lawns of the public schools. So was the subsequent loss of life. The rule written in blood of the Great War was that the higher a man's social position, the more expensive his education, the more likely he was to die. The reason was blindingly simple: public schoolboys, current or old, would step forward almost en masse to take up the most dangerous rank in the British Army, that of a second lieutenant or subaltern, the leader of the men in the trenches. And the more eminent the School, the more likely they were to be given this commission.

No other communities in Britain would suffer a greater death rate, and only the ancient universities would suffer a comparable one.[32] Over the course of the war, 12 per cent of those who served were killed or died of wounds. Against this:

WAR SERVICE FIGURES FOR SELECTED PUBLIC SCHOOLS

School	Numbers serving	Numbers killed	Per cent killed
Harrow	2917	644	22
Charterhouse	3200+	687	22
Eton	5650	1157	21

Uppingham	*2221*	*447*	*20*
Rugby	*3445*	*689*	*20*
Sedbergh	*1250*	*251*	*20*
Cheltenham	*3541*	*675*	*19*
Wellington	*3350*	*597*	*18*
Monmouth[33]	*330*	*43*	*13*

As few as 3 per cent of Harrovians, Carthusians and Etonians served in the ranks, whereas only half of Monmothians had commissions, hence the disparity of death. In these stark statistics there are greater tragedies. Charles Douie, when he asked after the boys who had been in his house at Rugby in 1910 found that 50 per cent of them had died. At Cheltenham College, the roll of honour included 33 pairs of brothers and two trios of brothers, from the families Lowry and Mather; there were two trios of brothers at Monmouth, the Watkins and the Davieses; of Marlborough's 733 war dead, three were the brothers Shaw.

After the Head's speech at Uppingham, the audience broke up and Roland Leighton and Vera Brittain took the chance to stroll together in the rose garden during the Head's garden party. Afterwards, Leighton wrote one of his first poems, 'In the Rose Garden':

Dew on the pink-flushed petals,
Roseate wings unfurled;
What can, I thought, be fairer
In all the world?

Steps that were fain but faltered
(What could she else have done?)
Passed from the arbour's shadow
Into the sun.

Noon and a scented glory,
Golden and pink and red;
'What after all are roses
To Me?' I said. [34]

For her part, Vera Brittain remembered Speech Day as

> the one perfect summer idyll that I ever experienced, as well as my last care-free entertainment before the Flood. The lovely legacy of a vanished world, it is etched with minute precision on the tablets of my memory. Never again, for me and for my generation, was there to be any festival the joy of which no cloud would darken and no remembrance invalidate.[35]

Even as Leighton and Brittain shyly strolled and talked in Uppingham's rose garden, the little local difficulty in the Balkans caused by the assassination of Archduke Ferdinand in Sarajevo was bursting its banks. Three weeks later the crisis began lapping at the shores of Britain.

Late July was traditionally the time for schools with OTCs to hold their tented summer camps, and 1914 was no exception. That year, however, there was none of the usual 'colossal picnic' levity amongst the 10,000 schoolboy warriors. Douglas Gillespie at the Inns of Court OTC for law students wrote on Sunday 2 August to his parents:

> We have no news to-night, and so I hope that there may still be some honourable way to peace. I don't want to fight the Germans, for I respect them, but if the country is drawn in, I feel I must go in too, and do the very best I can. In the meantime we shall stay here, training and manoeuvring for all we are worth. Good-night.[36]

Anthony Eden at the Eton College OTC camp at Aldershot remembered:

> In that year at camp the talk was all of war. Would there be one, would our country be involved, how long would it last and, only occasionally because the contingency seemed comparatively remote, should we personally have any part in it? ... A few mornings later the orderly corporals aroused us with the order: 'Pack your kit bags. We parade within the hour to march to the station and entrain for Windsor'. It was soon evident what had happened. Our adjutant, our instructors and, most serious of all, our army cooks had all vanished in the night. The British mobilization order had gone out.[37]

Disbanded, the Eton College OTC cadets went to their homes to await events. One of Eden's schoolfellows, Desmond Allhusen, found his elder brother sharpening his sword.

4 August. Fateful day. For all of the rumours of war, the actual declaration seemed unreal, a sudden burst of rain out of the bright blue of that deceptively long summer. The daily newspapers had the usual advertisements for holidays to the Rhine. Rupert Brooke was in a music hall when a scribbled message was thrown across the screen: 'War declared with Austria. 11.9'. Brooke recalled that 'There was a volley of quick low hand-clapping – more a signal of recognition than anything else'. Playing tennis in a holiday tournament at Littlehampton, Brian Horrocks, a student at Royal Military Academy Sandhurst was mildly irritated by the news since it threw him off his game; the thought uppermost in the mind of Horrocks, who had been a 'games addict' at Uppingham, was that his father would now find out that he had pawned his revolver.

Lord Kitchener, appointed Minister of War, had somewhat weightier matters on his mind. Due to the long British distrust of the military, a hangover from the Cromwellian dictatorship, the Regular army was a mere 250,000-strong. With this small, if perfectly formed, force Kitchener had to fight the field-grey German divisions marching through Belgium, as well as garrison the pink sprawling British Empire. Even if Kitchener added the 'Saturday afternoon' soldiers of the Territorial Force, the Reserve, the Special Reserve and just about anybody who had ever worn a uniform, only 733,514 could be placed under arms. The German army was 3.8 million strong. Of course, Britain had her Allies, but the French were the French, the Russians the Russians ... Kitchener determined to form a 'New Army', and obtained Cabinet assent to do so. On 6 August 1914 Parliament, in its turn, approved an increase of the establishment of the Army by 500,000 men. Within a week the first New or Kitchener Army of 100,000 men had volunteered and enlisted; by the end of October 1914, five New Armies had been sanctioned.

But who was to officer the expanded army? Some 500 officers in the Indian Army were prevented from returning to the sub continent, retired officers were 'dug out', and some New Army battalions, formed by any local worthy with enough clout to do so, appointed their own officers; the 13/The York and Lancaster Regiment (First Barnsley Pals) was commanded by a local solicitor, who was granted the temporary rank of lieutenant-colonel. After these, the War Office turned to the 'traditional source of supply', the public schoolboy, who was ready and waiting in the wings of history: on Monday 10 August *The Times* carried an advertisement for 2,000 young men of 'good general education' – code for public school – between the ages of 17 and 30 who were 'cadets or ex-cadets of the OTCs' to whom temporary commissions in the Army might be given.

Cometh the hour of national peril, cometh the boy soldier in his tens of thousands. There is no way of gauging exactly how many public schoolboys volunteered in August–October 1914, because not all schools kept records, but snapshots tell the story; at Newick House at Cheltenham College 50 out of 51 boys boarding there in 1910 volunteered; at Winchester, 531 of 594 leavers of the six years previous to the war were in khaki before conscription; school archivist upon archivist if asked the question 'How many boys volunteered for service?' responds, 'We think pretty much everyone'; Charles Carrington surveyed his contemporaries and concluded that they were 'all of one mind, excepting those persistent individualists who manage to keep out of step in every occasion'.[38] The volunteering was a phenomenon. 'Now, God be thanked who has matched us with His hour', versed Rupert Brooke on the declaration of war; he perhaps ought to have mentioned Thomas Arnold and R.B. Haldane in the same breath. Due to the public school reforms of Arnold and the OTC reforms of Haldane, Britain had a body of boys dedicated to, and trained in, the service of the country. Boys still wearing their OTC uniforms from summer camp, coursed through the recruiting offices; between August 1914 and March 1915, 20,577 officers were commissioned from OTCs and while some were holders of a university Certificate B, many were simply holders of the Certificate A from school. If that. Another 12,290 ex-OTC boys were serving in the ranks. Of the 247,061 commissions granted to officers from the start of the war to the end of the war over 100,000 had passed through one of Haldane's OTCs.[39] During the same period they led 5.5 million men.

One of the great fallacies of the Great War is that all those who joined the colours in 1914 did so in a rush and flush of jingoism. Doubtless some of the thousands of public schoolboys who eagerly sought to serve were fired-up on some primitive gut patriotism, but not all. Not even many. There was no sprint of flag-waving lemmings over the edge. Boys were willing to serve but the impact of their education was to make them reflect intellectually;[40] leaders, after all, need to be taught to think and think independently. While there was no doubt that the public schoolboys of Britain would heed their country's cry for help, their reasons for doing so were varied. Robert Nichols, educated at Winchester and Trinity College, Oxford, and commissioned in the Royal Artillery, analysed his compatriots' reasons for volunteering, and deduced that the spectrum covered: 1) A sense that England's honour was imperilled if she did not keep to her pact to protect Belgium; 2) Sympathy with France; 3) The desire which exists within almost every youth to suffer for others; 4) Love of England; 5) The 'Zeitgeist' of the time; 6) The pure spirit of adventure; 7) Curiosity; 8) The vague feeling that 'it was the right thing to do'; 9) Fear of the world's censure.[41]

For some volunteers Germany was an obstacle not an incentive; there were powerful cultural and economic ties between Britain and Germany. Anthony Eden's brother Timothy was in Germany learning German when war broke out and was interned. With Teutonic ancestry, and a fascination with Anglo-Saxon culture that would birth *The Lord of the Rings*, J.R.R. Tolkien was dismayed by the declaration of war in the August of the Deluge. At New College, Oxford, Arthur Heath spent his last evening before enlisting playing German music on his piano. Charles Sorley who, upon leaving Marlborough, had sojourned in Mecklenburg acquiring German, identified with Germany so strongly that he 'felt I was a German, and proud to be a German'. Another who had spent golden days in *Deutschland* was Rupert Brooke. In the autobiographical 'An Unusual Young Man', one of Brooke's lesser known pieces, he gives an *inkling* of the varying thought processes involved in electing for country in 1914. He is 'the friend' of the essay:

Some say the Declaration of War threw us into a primitive abyss of hatred and the lust for blood. Others declare that we behaved very well. I do not know. I only know the thoughts that flowed through the mind of a friend of mine when he heard the news. My friend – I shall make no endeavour to excuse him – is a normal, even ordinary man, wholly English, twenty-four years old, active and given to music. By a chance he was ignorant of the events of the world during the last days of July. He was camping with some friends in a remote part of Cornwall, and had gone on, with a companion, for a four-days' sail. So it wasn't till they beached her again that they heard. A youth ran down to them with a telegram: "We're at war with Germany. We've joined France and Russia."

My friend ate and drank, and then climbed a hill of gorse, and sat alone, looking at the sea. His mind was full of confused images, and the sense of strain. In answer to the word 'Germany', a train of vague thoughts dragged across his brain. The pompous middle-class vulgarity of the building of Berlin; the wide and restful beauty of Munich; the taste of beer; innumerable quiet, glittering cafés; the Ring; the swish of evening air in the face, as one skis down past the pines; a certain angle of the eyes in the face; long nights of drinking, and singing, and laughter; the admirable beauty of German wives and mothers; certain friends; some tunes; the quiet length of evening over the Starnberger-See. Between him and the Cornish sea he saw quite clearly an April morning on a lake south of Berlin, the grey water slipping past his little boat, and a peasant-woman, suddenly revealed against apple-blossom, hanging up blue and scarlet garments to dry in the sun. Children played about her; and she sang as she worked. And he remembered a night in Munich spent in a students' Kneipe. From eight to one they had continually emptied immense jugs of beer, and smoked, and sung English and German songs in profound chorus . . .

He vaguely imagined a series of heroic feats, vast enterprise, and the applause of crowds. . . . From that egotism he was awakened to a different one, by the thought that this day meant war and the change of all things he knew. He realised, with increasing resentment, that music would be neglected. And he wouldn't be able, for example, to camp out. He might have to volunteer for military training and service. Some of his friends would be killed. The Russian ballet wouldn't return. His own relationship with A—, a girl he intermittently adored, would be changed. Absurd, but inevitable; because – he scarcely worded it to himself – he and she and everyone else were going to be different. His mind fluttered irascibly to escape from this thought, but still came back to it, like a tethered bird. Then he became calmer, and wandered out for a time into fantasy. A cloud over the sun woke him to consciousness of his own thoughts; and he found, with perplexity, that they were continually recurring to two periods of his life, the days after the death of his mother, and the time of his first deep estrangement from one he loved. After a bit he understood this. Now, as then, his mind had been completely divided into two parts: the upper running about aimlessly from one half-relevant thought to another, the lower unconscious half labouring with some profound and unknowable change. This feeling of ignorant helplessness linked him with those past crises. His consciousness was like the light scurry of waves at full tide, when the deeper waters are pausing and gathering and turning home. Something was growing in his heart, and he couldn't tell what. But as he thought 'England and Germany', the word 'England' seemed to flash like a line of foam. With a sudden tightening of his heart, he realised that there might be a raid on the English coast. He didn't imagine any possibility of it *succeeding*, but only of enemies and warfare on English soil. The idea sickened him ... He thought often and heavily of Germany. Of England, all the time. He didn't know whether he was glad or sad. It was a new feeling.[42]

What was obvious in 1914 – although it has not seemed obvious to generations of historians since – was that German occupation of the Belgian and French coastlines would have allowed her to control Britain's liquid lifeline, the Channel. The imperilling of Britain was real. And, after occupying Western Europe, what was there to stop the Kaiser's army from invading England? When Edward Thomas, poet and instructor in the Artists' Rifles (and later a gunner officer in France), was asked why he was fighting, Thomas bent down, picked up a pinch of earth and said, 'Literally, for this'. Thomas thought Walton's *The Compleat Angler* the quintessence of book-bound patriotism, because in it 'I touched the antiquity and sweetness of England'. The nascent poet Wilfred Owen determined that the 'Perpetuity and Supremacy' of the mother tongue was the reason to take up arms.[43] Not sporty, a hopeless hypochondriac, Owen had attended an independent school in Birkenhead that was not a public school; a sojourn teaching in France was enough to qualify him as gentleman and he enlisted in the Artists' Rifles. Robert Vernede at thirty scraped in under the age barrier (it was later raised to thirty-five for men without prior Army service) and only asked that he might serve England as a gesture of gratitude:

All that a man might ask thou hast given me, England,
Yet grant thou one thing more;
That now when envious foes would spoil thy splendour,
Unversed in arms, a dreamer such as I
May in thy ranks be deemed not all unworthy
England, for thee to die.[44]

For still others, England was more than a green Eden in silver sea and the home of the language of Keats, it was the land of liberty. Uppingham Musketeer Victor Richardson was one of those who thought England and her Allies were 'God's instrument by which He will remove that spirit and doctrine which is the cause of such wars as this one'.[45] Vivian de Sola Pinto – his friends in the Army never managed such an exotic moniker and affectionately called him 'Gondola' – was utterly relieved by the redemptive, moral purity of the war: 'At last we were being asked to fight and suffer not for imperial aggrandizement or material gain but for justice and liberty.' Likewise, Tom Kettle, Irish nationalist, formerly MP for East Tyrone, opponent of Britain, took one look at the Kaiser's attempt to export his right-wing military dictatorship through the barrel of a gun and declared: 'This War is without parallel. Britain, France, Russia enter it purged from their past sins of domination.'[46] He urged his countrymen to join 'The Army of Freedom', meaning the Dublin Fusiliers of the British Army. Brooke, Thomas, Owen, Vernede, Richardson and Kettle all died for their visions of England. There was little ignoble about the volunteers of 1914. Their reactions were not those of a foaming-mouthed dog. They were idealists.

Robert Graves was as German as he was British; his ancestral surname was von Ranke. The summers he spent at his grandfather's manor house at Deisenhofer outside Munich 'were easily the best things of my childhood'. Nevertheless, the ex-Charterhouse boy found his loyalties easy to pin to the Union Jack because he was outraged by 'the Germans' cynical violation of Belgian neutrality'. The bullying of Belgium ran slap against the sacred code of fair play, and although he could discount 20 per cent of the stories of German atrocities in Belgium as wartime propaganda (an eerily accurate estimate as it turned out) it 'was not, of course, sufficient' and so he too went off to the recruiting office.[47]

In retrospect, Robert Nichols' survey of the volunteering impulse missed several reflexes. As David Cannadine tracked in *The Decline and Fall of the Aristocracy*, for decades before the Great War the patricians of Britain had suffered the slings of criticism for 'their monopoly of the land, unearned incomes, reactionary attitude to social reform, anachronistic possession of hereditary political power, and leisured lifestyle and parasitic idleness'.[48] The war gave them the opportunity to prove themselves, the chance for a last hurrah. Historically, war is what the aristocracy did, and did well; fortunately, they had kept the martial spirit ticking over by hunting and shooting. They paid a high price for their combativity. By the end of 1914 alone the First World War had done away with six peers, 16 baronets, six knights, 95 sons of peers, 82 sons of baronets and 84 sons of knights.[49] As hurrahs went it was strangely magnificent, and quite fuss-less.

Secondly, since the Army was a standard career for public schoolboys – particularly from schools such as Eton, Cheltenham and Wellington which had 'Military sides' or streams – volunteering in 1914 was not a step into the dark, it was a following of pre-ordained boot-marks. Stuart Graham, whose family had been soldiers for generations, recalled: 'Soldiers went to war; it was as simple as that'.[50]

Thirdly, aside from family history, aside from the chance of adventure 'on a heroic scale', Graham was astute, and honest, enough to identify another psychological reflex behind the trip to the recruiting office: 'the eagerness of a young man to test himself, to try out, as it were, his own guts'.[51] There was nothing new in that, of course. As Jacques said in his survey of a man's life in *As You Like It*, young warriors, boy subalterns, call them what you will are:

Full of strange oaths, sudden, and quick in guard,
Seeking the bubble reputation
Even in the cannon's mouth.

For his part, Roland Leighton thought anything other than volunteering 'a cowardly shirking of my obvious duty'.[52] To the public
school generation of 1914, their duty to defend Britain was so obvious,
so intrinsic to the bedrock of their being, that they scarcely recognized
it; hence in Robert Nichols' list of the volunteering impulses, it appears
as a 'vague feeling'.

But there was, after soul and mind had been engaged, and the
decision to volunteer made, a war to fight.

For the young man from the right background securing a commission in the Territorials, New Armies or Special Reserve was as
easy as finding a commanding officer to take him on. Robert Graves
obtained a commission in the Special Reserve of the Royal Welch
Fusiliers purely on the basis of having been in Charterhouse's OTC
and a good word from the secretary of the Harlech Golf Club. His
commission, because it was in the Special Reserve, was permanent,
and several boys who joined the same day were failed applicants for
Sandhurst getting into the Army 'through the back door'. As Bernard
Martin's headmaster temptingly pointed out to him, a benefit of the
Special Reserve was that the lower age limit was eighteen, and not
nineteen as in the Kitchener armies. 'So a miracle came to pass',
recalled the eager Martin; he was gazetted a second lieutenant in the
reserve battalion of the North Staffs the day after his eighteenth
birthday. Meanwhile, Etonian Peter Davies just tagged along with
elder brother George when he went to the recruiting office in Winchester:

'Where were you at school?'
'Eton, sir.'
'In the corps?'
'Yes, sir, Sergeant.'
'Play any games? Cricket?'
'Well, sir, actually I managed to get my eleven.'
'Oh, you did, did you?'

The Colonel, who had played for Eton himself in his day, now became noticeably more genial, and by the time he had ascertained that George was the Davies who had knocked up a valuable 59 at Lord's (which knock he had himself witnessed with due appreciation) it was evident that little more need be said.

'And what about you, young man?' he asked, turning to me.

'Please, sir, I'm his brother,' was the best I could offer in the way of a reference.[53]

It was enough. George and Peter Davies both obtained a King's commission in the Special Reserve of the 60th Rifles.

Nepotism was useful. Anthony Eden was considering the Grenadier Guards but then Lord Charlie Feversham, an in-law, wrote to him saying he was raising a yeomanry battalion in the King's Royal Rifle Corps. Would Eden like to take a temporary, hostilities-only commission and help? And perhaps command something in the battalion? The future prime minister drove around Country Durham in his father's yellow Benz helping recruit his own platoon. Although Gerald Brennan was going through a 'period of adolescent revolt' and not feeling unduly patriotic, he still wished to be in the war because it would be 'a great experience'. He recalled: 'I was therefore delighted when my father returned from Gloucester with a commission for me in the local Territorials.'[54] Jim Mackie, a young Regular officer in the 4/Somerset Light Infantry, wrote to his brother:

I heard the Colonel saying this morning that he wanted one more subaltern so I at once approached him and said that I had a younger brother who would like to join. He jumped at the idea at once and said he should be delighted to have a younger brother of mine in the regiment . . . send your birth certificate and medical certificate tonight because the Colonel is sending to the War Office to-morrow and if your certificates are sent up you will get gazetted more quickly . . . you need not wait till you are gazetted before you get your uniform but can begin at once.[55]

In London Dennis Wheatley's frantic attempts to secure a temporary commission were taken in hand by his father, who called in a favour from a friend recently elevated by the War Office from banking to the colonelcy of a Territorial regiment. Called in to interview with the colonel, young Wheatley explained that he was actually seeking a commission in the 4/Royal Fusiliers – at which the colonel exclaimed, horror-struck, 'But my dear boy … you cannot possibly go into the Fusiliers – they walk!' The colonel wrote Wheatley a chit for the First City of London Territorial Royal Field Artillery, which had stables of horses. At the unit's HQ at Handel Street, Wheatley was asked by the battery's commanding officer when he could report for duty:

> 'The minute my commission comes through, sir,' I replied.
> 'Have we got to wait for that?' he said. 'That may take a week or two. I need all the help I can get. I've got one or two other young fellows like yourself who have just applied for commission and they're coming along tomorrow morning to give me a hand. Could you come too?'
> Next morning, at nine o'clock I was on parade.[56]

School connections could be as useful as family ones. Still at his school OTC summer camp when war broke out, F.P. Roe was handed an application for a temporary commission by his commanding officer. All Roe's details had been filled in for him. Everyone else in the contingent received a form, likewise filled out for them. 'We all of us signed', he remembered, 'and the forms were dispatched to the War Office the same day.' Roe was appointed to a second lieutenancy in the 6th (Territorial) Battalion of the Gloucester Regiment.

But school was the stumbling block for R.C. Sherriff. After putting on his best suit, Sherriff went to the headquarters of the county regiment, and waited with others to be interviewed. He watched a Wykehamist walk away with a commission, then a boy from another famous public school. On Sherriff's turn, he too was asked the name of his school by the adjutant. 'I told him', wrote Sherriff,

> and his face fell. He took up a printed list from his desk and searched through it.

'I'm sorry,' he said, 'but it isn't a public school.'[57]

The fact that Kingston Grammar School had been founded by Queen Elizabeth I in 1567 was of no help. The adjutant said that there was nothing he could do. In all likelihood, if Kingston Grammar had been one of the 'posh' grammars with an OTC, Sherriff would have been accepted. As it was, Sherriff went off to another room, enlisted in the ranks, and 'it was a long hard pull before I was at last accepted as an officer'. In August of 1914 Sherriff thought the distinction drawn between candidates from public and grammar schools 'silly'; in retrospect he accepted:

> It was a rough method of selection, a demarcation line hewn out with a blunt axe; but it was the only way in the face of a desperate emergency, and as things turned out, it worked.[58]

Not everything about the public school code would have been alien to Sherriff the grammar schoolboy, because grammar schools were little other than cheap day-school facsimiles of the establishments organized by the Headmaster's Conference; they too stressed the Classics, sport, and cultivated loyalty through a House system.

Eyesight was Roland Leighton's problem in obtaining a commission. He tried first for the Regular Army but failed the eyesight test, then the Territorials ('where wearing eye-glasses would have been permissible') but they had more officers than required. With the persistence that defined his generation, he carried on writing letters and knocking on colonel's doors for eight weeks until he was approved for a commission in the 4/Norfolk Regiment on 7 October. Having suffered one-twelfth vision since the age of six, Paul Jones of Dulwich College, winner of a Balliol scholarship and a rugby fanatic, was never likely to pass the medical test for the infantry, and duly did not. He promised the commissioning board that he would remember faithfully to take spare spectacles into battle, but they worried about rain on the lenses anyway. Jones lived up to his own belief that 'the chief virtue of the public school system is that it teaches one to make sacrifices willingly for the sake of esprit de corps'[59] and settled for a commission in the Army Service Corps. And then spent two years doggedly working his way into a battlefield role; he eventually did so, as a Tank Corps commander. Another reject by virtue of his short-sightedness Vivian de Sola Pinto took the long view and departed for Oxford's dreamy spires; there he joined the senior OTC 'to prepare myself for the time when the rigid rule debarring myopics from the fighting forces should be relaxed'.[60] It was, and the 'spectacled subaltern' ended up as Siegfried Sassoon's second-in-command in 25/Royal Welch Fusiliers. In the meantime, he wore his OTC uniform to stop hysterical young women in the street pestering him to sign up.

Although decided on a career as a Regular soldier, Stuart Graham had spread his bets and applied for a Temporary commission too. Who knew which was the quickest route to the front in France and Belgium? He was studying at Jimmy's, a 'crammer' for those seeking a place at Royal Military College Sandhurst, when there arrived a large envelope marked OHMS. Inside was a large stiff piece of paper which read:

Temporary

GEORGE by the Grace of God, of the United Kingdom of Great Britain and Ireland and of the British Dominions beyond the Seas. King. Defender of the Faith. Emperor of India, etc. To our Trusty and well beloved Edward Fairley Stuart Graham. Greetings.

We, reposing especial Trust and Confidence in your Loyalty, Courage and Good Conduct, do by these Presents Constitute and Appoint you to be an Officer in Our Land Forces from the twenty-second day of September 1914. You are therefore carefully and diligently to discharge your duty as such in the Rank of 2nd Lieutenant or in such higher rank as We may from time hereafter be pleased to promote or appoint you to, of which notification will be made in the London Gazette, and you are at all times to exercise and well discipline in Arms both the inferior Officers and Men serving under you and use your best endeavours to keep them in good Order and Discipline. And We do hereby Command them to Obey you as their superior Officer and you to observe and to follow such Orders and Directions as from time to time you shall receive from Us, or your superior Officer, according to the Rules and Discipline of War, in pursuance of the Trust hereby reposed in you.

Given at Our Court at Saint James's the Twenty-first day of September 1914 in the Fifth Year of our Reign.
By His Majesty's Command
Edward Fairley Stuart Graham
2nd Lieutenant
Land Forces

He was in the War.

However, news from his father, Graham recalled, 'took some of the gilt off my gingerbread'; his father confessed to having been imprisoned years before for financial misdealing. Graham was not the family's real name; it was Cloete.

Horace Watkins, old boy of Monmouth School beside the languid Wye, was commissioned from Oxford University OTC into the South Wales Borderers on 22 August 1914; he was killed in action at Poelkapelle, Belgium, on 21 October 1914.

Death could come quickly to the public schoolboys who volunteered at the end of the Summer of 1914. And often. In the month that Watkins was killed, officer deaths on the Western Front began to run at the rate of 1 in 7, and officer casualties – that is those killed, wounded, missing or taken prisoner – at 1 in 2.

Boys in Britain, too young yet to enlist, were left in no doubt about the fate of those who had once shared the hallowed precincts and had since donned khaki. Every issue of the *Eton College Chronicle* carried a list of the fallen from the school in its 'Etona Non Immemor' column; on 19 November 1914, the deaths of 17 old boys were listed; a week later, 25 old boys. Every issue, more dead.

Four months later, in a 'The School at War' leader, the *Eton College Chronicle* noted:

And yet practically no one enjoys it [the war]. Nobody pretends that life at the front is in anyway enjoyable ... People no longer wish to join the Forces for the mere fun of it, and their action in thus joining becomes all the more admirable as their personal inclination towards it is less.[61]

Still they volunteered. The public schools would be the last bastion of the volunteering impulse. Long after the desire to freely serve had departed the rest of Britain, boys from the public schools carried on queuing for commissions.[62] In Autumn 1915 no Wykehamist went up to Oxford for the first time in 500 years.[63] When the commissioning system became 'choked up' with too many Chiefs for the number of Indians, public schoolboys, rather than miss the war, enlisted in the ranks. Some of the 'Pals' battalions of the New Army, such as 18–21 Royal Fusiliers, were actually and exclusively for recruits who had been to a recognized public school. The school OTCs, meanwhile, stepped up their efforts to prepare boys for service in the Army proper. (*The Cheltonian* reported in December 1914, alas, that 'The work of the Corps has been somewhat disturbed owing to the War Office having commandeered half of our rifles.') Possibly the last school to adopt khaki uniform, instead of 'the time-honoured blue', Monmouth announced a 'new phase' in the history of the Corps, with the 'introduction of NCO's lectures in School hours'. The desire of public schoolboys to serve the country in the time of crisis was mirrored in the boys' army, as well as the adult one; in July 1914 the parade state of Monmouth's Corps was 90; in December 1915 it was 130.

With the introduction of conscription in 1916, volunteering ended. Everyone of the right age and sufficient fitness and not in a protected occupation had henceforth to go to the war, like it or not. Although no longer able to express their feelings through mass volunteering, the public schoolboys of Britain maintained a passionate desire for war service. R.C. Sherriff's autobiographical play *Journey's End* has nothing by accident, and almost everything of the officer's life on the Western Front by design. The play is set in March 1918, just before the great German offensive. 'I hope we're lucky and get a youngster straight from school', says Lieutenant Osborne, 'They're the kind that do best.' They do, indeed, get a smooth-faced, keen as mustard, literature-loving, brave as a lion schoolboy. They get Second Lieutenant Raleigh, the mirror image of the public schoolboy who had volunteered at the war's start, four long years before.

II

Arms and the Gentleman:
The Training of the Officer

How great it was to be a temporary second lieutenant, gazetted to the KOYLI [King's Own Yorkshire Light Infantry], to have a cheque-book and an account at Cox's bank.

Second Lieutenant Stuart Cloete,
King's Own Yorkshire Light Infantry

There was something about a boy in uniform, the boy said to himself as he stood in front of the admiring mirror. Stuart Cloete was particularly taken with one item on his kit list:

I bought a sword. Imagine it. A sword like a knight in ancient times . . . All officers carried swords in those days. We even did sword drill.[1]

The sword made up for the slight disappointment of having to obtain his uniform from Moss Bros; the rush to uniform in late Summer 1914 meant queues out of tailors' glass doors, especially the ones generally favoured by officers, such as Pope and Bradley in Bond Street and Wilkinson's in Pall Mall. (When Cloete was able to trade up to 'a decent uniform', he went to Humphrey & Crook in the Haymarket.) Officers received an allowance of between £30 and £60 – and it was usually £50 – for their uniform and kit. Roland Leighton thought that £30 in 1914 would not cover everything, but acknowledged he 'was a bad financier'.[2] Charles Carrington found that £50 in 1915 'provided easily' for the all important sword, plus a revolver, two service-dress uniforms, a greatcoat and all the accessories.[3] Second Lieutenant Bernard Martin of the North Staffs recalled:

'Fifty pounds to spend on uniform!' exclaimed my elder sister when

I proudly held up the cheque sent by the war office. 'Fifty pounds will buy you enough clothes to last a lifetime.'[4]

Which might not, it suddenly occurred to 18-year-old Martin, be very long at all in wartime.

Pope and Bradley charged from £3 13s for a dress service jacket, but a uniform could be had much more cheaply. Dennis Wheatley's uniform for the Royal Field Artillery was run-up by his father's tailor, old Mr George in Portman Street; young H.E.L. Mellersh, another Londoner, recalled how it 'was flattering to one's ego to be fitted for a uniform at one's father's tailor'.[5] Becoming an officer was, for many of the volunteers, simultaneously a step into adulthood.

Smart regiments like the Guards had approved tailors, notably Andersons; the Royal Welch Fusiliers, although not quite of the Guards cut, had high standards too. Alas, Robert Graves had entered the emporium of what his adjutant considered 'an inefficient tailor', and he refused to let Graves be seen in France, regimental standards and all that. Not having the money for a new uniform, the eager Graves was left in a quandary; he solved it by boxing the regimental star, Lonsdale-belt winner Sergeant John Basham. At such pluck, Crawshay relented and put Second Lieutenant Graves down for the draft for the front, regardless of his sartorial inelegance.

Of coats for officers there was a variety. The greatcoat, which came down to the mid shin, had the admirable capacity to be a snug impromptu sleeping bag but was heavy; with the merest hint of precipitation it became sodden, despite maker's claims that it was 'waterproofed'. Bernard Martin's admirable tailor pointed out the greatcoat was perfect – if 'you expect to fight Germans round the North Pole!' He suggested instead a British Warm, a leather-buttoned reefer coat, costing £3 10s, the same as a greatcoat, although the equally venerable Mr George ran one up for Dennis Wheatley for a thrifty £1 7s 3d. The specially designed Burberry trench coat had a certain *je ne sais quoi*, though most outfitters supplied something similar – it was, for all its fashionability, merely a gabardine raincoat; Harrods' version of the trench coat, the 'Yeltra', was advertised as being 'absolutely weatherproof' and could be worn with detachable linings, in material from sheepskin to wallaby fur; the cost of the coat with the latter exotic option was 12 guineas.

There was no *absolutely* standard colour for uniforms. As Reginald Pound, a Territorial subaltern observed, shirts, ties, puttees were worn in various tones, 'from dark green to pale coffee'. Young subalterns in Territorial and New Army regiments also had the habit of infuriating choleric colonels by customizing their uniform in various ways. One favourite was to take the stiffener out of the service cap to produce a 'negligee' effect,[6] while Dennis Wheatley had his Bedford cord breeches made with the 'beautiful full cut' more generally associated with jodhpurs. The dandyism of boy subalterns was later gently satirized in the trench newspaper *The Wipers Times*, with a pen-and-ink drawing of a subaltern wearing trousers cut especially short so as to show off a generous amount of spotted sock. Above the drawing the caption read: 'Questions a Platoon Commander Should Ask Himself – Am I as offensive as I might be?' – a reference to a pamphlet of that title issued to all subalterns by a well-meaning general. (Bernard Martin considered the cartoon the 'best joke of the war'.)

The fashion for showing off socks was definitely too offensive for some; Second Lieutenant Jules le Verrier Constant was courtmartialled at Whittington Barracks, Lichfield, in July 1916 for 'appearing in Public dressed in mustard coloured socks & low brown Shoes and having his Trousers turned up at the bottom' contrary to regulations. The said socks were confiscated for a month, only to be returned when le Verrier Constant had rendered a written apology to his fellow subalterns.[7] The shoes Jules le Verrier Constant should have been wearing were Military (regulation) Brown and Khaki Canvas Shoes with leather soles. Infantry officers generally wore the Service Boot in barracks. In the trenches they wore leather knee-boots, or boots with puttees. Overdressed young officers were known as 'Nuts' or 'K'nuts'. There were many thousands of them.

It wasn't only decent tailors who were in short supply in the hectic days of summer 1914. Graham Greenwell, commissioned straight from his public school's OTC camp into the 4/Oxford and Buckinghamshire Light Infantry wrote home: 'I can't get a sword or revolver for love or money, though Harrods are getting me one. My old one

Rosa gave me is no good I'm afraid.'[8] Private purchase of kit by officers had a long history in the British Army, and was officially encouraged in 1914 whilst government suppliers staggered and collapsed under the strain. Manufacturers used department stores such as Army & Navy, and Selfridges to sell their wares; Harrods had a separate 'War Comforts Room'. The three most common pistols for British officers – all .455 inch – were the Mark V/VI Webley, the Colt New Service and the Smith & Wesson Hand Ejector. The cost of a Colt New Service revolver in Harrods' gun department was 90 shillings. Like Greenwell, Second Lieutenant Wheatley was short of his kit-listed Service revolver, until a family friend donated one: the friend was Chief Inspector French of the CID, who gifted young Dennis the Webley & Scott automatic he had just confiscated from a German spy.

Dennis Wheatley was among those bought an armoured tunic by a doting mother. No less than 18 types of body armour were commercially available, which toted such reassuring names as the 'Best Body-shield' and 'Wilkinson's Safety Service Jacket'. Wheatley's armoured vest consisted of:

> a number of oblong steel plates about one and a half inches by an inch linked together at the corners. These were sewn into the lining of the tunic where it covered the back, chest and stomach thus protecting one's vital parts from anything short of a direct hit by a bullet or shell splinter at close range. I demanded that armour should also be inserted in the lower front flaps of the tunic, as the parts this covered were of equal importance to me.[9]

When the shops ran out of kit, or if the allowance would not stretch, officers advertised in *The Times* for revolvers, wrist-watches and field glasses.

Of course, all this was the official Army uniform. New officers quickly became wise to 'unofficial' kit that would make their lives easier. Greenwell requested from his parents, in the same letter as above, a ruck-sack, 'like a Tommy's pack' because it made carrying equipment easier on the march. In the trenches all kit was adapted wildly. German pistols pilfered from the dead were much sought after.

A subaltern's pay in 1914 was 5s 3d, which was raised by Kitchener to 7s 6d a day ('a handsome gesture', thought Charles Carrington). Second Lieutenant H.E.L. Mellersh was pleased to find that he was allowed a 1s/6d Mess Allowance as well, plus a billeting allowance, making £210 per annum; as he had not learnt to drink yet, had only just started smoking ('the status symbol of growing masculinity'), he bought a share of a second hand motor bike with this heady wealth.[10] Further up the commissioned pole, a lieutenant received 8s 6d a day, and a captain 12s 6d. An advantage of overseas service was that pay increased by means of the special field allowance of half a crown a day; as a captain in France Charles Carrington earned over £300 a year; 'This was wealth', he considered. Allowances could be impenetrable, yet were welcomed when they did arrive. John Hay Beith likened allowances to a gift from a benevolent maiden aunt who:

> unexpectedly drops a twenty-pound note into your account at Cox's Bank, murmuring something vague about 'additional outfit allowance'; and as Mr Cox makes a point of backing her up in her little secret, you receive a delightful surprise next time you open your passbook.[11]

Nearly all officers were paid through an account at Cox & Co. at 16 Charing Cross, London. Generally junior officers were encouraged to live within their means, and the prudent and the frugal could even save money. Many an officer, however, struggled with their mess bills, especially officers in smart regiments. The wonderfully named Lieutenant Burgon Bickersteth, 5/Cavalry Reserve Regiment concluded, gloomily, 'I think messing will be an average 7/- a day if not 7/6'.[12] On transferring mid-war to the Household Cavalry Stuart Cloete calculated his mess bill at a daily drain of 12s/6d but:

> I must say I had never lived so well but then I had never lived with such rich men before ... We were messed by a contractor and had every known luxury – pate de foie gras, caviar, oysters, game, fruit, all wonderfully cooked ... [13]

Officers in less prestigious regiments could also feel the strain of keeping up with the Cazenoves as they wined and dined. Dennis Wheatley remembered that: 'It was the many rounds of drinks that kept me perpetually in debt, and a time came when I had to sell my Triumph motorcycle and sidecar.' After a year in the Army 19-year-old Graham Greenwell had to close his account with Harrods and Robert Jackson owing to 'financial straits'.

In Charles Carrington's mess there was a monthly guest night, at which the King's health was drunk; always conscious of the pennies, he was delighted to find that the cost was covered by an additional allowance of sixpence. When the senior officers withdrew from Carrington's mess dinner a 'rough house' would start up. 'Never again, I surmise', Carrington wrote, 'shall I climb round the room from mantelshelf to cornice to window ledge, without touching the floor, or drink a pint of beer standing on my head.'[14] Hi-jinx occurred in the mess of 4/Oxford and Bucks Light Infantry too; after J.P. Hermon Hodge rashly drew his sword to signal drinks all round, Graham Greenwell recalled 'We then had a fight with soda water bottles, in which I got soaked.'[15] They were very young.

Never such innocence again. Eighteen-year-old subalterns going straight from public school into the Army were invariably virgin soldiers. The Victorian corsets of Britain were loosening but not yet undone. Reginald Pound noted of the war years: 'Public behaviour between the sexes conformed to the pattern and proprieties of the waltz.' A teenage subaltern put his arm around the waist of a decent girl but no higher – and certainly not lower – and chaperones were not entirely ogres of the dim past. Dennis Wheatley pursued the wispy Pre-Raphaelite Barbara Symonds, a pupil at Streatham Hill High School where, as was the case with most girls' schools, the gals were not allowed to have boyfriends.[16]

Young officers tended to a highly romantic view of women: in the words of Sidney Rogerson, a twenty-two-year-old officer in the West Yorkshire Regiment: 'Women stood as a symbol of all that we were missing ... The point is that the longing was sensuous as opposed to sensual.'[17] Subalterns could be sharply censorious of any of their ilk who did pursue girls for the pleasures of the flesh. Second Lieutenant

H.B.K. Allpass, who had been in the Fabian Society at Oxford, complained that it had become a 'sort of social duty' to 'walk out with a girl', which he thought undignified.[18] Throughout the war Stuart Cloete searched for, and saved himself for, a 'Venus Aphrodite', which 'was the way many of us thought then'.[19] He found her, dressed as a Voluntary Auxiliary Detachment nurse, in an officers' hospital in London; they married in 1919, when he was twenty-two. Meanwhile, Guy Chapman and his fellow subalterns in 13/Royal Fusiliers were, they discovered, decidedly less 'habited to wayside pleasures' than their senior officers:

> Idling in the mess one afternoon, Sidney Adler, the most irresponsible of our group, suddenly remarked: 'X is with that woman again. He is a dirty dog. And he had that thing in our billet at Ballieul. And he's only been married a few weeks'. 'Too bad', we nodded in agreement. We felt that X was letting the battalion down.[20]

For the louche, there was always a girl who would lay down her body for her countryman. The lure of a well-cut uniform and the air of heightened mortality made a potent aphrodisiac. Dennis Wheatley, who regarded the mere thought of seducing Barbara Symonds 'as sacrilege',[21] was initiated into the pursuit of unchaste girls by his Battery commander, Major Inglis. Married and in his forties, Inglis habitually drove his four seater Rover over to Richmond, a popular promenading venue for crowds of young men and women from all over London. No woman, Wheatley recalled, 'between the ages of 16 and fifty was safe' from Inglis. Across in Maida Vale, senior officers in Cloete's battalion of the King's Own Yorkshire Light Infantry kept a girl called Mona. 'They had some system of apportioning out her time', Cloete recalled.

Junior officers had other, more pressing draws on their time. They needed to be trained.

What training the tyro officer received depended on when, and what, he joined. In the first Autumn of the war it was quite possible to get into uniform and be whisked to the front, purely on the basis of having been in the OTC at university or school. Naturally, any officer intending a Regular commission – a permanent career in the Army – enrolled at the cadet college of Sandhurst for the infantry, or Woolwich Arsenal ('the Shop') for gunners and engineers; both establishments introduced shortened courses in an effort to make more subalterns, faster. Subalterns entering the Special Reserve received permanent commissions, but were expected to be full-time soldiers only while hostilities lasted; afterwards they went on the Reserve list, from which they could be called up in the event of another emergency. A temporary commission was for the duration of the war only. Of the 1914 vintage of temporary and Special Reserve subalterns, most were trained *in situ* by their battalions. Boys who had done time in the OTC had a flying start – according to one Sandhurst instructor OTC boys were three months ahead of their peers who had not been in the Corps – although Robert Graves' stint in Charterhouse's OTC failed to stop him from the humiliation of saluting the Royal Welch's bandmaster.[22] Graham Greenwell was thrown in at the Ox and Bucks deep end: 'The Adjutant came up and made me drill the squad for half an hour yesterday and I got on remarkably well', he wrote to his mother. He added: 'My practice at camp helped me lot',[23] before earnestly reassuring her, 'You will be glad to hear that I am settling down all right … and have made one or two friends.'[24] The 4/Ox & Bucks, aside from being distinctly upmarket, was a Territorial battalion and part-time, but at least half-trained soldiers were reasonably plentiful on the parade ground. *In situ* training in New Army battalions could be particularly haphazard, because of scarcity of resources, and because they tended to have only the faintest peppering of experienced officers and instructors. Guy Chapman was one of the lucky bright-eyed subalterns of 1914; he attended an emergency month-long course at staff college, before joining his battalion for further training. He recalled his shock on first meeting the New Army:

It was not so much the circumstances; the dull little south coast watering-place in winter; the derelict palazzo, the headquarters, facing on one side the tumbling grey sea and on the other an unkempt field; it was not the men in shabby blue clothes and forage caps with their equipment girt about them with bits of string: it was the obvious incapacity and amateurishness of the whole outfit which depressed. The 13th Royal Fusiliers had been broken off from a swarm of men at the depot some three months earlier, and from then left almost completely to its own devices. It never had more than three regular officers, and those very senior and very retired, two drawn from the Indian Army and not one from the regiment. In consequence it had learned nothing of the traditions of its name – few could have told you anything of Alma or Albuerra – and knew nothing of its four regular battalions . . . Many officers displayed only too patently their intention of getting through the war as quietly, comfortably, and as profitably as they could manage.[25]

Future prime minister Anthony Eden arrived at Aldershot for training with his New Army battalion, and was equally depressed by his surroundings: 'The long lines of barracks interspersed with parade grounds succeeded each other in dreary rigidity. In the cold and rain of mid-winter the prospect was drab and dour.'[26]

His training matched his environment; much of it was uninspiring, and more of it was useless, because it was about open warfare and dated back to the Boer War, when all the information coming back from the front suggested that trench warfare was likely to be around for a while. A tragic result of inexperience occurred when an instructor placed a pound slab of TNT under a steel rail and shepherded the spectators back. Not far enough, alas. The 'convincing bang' sent fragments of rail further than anticipated; one of the spectators standing by Eden was killed.

Guy Chapman tried to make good his deficits in the training of the arts of war, by gobbling up the buff official pamphlets entitled *Notes from the Front*, but the advice therein was 'out of date before it was published'. Harold Macmillan (another future prime minister) found an aged gem in his military reading:

In the evenings we studied various textbooks. Infantry Training, Field Service Regulations, Manual of Military Law, took the place of ancient history and philosophy. Occasionally these researches revealed nuggets of pure gold. For instance, 'Officers of Field rank on entering balloons are not expected to wear spurs.'[27]

The making of a mass New Army between 1914 and 1915 was mayhem. Fortunately, as Scottish teacher and subaltern John Hay Beith (who wrote under the pseudonym Ian Hay) expressed in his personal record of the formation of the initial New Army, *The First Hundred Thousand*:

> The outstanding feature of the relationship between officers and men during all this long, laborious, sometimes heart-breaking winter has been this – that, despite the rawness of difficulties which are now happily growing dim in our memory, the various ranks have never quite given up trying, never altogether lost faith, never entirely forgotten the Cause which has brought us together. And the result – the joint result – of it all is a real live regiment, with a morale and soul of its own.[28]

He added that the juniors were very junior, 'but as keen as mustard'. They were. Guy Chapman considered that by 'a compound of enthusiasm and empiricism', the junior officers trained the battalion as well as themselves. There were thousands like them. One lesson that was 'drummed' into Chapman by the few Regulars around him was: 'Get to know your men and they'll follow you anywhere'. The trainee officer was encouraged to know the name and character of every man under him. One officer of the 8/Norfolk Regiment, recorded:

> The officers not only knew their men by sight and by name, and by their military proficiency, but knew many details of their private lives ... Thus was morale and esprit de corps of the battalion fostered.[29]

Charles Carrington recalled Major Lewis, second in command of 9/York and Lancasters, and a ranker promoted from the Guards. Carrington thought him at '42' a great age:

> Perhaps the best schoolmaster I ever had, Major Lewis impressed upon me and my friends one lesson at least, that young officers have no privileges and no rights but only duties. Woe betide any subaltern who ever so much as enquired after his dinner until he had seen his

men fed and made comfortable, or who kept them standing at attention when they might have been standing at ease.[30]

Paternalistic care by an officer for his men was a venerable tradition in the British Army, and would be deepened and expanded by the junior officers of the Great War.

His men. An officer remembered his first platoon for the rest of his life, no matter how long or short that life. Chapman thought the remembrance as vivid as 'one's first pantomime, Dan Leno as the Widow Twanky, and one's first tanning'. Ten years after the war, when he came to write his memoir *Goodbye to All That*, Robert Graves was able to say, 'I still have the roll of my first platoon of forty men'.

An officer would love his men. They would also be an exasperation and a shock.

Eighteen-year-old Graves recalled that his 'greatest difficulty was talking to the men of my platoon with the proper air of authority', unsurprisingly perhaps, when the platoon was in the Special Reserve of the Royal Welch Fusiliers and was full of re-enlisted soldiers, 'a rough lot of Welshmen from the border counties'. Wily old Regulars and Reservists, skins still tanned from service in Africa and India, could have a knowledge of King's Regulations that would reduce a subaltern to pulp.

Subalterns taking charge of a platoon of Territorials or New Army volunteers were likely to have an easier time. The 'Saturday afternoon' soldiers of the Territorials were an informal lot, neighbours in civilian life and used to helping each other when in khaki, regardless of rank. Anthony Eden, known as 'the Boy' because at eighteen he was the youngest subaltern in the company, found that few of his New Army platoon was over twenty-one; he thought their collective youth gave them an all-in-the-same-boat-pulling-together mood. Since Regular battalions of the King's Royal Rifle Corps could not spare NCOs, Eden's battalion selected NCOs from among the platoon on the basis of 'ability as best as we could judge it over a short span'.[31] Eden's platoon sergeant was Reg Park, 'a staunch and wise ally'. They fussed over and discussed the platoon together.

Meeting a platoon of predominantly working class men was often a severe culture shock for a boy fresh from public school. Subalterns were horrified by the foul language of their new charges. 'The men swore a great deal', recalled Stuart Cloete. 'Everything was qualified with bloody and effing. The butter, the bread, the Colonel.'[32] John Christie, an Eton maths master (and later founder of Glyndebourne opera house), commissioned in the King's Royal Rifle Corps, wrote bluntly to a colleague back at the school: 'The men say "fuck" all the time.'[33] Before enlisting Reginald Pound had considered 'bloody' a passport to Hell; the most 'dynamic epithet' in his social circles was 'bally'.[34] Not that his own vocabulary was beyond reproach; reporting for duty at an Army ordnance depot outside Cambridge, Pound was torn off a strip by his commandant, an old Indian major dug out of retirement, for using 'expressions of a petticoat origin'. These turned out to be anything the major considered non-Upper Class and falsely genteel. A particular bug-bear was 'taxi' instead of 'cab'.

Out of the chaos, some training order arrived. From January 1915, the bulk of would-be officers passed through a month-long course organized by senior OTC units, notably the Inns of Court OTC Unattached Battalion, or the Artists' Rifles. Commissioned, they then went on for more training at a Young Officers' Company.

The Artists' Rifles was the subalterns' factory *sans pareil*. Formed as a voluntary unit in 1859 by the painter Edward Sterling and the historian Thomas Carlyle, the Artists' Rifles had both fighting and training battalions during the Great War; the training tone was set by Lieutenant-Colonel William Shirley of 2/Artists' Rifles. Formerly of the Indian Army and a committed Christian soldier, Lieutenant-Colonel Shirley actively recruited officers from the traditional source – the public schools – rather than waiting for the polite knock from pale scrubbed hands on the door. In November 1916 Shirley wrote to headmasters of the public schools asking for the names and dates of birth of the eligible, so that he might 'have the opportunity of putting before them personally the advantages which the Artists' Rifles offer to men of the right class', adding that '6,000 of our cadets have gone on to commissions'.[35]

Thousands went on to Heaven, too. In the preface to the war memorial book of the Artists' Rifles Sir John French wrote:

> I may recall at this moment, without frivolity, the fact that these boys, all of them, looked death straight in the face laughing and smiling, and that the Artists earned at that time the soubriquet of 'The Suicide Club'.[36]

Shirley's Artists' Rifles were taught dash, duty and devotion to the men. His new boys were informed: 'Now that you have entered upon the service of your Country ... you must proceed to serve her with all your heart and with all your soul and with all your mind and with all your strength.' Shirley believed that an officer should always place his men's welfare above his own, while making himself their superior in all matters of the soul. He quoted Horace. '*Dulce et decorum est pro patria mori*.' Wilfred Owen passed through 2/Artists' Rifles; he may have come to doubt it was sweet to die for one's country, but he did not escape Shirley's dictum that an officer should serve his men to the end, which is why the poet chose to return to France after being treated for shellshock. Only weeks before his death in November 1918, Owen wrote to his mother:

> I came out in order to help these boys – directly by leading them as well as an officer can; indirectly, by watching their sufferings that I may speak of them as well as a pleader can. I have done the first.[37]

Everybody taking up the King's commission was taught the same *noblesse oblige*, because the British Army officer had combined pluck and paternalism for centuries. The close relationship between a junior officer and his platoon urged by instructors proved a crucial difference between British and continental armies in the dog years of 1917 and 1918. Shirley, the author of *Morale: The Most Important Factor in War*, however, did the urging particularly well.

H.E.L. Mellersh went from the Inns of Court OTC – a 'footling repetition' after school OTC – to a Young Officers' Company training unit based at Worcester College, Oxford, a journey made memorable by his taking a taxi, the first time he had ever been in a car. His typical day at the YOC consisted of parade, PT, lectures on tactics, military law and military history. When night operations were added, Mellersh discovered that:

> One evening I was so tired that I went to sleep in my room and totally missed my dinner. I was very sorry for myself, but it did not occur to me that I might do anything so rash and expensive and grown-up and sophisticated as go out and buy myself a meal.[38]

One of the difficulties in drill practice at YOCs was that the squad was made up of other young officers. Mellersh recalled:

> set in my turn to drill our Worcester College platoon, I found it incumbent upon me to correct one in the ranks. 'Jones there!' I began. 'I've got a handle to my name!' he shouted back. What a cad, what indiscipline! But I called him Mister Jones after that.

Edmund Blunden, at officer training unit in Sussex, encountered the same dearth of 'Other Ranks':

> We were so many that there were not enough 'other ranks' for us to play at officering, and the medical officer was exceedingly sympathetic in excusing us from duty, which would let us disappear into joyous Brighton – or I would sometimes walk home, 20 miles, in those days.[39]

Young officers were very fit. Training was not only designed to instruct them in the military arts, but to toughen them, since the prerequisite of service in the field was that the officer was bodily fit enough 'to bear the strain of war'. Route marches were physical endurance courses intended to push the cadet to the limit; at Halton Park, near Tring, Stuart Cloete and his fellow cadets emerged from their shivering winter tents to go on a march of 26 miles over snowy roads; it was done in 6 hours and 26 minutes. Six men died en route from heart failure.[40] Alexander Stewart, a 33-year-old planter from Malay granted a commission in The Cameronians Special Reserve, found running around Glasgow streets 'not much fun' and 'rather chilly'.[41]

The upshot of surviving officer training, Richard Talbot Kelly found on leaving Woolwich, was a 'physical fitness undreamed of before'.[42]

Then there were the horses. In the first years of the war, junior officers were taught to ride, because they might be elevated in rank one day to company commander – and captains rode – or need to use a horse in a communications or other emergency. H.E.L. Mellersh recalled:

> Undoubtedly, something of a test was the learning to ride, for few of the young officers were likely ever to have mounted a horse before. . . . We practised on the battalion parade ground, a large long field by the River Plym, but in the evening, when at least the troops were not there to see our discomfitures. No jumps were put up: but that was of no matter, for the field had a steep-banked stream running through it, and that the Adjutant found very apt for training and we trainees very conducive to falling off. I remember with what a glow of pride and relief I learnt to rise in the saddle and so not get jogged to a pulp.[43]

Geoffrey Thurlow fared less well in his equine studies:

> Never shall I forget Edward [Brittain] and myself setting forth in great splendour from some stables in Folkestone, to have our first riding lesson: and my horse bolting with me causing a realistic John Gilpin effect: the Canadian Tommy who restored my hat & handkerchief, which had floated away, without the vestige of a smile on his face always has my admiration.[44]

The year of the Somme saw all-change for officer training, with the creation of Officer Cadet Battalions; nearly all of the 107,929 temporary officers commissioned from February 1916 until the end of the war went through the four-month course of an Officer Cadet Battalion after serving in the ranks. Public schoolboys, however, could still skip into an OCB straight from their school OTC or after having done two months' training with the Inns of Court OTC or the Artists' Rifles. Meanwhile, Sandhurst and Woolwich continued to commission Regular officers, respectively 5,131 and 1,629 over the course of the war.

Henry Ogle was a corporal in the trenches with the Royal War-wickshire Regiment when his company commander announced that any NCOs and men wanting commissions should put their names forward:

> Many of us had discussed the pros and cons long before this. Officer's training would take a matter of months. That at least was something worth consideration on one side. On the other, no one with eyes or brains had any illusions about the life of a subaltern in this war. The fact that we were being asked told its own tale.[45]

Ogle decided to apply for training, and was approved by his Commanding Officer. He was sent for instruction at the 19th Officer Cadet Battalion, based at Pirbright:

> On arrival, all NCOs took down their stripes and all mounted a white cap band labelled 19th OCB. This was the only thing to distinguish an O[fficer] C[adet] from an ordinary soldier but it was very striking indeed.[46]

Gunner L.P. Hartley attended an OCB housed in Sidney Sussex College, Cambridge, finding it a comfortably pleasant change to the life he had known in the ranks:

> There we slept 4 in a room – instead of 30, as at Catterick, and 250 as in my first camp. I studied the infantry regulations and learned more or less, how to behave as an officer. But owing to some physical disability, I could never, marching, quite keep in step, and I remember our sergeant major walking alongside of me and pointing out this defect. But unlike what sergeant majors are supposed to be, and often are, he was a kindhearted man, and I owe it to him (I'm nearly sure) that I was called on to drill the battalion, a feat of which, from nerves and other reasons (e.g., lack of a resonant voice), I should never have been capable of, although the test was part of our schedule.[47]

The bespectacled Second Lieutenant Hartley passed out fit only for Home Service, 'which in my case meant defending the coast of East Anglia from possible German invasion'.[48]

Drill was designed to break the individual, instil discipline, and was regarded from time immemorial as being the most efficient way of controlling a heterogeneous collection of men. An ex-Balliol scholar, Hartley was perhaps fortunate to find such an accommodating drill instructor; another intellectual passing through the OCB system, Arthur Graeme West, found its mechanical sameness purgatory:

> This morning we had saluting drill for half an hour. It was the most pitiably comic parade I have ever seen, even here. First we were drilled in platoons: our official way of carrying the stick was outlined, and a special drill, by numbers, drawn up, for tucking the stick under the arm, taking it into the hand again, and cocking it up in the air. We practised in two movements:
> 1. Put the stick under left arm;
> 2. Cut the right hand away; then
> 1. Seize stick on the under-side;
> 2. Bring it smartly down to the side;
> We were then marched up and down the road saluting by numbers imaginary officers, thus:
> 1. Stick under arm;
> 2. Hand away;
> 1,2,3,4,5, put hand up;
> 6. Hand down;
> 1. Hand up to stick again;
> We did this for quarter of an hour, yelling out the numbers. On all hands were platoons rushing about in the same way.[49]

West was contemptuous about musketry instruction from a sergeant who had never handled a short rifle. He hated the shouting NCOs, and one of his fellow cadets bluntly informed the Company Sergeant Major that 'bullying would do no good with men like us, it simply makes us bored and indifferent'. By 'like us', the cadet meant middle and upper class men who were volunteers.

West's CO was unmoved. He informed the battalion that because they moved and talked on parade, he was devising a system of punishments, with deprivation of weekends the likely penalty. He went on to say that West and his fellows probably detested the Army. They must all do their best and fall into line.

West did. He swapped his cadet's hat with its white band for an officer's cap in the Oxfordshire and Bucks Light Infantry.

As the war progressed the working class began appearing in the officers' mess in greater and greater numbers, in a role other than servant.

Hitherto, an officer had been a gentleman. In 1912, 9 per cent of newly commissioned officers came from titled families and 32 per cent from country landowning families. Nearly all the rest glided out from upper middle class families − of the army and navy sort, of the professional sort, such as clergy, physicians, lawyers − via a public school, predominantly Eton, Cheltenham, and Wellington with their Army streams. Around 2 per cent of the officer corps were promoted rankers.

Although there had been some emergency appointments of rankers in 1914, the shortfall in officers was filled with the public school subalterns. When the blood of boy subalterns began to gush over the dull brown soil of Flanders and the chalk flecked earth of the Somme, promotions from the ranks began to accelerate. Too often it is supposed that all promoted rankers were horny handed sons of toil; they were not. Many were from among the thousands of upper and middle class boys and men who, having missed out in the great commissions rush of 1914, enlisted as privates, particularly in the Public Schools Battalions.[50] 'Smart' regiments anyway continued to maintain their social exclusivity by replenishing themselves from the cream of Sandhurst and being very picky about anyone with a temporary commission; when Henry Dundas (Eton) looked around the faces of his company of Scots Guards in 1917 he saw a Wykehamist, an Harrovian, an old boy of Beaumont (a Roman Catholic public school). Nevertheless, the war did see a marked influx of men into the general officer corps whose social occupations were not 'pukka', and who would not have had a sniff of a Territorial, let alone a Regular, commission in

July 1914. By 1918 about 40 per cent of officers came from working and lower-middle class backgrounds. Since they were now officers, these 'lower fraction' men, by the iron logic of the era, had to be accorded the status of gentlemen. The logic was still more iron clad; because their commissions were temporary, so must their social status be transient. Thus, they were 'Temporary Gentlemen'.

No sooner had Henry Ogle and his fellow cadets passed through the gates of Pirbright Officer Cadet Battalion than the Commanding Officer appeared and:

In his opening speech he told us that his job was to make us Officers *and Gentlemen.*[51]

To this end, a good deal of the OCB course concerned the teaching of etiquette and gentlemanly manners; Ogle recalled 'table manners try-outs', that while excruciating at the time, 'taught us that officers' messes were conducted in a certain way and the experience saved us from embarrassment later'. Arthur Graeme West was lectured: 'Not to go into pubs ... not to go about with obvious tarts, nor get drunk'.[52] One Temporary Gentleman, an ex-clerk in a Brixton office, recalled that the keynotes of training for officers were *'noblesse oblige*, sportsmanship and responsibility'.[53] Perhaps the most effective parts of the 'gentlemanlification' process at OCB, however, were the subtle and hardly recognized ones; many OCBs were in the refined settings of Oxford and Cambridge Colleges and the senior staff exuded old Army style. The gentleman's code was effortlessly rubbed into the 'TGs' by exposure; as Reginald Pound observed during the war, Temporary Gentlemen, by mixing with 'real' gentlemen 'developed a class consciousness that confirmed rather than diminished the old social patterns'.[54] In effect, the OCB course was a crash-lesson on how to be a public schoolboy, short of the inimitable accent. But the point of the course wasn't only to save everyone's blushes in the mess; it was to make lower-class rankers think like public schoolboys and have the self-confidence of public schoolboys. Up to this stage in their lives lower class rankers had been on the receiving end of orders; now they had to give them. They had to think for themselves. (Some OCB courses taught 'leadership'; at Sandhurst and the 'Shop' it was entirely assumed that the public school intake had this quality.)

When Robert Graves was temporarily an instructor at a Cadet Battalion, he and the other instructors administered a test to judge pass or failure of the course. The test was a game of soccer or rugby, and those 'who played rough but not dirty' and had quick reactions were commissioned.[55] In other words, those who could play the sports of gentlemen like gentlemen. Or, indeed, like public schoolboys.

Not everyone was convinced by the phenomenon of 'Temporary Gentlemen' or approved of the broadening of the social basis of the Army. Stuart Cloete, son of a banker and educated at Lancing, returned to active service in 1917 after injury. He joined the Reserve Battalion of King's Own Yorkshire Light Infantry at Rugeley on Cannock Chase:

> Officers who had seen no active service were, with one or two exceptions, running the show. Many of them came from the lower middleclass and had no manners, including table manners, of any kind. I was profoundly shocked by what I saw and heard. Officers in public places with shopgirls on their knees. The way they talked . . . when my room mate, a captain, said, 'I always wash me before I shave', I felt the bottom of the barrel had been scraped for officer material. The full tragedy of the Somme Battle was now beginning to show: thousands of public schoolboys who should have been leading troops had been killed in the ranks of such regiments as the London Scottish, the HAC [Honourable Artillery Company] and Queen Victoria Rifles.[56]

Cloete transferred to the Household Cavalry. Hampshire squire Colonel Sir Morgan Crofton remembered that lots of shellshocked 'TGs' were posted to East Africa, and had no idea how to behave like gentlemen; the Askaris called them 'shensi B'wanas' or 'low class masters'. 'One NCO wanted to know which tribe they were from.'[57] Captain Dalton, himself a promoted ranker and 'Temporary Gentleman' thought that by 1918 soldiers were accepting orders from officers who 1914 Regulars would have made mincemeat of.[58]

Yet overall the 'TGs' were accepted in the mess and acquitted themselves on the battlefield.

The literary epitome of the temporary gentlemen is Lieutenant Trotter in R.C. Sherriff's autobiographical play *Journey's End*. Trotter (a significant name), with his unseemly table manners and talk of jam pips getting behind his mouth-plate, is outnumbered in the officers' dug-out by four public schoolboys, but they think 'He's a genuine sort of chap'. And far superior, because of his bravery, to Hibbert, the well-spoken funk, trying to wheedle his way home. A real life public school officer, Charles Carrington was convinced that by the war's end the Temporary Gentlemen 'proved their worth ... by revealing their talent for responsible leadership, even though their accents were not refined'.[59] Sassoon, despite his many snobberies, acknowledged that in B Company Mess of 1/Royal Welch Fusiliers Evans, who licked his thumb when dealing cards and used the infra dig expression 'pardon' ('That "Pardon" became a little trying at times'), and Casson, who had been educated at Winchester and Oxford, were: 'Equally good when tested, these two merged their social incompatibilities in the end; both were killed on 26 September.'[60]

Throughout the war, the men would evidence a preferment for officers of the 'traditional sort', especially young swells, but the Temporary Gentlemen did not let the side down. As one pre-war Regular said with brutal candidness regarding Temporary Gentlemen: 'You can't make a silk purse out of a sow's ear, but you can make a good leather one.'[61]

The Temporary Gentlemen too played up, and played the game.

For subalterns training in their battalions, the training seemed to take forever. All they wanted to do was get to France. Roland Leighton wrote to Vera from the Esplanade Hotel, in dreary Lowestoft, in the first dreary winter of the war:

> It only makes me angry, angry with myself for being here, and with the others for being content to be here when men whom I have once despised as effeminate are sent back wounded from the front, when nearly everyone I know is either going or has gone, can I think of this with anything but shame?[62]

H.B.K. Allpass wrote in lighter tone in *Stars for Subalterns*, the camp magazine at Halton Camp on 26 March 1916:

> Of course every one wants the war to stop – abstractly; but I not having been out, don't want it to stop yet. A week in the trenches, one charge, the DSO (which is much more dignified than the VC) and a wound in the left arm is my own idea. (Providence, please note.)[63]

Providence did not note; Allpass was killed six months later.

To H.E.L. Mellersh's chagrin he spent nine months training with the East Lancashires before being drafted for France; during his time of 'over-long training' he became impatient, bored and lonely. Battalions constantly sent off young officers on courses (musketry being a favourite), bringing them back to teach the same subject in the battalion; the recycling economics were praiseworthy, but the flux made friendship tricky. When some 'Sandhurst pups' of his own age[64] debouched into the battalion, he found them to be a 'very close-knit and self-satisfied and bouncy bunch of pups at that.'[65] He enjoyed the pomp of guest night in mess, however, the singing of the national anthem, the passing of port ('strong stuff!') and

> then the final touch: a waiter with a box of snuff, a regimental tradition. 'You have to, sir!' Sniffings from the backs of hands. A few sneezes, a little laughter.[66]

Another 18-year-old, Bernard Martin in the Special Reserve Battalion of the North Staffs, had to deal with institutional loneliness; the North Staffs kept up the regimental tradition of not speaking in the mess to new subalterns for a fortnight. To cheer himself up, he read and re-read his commission. And at least Army discipline was no problem, 'fundamentally the same as public school'.

If not training, the young 'sub' might be posted to decidedly non-heroic duties at home, while the lumbering Army machine sorted out the order of battalions for France. Graham Greenwell's first job was the hum-drum one of guarding the Marconi Station in Chelmsford.

Edward Brittain, meanwhile, oversaw the digging of defensive trenches . . . at Wrotham in Kent:

> It is awfully boring for the officers having to watch the men dig and to measure as they go along; occasionally I dig myself but am not really supposed to, as we are supposed to superintend.[67]

Commissioned as a second lieutenant in the Manchester Regiment Wilfred Owen wrote:

> The sub. has a stiffish day's work: has to do the 'Third' Physical Training (i.e. most strenuous) at 6.15, carries pack on parade & march, and has a good deal of responsibility, writing, and ceremonial to fetter him. I had the misfortune to walk down the road to some Camp Shops when the men were 'at large': and had to take *millions* of salutes . . . My most irksome duty is acting Taskmaster while the tired fellows dig: the most pleasant is marching home over the wild country at the head of my platoon, with a flourish of trumpets, and an everlasting roll of drums.[68]

Owen had just taken the Army exam to qualify for service in the field. For this the officer 'must know, or have good knowledge of: DISCIPLINE; DRILL; MUSKETRY; TACTICS AND FIELD WARFARE; TOPOGRAPHY; BILLETING; MACHINE GUNS; INTERIOR ECONOMY AND MILITARY LAW; PHYSICAL DRILL; SIGNALLING; TRENCH WARFARE'.

All these headings had copious sub-sections: in 'Trench Warfare' the officer had to have a knowledge of 'Handling of commonest Bombs and Explosives; Telling off a Working Party and allotting a Task; Loopholing and revetting; Common types of Trenches and Dug-outs; Entanglements; Obstacles; The relief and handing over of a Platoon in the Trenches by day and night; Construction, repair, holding and capture of Trenches; Duties of a leader of a Grenade Party; Methods of training and employment of Grenadiers'.

You could take a boy to training, but you could not necessarily make him learn: Vyvian Trevenen's 41st Battery, Royal Field Artillery, was presented in France with one Second Lieutenant H.W. Copland.

'He has not had any training at all', Trevenen entered in his diary.

Impatient young officers, despairing of their battalion *ever* seeing action, pestered to transfer to units seemingly more likely to be sent out to the Western Front. After six months of letter-writing Roland Leighton succeeded in switching to the 7/Worcestershire Regiment, and went off to France in April 1915.

Harold Macmillan was another of the myriad impatient; believing that his Kitchener battalion was well down the list for dispatch across the Channel, he 'began to lose heart'. So he pulled some distinguished strings and got a transfer to the Reserve Battalion of the Grenadier Guards in March 1915. Were such personal, nepotistic favours reprehensible? In his memoirs Macmillan wrote: 'The only privilege I, and many others like me, sought was that of getting ourselves killed or wounded as soon as possible.'[69]

The long-wanted wire from the War Office with the order for France could come at any time. Douglas Gillespie of the 4/Argyll and Sutherland Highlanders received his order in Sunderland at 10.00 in the morning of 19 February 1915; by 4.30 in the afternoon he was sitting in a railway carriage puffing down through the Midlands, writing to his parents:

> Of course I know what this news means to you at home – for we have all the fun and excitement – and you have all the waiting, which is far, far harder, and it makes me ashamed that I have been so impatient with my own little worries at Sunderland, when I think how brave and good and patient you and Daddy have been all these months. I was always proud to be your son, but you have made me prouder than ever – and you and Daddy must remember when I am in France that my greatest help will always be to think of you at home, for whatever comes I shall be ready for it.[70]

Captain Lionel Crouch, a 28-year-old solicitor and Territorial officer, volunteered for foreign service ('I wouldn't be left behind for the world. I should feel such a cur') in August 1914 and then spent eight months of 'weary' training and digging with his beloved 1/Ox and

Bucks 'Terriers' while other Territorial battalions went off to France. 'Isn't it perfectly galling?' he wrote to his father from camp in Chelmsford. Finally, on 28 March 1915 the 1/Ox and Bucks received their orders for France. Crouch wrote to his father:

> Dear Old Dad . . . One more thing, if anything does happen to me for goodness sake don't go into mourning of any kind. There is nothing to mourn about.[71]

He also dropped a line to his mother, asking her to pass on his love to the rest of the family including Winkle, Dick, Gibbs and Cuthbert. (A pekinese, a terrier, a cat and a tortoise.)

By 'the inexorable decree' of the War Office, as frustrated subaltern Charles Douie expressed it, the age of officers serving in the field went up from seventeen to eighteen and a half, and then from 1915, to nineteen years old. (The reason for the raising of the age bar for field service was public disquiet over the youthfulness of many of the dead.) In that latter year Charles Carrington, below the age bar and in love with his platoon, was 'heartbroken' watching them march away to the station in August 1915 without him; he ' felt finished, disgraced and my war over'.[72] He was sent to the Reserve Battalion, which was full of supernumeraries, convalescents, shirkers and slackers. He escaped by getting an uncle in the 5/Royal Warwickshire Regiment to wangle a transfer; by this 'unusual – I think – irregular' switch from Kitchener's Army to the Territorials, he ended in the trenches facing Gommecourt Wood in time for Christmas 1915, 'secretly gratified that I had reached my goal irregularly, before my nineteenth birthday'.[73] In the confusing switch from one army to another Carrington's tender age had gone unnoticed. Not everyone was so gung-ho at being ordered for France. The order to go was one of those sudden moments of realization that the War was for real, not for playtime. Guy Chapman:

> I was loath to go. I had no romantic illusions. I was not eager, or even resigned to self-sacrifice, and my heart gave back no answering throb to the thought of England. In fact, I was very much afraid; and again, afraid of being afraid, anxious lest I should show it. Nevertheless,

I concluded that it was easiest to meet a fate already beginning to overawe, as an integral figure in the battalion I had been born into.[74]

For officers crossing to France the weight limit of personal luggage was 35 lbs total. Alas, as John Hay Beith wrote about the officer:

> He is the victim of his female relatives, who are themselves the victims of those enterprising tradesmen who have adopted the most obvious method of getting rid of otherwise unsaleable goods by labelling everything 'For Active Service' – a really happy thought when you are trying to sell a pipe of port or a manicure set. Have you seen Our Active Service Trouser-Press?[75]

In Beith's experience, the young subaltern tended to accumulate during his training, with a view to facilitating the destruction of the foe abroad:

> An automatic Mauser pistol, with two thousand rounds of ammunition.
> A regulation Service revolver.
> A camp bed.
> A camp table.
> A camp chair.
> A pneumatic mattress.
> A sleeping (or "flea") bag.
> A portable bath.
> A portable wash-stand.
> A dressing-case, heavily ballasted with cut-glass bottles.
> A primus stove.
> A despatch case.
> The "Service" Kipling (about forty volumes.)
> Innumerable socks and shirts.
> A box of soap.
> Fifty boxes of matches.
> A small medicine chest.
> About a dozen first-aid outfits.
> A case of pipes, and cigarettes innumerable.
> About a cubic foot of chocolate (various).
> Numerous compressed foods and concentrated drinks.

An "active service" cooking outfit.
An electric lamp, with several refills.
A pair of binoculars.
A telescope.
A prismatic compass.
A sparklet siphon.
A luminous watch.
A pair of insulated wire-cutters.[76]

To help subalterns avoid the *embarrassment de choix*, the 14th (Service) Battalion East Yorkshire Regiment gave officers going abroad a prescribed list of kit, which came in a shade under the recommended weight: A Wolseley Valise (a canvas sleeping bag that doubled as a holdall and named after the British general that invented it), a sleeping bag (Jaeger being the preferred manufacturer), blankets, cork mattress, pair of slacks, tunic, underclothes (complete set), a folding lantern. There was a touch of luxury in a pair of Jaeger slippers with leather soles. Recommended was a small mirror for shaving and only one hairbrush, 'weight being most important'.

III

I Like to Hear the Allyman's Shells:
The Journey to the Front Line

After two hours in an oily ship and then in a grimy train, the 'war area' was a haven of relief.

Lieutenant Charles Sorley, Suffolk Regiment

Women in white waving handkerchiefs on a packed platform. A military brass band playing. A scattering of civilian be-suited men, canes and hats, looking on proudly. A row of shining-faced troops leaning out of a railway carriage window. Smoke billowing sulphurous from the engine into a station's cavernous roof.

Only at the beginning of the war did the hero get the hero's send-off of photographic record. Second Lieutenant Brian Horrocks, barely eighteen, marched his men of the Middlesex Regiment down to the railhead at Chatham in balmy August 1914, amid cheering crowds, and 'felt like a king among men'. His only anxiety was the then commonplace one: that the war would be over before he got to it. Other gentlemen in England plainly did not want to be left abed; Horrocks arrived at Southampton docks with three more troops than he had been assigned.[1]

Two long war years later at Waterloo Station, Lieutenant Brian Lawrence of 1/Grenadier Guards found a 'good crowd' on the platform to see him off, but it was one of friends and relatives, and members of that other family, the regiment.[2] No cheering strangers. No photographers. No band. Charles Douie 'was not surprised, nor distressed' at the absence of ceremony at Victoria Station on his departure for France also in 1916, yet the lack rankled enough for him to remember it in his memoir of the war, written a decade after its end.[3] By 1916 indifference had settled on the public, the war had become routine. For those going to the war, their departure was anything but mundane, no matter the year. It was the adventure of a lifetime, which might bring a death time. In the circumstances every soldier wanted a little pomp.

A subaltern with the 1/Dorsetshire Regiment, Douie aptly entitled his account of the war, *The Weary Road*. The sheer numbing fatigue of the war, which would grind down the halest and heartiest of officers, began as soon as the officer climbed up the small wooden steps into the boat train for France, because the journey to the trenches was a locomotive and maritime marathon. Edward Brittain, Vera's brother and a lieutenant in 11/Sherwood Foresters, took 54 hours to reach the Flanders frontline from London in February 1916. He judged the time 'not bad'. The journey could take four sapping days or more.

During the Great War a thick and vast umbilical cord developed between Britain and her soldier children in France and Flanders. Nearly four million men entrained at Waterloo, Charing Cross and Victoria to pass along the railway artery to the south coast and from there across the Channel by boat; returning along the vein of the *funiculus umbilicalis* were the used up, those on leave, the injured and discarded. Fresh blood out, stale blood back. Less returned, because 750,000 men were buried in a corner of a foreign land.

By common acknowledgement, the British boat trains were decent enough (Pullman carriages were occasionally laid on) but slow enough, at six hours, recalled Second Lieutenant Guy Chapman of 13/Royal Fusiliers, for the excitement of boy subalterns to still as they began to suffer the 'juvenile softness' of hunger.[4] Wykehamist Douglas Gillespie neatly avoided the famine on the train by alighting and popping into his conveniently placed *alma mater* to have 'a very cheerful dinner with the Headmaster'. A fellow Winchester-educated subaltern, R.C. Hutchison, joined them.[5]

The real discomfort began at the embarkation port. Tiredness was already setting in; conversation had dried up ('shop' was rarely discussed); the shaven-headed men – if the officer was taking a draft across for the regiment – had become unruly; and many games of nap had already been played. On reaching the docks at Southampton or Folkestone, officers would clamber down, their packs on their backs, to the waiting grey-painted steamers on the grey sea. Also waiting would be the Maritime Loading Officer – who would, in all likelihood, announce a delay. There was a U-boat scare. The sea was too rough. There was a shortage of boats. Brian Lawrence waited for more than a day before boarding the *Marguerite*, a paddle steamer that in peacetime did the run to the Isle of Man. Embarkation, when it eventually came round, was prefaced by a police check of papers. Then, mounting the gangway, every officer and man was handed Lord Kitchener's message to troops proceeding on active service:

> You are ordered abroad as a soldier of the King to help our French comrades against the invasion of a common Enemy. You have to perform a task which will need your courage, your energy, your patience. Remember that the honour of the British Army depends on your individual conduct. It will be your duty not only to set an example of discipline and perfect steadiness under fire but also to maintain the most friendly relations with those whom you are helping in this struggle. The operations in which you are engaged will, for the most part, take place in a friendly country, and you can do your own country no better service than in showing yourself in France and Belgium in the true character of a British soldier.
>
> Be invariably courteous, considerate and kind. Never do anything likely to injure or destroy property, and always look upon looting as a disgraceful act. You are sure to meet with a welcome and to be trusted; your conduct must justify that welcome and that trust. Your duty cannot be done unless your health is sound. So keep constantly on your guard against any excesses. In this new experience you may find temptations both in wine and women. You must entirely resist both temptations and, while treating all women with perfect courtesy, you should avoid any intimacy.
>
> Do your duty bravely.
> Fear God.
> Honour the King.
> KITCHENER.
> *Field-Marshal*

On board, officers settled their drafts and issued lifejackets. As the ship pulled out of harbour, there was a moment of reflection. Always. Until then the war had never been quite real, and the train journey to the coast oddly reminiscent of a seaside holiday. As the white cliffs of England disappeared, 19-year-old Charles Douie was struck by the realization that, ineluctably, 'The hour of action had begun'. Lieutenant Vyvian Trevenen, a Regular in the Royal Field Artillery, wrote in his diary:

> Finished embarking at 9.30 a.m. and I then left England for the first time in my life. I wondered if I should ever return again. The sea was glassy and there was not a cloud in the sky. I could hardly believe I was going to war and it seemed more like a troop ship going out to India.[6]

Foreign travel, even amongst the privileged, was uncommon in early twentieth century Britain. For many of the Great War's officers such as Trevenen their first war and their first experience of an alien land were one and the same. Interest and anxiety swirled in the mind in equal measure.

Vyvian Trevenen did not return. His first trip abroad was his last.[7]

The troopships into which the soldiers were bundled were either commandeered paddle steamers or commandeered crude and bare cargo boats. Some army officers regarded the Channel crossing as one of the worst aspects of service on the Western Front. Overfull, the troopship ploughed into the tossing Channel, with Royal Navy destroyers and airships sailing alongside to protect against U-boats. There were many desperate aids against travel sickness – Lieutenant Alexander Stewart of the Cameronians swore by bromide – but the reality was that in anything other than the glass-flat conditions Trevenen encountered vomiting was ubiquitous. Second Lieutenant Robert Mackay of 11/Argyll and Sutherland Highlanders, after confiding to his diary that he: 'had no regrets, and did no moralizing as I saw the white cliffs of Dover recede from view', was promptly seasick. The journey made a strange democracy of the army as he, a mere subaltern, threw up over the rails with senior officers to the side of him.[8] As the most junior of junior officers Guy Chapman was stationed in the bowels of the boat; he could only find sitting space on the stairs and was jostled by everyone passing. The odour of sweat clotted between the decks. His nausea began to mount. Finally, he was relieved and he climbed wretchedly to the bows; 'Two destroyers flirted playfully round and about us, making signals at intervals. Someone began to talk about submarines. I didn't care. I looked down into the sea and was very ill.'[9] The misery of a bad crossing was graphically described by Lionel Crouch:

> Dearest Mother,
>   Oh, I've had the deuce of a time, as the parrot said when the monkey had plucked him. Our journey was uneventful as far as our port of embarkation, and then our troubles began. The boat was a small one with very limited accommodation, only a small smoking room for about 300 officers. The crossing was awful, more like purgatory than anything else, and if someone at Havre had offered me 100 down and another week's leave to go back that night I wouldn't have accepted his offer. I was awfully sick for seven and a half hours ; everybody was sick everywhere and on everything and everybody. Some officers were so bad that they didn't care, and lay down in it. Some officers had brought over some greyhounds; they were sick too. When we landed, I felt so weak that I could hardly stand, and it was twenty-four hours before I could face a smoke or anything but the very plainest things to eat. I couldn't possibly face those pork turn-overs, and swapped them for sandwiches.[10]

Even those not green-faced and gripping the rails were rarely comfortable. On board the *Marguerite* Brian Lawrence was pipped to the paltry two cabins by senior officers. 'We', he wrote, 'just had to settle down on the filthy deck as best we could on a part which was covered over by an awning; it was very hard sleeping, and draughty.'[11] Second Lieutenant Francis Hitchcock on a crossing from Folkestone, 'packed like sardines', slept on the saw-dusty floor of the bar.

It *was* possible to cross over in comfort, given good weather and a good ship. Eighteen-year-old John Glubb, a Regular with the 7th Field Company Royal Engineers, sailed on the *Hantonia*, which had the distinct advantage of being a real cross-Channel craft, indeed the very boat Glubb had taken to Normandy on holiday with his parents two years before. Frank Warren, promoted from the ranks, travelled across on a fast paddle-steamer, the *Princess Clementine*, sitting on a comfortable seat and 'basking in the sun' on the upper deck. If the sea was a mill-pond and one was in the Guards then one might even do the crossing in rare, rare style: after Second Lieutenant Harold Macmillan of the 4/Grenadier Guards had seen to the comfort of the 'Other Ranks', he and his fellow officers of No. 1 Company were ushered into the saloon of their craft. There, wrote Macmillan to his mother, was a full luncheon, 'with napery, crockery, silver, and all the rest'. The *maitre d'hotel* was Charles from the Ritz. 'We ate in a kind of rapturous silence from 1.30–3.30.'[12] The meal had been laid on by Captain J.A. Morrison, 'a man of equal wealth and generosity'. A Boer War veteran who had stepped forward to serve his country once more, 'Jummie' Morrison was best described as 'portly'. Morrison's morphology would later cause Macmillan problems under fire at Loos, because Morrison refused to do anything as uncomfortable and undignified as crawl, so he steadfastly sauntered amidst the shot and shell. Macmillan felt obliged to do the same as his commanding officer: 'I therefore walked about, trying to look as self-possessed as possible under a heavy fire.' Macmillan received an injury to the head, and a bullet through the hand.[13]

All officers leaving for the front were required to carry webbing and full pack, which left them fantastically upholstered. And so the enervated Guy Chapman came a 'cropper' disembarking at Boulogne:

> As I staggered on to the quay, burdened with a pack weighing 53lbs, a rifle, a revolver, field-glasses, a prismatic compass, 120 rounds of rifle ammunition and 24 of revolver, my newly nailed boots shot from under me and I clattered on the *pavé*.

The Regimental Sergeant Major bawled at him, but Chapman was too 'shattered' to assert his authority and picked himself up to meekly totter up the ramp.[14]

Most arrivals landed at Havre or Boulogne, although Rouen and Calais were also used. Wherever they landed the disembarked would be greeted with flocks of signs in flaming red letters: *Taisez-vous, méfiez-vous, les Oreilles de l'ennemi vous écoutent*. Looking at the signs Bernard Martin realized: 'Now I was in a country where war was a reality; here anyone could be a spy'. The war was getting closer.

An officer not destined to go straight to a unit – the majority of officers after 1916 – would spend the night in a transit camp outside the port, before proceeding by rail to Etaples and its environs, the dreary universe of the base depot, where regiments processed people and provided extra training. A vast tented city for 100,000 men on a wasteland of dunes, Etaples, considered Robert Mackay, was the 'last place on earth ... The atmosphere surrounding the place was rotten'. The base's ambience, Max Plowman noted to himself, was not improved by the dominating British cemetery, its ground 'smothered with wooden crosses'.[15] One of life's optimists, Charles Douie at least enjoyed the bracing winter dawns by the sea.[16] He was taken too with the sheer size of the encampment, 'which spoke of the growing might of the British Expeditionary Force'.[17]

The routine at Etaples was unchanging. Breakfast was at 5.45. From 7 a.m. to 5.30 p.m. officers and men alike were in the 'bullring' training grounds. The bullrings were the finishing schools of the British infantry soldier. Under the auspices of the 'Canaries', the permanent instructors with their signature yellow arm-bands, officers and men were given intensive instruction in drill (of course), fist-and-boots unarmed combat, trench-digging, running uphill, bombing, bayonet-fighting, and trench attacks. This facsimile warfare was intentionally physically demanding. On a single morning in 1917 Lieutenant Joseph Maclean went twice over Etaples' infamous 'final assault course' in full equipment.

> It is a series of rushes from trench to trench, the intervening space being strewn with barbed wire, high wire, shell holes etc., and they have fellows throwing huge fir cones at you all the time to represent bombs.[18]

Maclean was fortunate that the exercise only involved fir cones. Edwin Campion Vaughan recalled an exercise to repel trench-invaders at Etaples that involved lobbing practice bombs containing sufficient explosive strength to 'lay out any unlucky recipient'.[19] In retrospect, officers who passed through the bullrings would value the training given there. But hardly anybody forgave the brutal bullying by the NCO instructors or the indifference of the permanent officer staff, which dehumanized all who endured it. Wilfred Owen wrote to his mother of Etaples:

> It is a vast, dreadful encampment. It seemed neither France nor England but a kind of paddock where beasts were kept a few days before the shambles. There was a strange look on all faces in that camp; an incomprehensible look which a man will never see in England nor can be seen in any battle, only in Etaples.[20]

When troops at Etaples mutinied in 1917, few who had passed through the base depot were surprised. Captain Cyril Mason of the 60th Rifles wrote:

> A base camp is utterly different from one's own battalion, where officers and men are known to each other. In a base camp the men are constantly passing through ... The permanent staff of the officers is small. They are supposed to be helped by officers passing through, but officers passing through for one or two days cannot really be much help. In a base camp much of the routine work devolved onto the permanent base NCOs, some of whom abused their position taking bribes for privileges and leave passes.[21]

The riots at Etaples were a negative proof of the importance of the companionate bond between junior officers and 'Other Ranks': where no bond existed, things fell apart. The rioters exhibited no grudges against officers as a class; on the contrary frontline officers at Etaples were conspicuously well-treated by the rioters, who reserved their loathing for the Canaries.

At Etaples, officers in transit undoubtedly had an easier time than the men, not least because they were kept there for a shorter time, a week or so, as opposed to a month. Officers also had greater freedom of movement and less supervision; Edwin Campion Vaughan, having already learned the sly art of 'miking' [skiving], succeeded in missing all but one of the compulsory lectures, which gave him plenty of time to visit the delights of Paris Plage. Vaughan's stay was further enlivened by an officers' call to meet in the bullring in fighting order, where 800 troops had been assembled. Vaughan and his fellow officers were instructed to lead the men in a search for nine Australians who had escaped from custody and were 'committing outrages'. The hunt for Australians broke down and turned into one for rabbits instead.[22] Like many a subaltern in a base camp, Bernard Martin's preoccupation was to be posted to the front, and he fretted that: 'It would be tragic to be stuck at a base depot while the war petered out.' He need not have worried; this was 1916.

The end of the officer's stint at base was marked by his posting. An officer always hoped this was to a battalion of his regiment, even to the battalion of his choice, but he might well find himself attached to another regiment. When Robert Graves received his orders to go 'up the line' he was 'disgusted' to find himself posted not to the Royal Welch Fusiliers, but to the Welsh Regiment. Charles Douie of the Dorsetshire Regiment got the subaltern's short straw, and was sent off to an Entrenching Battalion digging a reserve line on the Somme: 'I accepted my fate with resignation,' wrote Douie, 'convinced that the digging of a reserve line must present greater reality than the tedious mock warfare and I would be nearer to my regiment and to the front line over which still rested an aureole of glamour.'[23]

Whether proceeding directly from the port or from the base camp, the journey 'up the line' was done by rail.

As every officer found after presenting his destination voucher to the Railway Transport Officer, the trains in France were an impenetrable, exhausting mystery. The trains went in inexplicable directions, they stopped for no reason. Sometimes they halted purely for the convenient financial arrangement of the driver and an accomplice who ran a snack stall. At Fontenettes, outside Calais, Douie's train took a rest. 'I gathered that engines usually expired at this point, as there was a hut presided over by a fairy godmother, supplied with unheard-of delicacies, real tea and pate-de-foie gras sandwiches.'[24] This was a lucky stop indeed, because the Army's notion of feeding passengers, Lionel Crouch discovered, was:

to chuck into each carriage a chunk of cheese, eight tins of bully beef, and about twenty dog-biscuits. There was no opportunity given of getting any food or drink en route.[25]

And when the trains did go, they went so, so very slowly. 'The train moved on', wrote Lieutenant Dennis Wheatley of the Royal Field Artillery, 'but only in a manner that one associates with native-run railways in the more desolate parts of Earth.'[26] Commonly people got off and walked alongside. John Glubb took seven and half hours to do the forty miles from Le Havre to Rouen which, being a 'sapper', he quickly worked out to be five and a quarter miles per hour.[27] The perverse habits and innate slothfulness of the trains meant that journeys to the front line took an apparent eternity. 'The journey up from base seemed absolutely endless', remembered the spectacled Paul Jones, going out as an officer in the ASC but still determined to shift to a fighting unit. Some examples of the escargot pace of the trains in France in wartime: on leaving Etaples at 4.30 p.m. on 12 September 1916 Robert Mackay arrived at Albert on the Somme at 6.30 p.m. on 13 September – a distance of 70–80 miles in 28 hours (a journey which takes an hour and half by car today); Graham Greenwell spent a day and three quarters on the train travelling the 200 miles from Le Havre to Ploegsteert ('Plugstreet' to the monoglot Tommies), his journey not improved by the Flanders landscape outside the window, its flat monotony broken only by occasional ruler-straight lines of poplars.

Travelling companions could be help or hindrance on the long journey to nowhere; Lionel Crouch shared a carriage with a French private who 'insisted on exhibiting a loathsome wound in his leg which he got last January and of which he was very proud. Luckily we had already had our breakfast.'[28]

The length of the journey grated with young officers keen to get to the front. The discomfort of the boneshaker trains affected all. When whole battalions were on the move, the men were loaded in livestock trucks with the indelible legend: 'Chevaux (en long) 8: Hommes 40'. Officers travelled in passenger carriages, which rarely had heating or lighting, although broken windows and soiled upholstery were fitted as standard. Consequently, deduced Sidney Rogerson, an infantry captain, there was 'little difference in degree of comfort between officers and men'; if anything, the men packed together on straw were probably warmer.[29] Frank Warren, risen from the ranks to a one pip officer disagreed: 'There are five of us in a 1st class compartment, and this is comfortable indeed compared with 42 [sic] in a horse truck!', he wrote in his diary. John Glubb lamented the carriages' lack of brakes, because every slowing and stopping of the train produced 'a succession of bang-bang-bangs all the way down the train, making sleep impossible'.

Of course, a wily veteran wanting to extend a leave or to delay an arrival in the trenches could take advantage of the lethargy and incompetence of the trains. Transferring – finally – from the Welsh Regiment to the Royal Welch Fusiliers in 1915, Second Lieutenant Robert Graves and a fellow subaltern took a leisurely, lunch-hopping 54 hours to travel 17 miles by train in Laventie sector.[30] Nobody batted an eyelid, because even if they had been rushing their journey might have taken as long.

And then the train arrived at the railhead. From there the officer travelling alone had to use his ingenuity to reach his destination. Chutzpah helped. Dumped in Hazebrouck, cavalry officer Burgon Bickersteth pestered the Medical Corps to give him a lift in an ambulance. Graham Greenwell borrowed a horse, as did Lionel Crouch. Gunner Richard Talbot Kelly alighted at Locon, behind the Festubert front:

> A small party of us found ourselves stranded at Corps HQ with Division still some eight or nine miles away. I was persuaded to go to Corps and ask for a motor bus to take us to the Divisional HQ. I was shown into a room, furnished as an office, bare and comfortless, where a young staff captain gave me a written order for a bus. That officer was the Prince of Wales.[31]

An iron rule of the Great War was that one could never absolutely judge a man's social rank by his uniform cover. Later in the war, while making his way into No. 12 Casualty Clearing Station at Hazebrouck, Second Lieutenant John Glubb graciously tipped the RAMC corporal who carried his bag for him; the RAMC corporal was the Earl of Crawford, the Premier Earl of Scotland, who, being too old for a commission, had enlisted as a private in the medical corps.

The railhead at Poperinge in the Ypres salient gave Bernard Martin his first shocking sight of war:

> My train to Poperinge stopped short of the station, setting before my startled eyes a panorama of chaos – a derailed train with carriages overturned across a great hole in the permanent way; a large signal box now a heap of charred timber with contorted machinery sticking from it; station buildings with holes in roofs and walls, and broken glass everywhere.[32]

Martin was informed by the RTO that he had no transport to offer him, because everything was being destroyed by 'Little Willie', a naval gun set up by the Germans somewhere in their rear. Shortly afterwards, while walking along and alone to join his battalion at the forbiddingly named Shrapnel Corner, Martin was shelled by the said Little Willie: 'I flung myself on the ground, pressing my body to the earth passionately. The world shuddered beneath me, a roar assailed my ears, my head seemed to split.' On finally daring to raise himself from the ground, Martin wondered if he had not been rather hasty in volunteering for service. The Webley & Scott pistol at his side 'seemed no weapon to aim at some ineluctable power from the sky'.

The officer alighting at the railhead with his battalion or with a draft would march to the frontline or the billets behind it. Formed into fours by platoons in company columns, the men stepped it out. Fifty minutes in the hour. Fifteen miles a day. At first the men would march with full discipline, then would come the order for 'easy', rifles would be slung more comfortably, and pipes and cigarettes lit. A column on the march would have the appearance of a smoking centipede as it pounded the stone *pavé* on the poplar-lined roads of France. There would be singing. At first.

Marching was truly the weary road. Bowed down with 60lbs or so of kit, men would fall out under the strain, feet bleeding from the friction of ill-fitting boots on the relentless unyielding stone, cramps in the legs, their heart beating out of its cage. A march that began with singing in the morning would end the day with silent, sullen 'sticking it' in driving rain or Saharan heat and dust.

It is a falsity too generally accepted that officers were spared the rigors of marching, by riding a horse or placing their baggage on a mess cart. Only company commanders rode horses (and not all company commanders could ride, or horses be found for them); Captain Lionel Crouch pounded along the *pavé* in April 1915 at the head of his 'Terriers', admitting that 'It was jolly hot work in a lambskin-lined British warm with all one's Christmas tree arrangements hanging on.' A 'Christmas tree' was a Sam Browne hung with binoculars, map-case, water bottle and other kit; on an officer with a skirted khaki jacket, the effect was indeed to look like a Yuletide fir tree. Subalterns invariably walked, which is one reason why suave Harrods, and other stores for gentlemen, sold such feet-soothing potions as Weerifoot tablets ('to soothe and tone up tired and tender feet') and Eez anti-septic foot powder ('Gives instant relief to tired, weary, aching feet, and is indispensable to men on the march'). Subalterns invariably ported their own packs; Roland Leighton recalled 'carrying the same heavy equipment as men in addition to revolvers, field glasses etc'.[33] A platoon commander, indeed, in an effort to help his men would often carry some of their kit as well as his own. While Guy Chapman's battalion of the Royal Fusiliers marched along, the boy subalterns, although as laden as the men, were 'energetically passing up and down the ranks, encouraging and cursing, sometimes bearing two, even three rifles of those found faltering'.[34] Edwin Campion Vaughan marching to billets, after 'cursing and encouraging' his exhausted men, ended up carrying an additional pack and two rifles; 'other officers were doing more or less the same', he recalled.[35] Siegfried Sassoon wrote in his diary of a 15 mile march to Villers Bocage in April 1917: 'I covered the last lap trundling two of them [his men] in front of me, while another one straggled along behind, hanging on to my belt'.[36] The captain on his high-and-mighty horse, meanwhile, would festoon it with the packs of staggering soldiers.

Noblesse oblige. The British officer marched on it. Naturally, self-interest might play a part in an officer helping a ranker with his kit.

Francis Hitchcock carried Private Farrell's rifle to allow him to play the bagpipes, the sound of which Hitchcock loved. The march could be a trial in the officer's mind, as well as his feet. Large files of marching men tended to bunch up, then string out, and even bang into the preceding file. Bad marching increased the 'concertina' effect, and was only overcome by the constant to-and-fro vigilance of the platoon commander whose chief duty on the march, recalled Max Plowman, was to 'keep the men properly closed up [and], taking no more than their correct amount of road space either way'.

The officer marching in the cocoon of his battalion was footsore and frazzled but free of an ordeal suffered by the officer travelling alone, who tipped up nervously on the doorstep of a unit about which he might know nothing. Like the new boy starting at school, the welcome he received that day touched his entire term. At the billet of the 2/Leinsters Francis Hitchcock was greeted by the Commanding Officer, Major Bullen-Smith, who 'shook hands with me and welcomed me to his battalion. This kindly greeting made me feel instantly at home with the Regiment.'[37] Charles Douie was relieved by his open-armed reception from the other subalterns of the Entrenching battalion on the Somme. 'I was tired, lonely, and very shy, and the ready hospitality warmed my heart.'[38] When he joined his regiment proper at Rainneville, the welcome was no less generous. Douie remained passionately loyal to his regiment, and to the rightness of the war. So did Hitchcock. It is perhaps not unconnected that they were both made to feel as though they fitted from the start.

Robert Graves had the other sort of first day at school. On joining 2/Royal Welch Fusiliers after his temporary attachment with the Welsh Regiment, Graves found that the Adjutant did not shake hands with him, offer him a drink, or say a word of welcome. The Royal Welch's peace time custom of taking no notice of newly joined officers for six months was more or less kept up. Hilary Drake-Brockman, a second lieutenant in 2/Royal Welch Fusiliers (he was attached from the East Surreys, and thus known as 'the Surrey-man'), explained to Graves: 'The Royal Welch don't recognize it [the war] socially'.[39] Subalterns in the Royal Welch were referred to as 'warts'. For a sensitive young man, who was a volunteer, such coldness stung. Graves grew a pride in being an officer in the awesomely able Royal Welch Fusiliers, but never quite forgot or forgave his reception from the Regulars, and never became an insider.[40]

The Guards regiments were yet more socially exclusive than the Royal Welch. Appointed as an artillery liaison to a battalion of the Grenadier Guards, Second Lieutenant P.J. Campbell was asked by the Grenadier's Commanding Officer whether he had been to Eton. No. Was he a Regular? No. After these two negatives the CO, Campbell recollected, 'appeared to take no further interest in me as a person'. Campbell was generous enough to admit that he was anyway impressed by the Grenadier's sheer professionalism. Guards officers were a tight family. Almost literally so. When Rowland Feilding, a captain in the Coldstream, took his first tour of trench duty in May 1915:

On either side of me I found relations. On my immediate left Percy Clive [a cousin] commanded a company of grenadiers, and the Coldstream company on my right was commanded by Rollo [another cousin]. I visited Percy at 4.30 on the morning of our arrival ... while I was shaving, Rollo brought Henry Feilding [another cousin] to see me. He is with a squadron of King Edward's Horse, which is acting as Divisional Cavalry to a territorial Division near here, and was paying a visit to Rollo in the trenches.[41]

Following the professionalization of the army in the nineteenth century, aristocratic officers had congregated in the footguards and Household cavalry; about 80 per cent of Guards officers were from families listed in Debrett's guide to the aristocracy. And Guards officers not related to each other by blood were often connected by a school tie from Eton or Winchester. Advancing at Arras in April 1917, Household cavalry officers were heard singing the Eton boating song:

Jolly boating weather,
And a hay harvest breeze,
Blade on the feather,
Shade off the trees,
Swing swing together,

With your bodies between your knees,
Swing swing together,
With your bodies between your knees ...

*

Raleigh: It's – it's not exactly what I thought. It's just this – this quiet
that seems so funny.

Osborne: A hundred yards from here the Germans are sitting in their
dugouts, thinking how quiet it is.

R.C. Sherriff, Journey's End, 1928

Almost everybody arriving in the trenches was surprised by what they were like.

The Western Front meandered for 450 miles from the dunes of Nieuport across the monotonous Flanders plain, over the rolling chalk hills of Picardy and Artois, along the high ridge above the Aisne, along the 'Chemin des Dames' (the carriage road built to enable the daughter of Louis XV to reach the Chateau de Bove), before heading south east to the Alps. From the North Sea to the Chemin des Dames was mostly British line; thereafter it was all French.

Generally, the Germans held the higher, drier ground and the better, deadlier, view. A melancholy necklace of 1000 war cemeteries into which the dead – or at least, those whose bodies could be found – were interred marks the front line today.

There was not a single line of trenches dug into the earth all the way. Geology did not allow it. Digging into the loam of the Flanders plain, with its crisscross of drainage ditches and high water table, produced an effect that would become dismally familiar: the trench welled with water even as it was being dug. 'Working party as usual at night', Francis Hitchcock wrote in his diary at La Brique. 'Discovered the new line which we had just finished, completely flooded.'[42] Trenches that looked dry in fair-weather could turn into canals in rain. At Hannescamps on the Somme, Guy Chapman lamented:

Lulu Lane became a vast conduit into which the trenches emptied their top waters. At the western end it was ten feet deep, lipping the berm. Saps filled up and had to be abandoned. I was not sorry to see west Spring Gun vanish. The cookhouse disappeared. Dugouts filled up and collapsed. The few duckboards floated away, uncovering sump-pits into which the unchartered wanderer fell, his oaths stifled by a brownish stinking fluid. . . . In spite of frenzied work, the floods began to gain on us. The pumps broke down.[43]

At Plugstreet, Captain J. Cohen 1/East Lancashire Regiment discovered:

Our trouble of course is drainage. This horrible country is made of mud, water and dead Germans. Whenever water is left in a trench it drags the earth down on either side and forms a fearful sticky viscous matter that lets you sink gently down and grips you like a vice when you're there.[44]

The bottom of the trench had planks running along, otherwise 'passage is impossible', reported Cohen.[45] At intervals there were 'sump-holes' to receive water to make it easier for baling. Wet trenches also had 'revetments' of timber or wattle along the sides to prevent them falling in. At St Eloi outside Ypres, Hitchcock found conditions worse than at La Brique; both Britons and Germans gave up their subterranean trench life and took to walking along the parapets; the Germans used to shout 'Good morning' to Hitchcock when he was on his rounds.

In the wettest of the wetlands, such as stretches of the Ypres salient and Neuve Chapelle, the trenches went above ground and not down into it. 'In England', Ivar Campbell wrote home, 'you read of concealed trenches – here we don't trouble about that. Trenches rise up, grey clay, three or four feet above the ground.'[46] Edward Brittain recalled trenches 'made almost entirely of sandbags in millions, not dug in at all', while Gerald Brennan wrote that the trenches at Le Bizet were 'a narrow parapeted lane of sandbags'.

Arriving at Plugstreet in 1915, trench novice Graham Greenwell was struck by the way the trenches 'zigzagged anywhere' – a safety feature to stop invading Germans having a clear line of fire along the trench, and to ensure that bomb blast from a direct hit was as confined as possible. The Germans were 40 yards away. Bernard Martin, 'very much the new boy', entered his first trench in 1916 to find it nothing like the illustrations in the *Manual of Field Engineering*; the trench, dug under fire by British when they first went to earth in October 1914, was: 'Irregular in depth and width, it had suffered many direct hits by enemy shells and was more or less always under repair.'[47]

Trenches? What trenches? After 1915 Charles Carrington's Division, the 48th (South Midland) never 'held a continuous trench line shoulder to shoulder'. Instead they defended in depth by well-sited posts supporting one another with cross fire. In the naked lunar land of Passchendaele in 1917, Captain Ulrich Burke of 2/Devonshires encountered:

> no trenches at all ... only a series of shell holes which had been reinforced with sandbags so that you could hide inside them. If, for instance, you wanted to urinate and otherwise, there was an empty bully beef tin kept on the side of the hole, so you had to do it in front of all your men then chuck the content, but not the tin, over the back.[48]

Heavy shelling could change the landscape within hours. Going around his sector at night with his sergeant major, Burke recalled 'when we left one shell hole we'd have to ask which way to go next, because each night the ground would have absolutely shifted'.

The British frontline at Vimy Ridge in March 1916 was another series of pockmarks in the landscape. Second Lieutenant Leslie Hill 1/6 City of London Regiment wrote: 'The trenches we are going up to are simply a line of shell holes about 120 yards from the Boche and no wire between – but we are quite ready for them should they come over.' There was, perhaps fortunately, for all Hill's bravado small danger of a German attack; the Saxons opposite Leslie Hill were operating a local armistice, 'and have made a compact with us, that if we do not fire, they will not'.[49]

Digging trenches could be nightmarish. Since the frontline ebbed and flowed according to the fortunes of the war, there was the distinct possibility that the digging of a new trench was an excavation of fallen soldiery. In late 1916 Captain Sidney Rogerson set his company of the 2/West Yorkshire Regiment to spade-work in the 'putrid bone yard around Vermelles'; his Yorkshire men, no frail violets, vomited copiously because corpses of soldiers were unearthed every few yards. Rogerson recalled:

> Most pitiful, the attempt to straighten a piece of trench broke into a dug-out where sat huddled three Scottish officers, their faces mercifully shrouded by the grey flannel of the gas-masks they had donned when death came upon them.[50]

On another occasion Rogerson was obliged to make his men 'dig like blazes all night' into the Somme land, despite them being already done up by a long tramp through the dark and the mud. 'Which was why I tried to explain things personally to every individual', recalled Rogerson. The personal touch by an officer always worked wonders. Within a couple of hours the Yorkshiremen had deepened their trench from four and a half feet to seven feet down.

· Evidently, Sidney Rogerson was the ideal officer in more ways than one. For all the vagaries of topography and battle, there *was* a model trench and as far as possible it was emulated in the fields of Flanders and Picardy and Artois. Hence Rogerson's encouragement of his men that black Somme night to keep digging. The textbook frontline or 'fire trench' was a minimum of six feet in depth, and three and a half feet wide. A parapet (from the Italian *parapetto*, to protect the chest) built up the height, usually with sandbags, on the German side by nine or so inches, while a parados (French *parados*, to protect the back) built up the rear. In such a trench a man could walk along out of sight of the German Mausers. To enable the British soldier to shoot Germans dead – his business, after all – a fire-step was built along the enemy side of the trench. As Graham Greenwell noted, trenches were not straight. Better yet than the zigzag design was the Grecian key pattern of short fire bays intersected by traverses.

To the front of the fire trench was the deserted continent of No-Man's Land, into which shallow ditches called 'saps' ran to observation posts, bombing posts and machine-gun positions. North of Bapaume, machine-gun officer Alec Waugh stared across a No-Man's Land a mile across, and his company suffered not a single casualty in a month.[51] Usually, No-Man's Land was around 200 yards wide on the British sector. Siegfried Sassoon wrote in his diary:

> No-man's land fascinates me, with its jumble of wire-tangles and snaky seams in the earth winding along the landscape. The mine-craters are rather fearsome, with snipers hidden away on the lips, and pools of dead-looking water. One mine that went up to-day was in an old crater; I think it missed fire, as the earth seethed and spumed, but did not hurl debris skyward in smoke as they usually do. But the earth shook all right.[52]

Behind the fire trench was the support trench. Behind the support trench was the reserve trench. Connecting them all was a winding series of communication trenches. So tangled was the skein of trenches that signboards were erected in the same manner as street signs in towns. There was some sense to the signs; trenches with 'way' in their name were communication trenches, whilst the thematic Saddle, Stirrup, Pommel and Bridle were alongside each other. Often, however, trenches were named by a regiment after an event in its recent trench history, or after a place name from home – both of which were mysteries to outsiders. Trenches also had the disconcerting habit of moving, according to the progress of battle. In an effort to guide the hapless, maps to the trenches were issued.

Even so men got lost. Douglas Gillespie wrote:

> We came out of trenches last night; only a short spell this time, but a busy one, and I seemed to spend half my time showing lost men and officers their right way in the trenches, for everyone loses their way in that maze.[53]

In the trenches men needed cover from the elements and from shells. During the first autumn of the war shallow 'scrapes' or 'funk holes' were gouged into the side of the trench; when it became obvious that the trench was, in the most optimistic forecast, a medium term proposition, 'dug-outs' became ubiquitous. Officers lived in separate dug-outs to the Other Ranks, usually one dug-out for all a company's officers, although platoon commanders sometimes had their own dug-out; Second Lieutenant Bernard Martin worried about this exclusivity, but his platoon sergeant reassured him that officers needed a separate and larger dug-out 'for personal belongings, your pack, and some official records and army forms'.[54] An officer's dug-out was also an office. Sensibly, on finding that the officers' dug-out in his new stretch of trench at Ypres was like 'a dog-kennel' Lieutenant Donald Kenworthy, Somerset Light Infantry, decided to build a better one:

> 4a.m. 10/4/15: – Started work on a new dug-out for officers, the old one being quite impossible, it being only eight feet long by seven feet broad and some four feet high; six of us used to try and feed in it at a time. There was only a small door, so it used to take about ten minutes crawling in on your hands and knees fitting in. Two of us used to live in it, and to add to the difficulty there were four props in the middle supporting the roof, which was gradually falling in owing to the weight of the earth on top. By working hard all day we broke the back of the best dug-out I have seen in the trenches, built after my own design. Down the centre – in between the props – ran a narrow table consisting of two planks, leaving room for two officers to sleep either side – and one underneath if necessary – or one officer to sleep either side and the rest of the space taken up with chairs. We could therefore seat about ten people comfortable [sic]; the people at one end had to be small, unless the chairs were low, and there was just room to stand at the other end.[55]

Captain Frank Watson on arriving in the Ypres salient also determined that DIY was necessary. His dug-out was adorned by a human foot sticking out of the wall. 'It was unpleasing to the senses and unreliable as a clothes peg, so I sacrificed one-sixth of my space by walling it up.'[56] Deciding that yelling out of the dug-out entrance for his servant five times before the latter replied was an indignity, Edwin Campion Vaughan fixed up a patent bell – a coil of wire attached to a milk tin holding a few stones in the servant's dug-out along the trench.[57]

Some dug-outs were never more than enlarged funk-holes.

Alexander Stewart on the Somme wrote in a letter home in October 1916:

> Am sitting in a hole dug in the side of a trench 5 feet by 3 feet with a board stuck up in the middle to help support the roof. At present there are two of us in here; later on I shall try to get my other officer in. It is raining and thick mud is at the bottom of the hole; outside in the trench the mud is about a foot deep and in many places up to one's knees. Across the entrance to this hole is hung a torn waterproof sheet covered in mud on each side; a heavy bombardment is going on and this place continually vibrates as the Boche is using big shells.[58]

So laden with mud was Stewart's overcoat that he thought it must weigh about 55lbs. He could not get any food cooked and rather expected a counter-attack.[59] At High Wood, again on the Somme, the officers' dug-out, Brian Lawrence wrote, 'consisted merely of a very narrow opening with a fairly long flight of steps leading straight down to a small floor space with a seat in it ... in fact the whole concern was exactly like a hansom cab'.[60] This was, at least, a mined dug-out which was generally safer than the 'cut and cover' sort, where a large hole was dug and then roofed with timber and earth. Or whatever came to hand.

At La Brique in the Ypres salient, Hitchcock's 'bugwarm' [dug-out] consisted of sheets of corrugated iron across the top of the trench, with sandbags on top to stop them blowing away. (He stole doors off abandoned houses as a weightier, denser alternative.) Brian Lawrence once sheltered in something similar, but with a thin layer of earth as the counterweight to the wind. The accommodation, he observed, was 'quite comfortable but ... not in the least shell proof'.[61] On those stretches of the front where the 'trench' was actually a sandbag barricade, dugouts were notoriously uncomfortable. 'Two walls of sandbags with a sheet of corrugated iron on top and an oil-sheet under it to make the whole waterproof' was J. Cohen's laconic description of his 'tamboo' at Ploegsteert.[62] Sandbag dug-outs, noted Stuart Cloete unhappily, 'leaked like sieves'.[63] Greenwell once found himself in an officer's mess in the Douve valley trenches that was nothing but an alcove sandbagged on two sides. Morgan Watcyn-Williams considered that a 'candle made all the difference in a dug-out. It helped us to see the rats instead of merely hearing or feeling them.'[64]

But officers' dug-outs could be cosy, if not actually chi-chi, particularly when cut from dry Somme chalk. (German dug-outs on the Somme were thirty feet deep; one reason why so many Germans survived the artillery barrage to fight on that bloody morning of 1 July 1916). At Hebuterne Graham Greenwell took over a dug-out built by the French. He wrote to his mother:

> There is a small bed with French lace curtains above it, three pictures over the bed – two of red coated huntsmen, or rather the French idea of them. At the foot of the bed there is a large and very handsome mirror in a heavy gilt frame; to the right there is a bookcase with a few books, including a History of Europe, a book on Geometry and a few other works on miscellaneous subjects. To the right of the table is a funny old French clock let into the dug-out with a painted face and a long pendulum. The floor is tiled and there is a little washing basin on a gaudily coloured sort of stand, and a door. [65]

It was perfect, considered Greenwell, save for one defect: the doorway faced the exact direction German shells came from.

Christopher Stone, a lieutenant with 22/Royal Fusiliers, encountered a dug-out at Cambrin with the same door-towards-the Hun problem. 'There's a most persistent blighter of a Bosche', he wrote, 'who has got his rifle sighted on the doorway of this dug-out and about every five minutes as I sit here I hear the ping of a bullet in the mud.'

Altogether more Hun-proof was Brian Lawrence's dug-out at St Pierre Vaast Wood:

> The dug-out was quite the best I have struck yet, absolutely safe as it was excavated underneath the Bapaume road, and there was therefore lots of good stuff on top of us. It was L-shaped, and had a large chamber leading out of one side of the 'L' which had a wood floor and matchboard walls. There were four bunks in it, a large table, some shelves and several chairs, so what more could one want.[66]

To make his comfort complete, there was a ceasefire along this stretch of the front: 'By common consent there was a sort of policy of live and let live, and neither side ever sniped. If either of us had begun to use our rifles, both front lines would have become untenable.'[67] These little local armistices were another of the surprises of the front. Even the all-out-war around Ypres, where the salient stuck tauntingly and dangerously into the German line, had its moments of silence. 'Somehow I had assumed continuous gunfire at the Front, shells falling on the trenches all day, and of course a regular rattle of rifle and machine-gun fire', wrote Bernard Martin. 'It was almost disquieting (so to say) to be told there were long periods when war was silent.'[68]

Beds in dug-outs were usually of stretched rabbit wire, although Graham Greenwell, before moving to Hebuterne, slept at the wryly named Hope Cottage on a box of straw. Just straw scattered on the ground was not unknown. There was worse. There was plain earth. A stove for warmth was sometimes fitted. Douie was pleased to be initiated, by officers he relieved at Usna Redoubt, into the arcane art of keeping the stove 'respectable': it was to pour rum on it. The carbon monoxide fumes produced from dug-out stoves were potentially lethal; Alexander Stewart was lucky to escape with his life when the flue blocked and the carbon monoxide began to gather.

Most officers' dug-outs betrayed some slight signs of someone having tried to cheer the place up. A few ever-so-slightly risqué drawings of girls from *La Vie Parisienne* or by Kirchner tacked up were common enough to be a cliché. Captain Bruce Bairnsfather's cartoons of 'Old Bill' and 'Young Bert' were another common fixture on walls, though Charles Carrington thought soldiers lost interest in him after the Somme. Captain Francis Sainthill Anderson, Royal Horse Artillery, agreed about Bairnsfather; he wrote in 1916, 'I don't find him nearly as funny as I used to. No one can accuse me of having a dull sense of humour, but there are subjects one simply can't joke about.'[69]

Charles Douie was impressed with the flowers growing in the grounds of Thiepval Chateau garden, through which his fire trench ran. He cut some of the flowers to lighten his dug-out. At Ypres

Captain Crouch did the same: 'I have got some rather pretty flowers in my dug-out. Wheeler [his servant] picks them for me. To-day he got two very nice narcissi which smell ripping.'[70] Viewed from the outside, Crouch was a typical 'hearty' (Marlborough, shooting, law, Territorial Force officer with the fashionable Ox and Bucks); inside him beat a botanist's heart. Arranged flowers were nice, he decided, but not as nice as a real garden in the trench. He wrote home:

> I have started a garden at my company headquarters [dug-out]. Will you please send as soon as possible two packets of candytuft and two packets of nasturtium seeds. My daffodils and hyacinths are topping.[71]

On one magnificent, Fitzcarraldo occasion, Crouch tried to improve a peasant's manure heap by planting it with bulbs. For his trench garden, meanwhile, Douglas Gillespie carefully transplanted wallflowers, pansies and peonies from a nearby ruined village; he reassured his parents that there were 'still plenty' of flowers left should anyone ever come back to the houses.

There were many officers who like Crouch, in the death and desolation of the trenches, tried to beautify their surroundings. Others maintained that it was rarely worth investing a lot of time on dug-out décor or trench prettification. Looking back over his diary for 1916 Lieutenant Charles Carrington calculated that he spent 101 days of that year in the frontline trenches – but he had 'moved house' 80 times. The constant shuffling around was another surprise of trench life. The Black Watch once served 48 days in the line unrelieved, but that was exceptional; on a usual tour of duty a company would spend a week in the line, a week in reserve and a week at rest, although individual regiments had variations on the theme. Units would also be transferred from quiet fronts to hot ones, and vice versa, to give everyone a break, everyone their moments under fire.

Flowers or not, an officer's dug-out was always better than that of the rankers, more spacious and private. This excited little jealousy, because the life of the officer in the line was more stressful and physically demanding than that of his men.

It was also shorter.

IV

Trench World:
Life and Death in the Trenches

I am not going to harrow you with accounts of life in the trenches:
enough to say that it is extremely dangerous (for the enemy is still
hostile), dirty and unpleasant; boring and dramatic at the same time . . .

Second Lieutenant Bernard Strauss,
The Buffs, Flanders, November 1915

In the trenches, there was more than one war. There was the war
against the Germans. There was the war against the elements, against
vermin, against boredom. Then there was the war against the exhaustion caused by the endless toil.

Officers worked during the day, they worked during the night. The
work never stopped. The officer was a beast of burdens. Captain Dunn
blithely informed Robert Graves when he joined the Welsh Regiment
at Cambrin of the routine in the line:

Our time-table is: breakfast at eight o'clock in the morning, clean
trenches and inspect rifles, work all morning; lunch at twelve, work
again from one till about six, when the men feed again. 'Stand-to' at
dusk for about an hour, work all night, 'stand-to' for an hour before
dawn. That's the general programme. Then there's sentry-duty. The
men do two-hour sentry spells, then work two hours, then sleep two
hours. At night sentries are doubled, so working parties are smaller.
We officers are on duty all day, and divide up the night into three-
hourly watches.[1]

Lieutenant Donald Kenworthy, Somerset Light Infantry, noted in his
assiduous diary a typical day in the Ypres salient in early 1915:

Tuesday 19th January 6 a.m. to 7 a.m. – Stood to arms until daylight.
This has to be done twice a day – once for an hour before dawn, and

again in the evening one hour at dusk. 9 a.m. to 4 p.m. –Company on fatigues, building new fortifications, improving old ones, carrying rations, digging, draining trenches, making corduroy path etc. 9 p.m. to 10.30 p.m. – Continued the work of the previous evening. This has to be done during darkness, as one is in full view of the Germans during daylight.[2]

Kenworthy was glad to be relieved, he confided to his diary, as 'after four days in the trenches doing the amount of fatigue work we are doing, one is in want of a rest. One starts work at 6am and finishes anytime after 12 midnight; hard at it all the time.' He had also, like Graves, shared the night watches.

A day in the life of Captain Geoffrey Bowen, 2/Lancashire Fusiliers, 3 September 1917:

8 p.m. Started [for the fire trench from the reserve].
9.30 p.m. Arrived.
11 p.m. Company arrived.
11 p.m – 3 a.m. Round the line.
3.15 a.m 4.15 a.m. Sleep.
4.15 a.m. – 6 a.m. Stand to.
6 a.m. – 9. Sleep.
9 a.m. – 9.30 a.m. Breakfast: bacon, eggs, tinned sausage.
9.30 a.m. – 10.10. Round line.
10.10 a.m. – 12. Reports etc.
12.30 p.m. Lunch: Steak, potatoes, beans, sweet omelette.
1.45 p.m. – 2.15. Daylight patrol.
2.15 p.m. – 2.30. Sleep.
2.30 p.m. – 3.40. Gup [chat] with C.O.
4 p.m. Tea, bread, jam.
4.30 p.m. – 4.35. Sleep.
4.35 p.m. – 5.10. Entertain 'Bowes'
5.10 p.m. – 5.15. Sleep.
5.15 p.m. – 5.25. Trench Mortar Officer reports.
5.25 p.m. – 6.15. Sleep.
6.15 p.m. – 6.35. Entertain Brian and Padre.
6.35 p.m. – 7.30. Sleep.
7.30 p.m. – 8. Round line.
8 p.m. – 8.15 Dinner: Steak, potatoes, tinned fruit and custard.

8.15 p.m. – 9. Round line.
11.30 p.m. – 12.30 a.m. Sleep.
12.30 – 2.30 a.m. Intensive sniping.
2.30 – 5 a.m. Sleep.[3]

An infantry officer in the Great War might forgive himself for thinking that he had signed on as a manager in an inglorious but dangerous clerking office. After 'stand to' in the hour before dawn, when the entire company was armed and alert against a German attack, the subaltern waited for the NCO in charge of the platoon's sections to report his men present and their rifles clean. At this good news, the officer dished out the rum ration of a quarter-gill (one sixteenth of a pint) per man. This was sent up by battalion quartermasters in brown earthenware jars marked 'SRD', the abbreviation for 'Special Rations Department', but universally and jokingly assumed to stand for 'Seldom Reaches Destination', 'Service Rum Diluted' or 'Soon Runs Dry'. The rum ration – it was Navy rum – was dispensed by the platoon commanders into hot tea and was intended as medicine; the ration was ordered by the divisional commander on the advice from his principal medical officer that conditions were sufficiently debilitating to require it. Most commanders sensibly granted the ration every day, no matter the weather.

After the doling out of the rum, there followed the observation of Trench Standing Orders. Topping the list was foot inspection, and the supervision of sock-changing and rubbing-in of whale oil to beat trench foot and frostbite. Then iron rations – the hardtack biscuits and bully beef (tinned corned beef) that were for emergencies, and only to be opened on the say so of an officer – had to be checked, sentries visited, ammunition stocks examined, gas-respirator drill to be practised. In a good trench, with clean rifles, there was little thereafter for the men to do, so they drifted into dug-outs to play cards, or sat on the fire-step smoking. Late morning was a favourite time for a visit from a senior officer; as Sidney Rogerson, a company commander in the tail end of the Somme, set off with the battalion's colonel to check dispositions along his gluey wintry trench, he enviously noted his men going off for some additional sleep.[4]

If not escorting colonels, the officer settled down in the dug-out to some serious paperwork, tackling the correspondence to and from HQ: casualty reports, work reports, RE indents, conduct sheets, intelligence reports ... In the Ovillers Trenches on 24 August 1916 Greenwell wrote to his mother: 'Thank Heaven we had a quiet night and day, but of course I was up all the time receiving and sending messages until I dropped asleep over the table.' During three days in the line in October 1917 in Arras (not a particularly 'loud' front at the time) Lieutenant Robert Mackay counted up the number of official communications that passed through his hands: 451.

The amount of communications was seemingly only surpassed by their irrelevance. During the middle of a German 'hate' on the Somme, Brian Lawrence was asked in a communiqué: 'Please state the number of expert rat-catchers you have in your company. This return to be in before 12 noon on Friday.' In the mud and misery Lawrence went around questioning the men; they, thinking there might be money in it, claimed in unfeasible numbers to be consummate pest-control operatives. Sitting in the company dug-out at La Boiselle, isolated by a grenade and shell barrage, Charles Douie received a breathless orderly at the blanket door: 'As I took his message I thought that it must be of vital importance. It proved to be, in fact, a futile routine message about the proportion of blankets per man in the present state of the weather.'[5]

Irked at the stupidity of being asked to inform HQ of the number of rats in his trench Colonel C.R.C. de Crespigny of 2/Grenadier Guards archly chose to make the 'rat return' real, and organized a three day rat-shoot. After leaving the rats to mellow in sandbags, he dumped them outside Brigade HQ.

Work could be a balm. Greenwell phlegmatically concluded that immersion 'in all the petty details of daily routine' at least helped the time pass quickly. In July 1916 Anthony 'Boy' Eden was called into company HQ to be told that there had been a naval engagement in the North Sea and that the *Indefatigable*, his brother's ship, had gone down. Survivors were few. If any. Sixteen-year-old Nicholas Eden had been a midshipman in charge of a gun-turret. Anthony Eden recalled:

It was fortunate for me that during these weeks [after Nicholas's death] I was heavily occupied with my two sets of duties as platoon commander and battalion bombing officer, or perhaps thoughtful seniors had arranged it that way. I was over-worked, with no time to think.[6]

More work! In the line, out of the line, a junior officer censored the letters home of the men. Every ordinary letter and postcard had to bear the signature of an officer, who was then responsible if the base censors discovered a breach of security. Since the BEF wrote 8,150,000 letters and field postcards in 1917 alone, censoring mail was another of the subaltern and the lieutenant's Sisyphean duties. Censoring could take an age, particularly if the censor was a novice like Edwin Campion Vaughan, who did not yet have the knack of 'glancing over the page and spotting censorable matter without reading line by line'.[7] The more seasoned Lieutenant Vyvian Trevenen, a Regular, censored 41 letters and 53 field postcards on 19 October 1914 but 'As I have long ago given up reading them, it did not take too long.'[8] Another Regular, Geoffrey Pollard, RFA, was more conscientious, with the result:

It is always with mixed feelings that I personally view the arrival of fresh paper, because the soldiers write such awful things in their letters, mostly rot, or else a repetition of a few remarks which they could quite easily put on a postcard, and I have to read them all through! But it certainly makes them happy, and that is the great thing.[9]

There were other great things to be had from censorship. Sitting around the dug-out table reading letters by candle ends Lieutenant Eric Marchant, a temporary officer with 7/London Regiment, initially found censorship irksome then of 'absorbing interest'. The 'execrable' spelling of the letters aside, he was impressed by their contents:

I suppose there is no better way of getting an idea of the spirit of the men and I won't deny that I was surprised at the tone of practically all the letters. The percentage that showed a realisation of religious truth and faith in God, was tremendously bigger than ever I suspected, and such phrases as 'we must go on trusting in God' were in dozens of letters I read.[10]

Ronald Leighton also stumbled over the lack of literacy in his platoon's letters ('prosaic and unimaginative'), but acknowledged that a few left him feeling 'like a Father Confessor'.[11] Censorship gave a secret, God-like look into a man's soul; out of the resulting glimpse came a better understanding of the men. With understanding came appreciation, came admiration, came even love. Second Lieutenant Robert McConnell in 1915, on a starlit boat bound for Gallipoli:

I have just censored the letters of my men. By Jove! If you could read some of those letters, they would do you good. The tenderness of those great, rough fellows is wonderful. I love them all for it.[12]

The sole intent of censorship was to stop the spread of military secrets; its unintended consequence was that, by revealing a man's personal secrets to his commander, the latter could better command; he could make allowances for the grieving, he could isolate the disenchanted, he could lighten the load of the tired. For an officer intent on leading by close bonds, censorship was more boon than bore. As Carrington observed, a 'subaltern in the trenches saw little of his platoon', since his duties tended to be towards the company as a whole, such as having special observation duties, or being the company officer in charge of feeding the men, and distributing the new drafts and instructing them in the ways of the earth world. Censoring the platoon's letters, in the circumstances of the trenches, was the platoon commander's best chance of keeping a spiritual watch on the soul of his flock. For an officer freshly arrived in trench land, censorship was the quickest, surest way of getting to know his men.

There was another accidental by-product of censorship: a gentleman officer, reading the letters of his predominantly working class men, was given a window on a foreign nation – the lower orders of Britain itself. Charles Douie, an Old Rugbeian, recalled:

In their [his men's] letters I saw for the first time a new world, with interests and standards of which I had previously no experience. Most of the letters were frank in a degree which surprised me. The world which I had known professed a hatred of sentiment, made a virtue of understatement, held in contempt anyone who in its expression 'wore his heart on his sleeve.' But I found the world of the private soldier wholly natural and without reserve.[13]

Old Etonian Harold Macmillan was another officer to have his privileged eyes opened by the censoring of his men's mail. On 30 August 1915 he wrote:

Indeed, of all the war, I think the most interesting (and humbling too) experience is the knowledge one gets of the poorer classes. They have big hearts these soldiers, and it is a very pathetic task to have to read all their letters home. Some of the older men, with wives and families, who write every day, have in their style a wonderful simplicity which is almost great literature. And the comic intermixture of official or journalistic phrases – the kisses for baby or little Anne; or the 'tell Georgie from his daddy to be a good boy and not forget him' – it is all very touching. They love to buy little things to send home – postcards, or little pieces of silk, or ornamental sewing work – And then there comes occasionally a grim sentence or two, which reveals in a flash a sordid family drama. 'Mother, are you going ever to write to me. I have written you quite ten times and had no answer. Are you on the drink again, that Uncle George writes me the children are in a shocking state?' . . . There is much to be learnt from soldiers' letters.[14]

Douie and Macmillan, like many others of their class temporarily in khaki and pips, would get to the end of the war in 1918 profoundly affected and enlightened by four years of contact with the lower class. Nowhere was that contact more naked than in the officer's reading of his men's personal missives to their mothers, brothers, sisters, fathers, and friends in the tenements of Glasgow and the tied-cottages of Dorset.

As for an officer's own letters, theoretically these were to be read by his commanding officer, but by gentlemanly convention they went straight to the anonymous base censor. Trying to beat the base censor with a coded message to indicate the sender's whereabouts – a military secret – was a common game. Roland Leighton put small pencil dots under certain letters in his epistles to fiancée Vera Brittain; John Ronald Tolkien used the same dot-under the letter system, while Malvern old boy Lieutenant Philip Brown employed sound play – he informed his parents he was 'near the town held by British *Arms entirely*' [i.e. Armentières].[15] More cunningly still, Captain John W. Jeffries, Durham Light Infantry, began a letter to his wife with the sentence 'Your presumption remains essentially sound', the first letters making 'YPRES'.[16] Most cunningly of all, Wilfred Owen contrived a letter to his mother where the end letters of a certain paragraph spelt 'SOMME'.

Some epistle-writers sanitized their war for home consumption; Captain Francis Sainthill Anderson of the Royal Horse Artillery believed that: 'The truth of the matter is everyone out here considers it only fair to one's womankind to hush up the worst side of it.'[17] But not everyone did. Wilfred Owen informed his mother in a letter of 16 January 1917, sent from the front at Beaumont Hamel:

I can see no excuse for deceiving you, about these last 4 days. I have suffered seventh hell.
I have not been at the front.
I have been in front of it.
I have held an advanced post, that is, a 'dug-out' in the middle of no man's land.[18]

Graham Greenwell's mother must have had nerves of carbon steel to cope with his dutiful but detailed letters during nearly three years of continuous frontline service. ('The Huns had turned on to the spot at which we had to pass their most appalling of all engines – the minenwerfer or mine-thrower. As I was about to go across I saw a blinding flash in front of me . . . the concussion hurled me backwards into a deep German dug-out.') The devoted Robert Vernede of the Rifle Brigade wrote to his wife describing two days of shelling, adding that he was 'rather doubtful as to whether I should tell you quite the unpleasantness like this; but I think it's rather good that nowadays, when women have so much influence, they should not be fooled with the rosy side of things only'.

What no one in the trenches wanted, however, was bad news from home. Bad news from home could be the straw that broke the spine of a man's morale. Roland Leighton was 'distressed' by a sentence in a letter of Vera's that his mother seemed 'changed ... worn, and very tired'. He immediately wrote off to 'Big Yeough Wough', his pet name for his mother (he was 'Little Yeough Wough'):

> It troubles me muchly. Qu'est ce qu'il y a ? Is it finances and family navigation ; or working too hard ; or myself ; or what ? Please do tell me. Is there anything I can do ?[19]

'Must say', wrote Robert Mackay home, as if to make the point, 'we do appreciate cheery letters out here'. Good news from home was craved like drugs; 'Write soon' was almost the universal sign-off of letters homebound; Robert Mackay was therefore thrilled to once receive 16 letters and newspapers in 24 hours. Major J.V. Bates RAMC wrote to his fiancée, Alice:

> Your letters really have been splendid, old girl. When things looked bleakest in Longueval an orderly would dash into my dugout dressing station with a breathless 'A letter for you sir!' and there would be one of yours for me to read in the middle of all that hell.[20]

Luckily, the Army post service had the efficiency of a Swiss clock and the persistence of the Pony Express. Graham Greenwell's doting mother sent him a letter on 22 September 1915; he received it on the 26th, despite being in a trench at Courcelles under shellfire.

The flowering of poetry in the Great War is well-recognized, but the war's blossoming of epistles is mainly a secret. The public and grammar school-educated subalterns, or failing them, public school and grammar school-educated rankers like Ivor Gurney, led the way in wielding the pen with aplomb. As the historian John Laffin has remarked, the letters by the boys-going-on-men of the 1914–18 generation surpass in artistry and 'quite unselfconscious erudition' the letters home by their counterparts in the 1939–45 war.[21] We will not get so many letters, of such quality, sent from a war front again. We will not again get letters like Ivar Campbell's observation of men in trenches:

The splutter of shrapnel, the red squeal of field guns, N.E.; the growl of the heavies moving slowly through the air, the cr-r-r-ump of their explosion. But in a bombardment all tones mingle and their voice is like machinery running not smoothly but roughly, pantingly, angrily, wildly making shows of peace and wholeness.

You perceive, too, in imagination, men infinitely small, running, affrightened rabbits, from the upheaval of the shells, nerve-wracked, deafened; clinging to earth, hiding eyes, whispering 'O God, O God!' You perceive, too, other men, sweaty, brown, infinitely small also, moving guns, feeding the belching monster, grimly, quietly pleased.

But with eyes looking over this land of innumerable eruptions, you see no line. The land is inhuman.

But thousands of men are there; men who are below ground, men who have little bodies but immense brains. And the men facing west are saying, 'This is an attack, they will attack when this hell's over,' and they go on saying this to themselves continually.

And the men facing east are saying, 'We have got to get over the parapet. We have got to get over the parapet – when the guns lift'.

And then the guns lift up their heads and so a long, higher song.

And then the untenanted land is suddenly alive with little men, rushing, stumbling – rather foolishly leaping forward – laughing, shouting, crying in the charge . . .

There is one thing cheering. The men of the battalion – through all and in spite of that noisy, untasty day; through the wet cold night, hungry and tired, living now in mud and water, with every prospect of more rain to-morrow – are cheery. Sometimes, back in billets, I hate the men – their petty crimes, their continual bad language with no variety of expression, their stubborn moods. But in a difficult time they show up splendidly. Laughing in mud, joking in water – I'd 'demonstrate' into hell with some of them and not care.

Yet under heavy shell-fire it was curious to look into their eyes – some of them little fellows from shops, civilians before, now and after: you perceived the wide, rather frightened, piteous wonder in their eyes, the patient look turned towards you, not, 'What the blankety,

blankety hell *is* this?' But 'Is this quite fair? We cannot move, we are all little animals. Is it quite necessary to make such infernally large explosive shells to kill such infernally small and feeble animals as ourselves?'

I quite agreed with them, but had to put my eye-glass fairly in my eye and make jokes; and, looking back, I blush to think of the damnably bad jokes I did make.[22]

Captain Ivar Campbell, Argyll and Sutherland Highlanders, was killed in action on 8 January, 1916, at the age of twenty-five. He had made up his mind to be a soldier all his life.

The officers of the Great War were a golden generation of lettrists.

The sniper's job, recalled Guy Chapman of 13/Royal Fusiliers, 'was to work independently and try to pick off any enemy leaders he could see' in the trenches. He added: 'That was what the Germans did to us and they had no difficulty as we wore officers' uniforms with long tunics, riding breeches, trench boots and Sam Browne belts. This was one reason why the officers' casualties were so high.'[23]

In the first year of the war, the Germans dominated sniping, not least because they dominated the European optics industry; by mid 1915, a British officer calculated, the BEF was losing 18 soldiers per day to sniping.[24] Around the same time the British government could only secure a paltry 1,260 telescopic sights on the open market. Consequently, Britain's own early sniping effort was led by individual enthusiasts; these were invariably officers with experience of game shooting, and who had the kit to go with it.

Sniping in the trenches was a way of war; it was also a way of killing time. Two birds with one bullet. In the Ypres trenches in winter 1914, Julian Grenfell of the 1/Royal Dragoons went off alone with his rifle:

Off I crawled, through the sodden clay and branches, going about a yard a minute and listening and looking as I thought it was not possible to look and listen. I went out to the right of our lines, where the 10th were and where the Germans were nearest. I took about 30 minutes to do 30 yards. Then I saw the Hun trench, and I waited for a long time, but could see or hear nothing. It was about 10 yards from me.

Then I heard some Germans talking, and saw one put his head up over some bushes about 10 yards behind the trench. I could not get a shot at him; I was too low down; and of course I couldn't get up. So I crawled on again very slowly to the parapet of their trench. It was very exciting. I was not sure that there might not have been someone there – or a little further along the trench. I peered through their loophole, and saw nobody in the trench. Then the German behind put his head up again. He was laughing and talking. I saw his teeth glisten against my foresight, and I pulled the trigger very steady. He just gave a grunt and crumpled up.[25]

The remainder of the Germans in the trench could not locate where the deadly shot had come from, and Grenfell was able to stealthily creep back to the British trenches, inch by inch.

On the next day, just before dawn, Grenfell slinked out again to the German trench: 'Then a single German came through the wood towards the trench ... He was coming along upright quite carelessly, making a great noise. I let him get within 25 yards and shot him through the heart.' Ten minutes later a group of Germans came ambling through the winter wood, and Grenfell shot the officer or sergeant who seemed to be leading them. Grenfell then 'went back at a sort of galloping crawl' to the British lines.

Later, he made two entries in his game book, after '105 partridges' at Panshanger, the family home: 'November 16th: 1 Pomeranian; November 17th: 2 Pomeranians'.[26]

The entries were less glib than they appear. For Grenfell game-shooting was not a passionless pot at abstract targets, but a means of getting 'back to real things, bringing the elemental barbaric forces in ourselves into touch with the elemental barbaric forces of nature'.[27] Killing a man on a shoot was an even more fundamentally human, sensual activity. 'One loves one's fellow man so much more when one is bent on killing him', reflected Grenfell, albeit half ironically. It also required, as evidenced by his stalking at Ypres, the same virtues as game-shooting: stealth, patience, careful observation of the quarry.

The sniping of the Pomeranians won Grenfell a DSO. Julian Grenfell adored war. 'Isn't it luck for me to have been born so as to be just the right age and in just the right place?' he wrote to his mother.

Lionel Crouch wished also to bag a German, desiring to hang a Pickelhaube helmet alongside his father's 'woodcock and snipe spikes':

> I had a go at shooting one of their loopholes this morning about fifty yards away. I had three shots, and then a German put a spade up and signalled a miss. This is quite true and not a *Punch* yarn.[28]

Crouch, certain that his shots had gone close to the loopholes, thought the Germans 'damn liars'. Like Grenfell, Crouch was a keen sniper. 'I could sit all day', he informed his family, 'waiting for a Bosche's head to appear. It is a far better sport than rabbit-shooting; the game is much more sly and can also hit back.' Major F. Crum of the King's Royal Rifles, and Major T.F. Fremantle and Lieutenant L. Greener of the Warwickshires were other sniping enthusiasts, but the sniper par excellence was Major Hesketh Hesketh-Prichard.

A former big-game hunter and Hampshire County fast-bowler, Hesketh-Prichard had been turned away by the Army on account of his age – he was born in 1876 – but pestered and persisted, and finally reached the front as an Intelligence Officer escorting war correspondents. In his luggage he packed 'scoped rifles'; his self-proclaimed mission was 'to irritate Germans'. After lobbying a gaggle of generals Hesketh-Prichard founded 'The First Army School of Sniping, Observing and Scouting'. As Hesketh-Prichard's account of a 'Hun-hunt' on 3 October 1915 makes plain, with the right skills and right equipment, a sniper could deal death over a considerable distance. At 3.10 Hesketh-Prichard saw, 420 yards away through his magnifying telescope, a German preparing a board to use as a rifle rest:

> At 4.15 we could see the brim of his cap, and he lighted a pipe – I could see the tobacco smoke ... Then he fired a shot resting his rifle on the board ... I think he was shooting a dummy plate ... Then at 4.55 he looked over, his chin resting on the parapet. The rifle was well laid, and I had not to move it more than an inch; then the shot. Later, a Bosche with a beard looked over, and this man was killed by the sergeant major ... [29]

Hesketh-Prichard's memoir of his time in the trenches, *Sniping in France*, was published in 1920; he was a delayed casualty of the war dying in 1922 from wounds received.

Hesketh-Prichard's First Army School of Sniping succeeded in professionalizing and declassing British sniping in the trenches. However, the allure of sniping for the officer who was bored or who wanted to find a romantic war in one endlessly dominated by the mechanized mass-killings of shells and machine-guns, never entirely faded away.[30] As the jobs of junior officers went, sniping was a favoured one.

Of course, the sniper sometimes found himself the sniped. Such was the demise of The Honourable Edward 'Bim' Tennant on 22 September 1916, aged nineteen. For his besotted mother, Pamela Glenconner, he never died. She wrote in her memoir of him, simply, 'Bim went on'. Looking through loop-holes or, especially, over the bags to see what the Germans were up to was always risky. Robert Graves sensibly sent home for a trench periscope, the most popular of the various models of which was 'The Adams Trenchoscope'. A convoluted tall box of mirrors, the Trenchoscope cost 10s 6d. A right-angled mirror with a clip that attached to the bayonet was the cheaper alternative.

In the earth world of the trenches, time was topsy-turvy. Officers came out at night more so even than in the day. This was especially true in the vicious salient at Ypres and on the Somme, where for long stretches of the war nothing could be done above ground during the hours of daylight.

The watch, which was usually divided into two stints among the 'subs', was only the beginning of the night's fatigues. 'The bane of our life was working parties, usually at night', remembered Anthony Eden. In summer there was the grass to be cut in front of the trench to improve the field of fire. There was always the wire in front of the trench to be maintained and, if a company had a 'windy' company from another regiment next door, it might well wire down the sides of its position as well. Like painting the Forth Bridge, wiring was a never ending occupation, because German shelling would constantly undo and demolish the wire. 'There are working parties almost every night', Second Lieutenant Douglas Gillespie, 4/Argyll and Sutherland Highlanders, lamented to his parents. Wiring was more than arduous work; it was dangerous work. Twenty-year-old Roland Leighton was mortally wounded by a bullet reconnoitring ground in front of a trench for a wiring party on 23 December 1915, the day before he was due for leave. Vera Brittain came off her night duty as a VAD nurse and travelled to Brighton to await Leighton's return. On Boxing Day, she was called to the hotel telephone:

> Believing that I was at last to hear the voice for which I had waited for twenty-four hours, I dashed joyously into the corridor. But the message was not from Roland, it was from Clare; it was not to say that he had arrived home that morning, but to tell me that he had died of wounds at a Casualty Clearing Station on December 23rd.[31]

Leighton's poem 'Villanelle' now stands encased at the Ploegsteert Memorial to the Missing:

> Violets from Plug Street Wood,
> Sweet, I send you oversea.
> (It is strange they should be blue.
> Blue, when his soaked blood was red ;
> For they grew around his head.
> It is strange they should be blue.)
> Violets from Plug Street Wood—
> Think what they have meant to me !
> Life and Hope and Love and You.
> (And you did not see them grow
> Where his mangled body lay,
> Hiding horror from the day.
> Sweetest, it was better so.)
> Violets from oversea.
> To your dear, far, forgetting land ;
> These I send in memory.
> Knowing You will understand.
> Your dear, far, forgetting land!

German shelling and the weather eroded the trench, so that had to be maintained too. Different regiments had differing rules as to whether an officer should join his men in manual labour. Edmund Blunden, then a field work officer with the Royal Sussex Regiment, was torn off a strip by the general for as much as carrying a duckboard to reinforce Red Dragon Crater;[32] in the Welsh Regiment, Graves was informed that labouring alongside the men was essential. But even in regiments where officers were forbidden to get their manicured hands dirty, they often navvied anyway, because standing or crouching around while the men wired or dug was cold and endlessly frustrating, and gave a nasty impression of loafing superiority. The importance of trench maintenance was captured in a letter by Second Lieutenant Cuthbert Aston of 1/Bedfordshire Regiment:

> It was fortunate that on Saturday night I had built up my trench and made the parapet very strong as on Monday afternoon and evening their snipers gave us no peace, but not a single bullet came through the parapet.[33]

In the pitch-tar blackness of the night, in which lights could not be shown for fear of magnetizing enemy fire, it was frighteningly easy to become disorientated whilst working on the trench, even when it was mere feet away. Labouring alone on an isolated section of the front line, John Glubb 'was seized with panic and completely lost my sense of direction. To feel yourself lost is a terrifying psychological experience which prevents all thought.'[34] He succeeded in orientating himself and avoiding wandering into the 'Bosche' line. So confident was Sidney Rogerson of the route from the frontline trench to Battalion HQ on Sunken Road trench he took no orderly with him; but after just a few steps in the 'black as pitch' Somme night he entered his 'worst nightmare' of being lost and dying alone in the mud; exhausted and his hands cut by blundering into wire, he eventually stumbled into Sunken Road by pure accident. There was perhaps a worse alternative to the darkness – the light as bright as midday when the Germans launched star shells, leaving the working party silhouetted on the moonlit lunar landscape. Little tricks of the trade,

Anthony Eden observed, were soon learned, 'for instance that it was safer to stand stock still if an enemy Very light caught you by surprise rather than drop flat on your face, when the movement might betray you'.[35]

Soldiers were smugglers as well as workers. Stores were brought in at night, stealthily, out of the sight of German guns, along the blackened labyrinth of communication trenches. Anthony Eden considered:

> The worst assignment that summer was to carry gas cylinders up the communications trenches and install them in our front. This took many weary and exhausting hours. The most disagreeable part of the business was that we had to wear gas masks rolled up on the top of our heads under our tin hats all the time.[36]

Two in the morning was the usual hour for a battalion to relieve and be relieved in the trenches. The day before going in to the trench company commanders would take a 'Cook's Tour', a short visit to the trench to get the lie of the land and the 'gen' from the battalion they were to relieve. On the night of the relief itself, the company going in would blindly stumble along the maze of communication trenches behind a guide who himself had only the haziest notion of his whereabouts. Men got stuck in the ubiquitous mud and separated. And thus lost. Lucky was the company who found a white tape to follow, put up by some enterprising sapper. Brian Lawrence wrote that:

> A trench relief is always a little difficult and perhaps the most dangerous part of the tour of duty, for except in very quiet lines you nearly always have some casualties. The object of the enemy artillery is at all times, and especially at night, to make the approach to the front lines unpleasant.[37]

Night-time was when most subalterns had their blooding. Night-time was when their courage was first truly tested. Night-time was when they were first sent out on patrol in No-Man's Land.

Officially, as far as the British were concerned, No-Man's Land did not exist; the front line was the lip of the German fire trench. From February 1915 Sir John French called for 'constant activity', even though the army was on the defensive, including denying the Germans the ground to their front by patrolling. [37] Not all regiments followed the injunction earnestly. On attachment to the Welsh Regiment, Robert Graves did not go on patrol once; on joining the Royal Welch Fusiliers he discovered that both battalions of the regiment made it 'a point of honour to dominate No Man's Land', twenty-four hours a day, every day. More, it was 'the regimental custom to test new officers in this way by going out on patrol, and none dared excuse himself'.[38]

Graves first went out on patrol at Laventie, accompanied by Sergeant Townsend, to determine whether a German sap-head was occupied or not. They found a wicker basket containing a jar full of mysterious liquid which they dragged back for laboratory analysis. Graves overheard the Colonel say afterwards that the 'new wart [Graves] seems to have more guts than the others'.[39] On 'finding that the only thing respected in young officers was personal courage' Graves went out on patrol often. He also slyly factored that patrolling at night was likely to provide him with the best chance of a 'Blighty' wound, because rifle fire in the dark was 'more or less un-aimed'; the timing would be good too, because there would be no rush on the dressing-station services as there was in battle.[40]

It was the way of the Royal Welch Fusiliers, as it was of all Britain's regiments, that an officer should lead the patrol, and that he would be accompanied by two or three men; German patrols, which numbered six or seven men, went out under an NCO. As one Royal Welch sergeant-major observed to Graves, German officers did not believe in 'keeping a dog and barking themselves'.[41] Neither did the Canadians, who also let their NCOs do the patrols. The British system of officer-led patrolling was one more reason for the disproportionate measure of officer casualties. Among the casualties were the missing, those hapless or luckless enough to drown in mud or stray into the German lines to become POWs. On successive nights, Edmund Blunden's battalion of the Royal Sussex Regiment had officers go missing patrolling at Ypres; Blunden was sent off one night to 'see what I could see' about their fate. In No-Man's Land he came under an artillery barrage and in trying to escape almost crawled into an unknown, occupied German 'sap' trench projecting out into the wire wilderness, which was probably the man-trap that was 'the secret of my predecessors' misfortune'.[42]

Alexander Stewart, no soft stripling at thirty-three, nevertheless suffered the novice subaltern's eternal preoccupation during his first patrol in No-Man's Land: 'The men I took out knew it was my first time out and I was afraid of them thinking I was afraid.' Despite his party making a hell of a noise, which started a private 'little war', he did not, he recorded all importantly, show 'funk'.[43]

Every bit of information a patrol could scavenge about the enemy was regarded as useful. Douglas Gillespie:

> Last night I took three men with bombs, and we got right up to the German wire. I have cut a specimen of it, which I shall send home as a souvenir, unless the Brigade Staff want it. We brought in a curious iron stake, which the Germans use for rigging up their barbed wire, made in one piece out of an iron rod looped while the iron is hot, so that the wire can be just threaded through the loops, and it has a corkscrew end, so that it can be screwed into the ground noiselessly, just as you screw in the stake which anchors a tennis net, only, of course, this is much thinner and shorter. I don't think it's stout enough to be of much use, but it's an interesting thing, and Major Hyslop, who is commanding while Colonel Gore is home on leave, sent down a message this morning to congratulate me, so I feel quite pleased, for of course information about their wire is useful.[44]

The first patrol of Lieutenant Arthur Heath, 6/Royal West Kent Regiment, meanwhile, was an enjoyable affair:

> There used to be a listening patrol in the old mine-crater near which the new mine had been exploded. I had to go out, as commander of that part of the trench, and find out what really happened, and what could be done about occupying the place or preventing the Germans from getting it. So I crawled out and reconnoitred. Do you know the policeman's chorus in 'The Pirates of Penzance' – 'with cat-like tread upon the foe I steal'? It was absurdly like that, I didn't know where the new mine had blown up nor where the old one was precisely … So I had to make my way round and look over the rim very anxiously and carefully, with a revolver in my hand, hoping that there would be no

Germans waiting to shove a bayonet at me. Lying down between the lines and hearing the bullets whiz over you is really not at all bad fun, and I quite enjoyed one place where I could be covered as I thought, and survey the German trenches about thirty yards off.[45]

Cat-like creeping, under the wire and through the discarded bully tins, then in and out of the shell holes, around shell-blasted remnants of farms, was indispensable to success. To avert the danger of bayonets rattling against tin hats, soft hats on patrol became the order of the night; the men jibed at discarding their tin hats because they offered protection against shell fragments should the Hun decide to order a 'hate' against the infiltrators; when Edwin Campion Vaughan could not find his soft hat and had to wear the hard one, 'the troops were a bit surly and the patrol was only a half-hearted affair'.[46] Undaunted, Vaughan carried on volunteering for patrols and at Fremicourt led a night patrol that disrupted a German working party, capturing their shovels as souvenirs:

This little jaunt has left us with our tails well up, and I, for one, am very keen on No-Man's Land. I fully appreciate the truth of the maxim that was dinned into us during training – 'Fighting patrols are the finest stiffeners of morale'.

Patrolling earned Vaughan a reputation as a 'fire-eater', which was instrumental in habilitating him into the company after a lacklustre and unsociable start. 'It may soothe you to learn', Vaughan was told by his company commander, 'that Colonel Hanson is very pleased with your patrol work, particularly because you volunteered. And, by the way, Berry's platoon is being attached to yours to get used to working in No-Man's Land.'[47] Hundreds of other gauche and green subalterns, like Vaughan, used patrolling as their passport to the respect of their company. Psychologically, patrolling also prepared officers for 'going over the bags' (as veteran officers called 'going over the top', the 'bags' being the sandbags on the parapet), because it forced them out of the protective atmosphere of the trench. As Anthony Eden observed: 'at the first scramble over the parapet, any man's body must feel pathetically conspicuous and naked'.[48] Better, then, to do the first leaving of the womb on a night patrol, rather than a 'show'.

Charles Douie considered that patrolling had another virtue: it 'introduced an element of excitement into the dullest trenches'.[49]

There was another nocturnal activity likely to bring interest to a quiet trench.

Trench raids became all the rage after the success of the Canadian hit-and-run attack at Douve River on the night of 16 November 1915, when a 70-man group broke into the German trenches, bombing their way along, before withdrawing with a clutch of prisoners; Canadian losses were just one man wounded, one killed, and he by 'a negligent discharge'.

Haig euphemistically called trench raids 'winter sports'; they were also coyly called 'minor enterprises'. Whatever the synonym used, trench raids combined a multitude of virtues – they pacified the French (who were always clamouring for a lessening of pressure on their bits of the front), they provided untrained troops with the experience of combat, and they tied down substantial numbers of Germans. Trench raids, as *Notes for Infantry Officers* pointed out, were also the lemon juice and sea breeze that would banish lassitude in the BEF:

> There is an insidious tendency to lapse into a passive and lethargic attitude, against which officers and all ranks have to be on guard, and the fostering of the offensive spirit, under such unfavourable conditions, calls for incessant attention. Minor local enterprises and constant occupation during the tour of duty in the trenches furnish the best means of maintaining the efficiency of the troops ... Constant activity in harassing the enemy may lead to reprisals at first, and for this reason is sometimes neglected, but if persevered in it always results in ultimate mastery, it gives the troops a healthy interest and wholesome topics of conversation, and it achieves the double purpose of raising the morale of our own troops whilst lowering that of the enemy.

Minor enterprise or not, British trench raids were always led by an officer; the Canadians once again left the dangerous aspects of the night shift to NCOs. Trench raids, for all their listed attributes, were not universally popular; Guy Chapman considered them 'costly and depressing', Blunden wrote that 'our greatest distress at this period was due to that short dry word "raid"'. And truly, few raids were as unambiguously successful as the Canadian raid on Douve River. When the Dorsets sent 86 men forward under the cover of a mine explosion on the night of the 26 March 1916 at Y Sap on the Somme, they returned with nothing tangible save 21 casualties.

Anthony Eden went raiding on the flatlands at Ploegsteert, his task the familiar one of identifying the enemy regiment opposite:

> Our plans were carefully laid. No-man's-land at this point was eighty to a hundred yards wide. I was to command the raiding party which was to be small. With three riflemen who knew the ground well, we would form the main body. Harrop [a sergeant] with two more riflemen would take up a chosen position in no-man's-land on our right and about half-way across. From there he could support us if we needed it when in the German trench, or cover our withdrawal. If necessary he could also create a diversion which might confuse the enemy.
>
> There was to be no artillery preparation. The essence was to be secrecy and surprise on a night with little moon. Two riflemen with an uncanny aptitude for night patrol, Arthur Pratt, known to us as 'Tiger', who happily survived the war, and Tom Liddell, who was killed within a week of the armistice, were chosen for the toughest job. They were each to cut a gap through the German wire. The third rifleman, who was a skilled bomber, and I would be with them, and the wire once cut, we would jump into the German trench and kill or capture the sentry. At the least we should get some identification mark. ... The first moves went according to plan. We worked our way across no-man's-land without incident, and Pratt and Liddell began to cut the enemy wire. This was tough and rather thicker in its long grass than we had reckoned. Even so we made good progress and there were only a few strands left to cut, so that we were right under the German trench, when suddenly, jabber, jabber, and without warning two German heads appeared above the parapet and began pointing into the long grass. We lay flat and still for our lives, expecting every second a blast of machine-gun fire or a bomb in our midst. But nothing happened. After a little more jabber, the heads disappeared and all was quiet again.

We lay without moving for what must have been nearly an hour. There were no abnormal noises from the German line nor was the sentry on patrol. Less than four minutes of wire-cutting would complete our task and I had to decide what to do next. I touched Pratt and Liddell to go on.

The job was just about done when all hell seemed to break loose right in our faces. The German trench leapt into life, rifles and machine-guns blazed. Very lights soared up and the place seemed to us as light as day. Incredibly none of the bombardment touched us, presumably because we were much closer to the German trench, within their wire and only a foot or two from the parapet, than the enemy imagined possible. As a result the firing was all aimed above and beyond us, into no-man's-land or at our own front line.

Once more we had dropped down into the long grass and made no move until the firing eased and the Very lights dimmed a little. Then I signed to my small section to begin to crawl back. Our first blow was at the old field ditch, a German machine-gun sputtered down it at intervals, so there was no choice but a slow creep back across the open, praying that no Very light would expose us too clearly. All went well for a while, and we were about fifty yards from our front line when I heard what seemed a groan at my left hand. Signalling to the others to go on I moved a few yards to investigate. There I found Harrop lying in the lip of a shallow shell-hole bleeding profusely from a bad bullet wound in his thigh and two riflemen trying to help him.[50]

Eden and three riflemen managed to stretcher Bert Harrop back to safety; he spent two years in hospital but survived.

Lieutenant Siegfried Sassoon watched a trench raid go out on 25 May 1916:

Twenty-seven men with faces blackened and shiny – Christy-minstrels – with hatchets in their belts, bombs in their pockets, knob-kerries – waiting in a dug-out in the reserve line. At 10.30 they trudge up to Battalion H.Q. splashing through mire and water in the chalk trench, while the rain comes steadily down. The party is twenty-two men, five N.C.O.s and one officer (Stansfield). From H.Q. we set off again, led by Compton-Smith: across the open to the end of 77 street. A red flashlight winks a few times to guide us thither. Then up to the front line – the men's feet making a most unholy tramp and din;

squeeze along to the starting-point, where Stansfield and his two confederates (Sergeant Lyle and Corporal O'Brien) loom over the parapet from above, having successfully laid the line of lime across the craters to the Bosche wire. In a few minutes the five parties have gone over – and disappear into the rain and darkness – the last four men carry ten-foot light ladders. It is 12 midnight. I am sitting on the parapet listening for something to happen – five, ten nearly fifteen minutes – not a sound – nor a shot fired – and only the usual flare-lights, none very near our party. Then a few whiz-bangs fizz over to our front trench and just behind the raiders. After twenty minutes there is still absolute silence in the Bosche trench; the raid is obviously held up by the wire, which we thought it so easy to get through. One of the bayonet-men comes crawling back: I follow him to our trench and he tells me that they can't get through: O'Brien says it's a failure; they're all going to throw a bomb and retire.

A minute or two later a rifle-shot rings out and almost sim-ultaneously several bombs are thrown by both sides: a bomb explodes right in the water at the bottom of the left crater close to our men, and showers a pale spume of water; there are blinding flashes and explosions, rifle-shots, the scurry of feet, curses and groans, and stum-bling figures loom up from below and scramble, awkwardly over the parapet – some wounded – black faces and whites of eyes and lips show in the dusk; when I've counted sixteen in, I go forward to see how things are going, and find Stansfield wounded, and leave him there with two men who soon get him in; other wounded men crawl in; I find one hit in the leg; he says O'Brien is somewhere down the crater badly wounded. On the way down I see the Colonel, sitting on his bed in a woollen cap with a tuft on top, and very much upset at the non-success of the show, and the mine disaster; but very pleased with the way our men tried to get through the wire.[51]

Sassoon won the MC for his attempted rescue of Corporal Mick O'Brien. When the news of his award came through, avuncular Dr Dunn of the RAMC sportingly took off his own white-purple-white ribbon for Sassoon to sew on. The later career of Siegfried Sassoon MC illustrated one of the prime dangers of nocturnal work in No-Man's Land; he was shot by a jittery British sentry as he returned to the line. Fortunately, the head wound was not fatal.

Raids there were aplenty. The overall effect, opined Captain

Meysey-Thompson of the 21/Kings' Royal Rifle Corps, was merely to keep the Bosche on the *qui vive*. He may have had a point. There were 310 raids during the battle of the Somme alone.[52] By 1916 the British were raiding by day as well as by night, and with a mixed bag of results; a daylight raid behind smoke and gas (which blew away) by the 55th Division on 28 June 1916 near Blaireville Wood netted one German helmet and a Victoria Cross for the ranker whose red-hot rifle staved off the pursuing Germans during the retirement. The British casualties were 50 out of 75. Francis Hitchcock, however, won his Military Cross for a diurnal raid at The Triangle, Loos, in 1917 which involved 5 officers and 80 'Other Ranks', shook the enemy's morale, captured 8 prisoners, killed at least 20, and identified the opposition.

Whether they were sent out by day or by night, there was never any dry-up of volunteers for raids. A clue to the continued attraction of trench-raiding was provided by its kit; it was specialized, unorthodox, made for close-combat. The box of dressing-up kit included balaclavas, blackened faces, muffled boots, knobkerries, knuckledusters, knives and coshes, as well as pistols (for officers); Carrington used a trench stick, 'a longish cudgel with which I can feel my way in the dark but which I've decorated at the business end with a binding of barbed wire, to make a more formidable weapon of it'.[53] Like sniping, trench raids brought back the individual, the human, into a war of numbers and impersonal forces. It was man-on-man.

Sleep, there was no sleep. J. Cohen wrote: 'We get our sleep not so much according to our inclination as when we are off work.' Which was rarely, when in the line. Captain Edwin Venning of the Royal Sussex Regiment calculated in June 1915 that during a week in the trenches 'my average of sleep has been $2\frac{1}{2}$ hours in twenty-four'.[54] Lieutenant Arthur Heath, Royal West Kent Regiment, estimated that out of 112 hours in the trenches he got twelve hours sleep, 'and that entirely in the daytime'. He added that 'I am naturally a very sleepy animal, and do not like losing my rest'.[55] 'I don't think I have slept for more than 4 hours in the 24 for the previous five days', Donald

Kenworthy entered in his diary at Ypres in April 1915. While he was stationed on the Somme, Sidney Rogerson 'snatched less sleep than they (the men) – my total for the three days was no more than six hours'.

Rogerson was a company commander. Somnolence on the Somme for company commanders was particularly paltry, as Alexander Stewart confirmed:

> For days on end the officers would get what almost amounted to no sleep. This deprivation of sleep particularly applied to company commanders who at all hours of the day and night were receiving and sending out orders and casualty returns, etc. Nearly all the hours of dark had to be spent visiting posts and positions.[56]

Robert Graves thought that officers over 40 needed less sleep than those under 20 (but that 40-year-olds 'had less resistance to sudden alarms and shocks'). Boy officers found the sleeplessness truly gruelling. Twenty-year-old Francis Hitchcock went so far as to write in his diary:

> Lack of sleep, to my mind, is the worst strain of warfare, and how difficult it is to keep awake. I was in charge of thirty lives and two Vickers guns, holding an important isolated post, and yet at frequent intervals I found myself leaning against the parapet beside me and I would be startled out of my semi-comatose state, to choke and cough with the dust and fumes from the cordite.[57]

Many officers would have disagreed with Hitchcock. For them shelling was the one unbearable strain, the sitting in the dug-out or trench, trapped, with no option but to pray and wonder. The pure hopelessness of it all. Julian Grenfell confessed that after shelling 'one's nerves are really absolutely beaten down. I can understand now why our infantry have to retreat sometimes; a sight which was a shock to me at first, after being brought up in the belief that the English infantry cannot retreat.'[58] Following heavy shelling at Hebuterne the usually phlegmatic Graham Greenwell was moved to write to his mother:

It is the sitting still throughout a solid day listening the whole time to shells wondering if the next will be on the dug-out or not which is so unnerving. I cannot understand what sort of men they are who can stand three or four days of continued bombardment. Of course, at the end the ones who are alive are absolutely demoralised.[59]

Greenwell thought one particular German meteor nastier and more nerve-racking than the rest of the aerial arsenal. This was the 'Minnie' or Minenwerfer, the German trench mortar:

The row these things make is incredible and I can hear nothing but the low whistle of heavy shells; every puff of the wind startles me and I feel as nervous as a cat.

For Charles Douie, like Greenwell:

The heavy shells were not so disturbing as the Minenwerfer bombs. The former came with a rushing sound and at a speed which made escape impossible. It was easy to adopt a fatalistic attitude in regard to them. The latter could just be discerned as they sailed through the sky, a nightmare of black blobs. By keeping unceasing vigilance one might avoid them. The temptation to keep this vigilance was considerable, as they annihilated anything within a few yards of their explosion. The strain of watching the flight of the bombs, combined with the appalling noise which often made speech impossible, and the constant deprivation of rest for many days on end, placed a great strain on the nerves. In practice the troops became so tired as to be indifferent and made little effort to safeguard themselves. The casualties were high.[60]

One of the strains on an officer during a bombardment was a strain that would become all too familiar – of having to control his nerves to present the face of pluck to his men. Second Lieutenant Robert Vernede of the Rifle Brigade:

It's an extra-ordinary sensation – every portion of the trenches seemed to have shells exploding over them and you were nearly deafened by the near ones. I really was in a great state of funk, but I'm not sure that it's avoidable. The least sensitive of the men, I fancy, are strung up to the last pitch, and I doubt if even T. was as cool as he looked, though looking it is all the battle under the circumstances.[61]

T.P.C. Wilson, Sherwood Foresters stated:

As to my own feelings under fire, I was horribly afraid – sick with fear – not of being hit, but of seeing other people torn, in the way that high explosive tears. It is simply hellish. But thank God I didn't show any funk. That's all a man dare ask, I think.[62]

Bim Tennant worried:

I don't think I showed I was any more frightened than anyone else. Perhaps I wasn't ... The strain was awful.[63]

Arthur Graeme West wrote of a day in September 1916: 'I shall always remember sitting at the head of this little trench, smoking a cigarette and trying to soothe the men simply by being quiet.' They were shelled for about five hours. Although he could have 'cried for fright' West 'did not betray any kind of weak feeling'.[64] Ex-Eton maths master John Christie read Spenser's *The Faerie Queen* to his men to calm them during a 'hate'.[65] Some officers found a strange but surprising comradeship with their men under fire. 'It was extraordinary how one got to know and understand the men under shell-fire', recalled Francis Hitchcock. At shell-blasted Hooge under a heavy bombardment, a private in his battalion of the Leinsters shouted in his ear, ''Tis different now beyont in Killyon, sir.' The man lived at Killyon, three miles from Hitchcock's home, but only in war did they find their first social familiarity of talking to each other.[66] Likewise, Robert Graves found in battle that some of the divisions in the Royal Welch Fusiliers, between senior officers and junior officers, between officers and the men, broke down 'as though we were all drunk together'.[67] Graves even called the adjutant 'Charley'. Out of the line, discipline reasserted itself.

*

The mud, the mud.

It was enough to make an ex-public schoolboy drop the habit of understatement. It was enough to make a strong man complain. Sidney Rogerson wrote about the shit brown mud of the Somme in November 1916:

> It was like walking through caramel. At every step the foot stuck fast, and was only wrenched out by a determined effort, bringing away with it several pounds of earth till legs ached in every muscle.
>
> No one could struggle through that mud for more than a few yards without rest. Terrible in its clinging consistency, it was the arbiter of destiny, the supreme enemy, paralysing and mocking English and German alike. Distances were measured not in yards but in mud.[68]

A single round of a few hundreds yards to check on sentries took Rogerson over two hours of strenuous effort; some days he had to walk the rounds twice, even three times. Once, as small compensation, the perambulation was pleasantly interrupted:

> Hall and I had walked a little further along to the right of the sector – we were standing talking in the front line when we noticed a scuffling of earth in the parados of the trench, and out fell a furry, fat little mole. It appeared as one of Nature's miracles that this blind, slow creature could have survived in ground so pounded and upturned. After holding him for a few minutes, and marvelling at the strength of his tiny limbs, we put him into his hole again to find his way back whence he'd come.[69]

At High Wood on the Somme that same barren winter, Brian Lawrence's Burberry coat became so plastered in entombing mud that his servant had to cut the earth off with a knife to locate the buttons and buckle.[70] Finding his Burberry caked stiff with mud, Max Plowman hacked off the skirt leaving the remainder looking 'like an Eton jacket with frills'. Mud infiltrated everywhere, even into the mind. Graham Greenwell told his mother:

> Everything has to be carried for miles across country and at night. No-one knows the way, all landmarks have been removed by shells

and mud; and not for a single moment are the guns silent. Such food as we can get is gritty with mud, our clothes are caked with it; we think mud, dream mud and eat mud.[71]

On another occasion Greenwell informed her: 'My hands are caked in mud, my body bathed in it, my soul is full of it. I can hear nothing but the steady drip of water, gradually washing away the remains of the dug-out.'[72] He tried burning 'ruban de bruges' to take away the smell of mud in his top-rate dug-out in Hebuterne, but it did no good. Second Lieutenant Bernard Strauss MC, The Buffs, lamented: 'Mud is the keynote of our life: mud, mud, mud, inches deep: on one's feet, clothes, and in one's food: mud everywhere: what a country ... '[73] The mud of France and Flanders was more than soul-destroying; it swallowed humans alive. Stuart Cloete lost a Lewis gunner who fell into a crater; the 'gun on his shoulder pushed him under and we never got him out'.[74]

Some of the winters of the Great War, especially the winter of 1916–1917, were amongst the harshest in France and Flanders' history. So, along with the rain that caused the mud, came an agonising cold, which bit early. Second Lieutenant Arthur Young of the Royal Irish Fusiliers wrote from the Somme in September 1916:

The night was bitterly cold. I have felt hunger and thirst and fatigue out here to a degree I have never experienced them before, but those are torments I can endure far better than I thought I could. But the cold – my word! it is dreadful ... [75]

Greenwell encountered cold in the trenches unknown to him 'even in Switzerland'. Finding his British Warm anything but, he succeeded in keeping 'quite warm' with the help of a leather jerkin over his uniform. His Burberry came in useful as a cover for sleeping. Charles Carrington donned the popular goatskin jerkin – 'like Robinson Crusoe's with the hair on the outside' – which was applauded for its insulating qualities but not for the perfume it emitted in the confines of the dug-out. Meanwhile, at St Eloi, Francis Hitchcock wore his goatskin jerkin inside out, otherwise the 'hairy side got soaked rubbing against the muddy trenches'.[76] Relatives were pestered to visit military outfitters for lines of clothing specially developed to be worn under Army coats: Harrods had the 'Adaptable' fur jacket for wearing under the British Warms, waterproof or greatcoat. The Adaptable had an outer cover made of khaki Italian cloth, or proofed poplin, lined with camel fleece (£2 10d), English lamb (£5 5d), Musquash flank (£5 5d), or wallaby, or natural Musquash (£37 10s). Sometimes one just had to make do and mend; Graham Greenwell fashioned sand-bags into leg warmers. In the cold and the wet trench foot and frostbite became endemic. 'Our great battle now will not be against the Huns, but against frost-bite', Lionel Crouch penned home in November 1915. Conditions were so bad that 'hostilities', he unhappily concluded 'were a wash-out'.[77] Indeed conditions were so bad, that they caused a 28-year-old gentleman officer in the Territorial Force to readjust his morality; 'I really don't think that swearing is bad language out here', Crouch told his mother.

To stop trench foot and frostbite, officers, like other ranks, rubbed their feet in hog's lard or whale oil (both of which greases could be turned into fuel for an emergency cooker in a can). The elements could make men living rough – which is what trench inhabiting really was – suffer in the summer too. Douglas Gillespie wrote to his parents:

> I see Mai thinks I have a sunny temperament; she would not get the same opinion from some of my men. I have been biting their heads off lately; too many flies, too little sleep, and too much work in a hot sun to keep a philosophic mind, and the men themselves get lazy, and want to spend their time grousing about the state in which their trenches have been left, instead of getting to work to put them right.[78]

In mid August 1916 the Somme went from desert to waterland. Trench illnesses caused by the days of rain sped two officers of the 2/Leinsters, Hitchcock recorded in his diary, to base hospital in a single day.

For some there was satisfaction to be taken in their endurance of the elements; they included Stuart Cloete:

> Days, weeks and months of it, living almost in the open, hunting and hunted with only vestigial shelter unless we were deep underground like animals – moles, foxes, badgers in our earths and burrows. I felt an enormous pride in my body for having stood up to the strain.[79]

Living inside the earth, encounters with its fauna were inevitable. There were rabbits that mockingly burrowed into funk holes, grass snakes that fled shelling to plop into front line trenches, toads that lived under the flare-box and Edmund Campion Vaughan was once faced, literally, with the expert mammalian sapper: 'I was disturbed', he recorded of one night in a dug-out in Spring 1917, 'for a long time by a mole which at intervals kicked earth down on to my face as he burrowed into the roof'.[80]

These were curiosities. Some of God's creatures were plain vermin. All trenches heaved shudderingly with brown rats, although Robert Graves maintained that the lines cut by the French into the chalk at Festubert produced the largest swarms. After the Royal Welch Fusiliers took over the line, Graves recorded: 'We always ate with revolvers besides our plates and punctuated our conversation with sudden volleys at a rat running at somebody's valise or crawling along the timber support of the roof above our heads.'[81] Doubtless the rat plague at Festubert was a result of French 'nonchalance': their habit of burying corpses too near the surface, if at all.

Guy Chapman, like other callow subalterns, never forgot his first night in a dug-out, with its inevitable rat interlude. After falling asleep on a bed of wire stretched on poles at Houplines:

> I came to the surface with a jerk. I could hear something scrabbling beside my ear. I turned my head and caught a glimpse of what looked like a small pink monkey, clambering up the wall. With a spasm of disgust, I threw myself off the bed and bolted into the mess, where I sat shuddering and retching until the subaltern on duty pushed his head in and called 'Stand-to'. I was not yet hardened to rats.[82]

At Calonne, nearly a year later, Chapman – now thoroughly inured to rats – lived amongst rats 'as big as kittens'.[83] There was always an argument as to where in the line the biggest rodents lived, just as there was to where the worst mud waited (Passchendaele? The Somme?). The rats of Vimy Ridge, Hitchcock swore, were a 'colossal size', bigger even than cats and 'almost as big as dogs'.[84]

Rats were indiscriminate eaters. In the trenches at Annaquin in June 1917 Alexander Stewart 'was much troubled by the rats coming and licking the brilliantine off my hair; for this reason I had to give up using grease on my head'.[85] Rats the size of 'buck rabbits' ate Anthony Eden's specially held-back Christmas treat of chocolate peppermint creams, despite him having positioned them in the dug-out next to his wolf-hound, Con. The latter was probably too sated by eating rat for sentry dog duty. Not the least of the problems of living in 'Ratavia', Tom Kettle pointed out was that:

You lie in your dug-out famished, not for food (that goes without saying) but for sleep, and hear them scurrying up and down their shafts ... They scurry across your blankets and your face.[86]

Rattus norvegicus, the Brown rat that pervaded trench world, did at least provide sport for bored junior officers. Richard Talbot Kelly and his fellow artillery subalterns held candlelit rat-shooting competitions (with revolvers) in the vast cellars of the derelict Festubert brewery, a venue which happened to be a favourite skyline target for German gunners; as Talbot Kelly and pals potted away, shell splinters and bullets whined through windowless rooms above them.[87] The pleasure of 'strafing' rats with a revolver was also known to Lieutenant Frederic 'Eric' Rees, 13/ Durham Light Infantry, who extended his rat-hunting repertoire with a use of the bayonet not envisaged by Lieutenant-Colonel Ronald Campbell in his famous 'The Spirit of the Bayonet' talks at base: 'A great trick with these rats is to put a bit of cheese on the bayonet and rest it on the parapet and when a rat starts nibbling pull the trigger – result no rat.'[88] Hitchcock merely used a brick.

The insect life of sub-terra was no less pervasive, or profuse. There were grubs that fell into meals, mosquitoes that caused bitten legs to swell like tree-trunks, earwigs that crawled over the face (did they really live in ears? suddenly became a question with meaning) and fleas that hopped in and out of valises. In summer, there were flies everywhere, the unburied bodies strewn across No-Man's Land a gargantuan food source for their pale, wriggling young. On the roof of his dug-out Alexander Stewart watched flies massing 'like a swarm of bees' and had to put a muslin net over his head when resting. Eating was a nauseating trial. 'Bloated flies poised determinedly over our food and swooped on it', recalled Chapman.[89] 'One sickened of these carrion eaters and inevitably of the food they would contaminate.'

More troublesome still, was the body-louse, *pediculus vestmentii*, the 4mm-long female laying daily batches of five eggs in the seams of clothing. When hatched, the lice, curiously like miniaturized grey scuttling lobsters, fed off the blood of their human host, breaking the skin and causing irritation. Men could become so sensitized that they could feel each louse, each bite. In the unsanitary conditions of the trenches, scratching at the affected areas risked impetigo and 'perihelia of unknown origin' (p.u.o.) also known as trench fever or nephritis, a louse-borne disease similar to typhus.

On first contracting lice, the typical reaction of the human officer host was embarrassment, until he realized that the louse was indiscriminate in its attentions and nearly everyone was infested to a degree. Cloete recalled that: 'Going through the seams of our clothes for lice as we sat on the fire-step became a pastime for all ranks.'[90] The shame lifted, only to be filled with dull resignation: lice were yet another enemy, one which bit-bit-bit maddeningly away at the mind. Alec Waugh thought that there 'are few conditions that demoralize one more than being verminous with lice'.[91] So desperate did Cloete become to be free of lice that he once bought a pair of trousers from a passing artilleryman, and put them on, still warm from the artilleryman's legs. In war, Cloete observed, one 'loses daintiness'.

There were counter-attacks to be made. Visible lice or 'chats' could be cracked between finger and thumb-nail – grooming usually done whilst everyone was companionably sitting around talking, the origin of 'chatting' – and the eggs killed by running a candle or lighted cigarette along the seams of the clothes. Chemical cures were much favoured. Edmund Campion Vaughan, who became infested after sleeping in a former German dug-out where the lice dropped onto his face at night, wrote home for naphtha balls. There was an array of proprietary, specialized anti-louse and flea insecticides. 'Vermijelli' was 'a preventative and remedy for lice and fleas' which was mixed with water at 1/- for a 1lb tin. The promising-sounding 'Maxem Belt No.2 or Vermin Destroyer (Medicated)' was worn next to the skin and claimed to kill vermin, and 'render the wearer immune from future attacks', as well as protecting against chills. In truth, the efficacy of the commercially available insecticides was minimal, which was an irritant in itself, yet another example of war-profiteering.

Water, water everywhere and not any drop to drink. Or wash in. Or shave in. Water had to be carried into the trenches, along with every other necessity. In a 'hot' sector very little water might be brought up by the carrying parties, and the precious amount that was delivered was reserved for tea. At first, there was a joyous liberation in not washing, it was a boyish escape from nanny and stiff-collar formality. Julian Grenfell wrote puckishly on May 1915, 'I have never been so well or so happy. I have only had my boots off once in the last 10 days, and only washed twice.' War, declared Grenfell, was 'a big picnic'. But the thrill of dirtiness soon palled, because the middle and upper classes were the great washed. Being mired in dirt was another morale sapper. In the trenches officers lived in, and slept in, their clothes.

Edwin Campion Vaughan recalled that unless officers could find a clean puddle, 'which was seldom', they did not wash or shave for days on end. He developed a skin rash from not shaving or washing. Sidney Rogerson and his fellow officers laughed at each other's beards over breakfast in their Somme dug-out; 'by common consent I won the prize with a really fearsome blackness which covered my entire face'. Four days later the Brigadier, who had only seen Rogerson hirsute in the trench, failed to recognize him when clean-shaven. Some regiments would do their damnedest to shave in the line. After being shelled all night, Anthony Eden set his platoon to repairing the sandbags and gaps in defences. His colonel, however, came up to say:

You haven't shaved this morning, Anthony, nor have the men of your platoon. 'No sir, not yet; it's been a pretty rough night'. He

nodded: 'I know, but you should all be shaved by nine. See to it next time'. I was rather dunched, but he was right.[92]

King's Regulations indeed instructed officers and men: 'The chin and the lip will be shaved, but not the upper lip'. Moustaches were mandatory for officers and men; only boys too young to sprout facial hair escaped the injunction. Despite all the pressing urgencies of 1916 some stickler still found the time to court-martial a subordinate officer for razoring his upper lip. The officer only avoided cashiering when the humane Lieutenant-General Sir Nevil Macready altered King's Regulations instead, so that the moustache was no longer required.

Unsurprisingly, the infectious diseases carried by lice, dirt, fleas and flies on bodies weakened by stress and rough living caused the sick list to lengthen exponentially. Finally, the young and the cheerful succumbed: after a year and half in the trenches Graham Greenwell was hospitalized on 15 November 1916; his last bivouac in reserve at Bazentin Wood had been constructed from bits of wood and water-proof sheets, while his boots were split from heel to toe. Francis Hitchcock, who had felt truly sorry for Lieutenant Clancy on his being transferred to mortars because 'he was not strong, and not fit for the strenuous life of a platoon commander',[93] was himself medically boarded with pleurisy after 20 months in the trenches. Even Cloete, proud like an Achilles of his strength, succumbed to the germs; he contracted scabies, 'a skin disease due to the dirt and very prevalent among the troops'. The cure was to be sent to hospital for a week and rubbed head-to-toe with a mixture of fat and sulphur. And then he was felled by trench fever; despite feeling ill for days, he valiantly and dutifully did not report sick because the company was short of offic-ers – until he could literally stand no more, and toppled in a dead faint on the duckboards. He was dispatched to hospital, at Wimerieux, near Boulogne. Infectious diseases could whip through battalions in medieval manner, not helped by the unsanitary habits of other bat-talions; Captain Dunn of the Welsh Regiment complained to Robert Graves that the previous occupants of their trench 'had left the whole place like a sewage farm'; he blamed 'slack officers'. Dunn's battalion duly got sick. On the stifling Somme at the end of July 1916 four out of five officers joining Chapman's 13/Royal Fusiliers disappeared with dysentery, the perennial soldier's ailment, within days. Chapman himself contracted the disease but sought a cure from a medic, who presented him with five black pills averred to 'cure an elephant'. They did cure Chapman.[94]

'This is a war of attrition', the Regimental Medical Officer informed Sidney Rogerson; the RMO was treating more men for 'p.u.o.' and frostbite on the Somme in 1916 than the effects of enemy action. The West Yorkshire Regiment (The Prince of Wales' Own) was not unique; hospital wards were full of cases unrelated to enemy action. In 1917, 6,025 soldiers were admitted to hospital with dysentery, 15,214 with nephritis, 1,660 with tuberculosis and 21,487 with frostbite. Other diseases also took a toll, among them anthrax with 8 admissions and enteric fever with 1,275. The majority of soldiers recovered in a base hospital and were returned quickly to the front to fight another day; some, like trench-fever sufferer John Ronald Tolkien, were invalided home on a 'Blighty boat', with its green stripes and red crosses, never to return to action; and some died. A measure of the harvest that disease gathered among the officers, who were generally physically fitter and more resistant than rankers, can be seen in the war dead on schools' rolls of honour. When Cheltenham College compiled its 'List of Old Cheltonians and Masters Who Have Served in the War' it found that, of its 656 war dead, no less than 66 had died of disease or accidentally.[95]

All this was 'routine' war. This routine war of patrolling, raiding, shelling and disease annihilated battalions before battle commenced. Joseph Priestley at Souchez in 1917 watched his company go down from 270 to 70 just holding the line. At Mametz Alexander Stewart's company of 1/The Cameronians lost five officers killed, wounded or invalided out between 15–19 July 1916 just holding the line. In the rain of Passchendaele more and more of Richard Talbot Kelly's battery suffered from ague, until 'I had only one sergeant left on his feet and I was the only officer left at the guns'.[96] In his diary of 1916, Charles Carrington, a typical young officer, recorded no less than ten days spent in hospital being treated for illness.

Lack of food did not help. The Ration Party – which might have to carry food for a mile and half from the transport line to the front line – on occasion failed to arrive at the front line at all, having got lost in a landscape where all landmarks had been removed by shells or mud, or else deterred by heavy shelling. 'All I can get to eat are dog biscuits', wrote Greenwell to his mother on 24 August 1916 from the 'vile' trenches at Ovillers. The 'dog' biscuits were the ration biscuits, of the thickness sold for canines, 'very hard, but still they do fill up the gaps'.[97] Lieutenant Bernard Martin once lived for nearly three weeks on bully beef, hard-tack biscuits and jam. Meanwhile, crouched around the stove in the company HQ in the St Martin-Cujeul trenches ('the nearest thing to living in a rabbit-hole that I've experienced'), Siegfried Sassoon and Randal Casson shared a solitary slice of bacon; Sassoon's 'fragment' fell off into the stove; he recovered it. He then finished, with Casson, 'our only surviving orange'.[98]

But any food was a crumb of comfort. Food sustained soul as well as body. The officers', and the men's, fight back against the woes of trench life began with food. Periods in the line, recalled Sidney Rogerson, 'were bounded by our meals'.[99]

Usually, in the fire trenches the officer ate the same food as his men, as brought up by the Ration Party. Captain Joseph MacLean, 1/Cameronians, recorded a typical day's menu in the front line in March 1918:

This morning breakfast was *café au lait*, (tinned) bacon and sausage, bread and marmalade, which is pretty good going in a place like this. Breakfast is the best meal of the day. For dinner we have to fall back on bully beef, while tea is generally tea, bread and jam [always, but always apple-and-plum], perhaps with sardines or something like that ... During the night the men get stew and tea, which is brought up for them in 'hot food containers', and also rum, and I take a share of each – and the last is not the least.[100]

The hot food was prepared in horse-drawn wheeled cookers behind the lines and was carried up in dixies or hay boxes, two men to a dixie, to be emptied into proffered mess tins. It was invariably a kind of stew.

Edwin Campion Vaughan enthused over the 'wonderful hot meal' that came in the dixies: 'These containers are a great boon to us, for the food arrives quite hot at the front line. In the past we have had to do any little cooking possible over a Tommy's cooker – if we had one.' A Tommy's Cooker was a small shallow tin with three fins for a stand, which burned solid methylated spirit; the Primus stove burned paraffin. Uncommon at the beginning of the war, the Primus stove, which was more powerful than the Tommy's Cooker, became a must-have object by summer 1915. In the absence of hot food from a Ration Party, there was generally a tin of that stalwart of Army catering, tinned meat and veg, known generically as Machonochie's, after the leading manufacturer, that could be fried.

To overcome the monotony and unreliability of rations, officers took supplements into the trenches. Rankers did too, but officers, because of their higher pay and generally wealthier background, had more, and more choice. There was sometimes jealousy from 'Other Ranks'; Bernard Martin overheard his batman, while cooking some tinned concoction bought from a French village shop, explain to a passing private who grumbled that officers had better rations than the rank and file:

This stuff is not much more than a flavour. Officers have the same rations as you and me and anyway my officer is used to better grub at home than us . . . it's hard for them to miss what they've always had.[101]

Provisioners in Blighty offered a service whereby hampers could be supplied direct to officers in France and Flanders; the officers' favourite victuallers were Fortnum & Mason's in Piccadilly and Harrods in Knightsbridge. In the event that these refined establishments were unaffordable, a relative or friend could be prevailed upon to send out food parcels. Robert Graves enjoyed the weekly Fortnum & Mason hampers of his company commander, Captain Thomas, despite the tendency of the battalion's forbidding second-in-command, 'who had a good nose for a hamper', to appear at the opportune time.[102]

Greenwell, whose mother was endlessly considerate, had food parcels dispatched to him almost weekly. Sometimes he made suggestions: in May 1915 he wrote: 'Good cheese of the small Dutch variety and chocolate are welcome, but Harrods will make suggestions. In Hermon's Company they have a hamper from Harrods weekly.'

Whether Mrs Greenwell caught the hint is unknown. The sort of Harrods' hamper Greenwell had in the open-sights of his longing could be found in the 'Acceptable Gifts for the Man on Service' pages of the store's mail order catalogue or on a personal visit to the store's 'War Comforts Department'. Harrods' 'Our Soldiers' Half Guinea Box' hamper contained:

1 tin	H[untley] & P[almers] Oval Digestive
1 "	C and B Jam
1 "	Marmalade
1 "	Sardines
1 "	Nestle's Café au lait
1 "	Bivouac Cocoa and Milk
1 "	B.F. Beef Cubes
1 "	Matches, containing 12 boxes
1 "	Potted meat
1	pkt Candles
1	carton Muscatels and Almonds
2	tablets Soap
1	Christmas Pudding

After two years in the trenches, Greenwell was nearly begging his mother not to stop her food parcels: 'they are very precious and my friends will joyfully eat their contents even if I don't. You see we share everything in the Company Mess.'[103] Pooling food parcels was ubiquitous and, according to Lieutenant F.P. Roe, the contents 'rationed out with the greatest impartiality'.[104] For Douglas Gillespie the receiving of parcels reminded him of being 'back at school again; we all share everything together'.[105] To his chagrin, his servant left a brace of grouse, sent from Scotland by his parents, on the side of the trench for a day and half in the sun, so they were 'past'. Generally,

Gillespie wrote, he ate 'far too much, because there is so little else to do'.

Perhaps the best parcels were the surprise ones, which came like gifts from Heaven. Subaltern John Reith recalled how:

> one evening a splendid box of candy arrived from a girl of whom I had never heard: others followed from her at regular intervals. It was not until the Spring when, being invited to tea at my home, she explained the mystery to my parents. Shortly after we had gone overseas a photograph of the officers was published in a Glasgow newspaper. This young lady and some friends allocated us out among themselves with this highly satisfactory result. I never met her.[106]

A good meal could perform wonders. At Courcelles Graham Greenwell was shelled for thirty-six hours and 'felt quite done up'. But, he informed his mother, 'after a really excellent English breakfast of porridge, kippers, and eggs and bacon, I feel a new man'.[107] His other failsafe method of reviving his spirits was to tell himself, 'Thank God I didn't go to the Dardanelles'.

Food was an obsession in the trenches. It could be eaten to stave off hunger, it could be eaten to provide comfort. Food could even be arranged to suggest domesticity amid the madness. Here is Greenwell, writing home from the trenches of St Ives in the Douve Valley in June 1915:

> The beautiful large cake has just appeared at our luncheon table at which I am writing, clean and cool and with only the distant crash of a gun and the very occasional ping of a bullet against the parapet to disturb me. On our table there is some nice nobbly lettuce in a bowl with some very loud onions, some cold beef, a bottle of white vin ordinaire and another of table water; a Dutch cheese, some small cheese biscuits, some tinned fruit in a bowl, jam and marmalade, and lastly your cake. On the sideboard there are numerous varieties of potted meats, cigarettes, chocolates, pickles, dates, acid drops, revolvers, field glasses, the Bystander, Punch and The Times, so we might quite well be in rooms at Oxford, mightn't we?[108]

At the smallest chance, with the slightest resources, an officer would throw a dinner party in his dug-out. The food, usually cooked by the officer's servant, was not the fare of home, not even of billets, and certainly not of the Savoy, but it could be relatively luxurious. In the front line at Hebuterne, Greenwell was delighted when his cook produced five courses: 'The jam omelette and the mushrooms on toast contended for the chief honour.'[109] Lieutenant Calford, 1/Durham Light Infantry, wrote home on 1 February 1916:

> Last night we had quite a 'do' in my dug-out. One of the Gunner officers came round to dinner and for the Front Line Trenches in the most deadly sector in the line Turtle Soup, meat & two vegetables & Apricots & Cream washed down with whisky & Perrier from glasses isn't bad.[110]

The food, in truth, was always less important than the company in the dug-out dinner party. The dug-out dinner party was conviviality, comradeship, and community within cramped walls; it was the upper-and-middle class social scene (the working class did not hold dinner parties) transferred across the Channel and placed underground. For young officers – and so many of them were teenagers – it was a chance to taste normal adulthood. Staging such cheery evenings, Greenwell wrote, 'makes the life out here quite tolerable'.

Of course, something alcoholic to drink made the party 'go'.

In the trenches, the men were forbidden any alcohol except the rum ration, although most company commanders dished out an extra tot before a 'show' or under sustained shelling, or to rankers and NCOs coming off a cold sentry duty. John Glubb routinely brought his drivers into his tent on wet nights, where 'I sat in my flea-bag and distributed a tot of neat whisky to each in my tin shaving mug'.[111]

Officers too drank the rum ration; they were also allowed to privately purchase spirits and alcoholic beverages and take them into the trenches. Nonetheless Charles Carrington did not think that officers' dug-outs were 'floating in liquor' and that: 'Whisky – at seven and sixpence a bottle, a subaltern's daily pay, was a rarity which we husbanded.'

Carrington's Company must have been unusually abstemious or penurious. Many officers had funds other than their Army pay, and anyway whisky was obtainable at a much lower price than 7s 6d a bottle; Harrods shipped cases of 12 bottles of bonded whisky to France for the equivalent of 3s a bottle. A dollop of whisky in water in a tin mug was the common social gesture to the newly arrived officer, a wartime echo of the pre-conflict norm of proffering the guest in a home a drink. A social-gesture whisky is pointedly what Lieutenant Osborne gives to the newly arrived subaltern, Raleigh, when he first enters the dug-out at St Quentin in Sherriff's *Journey's End*. Despite finding a gunner officer attached to his company irritating, Sidney Rogerson still extended 'the ordinary courtesies of the trenches in the shape of a cigarette and whisky and water in a tin cup'.[112]

But officers drank principally to relieve stress. Robert Graves thought that there was a direct correlation between the length of service in the trenches and the amount of alcohol officers consumed:

> The unfortunates were officers who had endured two years or more of continuous trench service. In many cases they became dipsomaniacs. I knew three or four who had worked up to the point of two bottles of whisky a day before being lucky enough to get wounded or be sent home in some other way.[113]

During the days of 24 September to 3 October 1915 in the offensive against La Bassée, Graves was on a bottle of whisky a day himself to soothe his nerves. Although he discounted himself from the offence, he believed that some company leaders had their judgement impaired by the befuddling effect of drink. If so, such occasions were likely rare; Alexander Stewart contended, in his three years of frontline service, he 'never saw any man the worse for wear from drink, and very many times the better for it'.[114]

Alcohol was certainly used as battle dope or Dutch courage. In *Journey's End*, Sheriff has the principal hero, Captain Stanhope, say: '... if I went up those steps into the front line – without being doped with whisky – I'd go mad with fright'. He spoke for an army of frontline officers. Lieutenant Arthur Graeme West, becoming fearful as shells landed, drank 'enough whisky to enable me to view the prospect with nothing but interested excitement, and really did not flinch as the shells fell'.[115] As a novice in the trenches Edmund Campion Vaughan got 'wind up' about a forthcoming attack and retreated to the dug-out where he had a whisky 'to dispel the images'.[116] Learning a valuable lesson, he later administered 'a whacking dose of rum' to an officer shuddering with fear during a 'hate', in order to put him to sleep. In recognition of the virtue of alcohol as a liquid aid to courage, one anonymous officer wrote with affecting honesty, if not artistic brilliance, the doggerel:

> In moments when the front is still – no hustling whizzbangs fly-
> In all the world you could not find a braver man than I!
> Yet on patrol in No-Man's land, when I may have to stalk a
> Benighted Hun, in moments tense I have recourse to [Johnnie] 'Walker'.
>
> 'Tis Scotland's best which helps me rest, 'tis Mountain Dew which stays me
> When Minnies rack my wearied soul, or blatant H.E. flays me,
> 'Twas by its aid that I endured Trones Wood and such-like places.
> In times of stress my truest friend accelerates my paces.[117]

Sometimes the gesture of a drink was as much a tonic as the alcohol itself. In August 1917 Vaughan, by then a trench veteran, was deeply touched when two officers struggled through the mud and snipers of Passchendaele to the shell-hole he was using as an HQ, and presented him with a bottle of whisky. Not far away across the same bloody battlefield, Guy Chapman sat in a pill-box on the Menin road being shelled for a day and half:

> Most of us were too numbed and lethargic to care whether rain or shells fell. Two of the mess servants and Crosby, a kindly, elderly subaltern, suddenly appeared at noon bringing us cooked food and whisky from the transport lines. They had come eight miles and vol-untarily risked their lives to comfort us.[118]

Whisky was the drink of choice of officers, but other drinks had their connoisseurs. John Glubb drank port, but thought: 'The trouble was that everybody used to drink so much of it. Powell, of the Northumberland Field Companies, once came in and drank a tumbler full at 11 a.m.!'[119] In the lines at Potijze, Cloete enjoyed a glass of port after lunch, adding: 'Dinner was like lunch, only more elaborate, with wine to drink, or whisky and soda, and it ended with liquors.'[120] Quiet times at the front, he considered 'were very pleasant'.[121] Edmund Blunden, when mess president, made 'a foolish error' in taste and took up to battalion HQ at Thiepval 'an ample bottle of Benedictine, but little whisky'. His colonel 'gazed as one in a trance at the deplorable bottle of Benedictine, and more in sorrow than in anger at me'.[122] In an anticipatory mood before the battle of the Somme, Chapman's company of the Royal Fusiliers took half dozens of vintage wine, bottles of brandy and curaçao, plus various 'other correctives' into the line.[123] Some officers had yet more expensive tastes. Like Vaughan and Chapman, Graham Greenwell was grateful to a brother officer for the thoughtful gesture of a drink; the drink which reached him at 2 a.m. in the front trenches, when he was soaked through and exhausted was a bottle of champagne. Greenwell was doubly delighted to discover that the champagne was none other than Heidsieck '06, 'the very best'.[124] Bim Tennant was another believer in champagne, especially 'when one comes in at 3 a.m. after no sleep for fifty hours. It gives one the strength to undress.'[125]

A humane or sensible platoon officer also turned a blind eye to the King's Regulations regarding alcohol and Other Ranks on the special occasions in the calendar. Brian Lawrence on the Somme on Christmas Day 1916 was one such:

> As we had a large supply of drink, I went round the company and distributed a bottle of port and a bottle of brandy to each platoon, strictly against regulations of course, but still I think it marked the occasion in a fitting manner, and did no harm.[126]

The company had just been visited by the CO to impress upon the men that there must be no festive ceasing of hostilities or attempts to shake hands with the Bosche. This was an injunction Lawrence had no difficulty upholding; withholding a drink for his men was another matter. One reason for the prevalence of alcohol in the trenches was that drinking water was chlorinated by the medical officer and tasted like medicine. Water suffered too from the manner of its transportation, as Sidney Rogerson discovered:

> Tea was being made for breakfast, and though I accepted an offer of refreshment which was very welcome I turned retching away after the first gulp. It tasted vilely of petrol. For miles in the rear there was no water either fit or safe to drink, and all supplies had therefore to be carried up to the front in petrol tins, a system which was all right only so long as the tins had been burnt out to remove the fumes of the spirit.[127]

They rarely were. Sidney Rogerson also highlighted the other problem with tea; on the Somme, it 'was impossible to light a fire during daylight without giving the enemy gunners a fresh target', meaning no hot water. Neat rum was the drink of the day.[128]

Nearly all officers smoked like troopers, however young or old they were. Before going out to France officers generally puffed on Turkish and Egyptian brands. 'In those days', suggested young Dennis Wheatley, 'only the lower classes smoked Virginian cigarettes.' In London Wheatley bought gold-tipped Turkish cigarettes, with a personal monogram, for 7/7 per 100. On the front line in France he puffed away at Virginians; too many rounds of drinks in the mess had brought impecuniousness. 'Could you arrange for 100 Abdullahs to be sent me once a week? I am run clean out of smokes', Captain Lionel Crouch scribbled home;[129] the former solicitor may not have been popular in the dug-out; the pungent smoke from Turkish cigarettes in a cave already thick with the fug of coke-fumes, sweat, wet clothes, and cooking was, many pointed out, too bally much, and was another reason, aside from cost, for the spread of Virginian cigarettes. Like everything else, cigarettes could be ordered in from emporia in Blighty. There were odd war brands of cigarettes, such as 'Glory Boys', 'Ruby Queens' and 'White Cloud' made from poor green tobacco, which were avoided in favour of the tried and sucked, such as Woodbines, Gold Flake and Black Cat. The upmarket purveyors manufactured their own brands; Harrods shipped their 'Special Virginia' ('Free of English and French Duty') to the man on service at 16/- per 1,000. A 'Tinder Lighter' at 3/- averted the perennial problem of wet matches. Older officers might smoke a pipe. Temporarily attached to the Royal Warwickshire Regiment on their first tour of duty in the trenches, 35-year-old Alexander Stewart noticed his charges getting 'windy' at night under shelling; so he got up on the parapet and walked up and down, calmly enjoying his briar. Not all pipe-smokers were of such an advanced age; 18-year-old Bernard Martin was an ardent puffer on a briar.

Although the Army liked to keep officers busy, there were aching periods of blank time. Anthony Eden recalled:

> There was so much waiting in the trenches. Waiting through the hour before dawn for stand-down, waiting for the battalion which was to relieve us, waiting for rations and for letters, waiting for leave, or the Blighty wound, or ...[130]

Charles Douie agreed on the essential boredom of trench life: 'The moments of exultation were few and very far between; the hours of monotony were interminable.'[131] Almost any variation in routine was welcome, provided it stirred no significant retaliation.

Food, drink and cigarettes were pastimes as well as comforts. But how else did officers kill time in the trenches?

Tempting though the picture is of a subaltern composing poetry by the light of a guttering candle in a dug-out, most of the soldier poets composed their verse in billets or on leave [see pages 243–4, 341–5]. The reason was obvious: 'One cannot be a good soldier and a good poet at the same time', wrote Lieutenant Sassoon in his diary in 1918. 'Soldiery depends on a multitude of small details; one must not miss any of the details.'[132] Tolkien was more blunt still: 'You might scribble something on the back of an envelope and shove it in your back pocket, but that's all. You couldn't write ... You'd be crouching down among flies and filth.'[133] Reading verse was a different proposition.

Convalescing from myalgia at an Officers' Home in Aire-sur-la-Lys, Bernard Martin saw to 'my delight' Palgrave's *Golden Treasury* in a shop window, promptly bought it and it became 'my most cherished possession'. Edmund Vaughan took Palgrave's *Golden Treasury* with him to France (as did countless other subalterns), while Bim Tennant and Charles Douie preferred *The Oxford Book of Verse*. Rupert Brooke's poems had a wide circulation, even if they were gifts from female relatives and friends rather than purchases; Roland Leighton wrote, in gentle reproof, to Vera Brittain apropos the Brooke poems she sent him: 'I used to talk of the Beauty of War; but it is only War in the abstract that is beautiful. Modern warfare is merely a trade.'[134] Richard Talbot Kelly read Byron of an evening. Guy Chapman showed a 'very young, very fair and very shy subaltern' from the Royal Sussex around Hedge Street trench, prior to the Sussex' take over: 'As we bade him good-bye, he shyly put a small paper-covered book into my hand. *The Harbingers*, ran the title, "Poems by E.C. Blunden"'.

The bashful subaltern was indeed the volume's author. Along with *The Harbingers* Chapman put into his kit bag Shakespeare, Evan Harington and Sir Thomas Browne. Anthony Eden considered the Christmas present sent out by his cousin Violet Dickinson, the anthology *The Spirit of Man* by Robert Bridges, 'a perfect treat for the sensibilities'.[135] Charles Carrington received a copy of Browning's *The Ring and the Book* from his brother at Cambridge and 'by the end of the tour we were fighting over my book and talking of nothing else at meals'. The love letters of Browning were the preferred reading of Lieutenant Robert Mackay, who read every volume whilst on active service, which he considered 'rather a feat'.

It was. Trench life had its boredoms to fill, but the discomfort of the earth world could distract even the most literary minded of officers. *Tristram Shandy* proved hard-going for Arthur Grame West because of 'how supremely one was occupied with food and drink'.[136] Among the tired and those wanting easy escapist distractions Kipling, H.G. Wells, Rider Haggard, O. Henry, John Buchan, Anthony Hope, and the racing novelist Nat Gould were the popular authors. To Lieutenant Burgon Bickersteth's dismay his servant 'pinched' the Gould novel he was enjoying; in its place Bickersteth read, 'British Freedom

1914–1917' by the National Council for Civil Liberties. (Serving with a cut-glass regiment, the 1/Royal Dragoons, Burgon Bickersteth is the proof of the difficulty of pigeon-holing officers; he had definite socialistic leanings.)[137] The magazines that littered the dug-out tables were *Bystander, Punch* (both featured the cartoons of Captain Bruce Bairnsfather, of Royal Warwickshire Regiment), *The Field* and *Tatler*. School magazines were regularly sent out to old boys; in July 1916, Paul Jones had 'The Alleynian [Dulwich College magazine] duly to hand. Its monthly War record for the old school makes splendid, albeit mournful reading.' He also enjoyed keeping up with the School's domestic news, particularly the sports results. Likewise, Captain Vivian Watkins, a Regular in 2/Monmouthshire Regiment, was able to write back to *The Monmothian* that: 'O.M.s [Old Monmothians] in the Battalion, of whom there are quite a number, were all very pleased to hear the good result of the Brecon match'. The *alma mater* was near the top of most public schoolboys' correspondence list; Charley Sorley touchingly signed off his letters to his old school, 'My love to Marlborough'.

Of the illustrated newspapers *The Sketch*, with its society gossip, was top of the pile. At the bottom of the pile, hidden from the impressionable and the padre, were risqué French books and *La Vie Parisienne*. The attempts of Richard Talbot Kelly's colonel to hide 'immodest' French books from the teenager were undone when Talbot Kelly unearthed them and promptly enlisted the French interpreter attached to the battery or translation work.[138] The infamous *La Vie Parisienne* was a humorous magazine with the sort of mildly erotic drawings of scantily clad damsels that were the stock-in-trade of the art nouveau artist Raphael Kirchner. Siegfried Sassoon was convinced that, aside from the London Mail, his fellow officers read little else but 'illustrated papers with pictures by "Kirchner" and (for a treat) *La Vie Parisienne*'.[139] (Sassoon's main reads included Tolstoy, because 'the battle pictures help me a lot'.) If Sassoon was being too sweeping and priggish, the phenomenon of callow subalterns staring goggle-eyed at Kirchner girls and the lingerie models in pen-and-ink adverts was well-known enough to be spoofed by the trench newspaper, *The BEF Times*, under the heading 'The Subaltern':

He loves the Merry 'Tatler,' he adores
The Saucy 'Sketch'
The 'Bystander' also fills him with delight;
But the pages that he revels in, the evil
Minded wretch,
Are the adverts of those things in pink and white.

They are advertised in crepe-de-chine
And trimmed with silk and lace;
The pictures fairly make him long for leave;
And while he gloats upon their frills, he cannot find the grace
To read the pars of PHRYNETTE, BLANCHE and EVE.
[...]
It's this war, that is responsible for
teaching simple youth
All sorts of naughty Continental tricks
And already he's decided, when it's over
That, in truth
He'll buy mam a pair of cami-knicks.[140]

The BEF Times was the descendant of The Wipers Times, the most famous of the unofficial, and usually satirical, trench newspapers produced by British soldiers in the war. The first issue of The Wipers Times sallied forth on 12 February 1916 after being printed under fire in a cellar in Ypres on an abandoned press judiciously looted by Captain F.J. Roberts and Lieutenant J.H. Pearson, both hostilities-only officers with the Sherwood Foresters. They appointed themselves respectively the editor and sub-editor. The price was 20 francs. Running to 23 issues, The Wipers Times has been likened to a school magazine; it was not like a school magazine, it was a humorous, trench-time version of the officer's standard light read, Punch. In The Wipers Times the temporary officer from the middle and upper classes held up an affectionate, parodying mirror – to himself:

TRY OUR NEW CIRCULAR TOUR
EMBRACING ALL THE HEALTH RESORTS OF
LOVELY BELGIUM

–o–o–o–

Books Of Coupons Obtainable From
R.E. Cruting & Co.,
London. Agents Everywhere.
–o–o–o–
Our expert Guides meet all trains, and our excellent system of G.S.
coaches will make you realize what travelling is.
–o–o–o–

BEAUTIFUL SCENERY ON ALL CIRCUITS.

–o–o–o–

NO SALIENT FEATURE OMITTED.

–o–o–o–

BOOK AT ONCE TO AVOID DISAPPOINTMENT.

The national newspapers, which soldiers could arrange to have sent out to them, were vilified for their propagandizing and falsehoods. Second Lieutenant Douglas Gillespie wrote home on 12 May 1915 'from the trenches':

> I have just been looking at a full-page photo in an illustrated weekly with the stirring title, 'How three encountered fifty and prevailed', and a footnote describing their gallant deeds in detail. The dauntless three belong to this regiment, but we were a little puzzled because we have never been at La Bassée, where their exploit took place. A close inspection showed that the trees were in full leaf, and that the men were wearing spats and hose-tops, which we have long since abandoned for general use. Finally, someone recognized the sergeant as our shoe-maker sergeant, and his companions as two men from our second line transport. They are usually at least three miles from the trenches, and the whole story is a lie from beginning to end, without a shadow of truth in it. It makes one distrust all newspapers more than ever, to catch them out like that. The photo must have been taken somewhere on the retreat last year (i.e. the retreat from Mons in August, 1914).[141]

Second Lieutenant A.D. Gillespie was killed in action at Loos in September. He had taken Dante's *Inferno* into the trenches to read, along with Bunyan's *Pilgrim's Progress*. When his effects were sent home, there was found a mark at the page of which this was the closing sentence:

> Then I entered into the Valley of the Shadow of Death, and had no
> light, for almost half the way through it. I thought I should have
> been killed there, over and over ; but at last day broke, and the sun
> rose, and I went through that which was behind with far more ease
> and quiet.

But not all leisure pursuits were solitary, far from it. Friendships
were easy in the closed world of the trenches; Bernard Martin considered that the 'intimacy' of the trenches, and the low expectation of
survival, 'led to an acceptance of the rights of every individual to an
opinion and personal habits'.[142] Whereas young H.E.L. Mellersh had
endured loneliness in the barracks in Britain, in the trenches he –
along with thousands of other subalterns – enjoyed companionship.
Confined space left no room, literally, for diffidence, while conviviality
was succoured by collective pastimes. Card games of the gambling
sort were always popular. Alexander Stewart played a variety of
patience called Gambler's Seven, where two people played against
each other, buying and selling the pack for 10 francs. He valued it as:
'A very good game for the trenches as it was short and took up very
little time or room, and it was a good game for a gamble.'[143] 'Slippery
Ann' and Pontoon were staples. Lieutenant Frederic 'Eric' Rees
13/Durham Light Infantry was one of numerous officers who lugged
a gramophone into the line. In his dug-out, he wound up the gramophone to play ragtime records, the sound of which floated out down
the trench and into No-Man's Land. Charles Carrington's dug-out,
meanwhile, enjoyed a 'sing-song':

> And what I remember best of that long winter in the trenches is
> snuggling round a charcoal stove in the dug-out, singing. We had
> a large repertoire of drawing-room ballads, 'nigger minstrel' songs,
> musical numbers from the revues then playing in London, folk songs,
> and the bawdy old soldier's catches that run right back to the eight-
> eenth century wars.[144]

Outside the dug-out there were pleasures too. Edwin Campion
Vaughan lauded a May morning in 1917:

The morning was absolutely gorgeous; the sun was frightfully hot but there was a delightful breeze which just caught our heads when we stood on the first earth step. The grass is about a foot long and thousands of poppies are swaying along the lips of the trench, whilst among the stems of grass are multitudinous wild flowers.

It was very pleasant sitting at our dug-out door or strolling along the trench chatting to the troops as they carried out their morning duties of shaving and cleaning buttons and rifles.[145]

The war was in colour, not in black-and-white, or even solely in red for blood and brown for mud.

On other quiet days Vaughan would lie out smoking, watching Jerry trying to shell the road junction. Once he joined two other officers wandering round the trenches sightseeing, enjoying looking at the corpses of dead Germans. Douglas Gillespie also sneaked out of the claustrophobic trench to lie in the sun:

I found a hollow in the ground where I could wriggle along through the orchard, out of view of the sniper. There are a lot of cherry trees which look as if they would blossom before very long, and it was nice to get away from our muddy trench, and lie on clean grass in the sun ; no flowers yet except daisies and celandines. Almost all the trees have had branches broken off by shells or bullets, but the tree under which I lay was a walnut, so perhaps the breaking will serve instead of a beating, and do it all the good in the world.[146]

One of Gillespie's fellow subalterns in 4/Argyll and Sutherland Highlanders shot the hares that inhabited No-Man's Land for the pot with his revolver. On a gentler note, they all enjoyed the company of their adopted trench cat, Sonia, and their terrier pup, the fantastically named Satan Macpherson. For the recently married Max Plowman there was companionship and solace in the stars: 'What joy it is to know that you [his wife] in England and I out here at least can look upon the same beauty in the sky. We've the stars to share,' he wrote.[147]

Graham Greenwell especially liked:

The peace that reigns from 3.30 a.m. [dawn in Spring] till about 9 o'clock [which] passes understanding, all the staff are in bed, the gunners are asleep and the intense atmosphere of the night and watching is relaxed, you can almost hear the Hun sausages sizzling over the way.[148]

You could also hear birdsong. Stuart Cloete believed that in the trenches 'the feeling that each day might be the last led to an immense appreciation of everything'. A love of birds, especially, runs like a golden, obsessive thread through officers' diaries and letters.[149] No-Man's Land offered, on many stretches of the Western Front, an oddly ideal avian habitat; after all, few humans ventured there in daylight. As the anonymous author of *A 'Temporary Gentleman' in France* observed, 'To show yourself in it [No-Man's Land] meant death. But I have heard a lark trilling over it in the early morning as sweetly as any bird ever over an English meadow.'[150] The birds of No-Man's Land were usually farmland birds, perching birds or the small hawks that preyed on them. Captain T.P.C. Wilson wrote on 27 April 1916 from 'a trench not very far from the Germans' to tell his mother he had just heard the first cuckoo.'[151] In his observation post at Plugstreet, Talbot Kelly had swallows nesting alongside his head, a sight he lovingly sketched;[152] his interest in drawing birds never left him and he later provided the illustrations for bird guides, including his own *The Way of Birds* and R.M. Lockley's classic *Birds of the Sea*. Meanwhile, Lieutenant Christian Carver of the Royal Field Artillery was amazed at the heron living beside him in the wasteland of the Somme in March 1917, adding in his letter to his brother, 'It is the last place *I* would choose'.[153] (It was clearly a time of natural wonders; his platoon had just 'chivvied a wild boar'.) But it was the songs of birds that truly uplifted the spirits: Denis Barnett, a subaltern in the Leinsters, wrote to his mother in 1915, 'It is lovely sitting in the sun, listening to the cock chaffinches and yellowhammers tuning up.'[154] Julian Grenfell took similar solace from birdsong, when lying out in a field at night, awaiting the order to move into battle, with nightingales trilling around him.[155] Douglas Gillespie was another bewitched by the nightingale:

Presently a misty moon came up, and a nightingale began to sing. I have only heard him once before, in daytime, near Farley Mount, at

Winchester; but, of course, I knew him at once, and it was strange to stand there and listen, for the song seemed to come all the more sweetly and clearly in the quiet intervals between the bursts of firing. There was something infinitely sweet and sad about it, as if the countryside were singing gently to itself, in the midst of all our noise and confusion and work; so that you felt the nightingale's song was the only real thing which would remain when all the rest was long past and forgotten. It is such an old song too, handed on from nightingale to nightingale through the summer nights of so many innumerable years.[156]

Fortunately for those who liked to hear the evensong of the nightingale, the bird was more common in France and Flanders than at home.

At home. The assiduous noting of bird life on the Western Front was more than a way of passing the empty hours in the walled world of the trenches. In *Journey's End*, Sherriff has Lieutenant Trotter hear 'a bloomin' little bird' as he goes about the trench. Trotter goes on to say:

Funny about that bird. Made me feel quite braced up. Sort of made me think about my garden of an evening – walking round in me slippers after supper, smoking me pipe.[157]

The sentiment is echoed in the poem 'Birds in the Trenches' by Lieutenant Willoughby Weaving, Royal Irish Rifles:

Ye fearless birds that live and fly where men
Can venture not and live, that even build
Your nests where oft the searching shrapnel shrilled
And conflict rattled like a serpent, when
The hot guns thundered further, and from his den
The little machine-gun spat, and men fell piled
In long-swept lines, as when a scythe has thrilled,
And tall corn tumbled ne'er to rise again.
Ye slight ambassadors twixt foe and foe,
Small parleyers of peace where no peace is,
Sweet disregarders of man's miseries
And his most murderous methods, winging slow

About your perilous nests – we thank you, so
Unconscious of sweet domesticities.[158]

The birds of trench land also moved Lieutenant E.F. Wilkinson to poetry, in 'To a Choir of Birds':

Green are the trees, and green the summer grass,
Beneath the sun, the tiniest leaf hangs still:
The flowers in languor droop, and tired men pass
All somnolent, while death whines loud and shrill.
O fine, full-throated choir invisible.
Whose sudden burst of rapture fills the ear!
Are ye insensible to mortal fear,
That such a stream of melody ye spill,
While murk of battle drifts on Auber's hill,
And mankind dreams of slaughter? What wild glee
Has filled your throbbing throats with sound, until
Its strains are poured from every bush and tree,
And sad hearts swell with hope, and fierce eyes fill?
The world is stark with blood and hate – but ye –
Sing on! Sing on! In careless ecstasy.[159]

Lieutenant Robert Sterling of the Royal Scots Fusiliers, winner of the Newdigate Prize at Oxford for his 'Burial of Sophocles', put a philosophical finger on why birding appealed:

I've been longing for some link with the normal universe detached from the storm ... I did find such a link about three weeks ago. The enemy had just been shelling our reverse trenches, and a Belgian patrol behind us had been replying, when there fell a few minutes silence; and I still crouching expectantly in the trench, suddenly saw a pair of thrushes building a nest in a 'bare ruin'd choir' of a tree, only about five yards behind our line. At the same time a lark began to sing in the sky above the German trenches. It seemed almost incredible at the time, but now, whenever I think of these nest-builders and that all but 'sightless song', they seem to repeat in some degree the very essence of the Normal and Unchangeable Universe carrying on unhindered and careless amid the corpses and bullets and the madness.[160]

To a people more connected to nature than us, the bird was reminder of home, symbol of life eternal, as well as hobby. Lieutenant Edwin Campion Vaughan performed what must rank as the most poignant 'thank you' to the birds of the trenches. On discovering a dead pigeon he and his platoon buried the bird, 'railing his grave with little sticks and chains of sedge grass, and in the coverlet of pimpernels we erected a tiny white cross'.[161]

There was always the option of breaking the tedium of trench life by 'ragging'. 'Everybody looks on the bright side of things out here; one can generally find something amusing in most things if one tries', insisted Captain The Honourable L. Playfair.[162] Practical jokes were always good value. In June 1917 Edwin Campion Vaughan played the junior officer's favourite jape: he dropped some German stick bombs in the officer's dug-out.

After having removed the fuse and detonators.

The trick was always best done on those whose nerves were fraying. Junior officers. They were, by and large, very young.

To Serve Them All My Days:
Leadership in the Trenches

'I am only here to look after some men.'

Captain Siegfried Sassoon, Royal Welch Fusiliers, 1918

The officer in the trenches was warrior and father. No matter how baby-faced the subaltern, he was expected to care for his men. As a style of command, benevolent paternalism in the British Army stretched back to Agincourt, when English lords aided the 'ne'er so vile' archers and pike-men; the French knights in the battle merely rode roughshod – literally – over their own peasant soldiers. Military paternalism was a combination of patriotism, with its acceptance of a common national interest, and knightly *noblesse oblige*; if anything paternalism in the British Army increased over the Victorian era, as Christian-minded boys from Doctor Arnold's reformed public schools entered the officer corps. By the twentieth century fatherliness was absolutely institutionalized in the Army, with officers having to sign certificates that their men's feet had been rubbed with grease, their socks changed and that they had eaten a hot meal.[1] Official training manuals informed platoon commanders that it was their duty to stand as 'a father to their men' but not to be a 'dry nurse'.[2]

Paternalistic officers could go to extraordinary ends for their men in the line; Guy Chapman recalled his colonel in 13/Royal Fusiliers dealing with a dry-sock shortage by looting the knapsacks of dead Germans:

Pipe in mouth he might be seen hopping, carrion-crow-wise, from body to body in the appropriately named Opaque Wood, returning home towards lunch time with his runner, their arms full of necessaries for the battalion.[3]

Occasionally Guy Chapman accompanied the colonel on these free shopping jaunts but generally found himself too queasy. The intestines of Robert Graves were more iron-clad; he scavenged amidst the corpses of Mametz Wood for German overcoats for his men to use as blankets. In a marvellous inverse of the master-servant relationship, Lionel Crouch watched a colonel of the Ox and Bucks carry his batman through waist-deep mud.[4]

But what really counted for the Other Ranks' morale and well-being was the little stuff officers did, day in and day out, the double tot of rum with a wink of the eye, the slipped cigarette, the kind word, the help with a letter. Junior officers, in particular, became consummate experts at organizing extra supplies for their men by cashing in on connections at home: Eton subalterns wrote to the School's *Chronicle* asking readers to supply football kit and indoor games,[5] while Graham Greenwell requested his endlessly accommodating mother to send a cheque to Mrs Overy's charity, which sent out weekly consignments of comforts to the men of 4/Ox and Bucks. Bim Tennant roped in his mother, meanwhile, as a wholesale cigarette provisioner for his men. Not that junior officers were averse to spending their own money on their men, perish the thought; Max Plowman and a fellow subaltern reached into their pockets to pay for their platoons to travel to a divisional entertainment at Molliens Vidames, a treat the men would not have otherwise had. Officers themselves were quite aware of the difference their kindnesses made. And by a virtuous circle the kindnesses they performed pleased them too. One night Siegfried Sassoon found some tea for five of his men who arrived late to camp:

Alone I did it. Without my help they would have had none. And I was proud of myself. It is these things, done for five soldiers, that make the war bearable.[6]

Necessity was the father of invention. Despite – perhaps, because of – their youth, junior officers deepened and extended the Army's traditional benevolence towards soldiers, and the reasons were two-fold. The men of the Kitchener armies, being high-minded volunteers or even uppity trade unionists, were not as naturally obedient as the old Victorian Regulars; over such proud men a hastily trained sub-altern, not long out of school, might struggle to impose traditional military authority. Leading by caring reins was a green subaltern's natural reaction to citizen soldiers; happily, in general, this style of command suited the Other Ranks. In return for respect and care, the soldiery accepted the officer's authority. Second Lieutenant Francis Snell, Royal Berkshire Regiment, a private tutor, wrote with pres-cience and honesty:

> ... I have to deal with men whose response to noble impulses has been strong enough to make them give up their homes and everything they value, from motives that must be wholly unselfish ...
>
> One must not be weak or vulgar, or toadying, or showing off, or sickly sentimental of course, but neither would one be those things with one's own social and military equals.
>
> One may stand in relation to these men as a father or an elder brother, in some cases; but such relations exist between com-missioned officers also. And quite as often the boot is on the other foot, even as officers and men. Nothing is more fatuous than the old military precept, that the officer must by every subterfuge keep up an appearance of omniscience, and that if he is 'caught out' or reveals his ignorance on any point, his hold over his men will be gone.
>
> Any sort of bluff of that kind will be detected by these men in an instant and they will despise you for it: – and serve you right too! They know what you are worth, and if you are fit to lead ... [7]

In a similar vein, Captain Sidney Rogerson believed:

> It had always seemed absurd to me to try and adhere rigidly to the conventional formalities of discipline in the trenches where officers lived cheek by jowl with the men, shared the same dangers, the same dug-outs, and sometimes the same mess-tins. Quite apart from the absurdity, I believed, and nothing I ever saw subsequently shook me in the belief, that the way to get the best out of the British soldier was for an officer to show that he was the friend of his men, and to treat them as friends. This naturally involved a relaxation of pre-war codes

of behaviour, but it did not mean that an officer should rub shoulders with his men at every opportunity, or allow them to become familiar with him. It meant rather that he should step down from the pedestal on which his rank put him, and walk easily among his men, relying on his own personality and the respect he had earned from them to give him the superior position he must occupy if he wished to lead. He had consequently to steer a delicate course between treating those under him as equals in humanity if inferiors in status, and losing their respect by becoming too much one of them. [8]

The 'delicate course' Rogerson trod was one followed by many a Great War officer; indeed it can be taken as the venerable model for officering in the trenches of the Western Front, the deadliest place the British have ever served. When an NCO showed rude 'familiar resentment', Rogerson took him before the CO, and the lance-corporal lost his stripe. Friendship but authority.

It wasn't only the Great Wars' officers who likened themselves to fathers, brothers and friends of the men. When Lieutenant Paul Jones, Tank Corps, was shot by a sniper one of his company, Gunner Phillips, said:

He was a grand officer and treated his men like brothers. He would never ask the men to do what he would not do himself. The result was that we would all have done anything for him. There are a few rough chaps in our battalion – men who know the guard-room – but even these yielded gladly to his influence, and liked him very much. No officer in the battalion was so loved and respected by the men. [9]

After Lieutenant Robert Tennant, King's Own Yorkshire Light Infantry, was killed his Company Sergeant Major wrote to his parents:

It was a very sad and downhearted set of men that I led out as a company that night, for we had lost our best friend, captain and companion. [10]

Father, brother, friend – whatever the chosen noun, it signalled the closeness of the bond between officer and man. To a greater extent than ever before, junior officers cared for and lived alongside their men; in consequence, junior officers often developed deep attachments to the men of their 50-strong platoon or 200-strong company. Love would not be too strong a word for such bonds and the depth of the bonds struck everyone who encountered them. When the headmaster of Cheltenham College gave the Memorial Service Sermon at the school in 1915 he admitted to being affected by the letters from men and NCOs praising his old boy officers, and went on:

> The thing that fills my heart with the greatest wonder and happiness is the splendid simplicity of fellowship with which our young officers from the public schools and universities have won their way into the hearts of the men whom they have been called upon to lead. They have led them like faithful and good shepherds, caring for their souls and bodies, tending them, helping them and laying down their lives for them. They have loved their men, and their men have loved them. Nothing has been written in all the history of warfare which more redounds to the credit of human nature. And what is the cause of it? I do not know. I can only say with profound thankfulness that I believe there is something in the atmosphere of the public schools where these boys were bred which has been breathing into their natures a humanity worthy of their Christian profession: what is it but the Spirit of God?[11]

Perhaps the purest expression of an officer's paternal love for his men in the Great War came in poetry, in the heart-rending form of 'In Memoriam, Private D. Sutherland' by Second Lieutenant Ewart Alan Mackintosh of the Argyll and Sutherland Highlanders:

> So you were David's father
> And he was your only son,
> And the new-cut peats are rotting
> And the work is left undone,
> Because of an old man weeping,
> Just an old man in pain,
> For David, his son David,
> That will not come again.
> [...]

You were only David's father,
But I had fifty sons
When we went up in the evening
Under the arch of the guns,
And when we came back at twilight-
O God! I heard them call
To me for help and pity
That could not help at all.

Oh, never will I forget you,
My men that trusted me,
More my sons than your fathers'
For they could only see
The helpless babies
And the young men in their pride.
They could not see you dying,
And hold you when you died.

Happy and young and gallant,
They saw their first-born go,
But not the strong limbs broken
And the beautiful men brought low,
The piteous writhing bodies,
They screamed 'Don't leave me, sir',
For they were only your fathers
But I was your officer.[12]

The devotion of an officer to his men could be a fatal devotion; Billy Grenfell of 8/The Rifle Brigade refused a safe appointment, partly because he could not leave a short-officered battalion in the lurch and partly because: 'The men are glorious. I do love them.'[13] He was killed leading a charge of his riflemen at Hooge. Captain W.B. Algeo, an 'Old Contemptible', received an offer of a staff appointment at Thiepval in May 1916. A colleague recalled:

Standing, looking over the valley of Ancre, he [Algeo] debated for a moment before turning to a subaltern and said, 'I can't leave these old men'.

He went up the line and lost his life hours later; one of his men tried to rescue him and, refusing to leave him, died at Algeo's side. Like Algeo, Captain Thomas Kettle was offered the chance of a staff post – and life – on the Somme. He wrote to his brother:

> We are moving up tonight into the battle of the Somme. The bombardment, destruction and bloodshed are beyond all imagination. I have two chances of leaving my Dublin fusiliers – one to take sick leave and the other to have a staff job. I have chosen to stay with my comrades. Somewhere the choosers of the slain are touching as in our Norse story they used to touch with invisible wands those who are to die. I am calm but desperately anxious to live.[14]

Kettle was killed in action the following day.

There were styles of command other than the new, improved companionate paternalism, and what suited a New Army battalion of the East Surreys might not suit hard-bitten Regulars in the Guards. A Commission in the pocket and pips on the shoulder, of course, provided inherent authority, as Donald Hankey, a public schoolboy who served in the ranks before accepting a commission in the Royal Warwickshires, noted:

> The commissioned officer, even in the citizen Army, has a good deal of prestige as long as he does not give it away. He appears by virtue of his immunity from manual work and competition, his superior dress and standard of living, to be a higher sort of being altogether.[15]

The intrinsic 'prestige' of the King's commission was amplified by upper class confidence; although the New Army men were less tractable than the old Victorian Regulars, they were still accustomed to a society of masters and servants, employers and workers. There was something naturally authoritative about a gentleman. Lieutenant Hugh Butterworth (Marlborough and University College, Oxford) of the Rifle Brigade wrote:

> The curious thing is that in civilian life they've [the men] probably cursed us as plutocrats, out here they fairly look to us. The other night

some time ago, I had some men and had to get somewhere I'd never been to before ... [but] before we started I was told to send the men with a sergeant. Said the sergeant to me, 'I wish you were coming sir, I don't know the way.' I said, 'My dear man, nor do I.' To which he made this astounding reply, 'Very likely not, sir, but the men will think you do and they know I don't!'[16]

Units in the British army, even up to battalion level, were highly individual, because they were influenced by the personality and tastes of their commanding officer; a poor, aloof commander sunk the 11/Argyll and Sutherland Highlanders into such doldrums by 1917 that the men became loud in their condemnations of him and in the following year, the mighty 2/Royal Welch Fusiliers had a CO who had become so hands-off that the sergeant major was oversleeping for parade.

Even so, the extra-companionate paternalistic style of command set a tone across the whole British Expeditionary Force during the Great War. On many occasions over the war soldiers would gripe about individual regimental officers, but there were no substantial rank-and-file refusals in the line to follow orders. The 'family' nature of the junior officer and his platoon sons, at the very juncture of the Army between Us (Other Ranks) and Them (the Officers), was a major contribution to cohesion of the whole tottering, gargantuan khaki tower. A curious, and unintentional, confirmation of the sticky-bond that junior officers made in the army between those above and those below, came when a socialist 'Soldiers and Workers Council, Home Counties and Training Reserve Branch' held a meeting in Tunbridge Wells – of all places – on 24 June 1917. The Council's number six demand was: 'We ask for a more generous treatment of younger Officers who, out of a daily casualty list of over 4,000, suffer the heaviest proportionate burden'.[17] The French army had no history or current practice of paternalism – and by 1917 was mutinying and disintegrating in the pressure cauldron of total war.

Inevitably, paternal love in the trenches sometimes had to be tough love. In March 1917 Corporal Bennett asked Edwin Campion Vaughan if he could be relieved because he had lost his nerve:

He was shaking with fear and I felt very sorry for him, but knowing that he would have to stick it and that if I showed any clemency the rot would spread, I told him he had to return to his post at once, and set an example to his men.[18]

Nineteen-year-old temporary company commander Graham Greenwell confirmed the necessity of strictness when he refused to let a man out of the line with a hint of frostbite, because 'if you begin sending them off to hospital with that, lots of them will develop it'.

As should be the case in 'families', the devotion of the father, no matter how tender his years, was reciprocated. By nobody's measure could Corporal George Coppard of the Machine-Gun Corps have been called a bosses' nark or sympathizer, but as he observed:

If an officer used brutal words, we would loathe him and meditate vengeance. If he spoke kindly to us or did us some service, we would all call him a toff or a sport and overflow with sentimental devotion to him.[19]

Proofs abounded. Teenage subaltern Edwin Campion Vaughan conversed with Private Taylor, the black sheep of his platoon, with a view 'to winning his confidence and helping him keep out of trouble'; henceforth Taylor and his pal Dawson were two of Vaughan's smartest and most loyal men.[20] When Major The Hon. Hugh Dawnay was killed attacking an enemy-held farmhouse at Zillebeke in November 1914 his men wept in grief. When the likeable Lieutenant Charles Douie suggested to his talented sergeant-major Jim Miller that the latter should try for a commission:

though I could hardly contemplate the loss of his support in maintaining the reputation of the company. I was more than grateful to him when he said that he would not take a commission so long as I was in command of the company.[21]

In August 1915 Lieutenant Harry Crookshank was buried alive when a German mine exploded under the Grenadiers' position; all day he lay under four feet of earth, where he could breathe but not make himself heard. The company commander sent a party up later to dig him out. He heard the rescue party say they were only looking for 'a poor bloody officer' and seem to abandon the search. Then he heard them say that Crookshank 'was not a bad bloke. Let's have another go'. Eventually, they found him and dug him out; henceforth Crookshank was known as Lazarus amongst his fellow Grenadiers. So firmly did one major establish his popular and benevolent stamp on 377 Battery RFA that when his exhausted men learned he was returning from hospital a cry went up 'The Major's back – he's ah richt – he's coming back', and they gained new motivation in dragging out a stuck-fast artillery gun:

> It was miraculous, men were on their feet, horses mounted, shovels seized and a start made to hack down the hedge. The ditch was filled with clods of earth, brushwood . . . We were the first battery out of the field.[22]

The history of medals awarded in the Great War is large with examples of 'Other Ranks' being awarded for gallant efforts in trying to save the life of 'their' wounded officers.[23]

Of all the relationships between officers and men, that between the officer and his valet and his NCOs were the closest.

Officially, commissioned officers had servants and warrant officers had batmen (from the French 'bat', meaning saddle pack), but few bothered to observe the nomenclatural nicety. The possession of a servant was a Country House prop to the gentlemanly lustre of the officer, but more meaningfully a servant freed his martial master from the petty cares of everyday living, so that the latter could concentrate on command. A batman cleaned his officer's kit, cooked his food in the line (if possible) and out of the line, toted his officer's valise around and might even act as his bodyguard in battle. In return, the servant was relieved of ordinary duties, including the hated sentry duty at night, and was paid directly by his master at 15s a month. Many valets had been in service in Britain and the Upstairs-Downstairs nature of the deal was familiar.

Siegfried Sassoon admired his servant and noted in his diary:

I have been saved from innumerable small worries and exasperations in the last ten weeks by my servant, 355642 Private John Law. He is the perfect servant. Nothing could be better than the way he does things, quiet and untiring . . . He is simple, humble, brave, patient and loving; he is reticent, yet humorous. How many of us can claim to possess these things, and ask no reward but a smile.[24]

Law was immortalized as Bond in *Sherston's Progress*. Meanwhile, Montague Cleeve's batman, Hampshire, 'was a marvellously attentive person who sought my every comfort . . . He kept me marvellously tidy and we became great friends'.[25] James Agate found his servant to be half tyrannical father and half golf-caddy, but he too had his efficiencies, making young Agate eat and sleep properly. When Agate appeared improperly dressed, his servant complained Jeeves-like, 'You do me no credit, sorr, rushing off in all your swarth and sweat.' When John Glubb was invalided to England and unpacked his kit, he saw all the patchwork Driver Reilly had performed on his clothes 'and realized how much trouble old Reilly had taken'. Glubb had selected Reilly as his batman, to give him an easy job.[26] Lieutenant N. Algeo of the 2/Leinsters had the good fortune to inherit as his batman Private Keegan, who became widely admired for looking after his 'master in great style'. If Algeo was short of anything, noted a slightly envious fellow officer, 'Keegan used to go scrounging round the other officers' kits to make up the deficiency!'[27]

A good servant had the eye of a magpie for scrounging. When Sidney Rogerson arrived at Camp 34 on the Somme ('a camp in name only – a few forlorn groups of rude tarpaulin-sheet shelters huddled together') Rogerson unofficially encouraged his men to pilfer anything and everything they could to make life drier and warmer. Some minutes later the Colonel hoved into view, with Rogerson's young servant Briggs sheepishly following behind. The Colonel congratulated Rogerson on his servant, and when Rogerson asked why, the Colonel replied:

Well, as I walked into the very commodious trench shelter reserved for Battalion Headquarters, I saw your man walking out at the other

end with the stove. And you hadn't been in camp five minutes! A good boy, that. But I'm sorry I could not spare the stove![28]

Edwin Campion Vaughan's valet was the doughty Private Dunham. After a day of desperate fighting Vaughan and his company finally captured the Springfield pill-box on Langemarck Ridge. Slumped exhausted inside, Vaughan asked Dunham what in hell he was carrying in the mud-soaked sandbag to which he was umbilically attached. 'Your rabbit, Sir!' Dunham replied stoutly. 'You said you would eat it on Langemarck Ridge.'

When they peeled off the sacking from the cold rabbit portion that Vaughan had sworn to eat when the ridge was taken, they found the meat to be filthy. It was consigned to black water which swilled around their legs in the pill-box's black bottom, full of refuse and dead Germans.[29]

As a cavalry officer Burgon Bickersteth had a servant for his horse (a groom) as well as a servant for himself; on arriving in France Bickersteth was pleased to find that his appointed man-servant was Wallace. 'I am told', Bickersteth informed his parents, 'that in the fighting line he never leaves one and is most faithful.'[30] When Wallace was wounded, Bickersteth was troubled because he could not find out to which hospital he had been admitted and could not therefore write to him. For Charles Douie his servant Chapman, who had served with the Sherwood Foresters in the Boer War and had rejoined at the age of forty-six, was more than a servant: he was 'a most loyal friend'.[31]

Loyalty cut two ways. On hearing of the death of Lieutenant J.F. Marsland 2/Leinsters his servant, Horrigan, was inconsolable and wept for days.[32] Private Hobbs wrote on the death of Welsh Guards officer Christopher Tennant, 'I lost a good master in Mr Tennant and I shall not have another one like him'.[33] When Lieutenant Hugh Munro was killed in September 1915 his batman made a last poignant entry into Munro's diary: 'A kind and thoughtful master to B. Graham'. As Hugh Munro's father proudly observed about his son's detailed four month diary of service in the trenches around Festubert, there was 'not a single "grouse" in it'. Private Fahy, a reservist from Birmingham, used part of his leave to make Robert Graves a silver cigarette case, engraved with Graves's name.[34] Completely out of the blue, Richard Talbot Kelly's father received a letter in July 1917 from his son's batman, Gunner Needham, which said simply:

> I am your son's servant, and I am sure you must feel proud to be the father of so brave and sporting a young officer. We are all very proud of him and hope we always have the luck to have him with us.[35]

Most movingly, Private Blacklidge wrote to the father of Captain John Charlton, following the latter's death at La Boiselle on the fateful 1 July 1916:

> You mention your son's death. It gives me pain when I have to think about it, it really was the hardest blow I have had all my life, one that I shall never forget. Your son, my late master, was more like a father to me than a master and I may tell you I thought there was not another man in the world like him.[36]

When the body of Lieutenant Noel Hodgson was recovered at the end of the first day of the Somme, that of his servant Pearson was found by his side. Hodgson had written (as Edward Melbourne) often and affectionately about Pearson in the *Spectator* and other papers. The regard was clearly mutual. At Zouave, Nash, the batman of the mortally wounded Gilbert Talbot, was killed trying to reach his master.

Not all officer and servant relationships were so smooth or so deep. Wilfred Owen had to dismiss a servant, which caused him anguish later, as the servant was killed on night sentry duty. Perennial sources of friction between masters and servants were familiarity edging into insubordination, incompetence, and the inadequate preparation of food. In Mason, the servant in *Journey's End*, R.C. Sheriff melded several lacklustre servant cooks of his frontline acquaintance; Mason forgets the pepper (commonly regarded as disinfectant, as well as a tongue-pleaser), opens a can of hated apricots, tries to pass off bully beef as 'cutlets' and never washes saucepans sufficiently, so that the tea tastes of onions. He is the very model for Baldrick in *Blackadder Goes Forth*.

Journey's End is a reminder that traditional gentlemen found the right touch of authority and friendliness easier; experience of dealing with servants, crammings of *noblesse oblige* and good manners – the precise point of which being to smooth relations between people – all helped. Temporary Gentlemen, not used to being served, tended to be tin gods or fawning chums before finding the middle man that was the master. It is the promoted-from-the-ranks Trotter in *Journey's End* who cannot quite get Mason to perform adequately and who engenders the thin edge of a disrespectful tone in the servant's voice.

Generally, junior officers had good relations with their NCOs. In most other armies platoons were led by NCOs and not officers; in the British Army a subaltern was put in charge of a platoon to lead but also to learn. The in-built understanding that the callow subaltern was learning on the job, tended to bring out the best in the platoon's NCOs who wanted to help 'their' officer, and by extension the whole platoon. The sergeant with his moustache flecked with grey giving the bright-eyed subaltern a quiet word of advice out of the corner of his mouth was almost a cliché. Shy Royal Sussex subaltern Edmund Blunden had a sergeant-major free of 'any feeling against a schoolboy officer' and a sergeant who, in defiance of military principles, invited him into his tent to 'join a party of old stagers whose bread and cheese was the emblem of an unforgettable kindness'.[37] For Brian Horrocks his sergeant Whinney was a 'mentor', which was exactly what a good NCO should be. Hugh Butterworth's sergeant was 'a tip top A1 regular' and jointly and harmoniously they scavenged and avoided bureaucracy, each giving the other tips; 'In fact we're a thoroughly immoral pair, but I believe we're knocking out a pretty useful platoon.'[38] 'Pair' was the operative word; more than ever, subalterns worked with their NCOs, rather than delivering orders from on high. Fortuitously, this daringly modern approach to leadership meant that some of the 'dash and devotion' of the public schoolboy rubbed off on the NCO; so when Britain ran near dry on public school subalterns and 'rankers' were elevated to the officer corps, some of the necessary values and styles had already stuck.

For his part poor Second Lieutenant Milton Riley of 8/East Lancashire Regiment had a 'sadistic specimen' of a Company Sergeant Major:

I stood on the fire-step appalled and probably wide eyed, with the inferno of an attack so near. Nearby was the sardonic CSM. In the presence of men of my platoon he said, with a nasty grin, 'When we go over on the 31st, I'm going next to you Sir'. Somewhat coldly I replied, 'Why sergeant-major?' Then came the punch line – 'Because Sir', he said, 'I like your wrist watch!'[39]

Riley was supported in his clash with the CSM by his immediate superior, Captain Cunliffe, who took a fatherly approach to his sub-alterns. Officers looking after officers, paternalism upon paternalism.

Inevitably, the Great War's infantry subalterns tended towards the enlightened, easy-going disciplinary style of the Territorials, rather than the austere type of the Regulars. Out of humanity and the necessity of keeping the platoon's loyalty, junior officers followed the disciplinary precept of Lieutenant Denis Barnett regarding his Irish Leinsters:

> They will only obey their own officers … they obey me all right so far – but they make magnificent fighters. The only way is to jump heavily on serious offenders, and condone little things.[40]

What worked for the feisty Irish Leinsters, worked for many infantry units. Everybody understood that serious offences, desertion especially, required harsh punishment, but the unease of officers – and not just juniors or New Army officers – at the fact that 'little' infractions of the King's Regulations for the Army could result in severe punishments led many to blind-eye indiscretions such as a dirty rifle in the line or drunkenness out of it. Although flogging had been abolished on active service in 1881 (in military prisons as late as 1907), Field Punishment No. 1 – popularly known as 'crucifixion' – allowed prisoners to be chained to a fixed object, subjected to hard labour and their pay to be forfeited; Field Punishment No. 1 was meted out on 60,210 occasions during the Great War. In the same period the death sentence was awarded 3,080 times (although commuted on all but 346 occasions). Amongst the officer corps there was distinct vein of feeling that Field Punishment No. 1 and the death penalty were inappropriate in a citizen army, save for rank mutiny and desertion in battle. If strict military punishments could be avoided, they frequently were, especially for a first offence; when Edwin Campion Vaughan found Private Dredge asleep on duty, he put him under arrest – until another officer pointed out that if Dredge was officially 'crimed' he would be taken before a Field General Court Martial and probably receive the death penalty. So they typically decided to frighten Dredge with a talking-to instead.[41] One middle-class ranker, Private Burrage, praised officers who did not 'make a song' about exhausted sentries sleeping in the trench, but woke them up with a cough or friendly kick so all could pretend the sentry 'was awake, Sir'.

Officers themselves were subject to discipline from a chain of command that stretched all the way up to Field Marshal Sir William Robertson, Chief of the Imperial General Staff. A brave junior officer might challenge the heavenly order on behalf of his men. Such 'presumption' was easiest for officers whose mind was not set on an Army career. Edwin Campion Vaughan harangued a staff officer for keeping his men out in the cold snow, Robert Graves had the temerity to criticize plans at a brigade level conference (when another officer backed him the attack was called off) and amid the maelstrom of the Somme Lieutenant Stuart Cloete faced down a brigadier:

He came up the line after an attack. We had fought hard and I had mounted my sentries, checked my wire and posted my Lewis guns, and he wanted me to turn out my men to inspect their rifles. I refused. He said I was under arrest. At that time I was so tired that I did not care. We had been in action for two days, had taken all our objectives and were waiting to be relieved when he turned up. The men were lying exhausted in all sorts of positions on the fire-step and floor of the trench. Only the sentries were alert.

I said: 'The men are done, sir. There are none in dugouts. They can stand-to in a minute. I've inspected their rifles. Everything is in order, sir.'

'Do you refuse?' he said.

'No, sir. Not if you will give me the order in writing.' Every officer is entitled to ask for an order in writing if he does not like the sound of it. To wake the men after what they had already been through would impair their efficiency. We had had a lot of casualties and were pretty thin on the ground.

'Consider yourself under arrest,' he said.

I said: 'Yes, sir.'

'By God, I'll have you court-martialled,' he said. 'The men are filthy, unshaven – filthy.'

I said: 'We've lost a lot of men. We've been fighting two days, and if the men are dirty their rifles are loaded and clean. They are ready for action, sir.'

The men in the trenches generally kept an old sock over their rifle-bolts to keep them clean. He had even taken exception to this.

He said nothing more but went off. One thing about him was his guts. He was the only general I ever saw in the line.[42]

The brigadier, when he had got over his occupational choler, was obliging enough to say of Cloete: 'We could do with a few more like that young chap.'

Rankers in the Army machine frequently felt themselves to be automata, or cogs, to be moved by the dictat of an unseen and careless hand on high. Robert Graves wrote that he and Sassoon believed that 'being commanded by someone whom they [rankers] could count as a friend – someone who protected them ... from the grosser indignities of the military system ... made all the difference in the world'.[43] It did. And there were thousands of thoughtful, brave, and compassionate junior officers like Graves and Sassoon, Cloete and Vaughan.

Staff officers, with their red collar tabs, raised mixed emotions among the frontline officers. Griping about the 'top brass' is, of course, as occupational a habit amongst junior officers as choler is amongst colonels. Shakespeare's Harry Hotspur complained:

> But I remember, when the fight was done,
> When I was dry with rage and extreme toil,
> Breathless and faint, leaning upon my sword,
> Came there a certain lord, neat and trimly dressed,
> Fresh as a bridegroom, and his chin new reaped
> Showed like a stubble land at harvest home.
> He was perfumèd like a milliner,

And twixt his finger and his thumb he held
A pouncet box, which ever and anon
He gave his nose, and took't away again; . . . . . .
And as the soldiers bore dead bodies by,
He called them untaught knaves, unmannerly,
To bring a slovenly unhandsome corpse
Betwixt the wind and his nobility.
With many holiday and lady terms
He questioned me, amongst the rest demanded
My prisoners in your majesty's behalf.
I then, all smarting with my wounds being cold,
To be so pestered with a popingay,
Out of my grief and my impatience
Answered neglectingly, I know not what —
He should, or he should not; for he made me mad
To see him shine so brisk, and smell so sweet,
And talk so like a waiting gentlewoman
Of guns and drums and wounds – God save the mark!

Lieutenant Siegfried Sassoon vented his spleen against the staff in poetry; 'The General' who did for Harry and Jack with 'his plan of attack' is believed to be modelled on Sassoon's Corps commander, Lieutenant-General Sir Ivor Maxse. Also moved to pour satirical ink on the staff was Sub Lieutenant A.P. Herbert, an officer in the Royal Navy's infantry, the Royal Naval Division:

So they are satisfied with our Brigade,
And it remains to parcel out the bays!
And we shall have the usual Thanks Parade,
The beaming General, and the soapy praise.

You will come up in your capacious car
To find your heroes sulking in the rain,
To tell us how magnificent we are,
And how you hope we'll do the same again.

And we, who knew your old abusive tongue,
Who heard you hector us a week before,
We who have bled to boost you up a rung-

A KCB perhaps, perhaps a Corps-;

We who must mourn those spaces in the Mess,
And somehow fill the hollows in the heart,
We do not want your Sermon on Success,
Your greasy benisons on Being Smart.

We only want to take our wounds away
To some shy village where the tumult ends,
And drowsing in the sunshine many a day,
Forget our aches, forget that we had friends.

Weary we are of blood and noise and pain;
This was a week we shall not soon forget;
And if, indeed, we have to fight again,
We little wish to think about it yet.

We have done well; we like to hear it said.
Say it, and then, for God's sake, say no more.
Fight, if you must, fresh battles far ahead,
But keep them dark behind your chateau door![44]

For every Ivor Maxse there was an opposite, revered general.
Charles Carrington's division was commanded by Major-General Sir
Robert Fanshawe. As far as Carrington was concerned, 'Fanny' was
like 'Chaucer's knight'; he spent more time in the front line than most
soldiers, 'and never let us down, never took unnecessary risks'. And
Plumer, commander of the Second Army, was admired by all. Graham
Greenwell gave the sensible, company-eye view of the brass hats; after
grumbling against their promotions, undeserved baubles, he added
that their existence usually did not matter because 'one can and does
run one's own show when in the trenches without much interference
save over the telephone wires, and they, thank God, are often cut'.[45]
Indeed, as the War progressed the increasing sophistication of infantry
tactics tended to devolve more power down to company and platoon
level, and thus more autonomy.

What were relations like between officers in the same company? In
an infantry company, commanded by a captain, there would generally

be four subalterns or lieutenants leading a platoon of fifty men each, with perhaps a Machine-Gun officer or a supernumerary. In his candid account of his war service with the 1/8 Royal Warwickshires, Edmund Campion Vaughan relates an incident in which his superior officer, Syd Pepper, condemns him for his 'arrogant unsociableness'. Pepper tells Vaughan:

> the only fun we can get here is what we make between us. There is no room for personal dislikes; if our social relations are bad, we will never work together and the Battalion will lose the leading position that it has always held in the division.[46]

Life in the tight-knit family of company officers tended to be cordial, and a wise company commander might bring pressure to bear to ensure that it remained so. After the tête-à-tête Vaughan swore to be 'a model subaltern'. The collective youth of the officers in a company was a great binding agent; when Robert Graves arrived at the 1/Royal Welch Fusiliers billets at Locon in November 1915, 'No officer in the company A was more than twenty-two or twenty-three years old.'[47] By 1917 casualty rates meant that most company commanders were not more than twenty. Understandably, older officers did not always sit easily in such youthful company, particularly when they were married; Second Lieutenant Edward Thomas, Royal Artillery, twelve years older than the others in his battery, wrote in one of his daily letters to his wife, 'how long it will be before I can be quite frank and natural with anyone'.[48] (A perennial problem for married officers was incessant questioning about how, *exactly*, one went about 'it'.) The young John Glubb pointed in his diary to some of the frictions caused by the great age of his sapper commander, Major McQueen:

> To us, his only failing is that he must be approaching forty years of age, whereas we are all in our teens or early twenties ... [49] There can be no doubt that McQueen is an extremely able officer, and one totally dedicated to his duty, to the exclusion of any idea of relaxation or amusement.[50]

Specifically, Glubb criticized McQueen for banning the men from drinking *vin ordinaire* (a dictat worthy of a 'Cromwellian proclamation to Ireland') and for not approving of 'such frivolities' as dinner parties. Neither did it seem to Glubb to be 'the game' for senior officers to ride horses while the men marched. A company commander at barely twenty Graham Greenwell was sent a 40-year-old subaltern school-master, who was a victim of chronic neuritis, had a sad lack of a sense of humour, possessed the 'opinion that he and most of us will all be dead in a fortnight'[51] and a kit collection that was a 'monument of stupidity'; it contained, *inter alia*, a Gladstone bag, a folding bath, and Dayfield body-shield. Greenwell found it difficult to place him: 'I can't put him with a boy half his age, though I am myself young enough to be his son.' Eventually, Greenwell concluded that 'the poor old man' should never have been sent out, was likely to adversely affect morale, so had him slyly sent home on medical grounds

Other occasional frictions in the fraternity of officers were caused by whether officers were New Army, Regulars or Territorials; old loyalties died hard. Regulars liked to be with Regulars and failing that option, preferred to be with Territorials. New Army officers with badly cut uniforms and suspiciously intellectual ideas joining Regular battalions could be asked to smarten up the first and drop the last. Regular officers who transferred to 'Kitchener's mob' in search of promotion – a Regular captain could expect to be a battalion com-mander in the New Army – tended to tread on toes until they accepted that the human material they now commanded did better with less military etiquette. Promotions and seniorities could be vexed issues; after temporarily commanding his company Lieutenant Guy Chapman determined he was 'not going to surrender the company without a battle' when a new captain was sent out; the 'tangle' was only resolved by the Adjutant, who pointed out that Chapman must lose the company, but as an emollient suggested that Chapman was attached to staff as a learner, a promotion of sorts. Class always lurked, but became less of an issue as the war wound its long way; at least one infantry officer, Hubert Essame of 2/Northants, thought that by 1918 junior officers formed a club 'based on mutual loyalty and trust from which distinctions of class had long since vanished'.[52] There was, indeed, 'no room for personal dislikes' in a dug-out or a battle; overall, officers worked as well alongside each other as they did with the men. If an officer was of cheerful disposition and joined in he could be forgiven almost anything; the sunny, all-hands-to-the-pump officer kept many another officer going. Guy Chapman enjoyed the company of fellow subaltern Walter Spencer, down from Oxford, and the possessor of a sardonic sense of humour 'which would encourage me during those miserable winter hours when soaking to the chest we waded up and down the line'.[53] Despite sending home one 'poor old man' Graham Greenwell was inspired by the 'quite extraordinary' Carew Hunt, a university lecturer who 'managed to throw himself entirely into this new and really horrible job'.[54] Few would deny the observation of Lieutenant Christian Carver, RFA:

> The power of being cheerful is worth much fine gold, and it helps on others no end. Without it no man can attain to leadership, whether in thought or deed.[55]

As with so much of the officer's commanding style, the sunny disposition, if not natural, had to be assumed. On the winter-blasted night of 10 November 1916, Sidney Rogerson was informed that his battalion was to relieve the 2/Devonshires in the front line; he received the news 'with a great show of enforced cheerfulness' as befitted a company commander.[56]

Only incompetents and obvious cowards received totally short shrift, and then only if they failed to accept advice and pull their weight. When an officer in Guy Chapman's 13/Royal Fusiliers played with a live bomb, then handed over a precious Lewis gun to another battalion, he was taken before the divisional commander, his commission removed and he was drafted into the ranks at base. Joining him was another officer from the battalion who, having been sussed as 'windy' by the Medical Officer, had obtained a chit enabling him to leave the line from the naïve MO of the neighbouring Rifle Brigade. Guy Chapman concluded of their punishment: 'It may have been cruel; but it was a necessity. The lives of others depended on it.'[57] Frequently, 'dud' officers in infantry battalions escaped disciplinary procedures and were quickly dumped elsewhere (trench mortar batteries being a favourite ground) or in the medical system, as Greenwell's unwanted schoolmaster subaltern had been. The Army always feared that both windiness and incompetence were contagions that spread from the top down, and the diseased body had to be removed. Anyhow and any way.

Young officers, fresh out of school, were thrilled to be leaders, and liked the responsibility of commanding a platoon. Time and the burdens of care were wilting phenomena, however, at company level, where the officer led 200–250 men, day in day out, in the trenches, out of the line. 'The only thing I don't like', wrote Lionel Crouch to his parents, 'is the responsibility of commanding a company. What I should love would be a roving commission to saunter around where I like.'[58] Julian Grenfell similarly disliked captaincy: 'I hate being a Captain: I would like to be either God or a General or a Lieutenant. I had such fun as Lieutenant.'[59] Nevertheless they stuck it, out of duty, and out of love for their men. The unsinkable Graham Greenwell, meanwhile, wrote to his mother on his elevation to company commander: 'Thank God the responsibility doesn't worry me, and seems to give me a new interest in life; but it may be rather a trying ordeal at first.'[60]

Thank God, indeed. The paternalistic Army officer drew a surprising amount of his mental support from the ultimate father.

There were few atheists in the trenches. In the face of death's metallic shards, officers called on God. The men of the Great War, it is often forgotten, were more religious than the British of today; in 1911 church attendance was 98 per thousand, in 2007 it was 54 per thousand.[61] And the Edwardian statistic fails to disclose the near perfect affinity between religion and the upper and middle classes – the classes from whom the officer corps were mainly drawn. It was the well-to-do who went to Church on Sunday, who said grace before meals, and who sat in boyish ranks on pews in the shivering chapels and halls of the public and grammar schools. For these people Christianity was part of the weft and warp of their being.

Overwhelmingly, officers were from the established churches. The

Churches of England and Scotland were not *quite* the top quarter at prayer, but in Edwardian and Georgian Britain a man's religion tended to be dictated by his class; the dissenting Protestant creeds, Methodism and Baptism and the like, were religions of the working classes. Roman Catholics were concentrated in the Irish regiments. There was also a blood link between the khaki and the clergy; about 10 per cent of Regular officers had fathers who were Anglican or Presbyterian priests, soldiering being among the few occupations that a gentleman vicar's son might take up and maintain his status.

In the trenches officers, like NCOs and rankers, were private in their religion, because it was the British way. Ostentatious displays of belief were faintly foreign, something the continentals, with their wars of religion, might do. Also, most officers belonged to the absolute mainstream of the Church of England, which was hardly demanding in its observance of rituals.[62] So, prayers were said silently, in the moments before zero hour or in the trembling of a shell-bombarded trench, and theological opinion was mostly confined to the confessional of the epistle home. Even comrades-in-arms, given the privacy of belief, did not correctly gauge the religious tendency of their fellows; Captain Robert Graves estimated that hardly one in a hundred First World War soldiers was 'inspired to religious feeling of even the crudest kind', whereas the inverse is more likely true. Sir John Baynes, in his meticulous study of the Scottish Rifles at Neuve Chapelle thought that the 'complete dissenter' from established religion was a rare specimen, and a Regular Army officer who paraded atheism would have been thought unreliable by his superiors and a bore by his peers.[63] The 'Morale Reports' from the Third Army of the BEF in 1916–17, based on readings of soldiers' letters, found that 25 per cent contained 'a definite expression' of religion.

Religious belief was personally sustaining. 'I find, in this sort of job', wrote the aptly named Lieutenant Christian Carver, RFA, from a battlefield in Flanders, 'that I have to pray good and hard, otherwise one would not keep going.'[64] It surely brought comfort to Richard Talbot Kelly, 52nd Brigade RFA, that his father wrote to him in July 1916:

Schoolboys at Eton College playing the Wall Game. The public schools of Britain produced a generation of officers for the Great War whose ideas of loyalty and courage had been honed in part on the playing fields of their *alma mater*.

An officer leads a contingent of the Officers' Training Corps on a march at Mytchett Camp, Surrey, 1910. Formed by R.B. Haldane in 1907, the Officers' Training Corps was established in most leading public schools, some grammar schools and the ancient universities to provide basic military training for the nation's 'natural' leaders.

From left, Uppingham schoolboys Edward Brittain, Roland Leighton and Victor Richardson at OTC camp. Dubbed the 'Three Musketeers' by Leighton's mother, the entire trio perished in the War. Uppingham suffered the loss of more than 20% of its old boys who served, 1914–18.

RIGHT: Anthony Eden (centre) at Aldershot, 1915, aged 18. A volunteer with a yeomanry battalion of the King's Royal Rifle Corps, the Old Etonian and future prime minister became a convinced 'One Nation' Conservative as a result of his service in the trenches.

LEFT: On the face of things, Territorial Captain Lionel Crouch was a typical 'hearty', being ex-Marlborough, a solicitor and a keen shot. But like other 'hearties' he had a deceptively sensitive hinterland, and planted his trench with flower bulbs and seeds to beautify it.

Students from Cambridge University's Officers' Training Corps have their rifles inspected at Mytchett Camp, Summer 1914. University members of the OTC could achieve a Certificate A, which enabled them to command a platoon in the Territorial Army. Many OTC cadets went straight from university precincts to the front line in France.

Led by a sergeant instructor, officer cadets – distinguished by their white hat bands – take a riding lesson at Aldershot. Cadets from a non-equine background tended to view riding classes with abject horror; Captain Robert Graves of the Royal Welch Fusiliers even preferred front-line service to riding school.

Officers finishing their leave say goodbye to their wives and family at Charing Cross. Leave was often sweet sorrow, as officers and men alike found it difficult to readjust to home life. There was also the anguish of parting anew from loved ones. Frank Crozier found saying 'goodbye' to his wife and child so painful he vowed 'never to come on leave again.'

British officers travelling by rail in France. Officers travelled in passenger carriages separately to their men, who were stowed in trucks marked 'Chevaux 8: Hommes 40.' Even so, there was little difference in comfort, since passenger carriages usually had no heating and broken windows were fitted as standard. The journey to the Front could take days, because French trains went at walking pace.

OPPOSITE: Officers tossing a colleague in a blanket on board ship, 1915. High jinx and high spirits were endemic among young officers. A favourite prank, best played on friends whose nerves were frayed by combat, was to roll defused German shells or grenades into their dug-out.

Second Lieutenant F. Forrester Agar and his bride Majorie Laird Collins, June 1917. Many young officers held a romantic, chivalric view of love and women and remained virgins until marriage.

A pillow fight at the Guards Division Sports Day at Bavincourt, June 1918. Sports and recreational events played an essential role in maintaining the Army's morale. The events were the work of the junior ranks of commissioned officers, not 'the top brass.'

British troops receive hot stew in the trenches near Cambrai. In the lines, officers generally ate the same food as the men, which was brought up by a Ration Party. A 'batman', however, might be prevailed upon to cook meals for 'his' officer and dinner-parties in dug-outs were a popular way for officers to while away an evening, even under shell fire.

Members of a wiring party set out to lay new wire. Unlike most other combatant armies, the British Army placed an officer and not an NCO in charge of wiring parties, patrols and raids. The leading role given to the British officer in 'routine' trench warfare was one reason for disproportionately high casualty rates amongst those with pips on the shoulder.

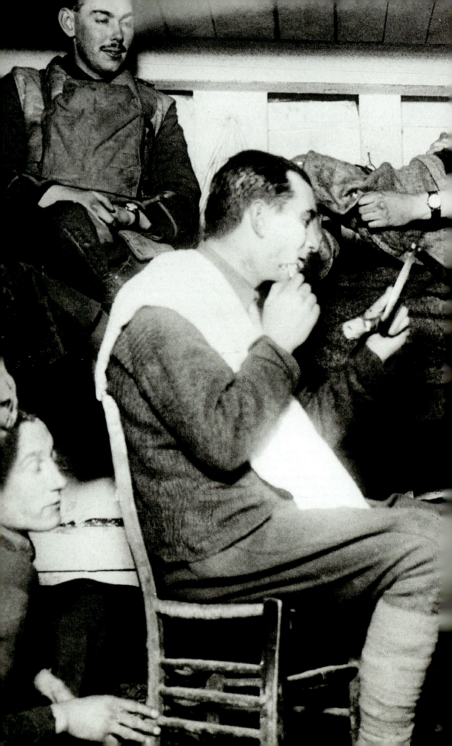

Officers of the 12/East Yorkshire Regiment wash and shave in a dug-out near Roclincourt.

An officer of the Royal Field Artillery feeds his pet duck outside a dug-out in Salonika. Pets in the trenches were common, though cats and dogs were the usual companion animals.

British infantry officers observe and mark the enemy's movements on a map at Pilckem Ridge, Belgium, 1917. By this stage of the war, officers were invariably issued with official glasses, revolvers, and rifles; at the beginning of the conflict, officers begged, borrowed or bought much of their own kit.

The mud. The mud. Officers wade through mud in a trench near St. Quentin, 1917. For officers, mud could turn a quick check on sentries into a gruelling two-hour wade.

A doctor dresses the wounds of Lieutenant Guy Morgan, Irish Guards, at a Regimental Aid Post at Pilckem Ridge, 1917. Contrary to myth, officers received no special treatment from the medical services on the battlefield.

The Officers' Quarters at Rastatt Prisoners of War camp, near Karlsruhe, Germany.
As many as 70 officers were crowded into each wooden hut. Forbidden from working,
officer POWs found boredom one of the main problems of life behind the wire.

Officer POWs captured during the Dardanelles campaign. At war's end all officer POWs were required to make a statement to the War Office explaining the circumstances of their capture. To the relief of the WO, nearly all the officers had been taken prisoner due to injury, ill luck or confusion on the battlefield, not to a lack of moral fibre. The highest standards of bravery and leadership had been maintained.

Officers of the 1st Royal West Kent Regiment pose for their picture a day before their attack on Hill 60, 1915. Four of the group were killed and five were wounded.

The tendency of youthful subalterns to 'dandify' their uniforms by such means as shortening the length of the trousers to expose lengths of coloured or spotted socks was satirized in the trench newspaper, *The Wipers Times*. The cartoon's punning title, 'Am I Offensive Enough?' referred to the title of an Army pamphlet from an attack-minded general.

QUESTIONS A
PLATOON COMMANDER
SHOULD ASK HIMSELF.

ENGRAVED BY SAPPER COUZENS R.E.

1: Am I as offensive as I might be.

A wounded British soldier making his first attempt to walk with artificial legs. The photograph was taken at Queen Mary's Convalescent Auxiliary Hospital at Roehampton House. The hospital specialized in fitting artificial limbs under skilled advice and taught men how to use them. At War's end, around 33,000 British Army officers were left disabled.

I can assure you that every day and many times a day we are all praying for you. I don't talk 'goody', dear boy, as a rule, do I? But this is the fact: everyone who knows and loves you thanks God that you have been able to do good work and preserve your nerve, and I feel sure you will come through safely and with honour.[65]

Prayers were sometimes cries for protection; more often they were a plea for courage. Donald Hankey, who saw life both from the ranks and the officer corps, thought: 'When he the Englishman first got to the front he prayed ... and he prayed that he might not be found wanting.'[66] There were also prayers for others. Captain John Llewellyn Thomas Jones, 3/London Regiment, a printer before enlistment, wrote in his last letter before his death: 'All I can say to you is that I thank God for giving me the best father in the world and two very dear sisters ... God bless you all and protect you is my fervent prayer.'[67]

Of course, if death was one's lot, Christianity offered the hope of existence after death. The belief in an afterlife was a widespread comfort in present dangers. Christianity could even make sense of the slaughter; after hearing of the death of Captain A.D. Hamer, 8/Manchester Regiment, one of his junior officers rationalized:

God has taken him unto Himself because he wanted him, because his blameless and exemplary life would satisfy God in a greater degree than most of us ...

John Glubb was among the soldiers who experienced a religious vision in the course of his service; his was on the road to Martinpuich in the bitter winter of 1917:

Suddenly I felt my whole self over whelmed by waves of deep and intense joy, which is impossible to describe. Never before had I experienced such a feeling of deep interior joy, so that I could hardly contain myself. I sat for what must have been several minutes, filled with the passionate joy of heaven itself – then the feeling slowly faded away.

I remembered how St. Francis of Assisi once said that perfect joy lay in being cold, hungry, exhausted and repulsed from the doors of every house at which one knocked. It was the depth of cold, misery,

weariness and exhaustion of that day in Martinpuich which had produced in me those waves of spiritual joy. I had given everything to do my duty and had held nothing back'.[68]

Whether a man believed in Heaven, whether a man believed that God would encase him in bullet-repelling armour in this life, whether a man believed that he was about God's work on Earth, there is little doubt that religion put steel in a man's spine. The first VC of the war was won by Francis Grenfell, Royal Artillery, whose daily reading during the retreat from Mons was psalm 121, 'I will lift up mine eyes to the hills';[69] Second Lieutenant Rupert Fellowes, 4/The Middlesex Regiment, a devout Christian, honorary secretary of the Church of England's Men's Society, won the VC at Hooge for five days of exemplary actions under fire, including personally bringing up ammunition and leading the rescue of two men wounded in No-Man's Land, which culminated in him walking along the trench top to encourage his men to hold fast under shelling;[70] William Bernard Vann, 1/6 Sherwood Foresters, a pre-war chaplain and assistant master at Wellingborough School, was awarded a posthumous VC for exploits which included the single-handed capture of a German field gun during the crossing of the Canal du Nord in September 1918; Britain's only double VC winner in the Great War was Captain Noel Chevasse, the regimental medical officer of 1/10 King's Liverpool Regiment. Chevasse was a staunch churchman, the son of the Bishop of Liverpool and the twin brother of an army chaplain.

Captain Chevasse was one of the small, but discernible, band of officers who wore their religion obviously, and who came out of the same mould as Gordon of Khartoum, Field Marshal Lord Roberts, Field Marshal Haig, and Generals Plumer, Byng, Rawlinson and Gough. For his religiosity, Lieutenant Burgon Bickersteth, 1/Royal Dragoons, was nicknamed 'The Bishop'. (He was the son of the Vicar of Leeds, and three of his brothers were in Holy Orders.) When Major Harry Bentinck, Coldstream Guards, was asked his opinion on moral standards, he replied: 'My standard is fixed by the regulations of my commanding officer, and my commanding officer is Jesus Christ.'[71]

These Christian soldiers marching as to war had a definite style of 'religiously infused' leadership.[72] All officers were nominally charged with the spiritual well-being of their men, but it tended to be the out-Christian who complied. Anglican padre Julian Bickersteth – Burgon's brother – believed that Christian officers had a bearing 'which placed them head and shoulders above their fellow officers' and however young they were they had to 'act as their [the men's] father and guide in everything'. One such Christian officer was Colonel Rowland Feilding, transferred from the Guards to 6/Connaught Rangers, who organized the distribution of crucifixes which had been blessed by the Pope to his men. Another Catholic, Edmund Campion Vaughan, arranged for the padre to say mass in the cellars where he was billeted, clearing out the non-Catholics first so the Catholics could go to confession behind a blanket.[73] In a report on Catholicism in the Army, a Catholic padre wrote:

> My experience of Catholic officers was very consoling . . . Officers led their men in religious practices as they did when they went 'over the top' . . . They came for Confession with parties of their men, whom they had zealously shepherded to the sacraments, and were the first to go down by the roadside on their knees for Confession . . . [74]

Officers of other denominations also did their spiritual bit for the men. John Reith, a staunch Presbyterian and regimental transport officer for the 1/5 Scottish Rifles, entreated twenty-two of his men to seek admission into the United Free Church. 'I was glad that these young fellows – walking in hourly jeopardy as they were – had been brought into this new relationship with God', he wrote.[75] On his way to Gallipoli Second Lieutenant Robert McConnell organized Bible readings for the men of his platoon, and:

> On Sunday I sat down to Communion with four other officers. It was a quiet little service. We went through the good old service and sang the old Communions Psalms. It did me good.

Before leading his men of 1/Royal Warwickshire Regiment over the top on the Somme in October 1916, the action in which he died,

Donald Hankey reportedly cried out, 'If wounded Blighty – if killed, the Resurrection'.

Hankey, an ex-Rugbeian missionary in the slums of Bermondsey in London before enlistment, had meditated on religion and life in the New Army in a series of articles published in the *Spectator* and *Westminster Gazette* and later collected as *A Student in Arms*. In his most celebrated essay, 'The Beloved Captain', Hankey penned a semi-fictionalized portrait of his company commander, Ronald Hardy, which stands as the paper ideal of the Christian officer. Hankey, who at the time was serving in the ranks, explicitly drew a connection between the officer's least favourite chore – examining the men's feet – and the New Testament. He wrote: ' ... there was in our eyes something almost religious about this care for our feet. It seemed to have a touch of the Christ about it, and we loved and honoured him [the captain] all the more.' Lieutenant-Colonel W. Shirley, commanding officer of that subaltern manufactury that was the 2/The Artists' Rifles, would have approved. He always maintained that an officer should have a Christ-like love for his khaki charges.

Christian officers of the Hardy sort could engender something more than the standard devotion of Other Ranks for a good officer; Hankey thought that Hardy's men would have earned the VC ten times over to save their beloved captain.[76]

There were officers for whom the soldier's soul was their profession. All chaplains of the established churches in the Army were officers holding the King's Commission; the most junior chaplain was a chaplain to the forces 4th class, the equivalent of the rank of captain. At the beginning of the war, the British Army had 117 chaplains; by the end of the war there were 3,475 Army chaplains of whom 1,985 were Church of England, 649 Roman Catholic, 303 Presbyterian, 256 Wesleyan, 251 Baptist, Methodist and Congregationalist, 16 Jewish, 10 Welsh Calvinist, and 5 Salvation Army.[77]

Along with generals in chateaux, military chaplains have not emerged well from the memory of the Great War. Since chaplains lived and messed with officers, they were viewed by the rank and file as 'Them' and not 'Us', while the inappropriately bloodthirsty preaching of the men like Dr William Williamson, Church of

Scotland, did nothing to endear; in April 1915 Williamson told a group of soldiers, 'Remember there is only one way to peace . . . it is through the bloodstained path of war.'

Soldiers made an exception for Roman Catholic priests, who were often working class. Guy Chapman:

> These Catholic priests impressed one. [Padre] Leeson never dropped a word of religion in my hearing; but one felt a serenity and certitude streaming from him such as was not possessed by our bluff Anglicans. Already there was a growing dislike of these latter. They had nothing to offer but the consolation the next man could give you, and a less fortifying one. The Church of Rome sent a man into action mentally and spiritually cleaned. The Church of England could only offer you a cigarette'.[78]

Chapman admired Roman Catholic priests because they went into the line under the obligation of administering extreme unction to dying men. Initially, Anglican chaplains were under an official instruction *not* to go into the line – hence Chapman's complaint – but in 1916 the Anglican padre's role was reformed, and he became assigned to forward field ambulances and main dressing stations. The chaplain as an unofficial RAMC helper henceforth became a familiar sight. In order to understand the lot of the men Padre Julian Bickersteth went further into battle than the field ambulance:

> I went out with a wiring party into no-man's land last Friday, got back at 4.00 a.m. – a most interesting experience. I was glad of it because I do so dislike the men to have to listen to someone who has not been with them under all conditions.[79]

He lived in the trenches in a 'humpy' (a tarpaulin bivouac), and eventually even went into action. So committed to sharing the lot of the troops was Chaplain Stafford Crawley (afterwards Canon of Windsor) that he used to go over the top with them, and was only stopped when the Divisional commander assigned a military police-man to keep him under control.

Out of the line Bickersteth took confirmation classes, set up a recreation room in an estaminet (patronized by 200 men a day), wrote to the parents of dead soldiers (he knew loss; his brother Lieutenant Stanley Bickersteth, 15/West Yorkshire Regiment, was killed in the slaughter of 1 July 1916) and comforted prisoners before execution. About one such execution by firing squad he wrote:

> As they bound him, I held his arm tight to reassure him – words are useless at such a moment – and then he turned his blindfolded face up to mine and said in a voice which wrung my heart, 'Kiss me, Sir, kiss me,' and with my kiss on his lips and, 'God has you in his keeping,' whispered in his ear, he passed on into the Great unseen God accept him; Christ receive him.' [80]

Still Julian Bickersteth's good work was not done. He led the Church parades that were compulsory for the men when out of the line, and he also set up churches in barns, caves and in the open air for voluntary Communion services. Such services left an indelible memory. At Henencourt Charles Douie recalled:

> A service was held in the barn on Sunday evening. The night was quiet, apart from the incessant muttering of the distant guns. A few candles gave a flickering light. Around the barn men's equipment and rifles hung on the shadowed walls. The Communion table was a rough wood packing-case. Yet the service was impressive, had indeed a splendour often absent in formal surroundings. Here the old prayers and hymns of far-off homes rose from men whose lives were forfeit of their own free will, while the guns throbbed a monotonous undertone. [81]

Cavalry officer Burgon Bickersteth might have had his own brother Julian in mind when he wrote:

> The padre is appreciated by the men in so far as he busies himself with their recreational and physical comfort, and respected if he visits the front line and shares their dangers. When he does both, he is loved. [82]

Julian Bickersteth was eventually promoted Senior Chaplain 56th Division and awarded the Military Cross – one of the 195 valour decorations made to Anglican chaplains alone, all of them tangible evidence of the forward role of the dog-collar officer.

Like King Gustavus Adolphus in the Thirty Years War, the British military authorities believed that 'The best Christian is always the best soldier, the more of Prayer in my army, the more of Victory.' So effective were some chaplains at raising morale that they were attached to formations judged to be lacking back-bone; thus was Padre G.A. Studdert Kennedy (nicknamed 'Woodbine Willie' for his promiscuity in handing out 'fags') sent to 42/East Lancashires, otherwise known as 'The Windy Forty Second'. Studdert Kennedy described his ministry as taking a 'box of fags in your haversack, and a great deal of love in your heart'.[83]

Given the public school, upper-class background of Anglican clergyman, it comes as no shock to find that a steady trickle de-frocked themselves and volunteered to fight on the frontline. Robert Callaway was a mission priest before returning to England to join the army as a chaplain. Dissatisfied with the role, he sought a combatant commission and joined the Sherwood Foresters. He wrote to his wife from the Somme on 2 September 1916:

I have never for a single moment regretted becoming a combatant. In one way I can say with St. Paul, 'I glory in the things which concern my own infirmities.' I am proud of just those very things which other people think must be a bore for me, e.g. Coming down in rank [as a chaplain he had been a captain], being under the orders of boys of eighteen, having to trudge along on foot, etc. and for that reason I rejoiced even when I gave up the Lewis Gun job, though everybody thought me a fool to do so.[84]

Lieutenant Callaway died eleven days later. He was aged forty-four.

The twin pillars of leadership in the trenches were paternalism and pluck. An officer might have all the paternalism, but if he did not have pluck he was 'no bon'. Only battle could tell.

VI

Over the Top:
Into Battle

I did not look forward into the future, since infantry subalterns had ceased to expect such a thing.

Charles Carrington, 1917

The trench was filthy, soaking, filled with the miasma of faeces and decaying bodies; but the trench was also earth-armour. When a man went 'over the top' or 'over the bags' onto the tangle-wire land above his head, he was exposed flesh in a storm of steel. The psychological effort required to climb up the scaling ladders and pegs at the side of the trench was immense; for the officer charged with leading the men over the top it was greater still. This was the loneliest time of his soldiering, and while he might have the support of his NCOs and platoon, the command was his, and only his; Siegfried Sassoon had a nightmare in which he led his men into battle – but when he turned around they had not followed him.[1] Such solitudinous anxiety dreams were commonplace. There were other worries. An officer might massacre drill, he might mess up the mess accounts, he might be pally with his men to the point of naiveté, but the one thing he could not fluff or funk was this supreme moment. He had to lead into battle with élan, if not downright nonchalance. It was expected. Not least by himself.

There was also the leaden knowledge that if anyone was to die that day it was likely to be him. By the Autumn of 1915 it had become apparent that officers were suffering disproportionate casualty rates in comparison with the Other Ranks. In the slagheaps around Loos, battalions had sometimes suffered the loss in action of all their officers; it happened to the 6/King's Own Scottish Borderers, who took twenty officers into the attack on the German line between Mad Point and Strong Point on 25 September 1915, and came out with none. Not one. In the 9th Division the period after Loos was known as 'The Reign of the Second Lieutenant' because nearly every company was commanded by a subaltern instead of a captain. The slaughter of the officers continued; of the thirty officers of J.R. Ackerley's battalion of East Surreys who went into the maelstrom of the Somme, only four survived.[2] Henry Dundas listed the officer casualties (killed, wounded and missing) for the Guards Division between 10–30 September 1916: Grenadiers 76; Coldstream 60; Scots 31; Irish 31; Welsh 16. A total of 214. 'Pretty shattering', wrote Dundas. He was himself shot dead by a sniper desperately close to the war's end in September 1918.

The official *General Annual Report of the British Army 1913–1919* makes the general point of officer losses in clinical, nameless detail:

	Percentage of officers killed	Percentage other ranks killed
1 Oct. 1914–30 Sept. 1915	14.2	5.8
1 Oct. 1915–30 Sept. 1916	8.0	4.9
1 Oct. 1916–30 Sept. 1917	8.5	4.7
1 Oct. 1917–30 Sept. 1918	6.9	4.0[3]

Another way of looking at the figures:

	Percentage of army holding commissioned rank at beginning of period	Percentage of officers among killed
4 Aug. 1914–30 Sept. 1914	4.4	8.1
1 Oct. 1917–30 Sept. 1918	3.6	6.2

Officers were also more likely to be wounded. In the period 1 October 1914 to 30 September 1915, 24.4 per cent of officers were wounded compared to 17.4 per cent of other ranks. Of the 234,000 officers who served in the Army during the Great War 37,484 died in action or of wounds.[4]

Of the officer corps, officers above the rank of captain did not usually lead in the line. Consequently, the overwhelming burden of the death rate was borne by subalterns, lieutenants and captains. Being a platoon commander in the infantry was unquestionably the most dangerous job on the Western Front. Any junior officer suffering under the pleasant illusion that his life was of any importance, would be swiftly disabused; waiting to go over at Hooge, Lieutenant Gilbert Talbot of 7/Rifle Brigade, son of the Bishop of Winchester, ex-President of the Oxford Union, was told by his colonel: 'Remember, you are responsible for fifty-two lives. Your own doesn't count.'[5] Talbot was mortally hit by a bullet in the neck in the charge; his brother, Reverend Neville Talbot, named the soldiers' rest house in Poperinge after him.

'After the fighting I have seen', wrote Julian Bickersteth in September 1916, 'I am quite convinced that no subaltern stands a chance of avoiding becoming a casualty out here. He simply must be killed or wounded sooner or later.'[6] Few infantry officers from Loos onwards went over the top with an expectation of avoiding injury or death, and less still after the first of July 1916, when 993 officers were scythed down like so many stalks of greening Somme wheat, among them Bickersteth's brother Stanley. 'Our lines were forfeit, and we knew it', said Charles Douie of the subaltern's lot in 1916. The conviction that a subaltern's only future was a hospital bed or interment in the soil of Flanders or France was as pardonable as it was universal. During the worst times on the Western Front – such as Second Ypres, Loos, the Somme, Passchendaele – officers were 'pouring through battalions'; when Lieutenant Francis Hitchcock of 2/Leinsters looked through his diary of Loos and the Somme he worked out that a company officer's life in the battalion worked out at just under six weeks.[7]

Fear nagged at the mind of the officer before battle. Fear of death, certainly, but more the fear of showing fear, the fear of failing to be the good officer. In a bivouac in the Bois des Tailles on 29 June 1916, Lieutenant Noel Hodgson, a 23-year-old officer with the

9/Devonshire Regiment, penned 'Before Action', a poetical cartograph of the worries that filled the mind of the Great War platoon and company officer:

> By all the glories of the day
> And the cool evening's benison,
> By that last sunset touch that lay
> Upon the hills when day was done,
> By beauty lavishly outpoured
> And blessings carelessly received,
> By all the days that I have lived
> Make me a soldier, Lord.
>
> By all of all man's hopes and fears,
> And all the wonders poets sing,
> The laughter of unclouded years,
> And every sad and lovely thing;
> By the romantic ages stored
> With high endeavour that was his,
> By all his mad catastrophes
> Make me a man, O Lord.
>
> I, that on my familiar hill
> Saw with uncomprehending eyes
> A hundred of Thy sunsets spill
> Their fresh and sanguine sacrifice,
> Ere the sun swings his noonday sword
> Must say good-bye to all of this;
> By all delights that I shall miss,
> Help me to die, O Lord.[8]

Two days later Hodgson was killed at Mametz Wood by a machine-gun bullet through the neck.

There was plenty of time for preying nags and gnaws because the 'Pushes' of the Great War were planned to the nth degree and came with long days of notice. Planning and preparation for a 'push', however, was at least time out of the front line.

The first official intimation of a major action would be a meeting of all officers of the division; before Loos, Harold Macmillan recalled that the Corps Commander addressed the officers in the public square of a village near Blendecques. To Macmillan's bemusement the open-air lecture went into considerable detail; 'Indeed, it was alleged by some of the more cynical of our officers that smiling matrons, leaning out of the windows of the houses, could be seen releasing pigeons at a frightening rate.'[9] After the divisional meeting, troops practised on mock-ups of trenches to be attacked, made from aeroplane photographs, and had refresher courses in such martial arts as bayonet-fighting and bomb-throwing. A culinary clock marked the approach of battle for Other Ranks; the more niceties there appeared on the billet menu, the closer they were to battle.

In the shadow of battle some of the battalion's officers would be named for the 'LOOB', the 'Left Out Of Battle' reserve. The LOOB was a cadre of around 10 per cent of the battalion's strength, from which the battalion could be rebuilt if casualties were high, as they so often were. Although selection for the LOOB meant the chance of life, selection for it could be weepingly unpopular. Charles Douie attended a meeting of officers of the 1/Dorsets in Blackhorse Bridge dug-out on the Somme, at which the duties in the attack were dispensed to subalterns. Some of the tasks were plainly, cruelly beyond reason, notably one which involved lugging a Bangalore torpedo under the German wire, exploding it, and then consolidating the lonely position; the subaltern accorded the task was wryly amused. 'The only protest at the allotted duties', recalled Douie, 'came from one of the subalterns detailed to remain in reserve, who was so upset he breached discipline by raising his voice. The adjutant, on this occasion, ignored the breach.'[10]

Brave and dutiful boys abounded. The nameless subaltern in the Dorsets who protested about being placed in the LOOB would have sympathized with Anthony Eden of the King's Royal Rifle Corps, also placed in the LOOB, also on the Somme:

The following afternoon our company commander sent for me and told me that a new order had just come down from division limiting the number of officers and N.C.O.s we were to take into action. As a consequence, each company had to leave behind two officers and a senior sergeant as well as a percentage of junior N.C.O.s. In our last weeks at Plugstreet and since, one or two junior officers had joined us and I imagined that these would be left out of the battle. So I asked casually who was to stay behind. He said, 'You, Boy,' and mentioned another comparatively senior officer. I was outraged and exclaimed that he could not possibly leave me behind. I had been with the battalion since its early days, I had helped to recruit my platoon, I could not desert them in their first major action.

Joe Pitt said he knew this would be my reaction, but the decision was not his. Which officers to take and which to leave behind had been a carefully considered decision of the colonel's in conclave with Foljambe and the adjutant. I was not to be appeased and asked to see the colonel.[11]

Eden saw the colonel, Charlie Feversham, but the colonel refused to budge. A few days later, on 15 September, Feversham was killed leading his rifleman at Gird Ridge.[12] Likewise, Guy Chapman was crushed to be left out of the line on the Somme, not once but twice, the second time on being ordered to 63rd Brigade HQ for a course of instruction in staff duties.

Now to be once more left out of the line, while more recently joined officers went into action, seemed to me a stain on my pride – or was it my vanity? ... It gnawed at me while I sat in outward tranquillity beneath a bank in the valley.

On saying goodbye to his company, he could not meet the eyes of the CSM.[13]

Those going to battle sometimes had their heads shaved; Bernard Martin's battalion, camped at the Sand Pits, an open down on the Somme, was coiffeured as close to the 'scalp as clippers could cut'.[14] Looking around him Martin enjoyed the 'gentle valleys' of the Somme's landscape, so different to flat Flanders.

Many would wish to make their peace with God. Held in a mud-floored barn or out in the open field, the voluntary communion service on the eve of battle was always intense; Padre Julian Bickersteth noted approvingly that 'officers in large numbers turned up'. A good sermon could kindle fire in the belly, as well as lend a spiritual arm of comfort. (Although Robert Graves once encountered an officer who swore that the best pre-battle sermon he ever heard was on the commutation of tithes, which took the men's minds right off the looming battle.) 'I went to a service on the side of a hill this morning, and took the Holy Communion afterwards, which always seems to help one along a bit doesn't it?' wrote 'Bim' Tennant to his mother on 20 September 1916.[15] Tennant was one of those bowed heads in the photographs of communicants at the Somme who were praying, yet in hindsight seem to be placing their heads on some invisible executioner's block of youth. He was killed two days later, aged nineteen. A brother officer, Harold Macmillan, thought Tennant 'seemed to illustrate in his person all the Elizabethan ardour that still gave some enchantment and excitement to war', and 'left to all who knew him a lasting memory'.[16]

In his letter to his beloved mother, Lieutenant The Honourable Edward Wyndham Tennant spoke also of sacred succour of another sort, 'the spirit of the Brigade of Guards'.[17] On the day before a Push, when the universe in the head to-ed and fro-ed with alarms, regimental pride was an unfailing morale raiser and was the motif of the colonel's address to the battalion, the men mustered at ease on three sides of him. Lesser officer-beings than the colonel on his horse relied on the old standby of humdrum humour to maintain spirits. Lieutenant Edwin Campion Vaughan:

The whole day we were busy, examining gas-masks, rifles, Lewis guns, field dressings, iron rations, identity discs, etc, and trying to joke with the troops despite the gnawing apprehension that was numbing our minds. Early in the evening I changed into Tommy's uniform and tried to prepare for every contingency – spare laces and string in one pocket, spare pencils in another, scissors in my field dressing pochette, rations and cigarettes in my haversack with my maps, small message maps stuffed into my respirator satchel, and a pocketful of revolver ammunition.[18]

Vaughan climbed into a private's uniform because in early 1916, in an effort to staunch the haemorrhaging of platoon and company commanders before German guns, officers going into action were ordered to camouflage themselves as Tommies. Specifically, Army Manual SS135 *The Training and Employment of Divisions*, instructed 'All infantry officers taking part in an attack must be dressed and equipped exactly like the men. Sticks are not to be carried.' Only the bronze star on each shoulder showed that the subaltern was an officer. Dressing as a Tommy dismayed Graham Greenwell, who thought such disguise was a sad departure from the 'Nelson Touch' – all decorations won in battle and worn in battle. Colonel de Crespigny in 2/Grenadier Guards mutinously refused to follow the order and continued to wear a gold-peaked cap and spurs into battle. 'But he had a charmed life', recalled Harold Macmillan, 'and survived the whole war from beginning to end.'[19] Boy-subalterns in Tommy's kit in the heat of battle would have a devilish job to persuade eddies of unfamiliar troops coming their way to take orders from them; still, the dress-like-Tommies order undoubtedly lowered the death rate amongst frontline officers, although it never equalized it down to that of the men they led, not least because an officer would still carry distinguishing kit – such as a revolver – and his actions would betray his status, as well as court his death.

The day before battle was the shortest day. Time did not fly. It ran and slipped away, uncontrollably. Intentionally, everyone was kept occupied on the equipment checks mentioned by Vaughan, yet there always seemed time to dwell on one's possible, if not likely, extinction. With the last letter home, 'only to be opened in the event of my death', the officer made his *salvete*. More than the will lodged with the adjutant, the last letter was the testament of a man.

The passing of the years has done nothing to diminish the tragedy and dignity of the last letters of the fallen from the Great War. Nothing at all. Here is Second Lieutenant John Engall, 16/London Regiment:

Friday, 28th [30th] June, 1916.

My dearest Mother and Dad,

I'm writing this letter the day before the most important moment in my life – a moment which I must admit I have never prayed for, like thousands of others have, but nevertheless a moment which now it has come, I would not back out of for all the money in the world. The day has almost dawned when I shall really do my little bit in the cause of civilization. To-morrow morning I shall take my men – men whom I have got to love, and who, I think, have got to love me – over the top to do our bit in the first attack in which the London Territorials have taken part as a whole unit. I'm sure you will be pleased to hear that I'm going over with the Westminsters. The old regiment has been given the most ticklish task in the whole of the Division; and I'm very proud of my section, because it is the only section in the whole of the Machine Gun Company that is going over the top; and my two particular guns have been given the two most advanced and therefore most important, positions of all – an honour that is coveted by many. So you can see that I have cause to be proud, inasmuch as at the moment that counts I am the officer who is entrusted with the most difficult task.

I took my Communion yesterday with dozens of others who are going over to-morrow; and never have I attended a more impressive service. I placed my soul and body in God's keeping, and I am going into battle with His name on my lips, full of confidence and trusting implicitly in Him. I have a strong feeling that I shall come through safely; but nevertheless, should it be God's holy will to call me away, I am quite prepared to go; and, like dear Mr le Patourel I could not wish for a finer death; and you, dear Mother and Dad, will know that I died doing my duty to my God, my Country, and my King. I ask that you should look upon it as an honour that you have given a son for the sake of King and Country . . .

I wish I had time to write more, but time presses . . .

I fear I must close now. Au revoir, dearest Mother and Dad. Fondest love to all those I love so dearly, especially yourselves.

Your devoted and happy son,

Jack

Engall, who had been educated at St Paul's, was killed in action on the first day of the battle of the Somme, 1 July 1916.[20]

Douglas Gillespie wrote to his father on 24 April 1915:

Before long I think we shall be in the thick of it, for if we do attack, my company will be one of those in front, and I am likely to lead it; not because I have been specially chosen for that, but because someone must lead, and I have been with the company longest. I have no forebodings, for I feel that so many of my friends will charge by my side, and if a man's spirit may wander back at all, especially to the places where he is needed most, then Tom himself will be here to help me, and give me courage and resource and that cool head which will be needed most of all to make the attack a success. For I know it is just as bad to run into danger uselessly as to hang back when we should be pushing on.

It will be a great fight, and even when I think of you, I would not wish to be out of this. You remember Wordsworth's 'Happy Warrior':

Who if he be called upon to face
Some awful moment to which heaven has joined
Great issues, good or bad, for human kind.
Is happy as a lover, and is attired
With sudden brightness like a man inspired.

Well, I never could be all that a happy warrior should be, but it will please you to know that I am very happy, and whatever happens, you will remember that. Well, anything one writes at a time like this seems futile, because the tongue of man can't say all that he feels – but I thought I would send this scribble with my love to you and Mother. Always your loving
Bey. [21]

He fell at La Bassée the next day, leading the charge.

Not all who went over the top were the young and the gallant. Lieutenant John Coull, 23rd Battalion, Royal Fusiliers, was the middle-aged and gallant:

France. 2.4.17 1p.m.
My dear boy Fred,
This is a letter you will never see unless your daddy falls in the field. It is his farewell words to you in case anything happens. My boy I love

you dearly and would have greatly liked to get leave for a few days to kiss you and shake hands again, after a few months separation, but as this seems at the present moment unlikely, I drop you this few lines to say 'God bless you' and keep you in the true brave manly upright course which I would like to see you follow.

You will understand better as you get older that your daddy came out to France for your sake and for our Empire's sake. If he died it was in a good cause and all I would ask of you dear boy, is that you will keep this note in memory of me, and throughout your life may all that is good attend you and influence you. May you be strong to withstand the temptations of life and when you come to the evening of your days may you be able to say with St. Paul 'I have fought the good fight'.

Goodbye dear boy and if it is that we are not to meet again in this life, may it be certain that we shall meet in another life to come, which faith I trust you will hold on to and live up to.

I remain ever
Your loving Daddy
J.F. Coull[22]

John Coull survived the battle for which the above letter was written 'in case', but fell on 30 September 1918. He was forty-three.

Second Lieutenant Glyn Morgan, Royal Welch Fusiliers, wrote to his father on 30 July 1917, on the eve of going over the bags:

I am quite content to die for the cause for which I have given up nearly three years of my life, and I only hope that I may meet Death with as brave a front as I have seen other men do before.[23]

Fear of failure, fear of not being brave – both bored away at the officer's mind, to run out in constant lines of anxiety in letters home. 'All I hope is that I don't fail – for I must confess I'm a bit of a coward to use a strong word: not so much for myself but for the men under me am I afraid. Still let's hope for the best', wrote Geoffrey Thurlow.[24] His friend Edward Brittain was equally troubled: 'I do not hold life cheap at all and it is hard to be sufficiently brave, yet I have hardly ever felt really afraid. One has to keep up appearances at all costs even if one is.'[25] Captain Hanbury-Sparrow of 2/Royal Berkshires recalled the effort required to conquer his nerves even to look over a parapet:

For very shame's sake pull yourself together, man ... Set them an example. With a dozen pairs of eyes watching you, you unstrap your field-glasses and, kneeling, look over the parapet.[26]

In the count-down to battle, through battle itself, the subaltern, in Charles Carrington's memorable phrase, possessed a 'strange sense of dual personality' in which:

Always the struggle within, fought behind the dark curtains which screen the hidden springs of conduct, was more real than the physical struggle without and the practical details of life passed by like an illusion.[27]

Some forwent the writing of a last letter. 'Did not, however, leave any addresses or messages behind because I believed it unlucky', recorded Robert Mackay in his diary. Luck, one needed luck. And if not luck itself, an enticer of luck, a charm or amulet. Harrods sold a 'fumsup' lucky charm of a miniature baby in rolled gold for 3/6. Most officers preferred something personal, or religious. Second Lieutenant P.E. Lewis in Guy Chapman's company, who had been commissioned from the ranks, always wore a garment of pink silk in battle; by 1918 it was chiefly held together by Smith's willpower but it 'bore him magically through' until the maelstrom was over.[28] A good Catholic, Edwin Campion Vaughan, after putting on his Tommy's jacket, 'saw that my rosary was sewn into my tunic with the sovereign that Marie had given me for luck, and that my holy medals were firmly attached with my identity discs to my braces'.[29] Vaughan then handed his money and cigarette case to CQMS Braham, so that if he fell 'Jerry would not have them'. Corporal Hill made Francis Hitchcock a cross made out of a copper bullet to wear as a charm around his neck. Hill said Hitchcock would not be killed while wearing it. He was right. Surely the luckiest charm belonged to Arthur Smith, a staff officer, who carried in his tunic a copy of the Bible given him by his father, which had lines from the 91st psalm on the flyleaf: 'Because thou hast made the Lord thy refuge. There shall no evil befall thee. For he shall give his angels charge over thee to keep thee in all thine ways.'

Smith was hit by a piece of shrapnel that cut through the Bible until that page in the psalms from which the text was taken. He wrote the event 'was a very significant thing and encouraged my faith'.[30]

Charms and amulets were not 22-carat guarantees of luck. Bim Tennant carried 'four photies' of his mother and a 'little medal of the Blessed Virgin into battle' to no avail.

Suddenly it was the night before battle. At Passchendaele in October 1917, Frank Warren had the last minute reprieve that was the secret hope of some:

> In the evening news comes through that the attack has been put off or given over to other troops. We can only feel much relieved, for our task would have been no easy one![31]

Soldiers not reprieved, soldiers who had marched on to the edge of the battlefield, spent the last night in rough billets within the sound of guns. On this night the men crowded together had an advantage over the junior officers, several to a tent. There was a sense of safety in numbers. But three, two, or – perish the thought – one officer to a room, and the horizon reduced ineluctably to self. Edwin Campion Vaughan lay in a tent with two others, listening to the rain beating on the tent and the booming of the guns. One of the others got drunk and melancholy. As for Vaughan:

> I could not sleep, but lay awake thinking and wondering about the attack, fancying myself blown to bits, or lying out on the wire with a terrible wound. It was not until dawn that I dozed off and slept fitfully until 9.a.m.[32]

Oddly, although dawn meant battle was closer, matters always looked better in daylight. Despite being scared in his tossing dreams of the previous night, Vaughan woke to find that the fear had gone and he was able to eat a hearty breakfast of sausages and bacon.

More preparations, then the march into the battle area, the column wreathed in smoke from the men's cigarettes and pipes, all through a chaos of traffic, of men and artillery, of signallers running out cable lines. Harold Macmillan wrote: 'The line of troops passing in front of us seemed never ending. To add to our discomfort it poured steadily all those six hours. We got a cup of tea while waiting, but otherwise no food, except chocolate.'[33] As troops entered the battle zone, they would encounter German shelling designed to break up the attack before it began. At Loos the whole of the Brigade of Guards went forward in full view of the Germans on the high ground and were heavily shelled for nearly two miles on the approach from Vermelles. The Guards historian wrote: 'Perfect order was maintained. Nothing more splendid has ever been recorded in the annals of the Guards than the manner in which every battalion in the Brigade faced this trying ordeal.'[34] It was Macmillan's baptism of shelling; 'I must confess that for many months and even years I would dream of it'.[35] On entering the communication trenches platoons would be guided along, shuffling, at snail's pace; Lieutenant F.P. Roe recalled the scene approaching the frontline trench on the Somme:

Every single yard of the communication trench up to the front line was impassable and the confusion was indescribable. Reinforcement troops and working parties with material and ammunition were trying to make their way forward against a stream of troops coming out of the line, including stretcher-bearers with casualties, walking wounded and exhausted troops coming out after a spell in the front line.[36]

On finally reaching the frontline trench or more likely a specially-dug trench just behind it, officers would order their platoons to rest. Often the Zero Hour was the next dawn, when the night was at its coldest, so there could be tense black hours of waiting. The men crouched around in the dark, smoking if there was an artillery bombardment of the German positions, but if the attack was a stealthy secret – as attacks increasingly were from late 1916 – they could only twiddle their thumbs. At Passchendaele, Lieutenant Angel of the Royal Fusiliers was confronted with an officer's nightmare:

Everyone was on edge and as I crawled up to one shell-hole I could hear a boy sobbing and crying. He was crying for his mother. It was pathetic really, he just kept saying over and over and again. 'Oh Mum! Oh Mum!' Nothing would make him shut up, and while it wasn't likely that the Germans could hear, it was quite obvious that when there were lulls in the shell-fire the men in shell-holes on either side would hear this lad and possibly be affected. Depression, even panic can spread quite easily in a situation like that. So I crawled into the shell-hole and asked Corporal Merton what was going on. He said, 'It's his first time in the line, sir. I can't keep him quiet, and he's making the other boys jittery.' Well, the other boys in the shell-hole obviously *were* jittery and, as one of them put it more succinctly, 'fed up with his bleedin' noise'. Then they all joined in, 'Send him down the line and home to Mum' – 'Give him a clout and knock him out' – 'Tell him to put a sock in it, sir'.

I tried to reason with the boy, but the more I talked to him the more distraught he became, until he was almost screaming. 'I can't stay here! Let me go! I want my Mum!' So I switched my tactics, called him a coward, threatened him with court-martial and slapped his face as hard as I could, several times. It had an extraordinary effect. There was absolute silence in the shell-hole and then the corporal, who was a much older man, said. 'I think I can manage him now, sir'. Well, he took that boy in his arms, just as if he was a small child, and when I crawled back a little later to see if all was well, they were both lying there asleep and the corporal still had his arms round the boy – mud, accoutrements and all. At zero hour they went over together.[37]

At Ginchy, Second Lieutenant Minchin received the officer's other pre-push nightmare; the undertaking of a preliminary action. By moonlight Minchin successfully drove off a German machine-gun stronghold from the orchard on the Ginchy-Flers road.[38]

Next in the descending schedule to 'going over the bags', the runner from battalion HQ arrived with the synchronized watch. The ticking down to Zero Hour began, inexorably. So did obsessive watch-watching.

Tick. Cloete recalled his platoon being 'very still', staring into the darkness in front of them hoping that the enemy's wire had been cut. Men started praying.

Tick. If there was a continuous Allied artillery barrage storming overhead the noise and spectacle would mesmerize the soldiers. Edmund Blunden likened the shelling to 'a flooded Amazon of steel' roaring immensely fast over his head.[39] Stuart Cloete on the Somme recorded: 'The shells went over like a gale above us. Among them we could hear the big ones – howitzer projectiles – that sounded like passing trains. We went on looking at our watches.'

Tick. An electric moment, the order to fix bayonets. For many, this was the moment when they knew there would be no reprieve, no cancelled order. There was no going back. There was only going up and forwards. Lieutenant Robert Nichols caught the moment in verse:

A sudden thrill.
"Fix bayonets."
Gods! we have our fill
Of fear, hysteria, exultation, rage—
Rage to kill . . . .

My heart burns hot, whiter and whiter,
Contracts tighter and tighter,
Until I stifle with the will
Long forged, now used—
(Though utterly strained)
O pounding heart,
Baffled, confused,
Heart panged, head singing dizzily pained
To do my part.

Blindness a moment. Sick.
There the men are.
Bayonets ready: click !
Time goes quick;
A stumbled prayer . . . somehow a blazing star
In a blue night . . . where?
Again prayer.
The tongue trips. Start:
How's time? Soon now . . . .[40]

Tick. With ten minutes to go the officer would pass along the trench checking the men's equipment, a practical necessity that had the benefit of making the men *feel* prepared. As he went he would, as so often in times of danger, tell 'damn silly jokes to put everyone at ease', in the words of Alexander Stewart.[41] Along with reassuring words, the officer doled out tots of rum. At High Wood Stewart's platoon sergeant came up to him to confess that his nerves had gone. 'The poor chap seemed very upset so I gave him a drink [of rum] from my flask. In a minute or so he was as right as rain and full of gratitude.' (Stewart thought that the 'blasted blackguard' on the staff who tried to stop the soldiers' rum ration 'should have been taken to High Wood and chained there for a week'.[42]) A self-administration of rum or whisky was not a bad idea, either. Few officers failed the greatest test of their life, and it does not matter that some of their support came from a flask. Guy Chapman recalled one who did funk it, literally crapping his trousers. 'He was last seen running down the road past Mametz Wood, his belt in one hand, his stick agitated in the other, calling on his batman to follow him. The battalion ensconced in the angle of a quarry jeered.'[43]

Tick. The men's equipment checked, the officer would double-check his own kit. Stewart wrote: 'As Zero time drew near I saw that my revolver was loaded, a rifle also fully loaded with one in the breach and bayonet fixed slung over my shoulder, my gas mask in the alert position under my chin and my coat collar turned up.'[44] The latter sartorial touch was another attempt to look more like a Tommy.

Tick. Few officers in the trenches tried to emulate Henry V at Agincourt. The noise of the artillery barrage and counter-barrage was too great anyway. A pithy Nelsonianism would do. Billy Grenfell at Hooge told his men before going over the parapet: 'Remember you are Englishmen. Do nothing to dishonour that name.' Lieutenant Arthur Heath 6/Royal West Kent Regiment, a former WEA lecturer wrote:

> The men were a good bit scared ... My job seemed to be to steady things a bit and it would have been a fine occasion for a dramatic speech. The only remarks that came to mind, however, were 'Sentries look to your periscopes and the rest keep low.' It was prosaic, but the

opportunities for romance do not occur to you in the moment – at least, they didn't to me. After all, it is no use saying 'Remember Waterloo' to my men, for most of them have never heard of the battle, and would think I was referring to the railway station.[45]

Heath was killed in action on 8 October 1915, his twenty-eighth birthday.

Tick. Cloete remembered repeatedly glancing at the luminous face of his watch. 'How funny to live by a watch, minute by minute, as if I were going to catch a train.'[46] More prayers. Anthony Eden silently begged: 'Please God, if I am to be hit let me be slightly wounded or killed but not mutilated.' Eden reflected that death did not seem so bad, because two of his brothers and many of his friends had died, and therefore extermination seemed 'if not normal, at least acceptable'.[47]

Tick. Now with a bare few minutes to go, it was time for the officer to light the all important pipe or cigarette. Captain William Branks Wilson, The Cameronians, recalled:

> At 7.45 we got word to go over in three minutes and wait 1,000 yards in front of our barrage, so, lighting a cigarette, off we went . . . [48]

The pipe or cigarette was an indispensable prop for the officer. A cigarette or pipe could literally help keep the upper-lip stiff. Captain T.P.C. Wilson, 10 Sherwood Foresters, wrote:

> Someday I'm going to write a 'paper' on the 'psychology of the cigarette'! It fills the place in a man's life, out here, which the snuff box held with the old French aristocrat. It helps a man to go to his death with a brave hypocrisy of carelessness, just as it helped the aristocrat go daintily to the guillotine.[49]

Edwin Venning thought that the cigarette fixed in the mouth was such a cliché that it helped the Germans identify the smoker as an officer.[50]

Tick. An officer must not show fear, because fear is contagious. A private of 32nd Field Ambulance recorded the disastrous effect of having nervy officers in the line:

You could see the spreading dismay as the ordinary Tommies recognised their own fear and hesitation in the eyes of these one-pip striplings [subalterns]. Men under fire . . . watch each other with nerves on edge. 'Blimey! Even the bloody officers are lost!..'[51]

Keep the upper-lip stiff, then. In the last seconds, Nichols willed himself into composure:

Gather, heart, all thoughts that drift;
Be steel, soul.
Compress thyself
Into a round, bright whole.

I cannot speak.

Tick. Cloete:

The whole of our front is scarlet and yellow with bursting shells, black with the thrown-up soil of the German trenches. One minute to go. I watch the second hand of my watch. I put the whistle in my mouth and blow.[52]

Zero Hour. The time to climb the slimy boxes, ladders and pegs on the side of the trench. Robert Nichols:

Time! Time!

I hear my whistle shriek
Between teeth set,
I fling an arm up,
Scramble up the grime
Over the parapet!

I'm up. Go on.
Something meets us.
Head down into the storm that greets us.
A wail!
Lights. Blurr.

Gone.
On, on. Lead. Lead. Hail.
Spatter. Whirr. Whirr.
"Toward that patch of brown,
Direction left." Bullets: a stream.
Devouring thought crying in a dream;
Men, crumpled, going down . . . .
Go on. Go.

Nichols who participated in the battle of Loos, was later invalided home with shell shock. The prime reason for the high casualty rate of officers was that in battle officers led from the front. In the words of Brigadier Frank Crozier an officer needed three seconds lead over the men, so he could say 'come on' instead of 'go on'.

It was always hoped that the British barrage would destroy the German infantry in their trenches. It seldom did. Climbing over the parapet, the whole body of a man was exposed to the German counter-barrage, to rifle fire, to the machine-guns set to sweep along the trench top. 'We are like men naked. The walls of the trenches were our clothes', thought Cloete as he began his peregrination across No-Man's Land.

No one was more naked than the officer because the recovering, surviving Germans sought him above other men for their sights. German riflemen and machine-gunners believed that if the British officer fell his men, leaderless, would not come on. The assumption held grains of truth; the British Army, faced with sometimes unpre-possessing human material for its private soldiers, had long organized the platoon as a tightly drilled unit to be controlled by a subaltern. NCOs were not expected to show initiative. The system had its virtues − proven by the colouring in pink of a quarter of the world's map − but its vice was that in battlefield action it did peculiarly require an officer. The Germans had divined this; the British already knew it; Robert Graves participated in a discussion in the officers' mess at Harfleur base camp where it was agreed dispassionately that the Catholic Irish and Highland Scots were 'useless' without officers.[33] In the messes of the Leinsters and Argylls there were doubtless men who believed that Graves' own regiment, the Royal Welch Fusiliers, was less than perfect when officer-less. And the broad-brogued men from Ireland and the Highlands would have been right. Even British regiments with battle honours as long as a coal train needed an officer to make them go over the top. Or to make a stand.[54] Of course, there were NCOs with initiative. At the end of an 'exceptionally bloody offensive' in September 1917, Sergeant Tom Liddell in Anthony Eden's King's Royal Rifle Corps 'took over command [of a company] as if this was the most natural event in the world, rallied his riflemen and led them to the objective which they consolidated and held'.[55] The Liddells, though, were the exception. The British Army was an army led by officers. On patrol. On raids. Into battle.

Lieutenant J.R. Ackerley 8/East Surrey Regiment, went 'over the bags' on the sunny first day of the Somme:

> The air when we at last went over the top in broad daylight, positively hummed, buzzed and whined with what sounded like hordes of wasps and hornets but were, of course, bullets . . .
>
> Many of the officers in my battalion were struck down the moment they emerged into view. My company commander was shot through the heart before he had advanced a step.

Ackerley ran forward 'bent double', because he feared a 'bullet in the balls'. His platoon was still scrambling out of the trench, when he was hit in the arm.[56]

Lieutenant Edward Liveing, London Regiment, likened the sound of German machine guns on the Somme to a 'continuous hissing noise . . . like a railway engine letting off steam'. On top of the parapet he signalled forward with his rifle; 'If I had felt nervous, I did not feel so now . . . I felt as if I was in a dream, but had all my wits about me.'[57]

Along the line, on both sides of him, Cloete could see men climbing out and moving forward, their rifles at the port, bayonets glinting in the dawn. There was always relief when the men obeyed the signal to advance. Vaughan wrote:

> Dully, I hoisted myself out of the mud and gave the signal to advance, which was answered by every man rising and stepping unhesitatingly

into the barrage. The effect was so striking that I felt no more that awful dread of the shellfire . . .[58]

Courage for an officer in battle was a many way relationship; Vaughan gave courage to his men; watching them rise gave him courage; later in the battle he would find his spine steeled by the (apparently) nerveless Captain Taylor, giving orders from a captured dug-out as chips of concrete rained on him as German shells hit home.

The men walked in lines towards the German trenches because such a drill-like formation, reminiscent of the parade ground, gave them familiarity and comradeship amidst the demonic din and pullulating earth. They walked in lines so that, if they were following a 'creeping' artillery barrage, the officer could control the pace of all, and ensure that the men did not enter the backsplash of the barrage, but also did not lag so far behind it that the Germans had time to recover after the barrage passed over their heads. And finally, the men walked in lines, so that when they arrived at the German trenches they did so in killing, critical mass, not ones and twos.

As the men walked forward, instinctively a little crouched ('resembling supplicants rather than the vanguard of a great offensive' thought Captain Graham Seton Hutchison of the Machine-Gun Corps) the officer would become conductor, waving and shouting to his men, to maintain the line. Wilfred Owen wrote:

I kept up a kind of chanting sing-song: Keep the line straight!
Not so fast on the left!
Steady on the left!
Not so fast![59]

Inevitably, the arm gestures the officer employed to maintain formation – the swinging of the rifle through the air for 'Forwards!', the swinging left arm for 'Hold back on the left!' – would betray him to a keen-eyed German rifleman. At Arras, Alexander Stewart tried to direct the last lap of the attack from a little hillock with a whistle – another giveaway – but found in the pandemonium that it was useless 'to attempt to influence any except those in my immediate neighbourhood, so with revolver in hand I pushed on knowing that those near would follow me into the trench and that others further down the line would follow in their own sweet time'.[60]

Courage is contagious. The officer with his cigarette or pipe, the epitome of grace under fire, was indispensable in beginning and main-taining the momentum of the line. Other Ranks followed their officer over the top for many reasons – from the desire to be brave in the eyes of their friends, to regimental pride – but loyalty to their paternal officer and the inspiration of his daring were paramount. Captain Nevill's famous kicking of footballs on the Somme was not so stupid as it seems; it was a gesture of magnificent nonchalance, one which also distracted the men from bullets and shells.[61] One ranker remembered another inspirational officer:

> My old colonel walked in front of our ragged line and gave the signals by a wave of his cane. We had no cover and advanced in open order under terrific fire – a few paces forward, then flat on the ground and, on each upward wave of the colonel's cane, forward.

Private Jimmy Walton of 11/Suffolks was much taken with an officer who rallied men at Lochnagar Crater on the Somme:

> 'Gentlemen, we're going to be faced with a counterattack. We stand and we fight.' He might have been on a barrack square – so calm, so collected.[62]

The approval of Private Frank Richards, an 'old sweat' in 2/Royal Welch Fusiliers, for two brave young officers in the battalion rings clear in his memoir:

> The following morning one hundred bombers of the Battalion under the command of Mr Sassoon were sent to the Cameronians to assist in a bombing attack on the Hindenburg Trench on our right. A con-siderable part of it was captured but was lost again during the day when the enemy made a counter-attack. During the operations Mr Sassoon was shot through the top of the shoulder. Late in the day I was conversing with an old soldier and one of the few survivors of old B

Company who had taken part in the bombing raid. He said, 'God strike me pink, Dick, it would have done your eyes good to have seen young Sassoon in that bombing stunt. He put me in mind of Mr Fletcher. It was a bloody treat to see the way he took the lead. He was the best officer I have seen in the line or out since Mr Fletcher, and it's wicked how the good officers get killed or wounded and the rotten ones are still left crawling about. If he don't get the Victoria Cross for the stunt I'm a bloody Dutchman; he thoroughly earned it this morning.' This was the universal opinion of everyone who had taken part in the stunt, but the only decoration Mr Sassoon received was a decorated shoulder where the bullet went through. He hadn't been long with the Battalion, but long enough to win the respect of every man that knew him.[63]

At Polygon Wood, Frank Richards saw 'Young Mr Casson' lead the way 'as cool as a cucumber'. Second Lieutenant Randal Casson was killed in action on 26 September 1917; a photograph of him rests in a display case in the museum above Tyne Cot cemetery on the bony animal spine that is Passchendaele ridge.

Lieutenant Harold Macmillan was blasé about the gallantry of his ilk:

When one is in action – especially if one is responsible for men under one's command – proper behaviour, even acts of gallantry are part of the show. One moves and behaves automatically as a member of a team or an actor on the stage.[64]

Fortunately, the courage of the officer – often just a mask, learned from school and home – received a chemical boost as the line advanced. Many officers wrote of their 'joy', or whatever synonym came to pen, as the line advanced through the maelstrom. Arthur Young, who had been dreading going 'over the bags' at Ginchy, found:

That numbing dread had now left me completely. Like the others, I was intoxicated with the glory of it all. I can remember shouting and bawling to the men of my platoon, who were only too eager to go on.[65]

Wilfred Owen thought there 'was an extraordinary exultation in the act of slowly walking forward, showing ourselves openly'. Such exultation was a chemical high caused by the rush of adrenaline. Macmillan found himself in a 'kind of daze that makes one impervious to emotion'. On one occasion, Stuart Cloete found no adrenaline, just pure, distilled anger. The trenches his company had taken had been lost, and they were ordered to re-take them, which entailed a five mile march back through mud to get to their own line:

> This was my worst battle. I was so angry, so exhausted, so certain my number was up, that I didn't even care and had fought in the open, on top of the trenches, with a party of men who felt as I did, bombing and shooting our way along, killing Germans like a fish in a barrel. They could not get us.[66]

In danger and stress men's loyalty to a brave and determined officer increased; he became an idealized warrior figure to be followed – even unto death. After having already personally led two platoons in the clearance of Germans from their position at Vieux Berquin, Captain Thomas Pryce MC and Bar, 4/Grenadier Guards, occupied the position and with 40 men repeatedly held off battalion strength attacks. The enemy brought up field guns to 300 yards of his line, and fired over open sights. The citation for his posthumous VC read:

> At 6.15 p.m. the enemy had worked to within sixty yards of his trench. He then called on his men, telling them to cheer, and charge the enemy and fight to the last. Led by Captain Pryce they left their trench and drove back the enemy with the bayonet some 100 yards. Half an hour later the enemy had again approached in stronger force. By this time Captain Pryce had only seventeen men left and every round of ammunition had been fired. Determined that there should be no surrender, he once again led his men in a bayonet charge, and was last seen engaged in a fierce hand-to-hand struggle with overwhelming numbers of the enemy.[67]

But the officer's example was not always enough; Edward Brittain on that fateful 1 July 1916 had to return to the trenches twice to exhort his men to follow him over the parapet. Wounded by a bullet in the thigh and by a shell splinter he was awarded the Military Cross. If the men would not move out of the trench, if the advance started to falter amid the shell-bursts, the tortured terrain, the stream of wounded coming back from a previous line, the officer would drive the men from the rear. Like cattle. At Langemarck Ridge, Vaughan discovered his men taking shelter behind tanks, so he and his sergeant major, Merrick, had to 'curse and drive' them out. Momentum was regained. They were cheered by the wounded as they passed. 'Go on boys! Give 'em hell!'[68]

Sometimes an officer had to threaten to use his revolver. Or even use it. Captain Edwin Venning wrote:

> I remember falling about 10 yards ahead of my Company with a slight shrap hit in the back, that didn't even draw blood, and the shock of the revolver at my waist being broken by a bullet; then I heard my sergeant-major's voice (he's one of the finest men I know) saying, 'Where are you, sir?' He said, 'That's right, sir, I'm with you when we get up again.' Well, we did get up again, and I had to drop back owing to difficulty in getting my remaining men on. I had a shot at one, and missed him, but it settled the rest, a man by me shouting, but he had his head and shoulders taken off; they sagged back from him, you know, riddled in a line, and I fell behind the rest of his body just in time. Then my men broke, and I remember standing somewhere in front of the German trenches, with a wounded pal's revolver, that he slipped into my hand, yelling at my men some of the filthiest language ever heard. They were appalled, and I rallied a dozen or so; as it happened, they were all killed almost at once, and I was left, so far as I could see, alone.[69]

At Gallipoli, Second Lieutenant G.R.D. Moor of the 2/Hampshires shot four British infantrymen to prevent a rout. Such instances of officers being forced to shoot their own men are blue-moon, minutely rare. Any subaltern running away could expect nothing more or less than a bullet himself; Brigadier-General Crozier shot dead a fleeing subaltern in April 1918.[70] Over the course of the entire long, dragging war a mere two British Army officers were found guilty of cowardice or desertion in the face of the enemy and executed.

In Venning's seemingly inconsequential phrase 'I had to drop back owing to difficulty in getting my remaining men on' lay an officer's death trap. An attack, even one over a hundred yards, could take hours if inertia and confusion set in, or the men fell back. Traversing the battlefield to collect men gone to ground meant repeating journeys, meant making extra journeys, meant that an officer was spending more visible time in the firing line. He was consequently increasing the risk of his own death.

In the mayhem of mid battle, the officer might well have to take command of men whose officer was *hors de combat*. Cloete recalled; 'I was exhausted, commanding a company of less than a hundred men, many of them not even in my regiment. This always happened in a show. Men got isolated, lost, and joined up with the nearest officer they could find.'[71] At Villers, Faucon Greenwell (who had 'become rather bloodthirsty of late') led a bayonet charge through the April snow, but 'swarms of Berks came surging in, and we got into a frightful muddle . . . I found myself in command of practically a whole company of Berks as well as my own, as they had lost a good many officers.'[72]

If wounded, much depended on how bad the officer's injury was. After being hit going forward, Lieutenant Ackerley was happy that 'my platoon, in which I had taken much pride, could now look after itself'. Some officers, however, were so absorbed in their commands that they would continue to direct and encourage, despite wounds; Frank Warren was hit by a glancing bullet to the head during the German's great offensive of 1918:

> Several men come running round me, including Sgt Page of 'C' Company who asks me if I have a shell dressing. I tell him 'No' and beg him not to let a crowd assemble, or it will draw fire and someone else will be shot.[73]

Lieutenant Raymond Asquith of 3/Grenadier Guards, shot in the chest during the battle of Flers-Courcelette, indifferently lit a cigarette so his men would not be disheartened by seeing that he was injured. He died on the stretcher shortly afterwards. Asquith had given up a staff job so he could return to active duty with his battalion and lead his men in action. On his headstone in the Guards cemetery at Guillemont is the inscription: SMALL TIME BUT IN THAT SMALL MOST

GRATEFULLY LIVED THIS STAR OF ENGLAND. In the attack at La Bassée in September 1915, Captain A.L. Samson of the Royal Welch Fusiliers was hit and lay groaning about 20 yards from the front trench. There were several failed attempts to rescue him, with two officers and one man killed in the doing. In the end his own orderly crawled out towards him – Samson waved him back, saying he was beyond rescuing. He sent his apologies to the company for making such a noise. When his shot-riddled corpse was recovered it was seen that he had forced his knuckles into his mouth to stop himself crying out and attracting any more men to their deaths.[74] Samson's action epitomized one of the deep-seated leadership traits of the British frontline officer: concern for his men's lives.

The German wire. Attacks so frequently suffered the fate recalled by Second Lieutenant Norton Hughes Hallett:

> We reached the wire, but found it absolutely uncut and far too thick to ever get through. For about two minutes we hacked at it, the men falling by scores the while; then I am told the remnant retired as best they could to the sunken road, though without me.[75]

He had been hit and thrown head first into a shell hole. On a good day, when the wire had been cut by artillery barrage or by a party out in the night before, the officer would lead or shepherd the men through the gaps. Again there was personal danger in his signalling. Over the final yards, the officer would begin a running charge. At five yards out Edwin Venning 'started a fire fight with rifles and machine-guns'. It was essential to close at speed, the officer firing his revolver, the men firing their rifles, their bayonets belligerent. They would scream and shout, unless they were wearing gas masks. Stuart Cloete wrote:

> Orders came to put on masks. We became strangers to each other. The horrible sticky treated flannel stuck to our faces. The end of the mask was tucked into our tunics. The bloody tit, like a baby's comforter, in our mouths. The clip on our noses. Fight? How the hell did you fight in these things? The goggles fogged. A regiment of ghosts, of men from Mars, we charged into the German trench, silent because we could not shout, and fought silent, mute as bulldogs, and took it.'[76]

Robert Nichols recalled the descent into the German trench:

Ha! Ha! Bunched figures waiting.
Revolver levelled: quick!
Flick! Flick!
Red as blood.
Germans. Germans.
Good! Oh, good!
Cool madness.

In the heat of the attack, few balked at killing, because the self-pre-servation of the officer – and his men – depended on it. In the heat of attack, only the Germans with hands held to Heaven screaming 'Kamerad! Nicht Schiessen!' would escape the cool madness. Some-times there was just hot madness. At High Wood on the rolling Somme downland, Graham Seton Hutchison led a textbook minor attack, short rushes using cover, into the German trenches, where he and his men bayoneted surrendering German troops: 'I was a murderer, breath coming in short gasps, teeth set, hands clenched round my rifle, nerves and sinews tense with life. An eye for an eye, a tooth for a tooth.' Of the fears that picked away at the boy subaltern, there was always the fear that one might not be able to do the ultimate soldier-man's job: Kill. Charles Carrington, behind a Lewis gun, was 'utterly happy to find I could do this thing killing and was not afraid'.

War always poses the possibility of being a comedy of terrors. Lieutenant John Christie reconnoitred a German trench with a party of bombers:

Got a bomb in my right hand and a rifle in the left, on we went [and] met a German ... [we] Both came round together, 10 yds apart. He hesitated, so I lobbed the bomb at his feet without pulling the string, too stupid for words. Shot at him with the rifle and Holloway with his revolver. Didn't get him ... my part in the show was very discreditable [...] I think I don't understand it myself. I don't usually get excited.[77]

At Passchendaele, one of the biggest battles in history, Alec Waugh sat in an abandoned German pill-box on the front line for four days and did not see an enemy soldier as the battle coursed out of sight around him.

After storming the trench, officers and men alike would be consumed by thirst, hunger and exhaustion. Yet the conquered trench or ground had to be defended from a counter-attack, because the Germans were inflexible and always tried to recapture lost territory. Therefore the men needed to be ordered to dig-in or reverse the fire-step, so it was facing the German direction. Arthur Young at Ginchy:

> McGarry and I were the only two officers left in the company, so it was up to us to take charge. We could see the Huns hopping over the distant ridge like rabbits, and we had some difficulty in preventing our men from chasing them, for we had orders not to go too far. We got them – Irish Fusiliers, Inniskillings and Dublins – to dig in by linking up to the shell-craters, and though the men were tired (some wanted to smoke and others to make tea) they worked with a will, and before long we had got a pretty decent trench outlined.[78]

After capturing their objective at Ginchy, the Grenadier Guards discovered a tiresome machine-gun on the left flank. Lieutenant Macmillan went out 'to silence it'. He was successful, but was shot in the left thigh by the machine gun. Macmillan rolled into a shell-hole, where he alternated between unconsciousness and reading Aeschylus' *Prometheus* in Greek, having had the foresight to bring along the book in his top pocket. 'It was a play I knew very well, and seemed not inappropriate to my position.' He lay out for twelve hours before being rescued.[79] The wound would not close properly, and he was in and out of hospital for the next four years.

By this end stage of battle, officers would only be alive in ones or twos, no more, and quite often it would be the most junior officers left fighting and leading, purely because there were more of them to begin with, four or five to a company, compared with the solitary captain. Nineteen-year-old Second Lieutenant Cloete recalled:

> I ended up the only officer in the battalion, with the trench cleared of Germans, and then handed over to a major of another brigade who had come to reinforce us, but he gave us no credit.[80]

At Gird Ridge on the Somme, Eden recalled that, after all the senior officers were killed or wounded, 'it says much for the subalterns that they were able to rally their units and dig in for the night without losing much ground'. The devil-may-care bravery of boy subalterns on the Somme was an imperishable, fifty-year-old memory for ex-Lance Corporal S.A. Boyd of 10/Royal Fusiliers:

> My lasting impression of the Somme battle is the fine young officers who led us so well. They were extremely brave but so young, many under the age of 20.[81]

The Somme played a significant part in the destruction of the German army in the field and allowed the British to develop tactics that won the war. Like Loos, it was fought at the insistence of the French. From the other side of No-Man's Land, Captain von Hertig thought the Somme 'the muddy grave of the German army and the infallibility of German leadership'. In the battle of attrition that was the Somme, junior officers played the indispensable, major role.

With the position secured against the inevitable German counter-attack, it was time to turn to food, drink, and cigarettes. On top of Langemarck Ridge at Ypres, Edwin Campion Vaughan – another subaltern who was the last officer left standing in his company – and his surviving men enjoyed a gift sent up in the rations by General Fanshawe, which consisted of a special meat and vegetable meal in a self-heating can called 'Autobouillant'. The troops blessed 'Fanny' for the thought.

With no rations in sight, Arthur Young ordered his men to pilfer the dead enemy of their rations:

> The only food we could get was Hun black bread, which we picked up all over the place; also Hun tinned sausages and bully beef. We had to lift up some of the dead to get at these things. Some of them had water-bottles full of cold coffee, which we drank. We all craved a smoke. Fortunately, the Hun haversacks were pretty well stocked with cigarettes and cigars. I got a handful of cigars off a dead Boche, and smoked them all morning. Also a tin of cigarettes. His chocolates also came in handy.[82]

Young Charles Carrington also did some plundering. After taking the Winchester pillbox at Broodseinde in October 1917 ('all-in wrestling in the mud') he relieved the German officer who had commanded the post of his automatic pistol 'because I thought it was a better weapon than our Webley revolver'.[83]

Then the long wait, holding the captured trench, until the relief came. When it did, finally, arrive, the handing over of responsibility led to a cessation of adrenaline. Adrenaline kept the lid down; with the lid off, emotions could boil over. Edwin Campion Vaughan showed the relief around the ex-German trench, then had a temporary fit of hysterics: 'After a while I realized that it *was* hysterics – that it was a temporary madness that kept me dawdling in the shell-fire, a disinclination to return to the reality of a new life out of the line'.

At the end of battle, Edwin Venning 'came near to blowing my own head off with my revolver'[84] but saving a wounded Northumberland officer proved a saving distraction. Stress amid death was not the monopoly of the infantry, as Basil Henriques, a tank officer in the red harvest of the Somme, remembered:

> The nervous strain in this first battle of tanks for officers and men alike was ghastly. Of my company one officer went mad and shot his engine to make it go faster; another shot himself because he thought he had failed to do as well as he ought; two others had what I suppose could be called a nervous breakdown.[85]

As the survivors staggered out through the darkening battlefield, they were assailed by the groans and wails of wounded men. Edwin Campion Vaughan heard:

> faint, long, sobbing moans of agony, and despairing shrieks. It was too horribly obvious that dozens of men with serious wounds must have crawled for safety into new shell-holes, and now the water was rising about them, and powerless to move, they were slowly drowning.[86]

At Delville Wood, Second Lieutenant Bernard Martin saw:

The whole blasted slope clotted to the very edges with dead bodies, too many to bury, and too costly, the area being under constant fire from artillery. This awful display of dead men looked like a set piece, as though some celestial undertaker had spaced the corpses evenly for interment and then been interrupted. Several times I picked my way through this cemetery of the unburied.[87]

On leaving the battlefield the company would assemble for temporary roll-call. How many reported would vary wildly.

The need then was for sleep. Just sleep. After Loos, Richard Talbot Kelly fell 'instantly into a dreamless sleep for seven or eight hours', on a mattress on the floor of an empty room in the mine manager's house. His 'A' Battery had, with the Brigade's T Battery, been the last in the history of the British Army to gallop into action.

On awaking, there was sadness or elation, depending on the fortunes of war. After the Oxford and Buck's bayonet rush at Villers Faucon in April 1917, which secured a ridge in front of the Hindenburg Line, Graham Greenwell was ecstatic, and busied himself sending in the names of NCOs for awards. He added in his missive to his mother:

Our captured guns are fine trophies and I have already had them stamped "Captured by 'B' Company 1/4 Oxford and Bucks Lt. Infty[88]

Alec Waugh, after Passchendaele, enjoyed the common emotion of war virgins: 'We had survived our test. We had been bloodied.' They were a bloody fine mob. Regimental pride – little could touch it.

But even in the bright lights of victory there were dark, grieving shadows. The taking of Langemarck Ridge by Edwin Campion Vaughan's 1/8 Royal Warwicks in August 1917 was successful, although at high cost. He busied himself, with one of the dread chores of the officer post-battle:

My next few days were very busy. I had casualty returns to render, deficiencies to replace, reorganization to carry out and – worst of all – letters to the relatives of fellows who had been killed.

While writing the casualty reports for D company he faltered and finally stopped; instead he sat in his tent and 'drank whisky after whisky as I gazed into a black and empty future'.[89]

For units annihilated by action, such as 3/4 Queen's, which lost all twenty officers who attacked at Zonnebeke in the Ypres salient on 4 October 1917, there was the task of rebuilding, by integrating and training new drafts. Promotions were rapid in the circumstances of massacre. Looking around the wreckage of 21/King's Royal Rifle Corps the CO said, 'Eden, you'll be adjutant'. Anthony Eden protested that he knew nothing about the role. 'Never said you did', came the curt reply; Eden was nineteen. Fortunately the 21/King's orderly-room sergeant, Arnold Rushworth, became Eden's 'right hand man and no small part of my brain as well'. Like Eden, Charles Carrington was adjutant at the tender age of nineteen; 'I'm sure that at just nineteen years old I was a bad adjutant', he wrote to his mother.

What saved the haemorrhaging of subalterns was a re-organization of tactics. In the new manual SS143, *Instructions for the Training of Platoons for Offensive Action*, 1917, riflemen were no longer organized for trench attacks as one long wave but in sections, being led forward by the bomber and rifle sections, with the Lewis gun and rifle grenade sections following close on behind. The platoon commander no longer stood in front of the men, but behind the first line and in front of the second. He now shepherded the men. Platoons became tactical, multi-armed units in their own right, deployed not in rigid lines, but in more or less flexible 'waves'; first went the skirmishing wave, then the second or 'main weight' wave, followed by reinforcements, and lastly a wave of troops to hold the captured territory. The new manual gave junior officers more responsibility and initiative, because they were expected to cooperate with, and provide mutual supporting fire for, neighbouring platoons. If anything, the re-organization strengthened the officer-man bond. With more autonomy, platoons increased their 'family' nature and identity. And because the subaltern decided who did what in the platoon – a matter of life and death – his paternal power was increased.

***

Better far to Pass Away
And welcome Death, if we should meet
And bear him willing company
Lieutenant Richard Dennys, Loyal North Lancashire Regiment

After the business of battle, there was another sort of roll call: the roll call in the mind. Bullet fodder, enervated by trench life, bowed by responsibilities, why did officers carry on fighting? A man's reasons for continuing the war were not necessarily the same as those he gave when going through the door of the enlisting office.

The familiar topography of morale in the Great War runs uphill to Loos in 1915, slips slightly towards the Somme in 1916, plummets to Passchendale in 1917, plunges again to the German offensive of 1918 and staggers flat towards the Armistice. Undoubtedly some who experienced battle had their faith, in God and in the Cause, almost literally blasted out of them. Lieutenant Peter Layard, Suffolk Regiment, wrote in March 1916:

> I rather hate watching these strafes in a way, because you think of all the poor men being broken and killed – and for what? I don't believe even God knows.
>
> Any faith in religion I ever had is most frightfully shaken by things I've seen, and it's incredible that if God could make a 17-inch shell not explode – it seems incredible that he lets them explode ... We kill them [the Germans] because they'd kill us if we didn't and vice versa, and if only we could come to an ordinary agreement – But we can't.[90]

Horrified that his brother had volunteered to come out as a 'Tommy', Second Lieutenant Ernest Routley MC – who had been in 'the Push' at the Somme and three bayonet charges wrote:

> You probably think it's a very fine thing to come out here and be killed. Well, just wait. It isn't being killed that worries you; it's the waiting for it. Just wait until you hear you have got to attack, and then as you are waiting your turn to go over the top, you see your pals get cut down by machine gun fire, and then see if you think it's a glorious thing to die. It would be glorious if you could have a fair fight, but it's absolute

murder here and you don't get a sporting chance. If only I could get home out of it, I would give up my M.C. and commission and all I possess . . . [91]

Ernest Routley was killed on 7 October 1916. Old Etonian Henry Dundas, a lieutenant in the Scots Guards, commented acerbically, on 19 September 1916:

What a wicked thing this damned war is. I should like to have pointed out to me just precisely where all the honour and glory lies. It is curiously elusive.[92]

Influenced by pacifist Bertrand Russell's pamphlet *Justice in War Time*, Lieutenant Arthur Graeme West despaired of the war to the black degree that he contemplated suicide, but forbore because 'I would pain many people'. On leave, he wrote a letter resigning from the Army, but at the last second plucked it out of the postman's hands. In France, in his tent billet at Ville-sur-Ancre, he observed:

Most men fight, if not happily, at any rate patiently, sure of the necessity and usefulness of their work. So did I – once! Now it all looks to me so absurd and brutal that I can only force myself to continue in a kind of dream-state; I hypnotise myself to undergo it. What *good*, what *happiness* can be produced by some of the scenes I have had to witness in the last few days?

Even granting it was necessary to resist Germany by arms at the beginning – and this I have yet most carefully to examine – why go on?

Can no peace be concluded?[93]

He was an atheist, and the shiny, happy pro-war poets in uniform suffered the slings of his loathing:

GOD! How I hate you, you young cheerful men,
Whose pious poetry blossoms on your graves
As soon as you are in them, nurtured up
By the salt of your corruption, and the tears
Of mothers, local vicars, college deans,

And flanked by prefaces and photographs
From all your minor poet friends – the fools –
Who paint their sentimental elegies
Where sure, no angel treads; and living, share
The dead's brief immortality . . . [94]

West was killed near Bapaume, at stand-to on 3 April 1917.

Burgon Bickersteth, 1/Royal Dragoons, also thought that peace should be given a chance, writing on 5 May 1917:[95]

> Personally, as I have felt for months, and feel even more strongly now, we have to a large extent gained the objects for which we went to war, in spite of all the foul inhuman behaviour of our enemy, we should be doing the right thing (and also the most advantageous thing) if we at any rate opened negotiations with a view to peace. I do not think going on fighting is a responsibility which any human shoulders should try to bear.

After being treated for shellshock, Max Plowman asked to be relieved of his commission on grounds of religious objection to the war; he was dismissed by the Army after a court martial. Siegfried Sassoon went beyond private disgust at the war to public protest. On convalescent leave for the shoulder wound he suffered in the second Battle of the Scarpe, Sassoon was encouraged by the pacifists who fluttered around Lady Ottoline Morrell's Garsington Manor to make a Declaration against the War. Published in *The Times* on 31 July 1917 the Declaration stated:

> I am making this statement as an act of wilful defiance of military authority, because I believe the War is being deliberately prolonged by those who have the power to end it. I am a soldier, convinced that I am acting on behalf of soldiers. I believe that this War, on which I entered as a war of defence and liberation, has now become a war of aggression and conquest. I believe that the purpose for which I and my fellow soldiers entered upon this war should have been so clearly stated as to have made it impossible to change them, and that, had this been done, the objects which actuated us would now be attainable by negotiation. I have seen and endured the sufferings of the troops,

and I can no longer be a party to prolong these sufferings for ends which I believe to be evil and unjust. I am not protesting against the conduct of the war, but against the political errors and insincerities for which the fighting men are being sacrificed. On behalf of those who are suffering now I make this protest against the deception which is being practised on them; also I believe that I may help to destroy the callous complacency with which the majority of those at home regard the continuance of agonies which they do not share and which they have not sufficient imagination to realize.

The Declaration did not spark an outbreak of peace; Sassoon's conviction that he was speaking on behalf of the soldiery was a solipsism. As his fellow Welch Fusilier, Dr Dunn remarked:

Sassoon gave a moral flavour to a gibe everywhere current at the front for a couple of years, that a lot of individuals in cushy jobs don't care how long the war lasts ... But I have not heard any stop the war talk among front-line troops.[96]

The Army treated Sassoon lightly; his friend and fellow Welch Fusilier Robert Graves pulled strings and persuaded the authorities to have Sassoon medically boarded, with the result that in July 1917 Sassoon was sent to Craiglockhart War Hospital, Edinburgh, officially suffering from 'shellshock'.

Voices of protest and despair like Plowman's, Sassoon's and West's were minority voices in messes and HQs. West glumly recognized this himself when an officer said 'half-ashamedly' that he had come to the conclusion that the war was very silly and everyone should go home. 'Nobody took any notice of what he said', recorded West, 'or else treated it laughingly.' Even in the bleakest period of the war between Passchendaele and the Spring Offensive, an analysis of soldiers' letters home undertaken by jittery top brass showed the split between the doomsayers and the optimists to be equal in Second Army; elsewhere morale was solid.[97] The topography of soldiers' morale in the Great War cannot be charted precisely, because the spirit of battalions and individuals was rarely constant, and went up and down, sometimes by the day. Young officers usually had the psychological buoyancy of cork, and a good meal after a bad shelling would be enough to bring them floating back to the surface. A period out of the line, a leave, a successful engagement, a promotion could salvage even the leaden hearted from an ocean of depression. Given the command of a company in August 1917, Henry Dundas, who a year before had written off the war as 'wicked', was 'more pleased than I can say'.[98] The ensuing 'biffs' were 'extraordinarily good'. Like many a company commander coming out of battle, he thought 'We really are magnificent'. Sassoon himself returned to the Western Front in July 1918, a self-confessed 'Happy Warrior'. Lieutenant Vivian de Sola Pinto, who served under Captain Sassoon, was struck by 'the curious paradox that the author of *Counter-Attack*, which had just been published, that volume full of bitter indignation at the hideous cruelty of modern warfare, should also be a first-rate soldier and a most aggressive company commander.' The 'pacifist' Sassoon was a dedicated believer in the old Royal Welch code of demonstrating superiority over the Hun by spunky patrolling of No-Man's Land.

The morale of the British soldiery never imploded, neither did it slide down as steeply as often supposed. That said, by 1917 exaltation had been largely replaced by weariness. Captain Desmond Allhusen, 8/King's Royal Rifle Corps, wrote about the year 1917, the year of Passchendaele:

> The future seemed to be an endless vista of battles, each worse than the last. We still felt that one day we would win, but had stopped saying so. The war was the only real and permanent thing, thriving and increasing in a world that was going to ruin. All our discussions ended by complete agreement on one point: that whatever might be the end for nations, our destinies were clear enough. We would all be hit, and if we recovered we would return and be hit again, and so on till we were either dead or permanently disabled. The ideal was to lose a leg as soon as possible.
>
> Perhaps we were unduly pessimistic, as two or three out of the twenty-five officers did survive uninjured to the end of the war. At that time it seemed impossible to believe that anybody could survive that long.[99]

So why did the British officer, almost to a man, 'stick it'?

Captain Claude Templar had the Saxon love of battle that dimmed yet never entirely died during the Great War, despite the slogs of the Somme and Passchendale. A Regular with the Gloucestershire Regiment, Templar was wounded and taken prisoner in December 1914. After escaping from Germany in 1917, he headed straight back to battle. A warrior standing in the shield wall at Maldon would have understood the sentiments in this letter of Templar's:

> When I was locked up in Germany I used to pray for this moment; I used to dream of the romance of war, its wild strange poetry crept into my soul; I used to think that the glory of going back to the beautiful adventure was worth any price. And now it's all come true, just like things happen in fairy tales. I go into my dream country like a baby, eyes wide with wonder, ears strained to catch every note of the magic music I hear there. In my dream country is a piper like Hamelin's piper and I follow him. I follow into his cavern a spell-bound child, and I come out at the other end a warrior fully armed, longing for the day that my mettle shall be proved. And often I fail and then I must cross over to the dream country and I must drink romance from the music of the magic piper. And when I come out of the cavern again perhaps this time *I win*. The romance of war and love. That is what the music tells me. And I resolve to be a worthy warrior. To fight to the finish, to love to the finish, to sacrifice everything but never honour. And to do all this with no hope of payment, but as a volunteer, just for the beautiful poetry of it all.[100]

Templar was killed on 4 June 1917.

The thrill of war was not lost on the bespectacled Lieutenant Paul Jones, who had slowly but grittily worked his way from the ASC to the Tank Corps. He wrote on 27 July 1917:

> *P.S.*–Have you ever reflected on the fact that, despite the horrors of the war, it is at least a big thing? I mean to say that in it one is brought face to face with realities. The follies, selfishness, luxury and general pettiness of the vile commercial sort of existence led by nine-tenths of the people of the world in peace-time are replaced in war by a savagery that is at least more honest and outspoken. Look at it this way: in

peace-time one just lives one's own little life, engaged in trivialities, worrying about one's own comfort, about money matters, and all that sort of thing – just living for one's own self. What a sordid life it is! In war, on the other hand, even if you do get killed you only anticipate the inevitable by a few years in any case, and you have the satisfaction of knowing that you have 'pegged out' in the attempt to help your country. You have, in fact, realised an ideal, which, as far as I can see, you very rarely do in ordinary life. The reason is that ordinary life runs on a commercial and selfish basis; if you want to 'get on,' as the saying is, you can't keep your hands clean.

Personally, I often rejoice that the War has come my way. It has made me realise what a petty thing life is. I think that the War has given to everyone a chance to 'get out of himself,' as I might say. Of course, the other side of the picture is bound to occur to the imagination. But there! I have never been one to take the more melancholy point of view when there's a silver lining in the cloud.

Certainly, speaking for myself, I can say that I have never in all my life experienced such a wild exhilaration as on the commencement of a big stunt, like the last April one for example. The excitement for the last half-hour or so before it is like nothing on earth. The only thing that compares with it are the few minutes before the start of a big school match. Well, cheer-oh![101]

Guy Chapman admitted to 'shrivelling fear' but at the same time being fascinated by war:

Once you have lain in her arms you can admit no other mistress. You may loathe, you may execrate, but you cannot deny her. No lover can offer you defter caresses, more exquisite tortures, such breaking delights. No wine gives fiercer intoxication, no drug more vivid exaltation.[102]

For Bernard Adams, the 'deadly fascination' of war made war endurable: 'Throwing a bomb, firing a Lewis gun, all these things were pleasant.' Injury, and eight months at the front, did nothing to dent Adams' belief in the rightness of the war. He steadfastly maintained we 'are fighting for just motives, and have already baulked injustice'. An old boy of Malvern College in the cockpit of England that was

Worcestershire, Adams was killed leading his men into battle in February 1917.

Lieutenant Hugh Butterworth also enjoyed the thrill of war:

> They all [the men] were right over the parapet firing like blazes, my humble self standing half on the parapet and half on the parados with a revolver in one hand and rifle near the other and a cigarette going well, using the most unquotable language. Do you know that really was a good moment. I can't pretend to like bombardments, nor war generally, but that really was a moment when one 'touched top' (as opposed to 'touching bottom'), but you'll feel that it was an interesting moment in one's life. I felt absolutely as cool as ice during that part, one was so worked up that one felt that one could stick anything out.[103]

In his last letter home, written as he sheltered with his men in the cellar of a forester's cottage in northern France, Lieutenant Wilfred Owen wrote: 'It's a great life, you would not be visited by a band of friends half so fine as surround me here.' He had already 'fought like an angel' in machine-gunning a German position. Another who enjoyed the companionship and adrenaline of combat was Harold Macmillan; 'it cannot be denied that to the individual war may and does bring an extraordinary thrill – a sense of comradeship – sense of teamship and a sense of triumph.' Decades after the war he harboured 'a certain contempt' for those in England who had voluntarily missed their chance to serve.[104]

Patriotism remained a constant thread in the reasons why to fight and, if need be, to die. A former university lecturer, Captain Bill Bland, 22/The Manchester Regiment (7th Manchester Pals), wrote to his wife:

> Think of the *cause*, the cause. It is England, England, England, always and all the time . . . I am here and I shall either survive or not survive. In the meantime, I have never been trulier happier.
>
> P.S. Hardship be damned! It's all a long blaze of glory.[105]

Two weeks later he was killed on the first day of the Somme.

Christian Carver was another ardent patriot. 'I always feel', he penned, 'that I am fighting for England, English fields, lanes, trees, English atmospheres, and good days in England – and all that is synonymous for liberty.' Elevated from the ranks of the Honourable Artillery Company to a commission ('I was one of the proudest men in the world'), Alfred Pollard was 'prepared to strain every nerve to attain' a British victory. He did not lie; the former pupil of Merchant Taylors' won, successively, the Distinguished Conduct Medal, the Military Cross and Victoria Cross.[106]

On the wintry Somme, Lieutenant Palmes exclaimed to his fellow officers, 'It's better to face up to it, and be ready to defend your life and your heritage rather than lie down and bleat about peace while someone walks roughshod over you.' Sidney Rogerson wrote later that 'Palmes was expressing very succinctly sentiments with which we all agreed'.[107] Subaltern Percy Boswell 8/King's Own Yorkshire Light Infantry concurred; in his last letter home, on 30 June 1916, he wrote that if he was killed on the morrow 'I shall rest content with the knowledge that I have done my duty – and one can't do more.'

A filip for patriotism came from German barbarism. After the sinking of the *Lusitania*, Douglas Gillespie exclaimed to his parents, 'It's no use protesting against them now, except with the bayonet.'[108] Despite an admiration for the German as a soldier, British troops were shocked to the moral core by the Germans' scorched-earth retreat to the Hindenburg Line, in an operation named after the vituperative dwarf Alberich in Wagner's *Der Ring der Nibelungen* operatic cycle. Edward Spears recalled:

> It was as if Satan had poured destruction out of a gigantic watering-can, carelessly spraying some parts of the land more than others ... Everywhere in these ruined villages women's clothing lay about, underwear so arranged as to convey an indecent suggestion, or fouled in the most revolting way.[109]

A sign left for British troops read: 'Don't be angry. Only wonder.' They did wonder, and when they had wondered about the mass shootings of Belgian citizens, the sinking of the *Lusitania*, poison gas,

Operation Alberich, they became braced in their desire and belief that Britain *must* win. A hatred of the 'Hun' crept into the soul that had not existed in August 1914. Second Lieutenant Norman Taylor, 1/Surrey Rifles wrote:

> I am now beginning to realise the genuine hatred of Germans one gets after a year or so of this, which one cannot understand when one first comes out. You have no idea what a subtle thrill there is on a good moonlight night, a Hun working party perhaps faintly silhouetted and opening a sudden burst of fire with a gun on them.[110]

Lieutenant Archibald Don, a sympathizer of the left-wing Union for Democratic Control and no jingo, believed: 'It is just because the beating of the Germans is essential to the cause of humanity that the war is bearable and quite worth it.'[111] Captain Henry Dillon, a Regular, was filled with absolute rage for the Kaiser and his doings:

> I don't care one farthing as far as I am concerned, but the whole thing is an outrage on civilisation. The whole of this beautiful country devastated. Broken houses, broken bodies, blood, filth, and ruin everywhere. Can any unending everlasting Hell fire for the Kaiser, his son, and the party who caused this war repair the broken bodies and worse broken hearts which are being made? Being made this very minute within a few hundred yards of where I am sitting.[112]

A better world was the dream that sustained Lieutenant Edward Chapman, 20/Royal Fusiliers in February 1917:

> But I think it will be better after the war than it ever was before. We must have learned a wisdom that nothing else could have taught us. And when we get home again we shall have the happiness of men who have seen terrible things, who have been in hell, and have come back to a blessed haven of peace. Different from the old careless happiness, but more permanent.[113]

Dull resignation to the war was the lot of many officers in 1917, only to be lifted with the return of mobile warfare in Summer 1918. Stuart

Cloete asked: 'What upheld us? Pride in our regiments, and stubborn refusal to acknowledge we were beat.'[114] Alec Waugh believed: 'There was the feeling that we owed it "to the fallen" to continue fighting until victory was won.'[115] Looking back at the war, Eden thought that the 'stubborn refusal' was helped by a combination of factors, including an 'unshakeable conviction' in final victory and the 'evidence we saw of enemy losses'. Nothing breeds success like success. An officer could not quit, not just because of the personal fear of punishment, but because of the shame it would bring, to the regiment, to his family, to his school. As Captain Stanhope said in *Journey's End*, in a speech that spoke for a regiment of officers: 'Just go on sticking it ... it's the only thing a decent man can do.'[116]

For his part, Edwin Venning thought that officers were happily too busy to think: 'The "Why?" and the "What is it all about" trouble only the few.'[117] One of the 'few' was Victor Richardson, who wrote to Vera Brittain:

I often wonder why we are all here. Mainly I think, as far as I am concerned, to prevent the repetition in England of what happened in Belgium in August 1914. Still more perhaps because one's friends are here. Perhaps too, heroism in the abstract has a share in it. But the outlook of 90 per cent of the British Expeditionary Force is summed up in the words of two songs ...
'We're here because [...]
We're here'
... The second is ... 'I'm here and you're here/So what do we care'.[118]

Religion continued to play its hidden role in the mental springs of the officer. In the field at Guillemont on the Somme on 4 September 1916, Captain Thomas Kettle, 9/Royal Dublin Fusiliers, wrote 'To my daughter Betty, the Gift of God ':

In wiser days, my darling rosebud, blown
To beauty proud as was your mother's prime,
In that desired, delayed, incredible time,
You'll ask why I abandoned you, my own,
And the dear heart that was your baby throne,

To dice with death! And, oh! they'll give you rhyme
And reason: some will call the thing sublime,
And some decry it in a knowing tone.
So here, while the mad guns curse overhead,
And tired men sigh, with mud for couch and floor,
Know that we fools, now with the foolish dead,
Died not for flag, nor King, nor Emperor,
But for a dream, born in a herdsman's shed,
And for the secret Scripture of the poor.[119]

Above and beyond all these reasons, there was one reason why the officer did not quit. Kettle had put the finger on it himself in the letter to his brother the day before he died: 'I have chosen to stay with my comrades.' The chivalric, paternal code of the officer was hard to escape. One had to fulfil the duty of care. Wilfred Owen and Siegfried Sassoon had tried to escape, but could not and had both willingly returned to front line service. In Sassoon's words:

Love drove me to rebel.
Love drives me back to grope with them through hell . . . [120]

Both Siegfried Sassoon and Wilfred Owen won the Military Cross (MC), the gallantry award instituted in 1914 for warrant officers and commissioned officers below the rank of major. There were more rewards for courage available to officers; the Distinguished Service Order (DSO), instituted in 1886, could be awarded for either acts of bravery or acts of committed service in the backroom, making it difficult to know whether the bearer was a pen-pusher or bayonet-pusher. The Victoria Cross was open to all ranks for the highest deeds of valour, as was the lowest award, a Mention in Dispatches. Wound stripes, again given to all ranks, were not strictly awarded for bravery, but they did at least show one had been in action. Harold Macmillan wore his proudly on his cuff.

For MCs and DSOs there was a set quota on the Western Front; in mid 1917 it was 500 MCs per month and 200 DSOs. Who got a medal, and for what, was a sore tooth of frustration. Officers in Regular regiments were convinced that they did not get their fair share. Lieutenant Charles Nye, 1/Royal Inniskilling Fusiliers, wrote:

> I'm glad I'm with a regular regiment. You don't know what it means in action. You can always depend on your men standing by you whatever happens. Although there are only about one fifth of the decorations given as are given to the new lot. What regulars do as a matter of course the others think worth a military cross.[121]

On joining the Royal Welch Fusiliers Robert Graves was bluntly told not to expect a medal.

All company commanders, be they Regular, Territorial or Kitchener's Army, were unlikely to win an MC because, as with all gallantry medals, the heroic deed had to be witnessed by a superior officer. Which was difficult when one's superior was, in all probability, sitting in Battalion or Division HQ on the end of the phone and not stumbling alongside through No-Man's Land. 'A Company Commander's job', lamented Lionel Crouch, 'is the worst in creation. He is responsible for everything and gets all the kicks if things go wrong, but he never has a chance of a "mention" [in dispatches] much less of a medal.'

Bernard Pitt, Border Regiment, put his lack of a medal down to pure ill fortune:

> I have so far escaped injury, and have seen very heavy fighting in different parts of the line. I was recommended for the Military Cross, but my usual bad luck intervened to relegate me to 'mentioned in dispatches' only.[122]

In truth, the dishing out of medals did follow one fast rule: a successful 'show' was more likely to generate a ribbon to sew proudly on the tunic than a shambles. Some officers almost single-handedly created 'a good show', and no one grudged them their gong. Lieutenant J.V. Holland of The Leinster Regiment on leaving the Base Camp at Etaples told his comrade Francis Hitchcock: 'I am going to get one of two things, a Victoria Cross or a Wooden Cross.' It was no idle boast: He got glory and not death, winning the regiment's first VC in the war, by leading half a platoon through a 'friendly barrage' and clearing a large part of Guillemont village, capturing fifty prisoners and killing scores more. In the phrase of the *London Gazette*, Holland 'undoubtedly broke the spirit of the enemy'.[123]

Second Lieutenant Henry Ogle, Royal Lancaster Regiment, received his MC from the King in person at Buckingham Palace:

> We were marshalled in the correct order for the ceremony and slowly moved along the corridors which led directly to the top, or dais, end of the big room. As we moved forward we could see King George V and Queen Mary on the dais, I think under a canopy but I was too scared to observe closely. We had to march in turn to the steps in the middle front of the dais, turn left, ascend the steps and bow. Then His Majesty pinned the decorations to our tunics, said a few words and shook hands. Then, after another bow, we backed down the steps, turned right and marched off. While we marched to the dais there was just time for an officer of the Royal Household to read the citation. Upon this the King had to base his few words. Mine read as follows:

> 'Second Lieutenant Henry Ogle, Royal Lancaster Regiment.
> He carried out numerous patrols with his party of Scouts, bringing back most valuable information. It was mainly due to his daring and able reconnaissance in a locality infested with enemy snipers and machine-guns that it was possible to establish a line on the left centre of the brigade.'

> The King said, 'You have worked hard for us under dangerous conditions. Well done.'
> After leaving the Throne Room, in which we were acutely conscious of a seated assembly of distinguished looking people, we turned right to a room where liveried attendants stood at a long table covered with little leather cases of different kinds. One of these men *snatched* my Military Cross, *clapped* it into a purple case which he *thrust* into my hand, and then immediately turned to snatch the next.[124]

Ogle wrote in his memoir of the war that he was disappointed to see that the Cross had not been engraved with his name, rank and regiment, like his other medals. 'And so, like a proper soldier, I end this narrative with a grouse.'

The lack of a medal spoilt the Armistice in 1918 for H.E.L. Mellersh, on leave in London. As the crowds celebrated around him in Whitehall he felt dissatisfied:

> I should have liked to have done a bit more since retiring from the March retreat; I should have liked to have won that MC. A munitions girl passed me; and she called 'What's the matter? – cheer up!!' Was I looking as gloomy as that?[125]

There were unofficial awards that did something to quicken the proud heart. At Third Ypres, Alexander Stewart did such a grand job leading the stretcher bearers, that they went to the Adjutant to praise him. Thereafter the attitude of the older majors and captains in the battalion softened towards him. 'Their speech lost a curious harsh element.' He had respect. He had become 'one of us'.

Many brave officers, their deeds unknown or the medal quota used up, received only the cross of wood. Lieutenant Cyril Winterbottom 1/5 Gloucestershire Regiment, thought this cross the finest cross of all. In the trenches at Hebuterne, in the bloody July of 1916, he wrote:

> Rest you content, more honourable far
> Than all the Orders is the cross of Wood,
> The symbol of self-sacrifice that stood
> Bearing the God whose brethren you are.[126]

VII

It's a Long Way to Tickle Mary: Rest and Leave

Release

A leaping wind from England,
  The skies without a stain,
Clean cut against the morning
  Slim poplars after rain,
The foolish noise of sparrows
  And starlings in a wood –
After the grime of battle
  We know that these are good.

Death whining down from heaven,
  Death roaring from the ground,
Death stinking in the nostril,
  Death shrill in every sound,
Doubting we charged and conquered –
  Hopeless we struck and stood;
Now when the fight is ended
  We know that it was good.

We that have seen the strongest
  Cry like a beaten child,
The sanest eyes unholy,
  The cleanest hands defiled,
We that have known the heart-blood
  Less than the lees of wine,
We that have seen men broken,
  We know that man is divine.

Lieutenant W.N. Hodgson
(Composed While Marching to Rest-Camp After Severe Fighting at Loos)

Coming out of the line, it was the pleasure of small things that were looked forward to. 'I think only those who have been in the front line', Second Lieutenant Edward Chapman informed his family in winter 1917, 'can realize how delightful ordinary things are. What a blessed thing sleep is; the relief of *not* being shelled. And how nice it is to have clean hands and wrists.'

Douglas Gillespie was taken with the change in smells, on leaving the trenches:

> I always like walking on a summer night, and there's a peculiar pleasure in it when you are leaving the trenches. The rain had cleared off, and the moon was full. We fell in quietly on a road just behind the trench, as soon as the sentries had been relieved, and moved off by a track through the deserted fields. The first few hundred yards are always a little anxious, for there is a chance that a star-shell or search-light will discover you, or that the clink of rifles or shuffle of feet will be heard. But all went well, and we soon lost sight of the braziers and line of twinkling lights, which is all you see of the breastworks from behind at night. It was very still and quiet, with a smell of summer in the air, a change from the trenches, which often smell of chloride of lime, if they do not smell of something worse, and the crack of the rifles sounded fainter and fainter behind us, while, at long intervals, a bullet would come lisping past. Presently we reached a road, still showing white, in spite of the weeds invading it from either side, and followed it for a mile or more, parallel to the firing line, with star-shells lighting up the level ground and rows of poppies in the distance.[1]

Billets for those 'resting' from frontline service were arranged by the billeting officer or NCO, in liaison with the French. What everyone wanted, from humblest New Army private to the most aristocratic Guards colonel, were domestic billets in a village with an estaminet, with its on-tap refreshments, and the sights and sounds of civilian life. And that was the problem. Often a battalion found itself in competition with another, as Lieutenant Roe discovered:

> We arrived in the pouring rain after dark one evening. Our billeting officer pointed to a farm area and pointed out where we were to spend the night, only to be told that some other unit had got there first. Our

claim having been jumped, there was no other sheltered accommodation available ... so we just marched into an orchard.[2]

A hard-nosed billeting official was a treasure, someone who went ahead, bargained with the locals, marking the deal with a chalk mark on the door – 'four officers and eight servants', 'two platoons A.Coy.'– so as each tired platoon arrived it wheeled mechanically to the right place. The job of billeting officer was temporary, and allocated on the Buggins Turn principle; if one lasted long enough, one would likely get a go. Eden, billeting officer for the battalion when it went to Francières on the Somme, enjoyed cycling around in the sun with the local gendarme allotting the accommodation, but considered it 'an invidious exercise which was likely to earn me some criticism when the battalion arrived'.[3]

The army adage of horses first, men second, officers third was nowhere more true than in billeting. Only when the horses were fed and watered, the men were settled, did officers turn to their own accommodation. Officers slept in quarters separately from the men, and the more senior the officer the better the billets he was likely to be allocated. There was fierce competition from the locals to house officers, for the simple reason that the going rate for accommodating an officer per night was five francs; for a ranker it was one franc. The superior boarding-rate notwithstanding domestic billets for officers were, in the word of John Hay Beith, best characterized as 'promiscuous'.[4] They were anything and everything. In his first week in France, Beith slept in 'chateaux, convents, farm-houses and under the open sky'. Second Lieutenant Bernard Strauss was another temporary castle-dweller:

> We are out of the trenches now for a rest in a deserted chateau; oh! the joy of being warmly within four walls again, even if Monsieur Le Comte, who I believe was a German, has not left behind him any of the appendages of civilized life: still there are fires, and good food to be consumed – and a real lavatory with a real plug.[5]

Francis Hitchcock, in some top hole billets in a deserted – but still intact – house on the Poperinge road, found 200 bottles of good red wine in the cellar.[6] As if to prove the promiscuity of billets, he was later billeted in dug-outs cut in the ramparts by the Menin gate in ruined Ypres, as was Harold Macmillan. In Corbie, Sassoon was also at the bottom end of the billeting-spectrum, 'an airless cupboard over a greengrocer's shop ... The room reeked of onions and made no pretence of having a window.'[7] Douie slept in a corner of the cold school house at Frechencourt, where a 'biscuit tin, heaped with charcoal, improved the outlook, if not the atmosphere'.

Even the dreamed-of, hoped-for estaminet could be less than impressive, as Donald Kenworthy noted in his daily diary:

> We only have one room, which has to hold four officers and three servants, and all the cooking has to be done on the stove. We have to sleep on the floor of course, but are lucky enough to have mattresses of sorts.[8]

Whatever an officer's longing, the billet he was likely to draw in the first years of the war, especially in Flanders, was one of the peasant farms that studded the landscape every hundred yards or so. 'We are in the usual farm', wrote Douglas Gillespie,

> with the usual midden in the middle of the court-yard ; there is a big dog there too, chained to his barrel, who is having the feast of his life on scraps of bully beef. All these French farms have a wheel outside, in which the dog runs round and round, pumping water or working a hand-mill. I could never make out how the wheel worked at first, for it seems to be a dog's holiday just now.[9]

The single-storey, red-brick peasant farms of Flanders, with their square courtyards and middens would become one of the permanent fixtures of the officer's mind, along with dining by candlelight in a dug-out, dead and bloated horses, pounding along Roman straight *pavé*, and artillery wheel to wheel. Some were struck too by the echoes of history. The British had been in Flanders before; discarded Brown Besses from Wellington's Waterloo campaign were sometimes unearthed by trenching parties. And before the Iron Duke, Corporal John had ridden the land. Sitting in his farm billet, Charles Douie wondered whether during Marlborough's campaign in Flanders 'in this very farm-house had sheltered infantry soldiers as tired and as soaked as my little party'.[10]

The Other Ranks would be accommodated in the hay barn, the officers in a room in the house from which the children had been shooed. Joseph Lee versed the prevailing view of the welcome, if primitive, farm billet:

> A roof that hardly holds the rain;
> Walls shaking to the hurricane;
> Great doors upon their hinges creaking;
> Great rats upon the rafters squeaking –
> A midden in the courtyard reeking –
> Yet oft I've sheltered, snug and warm,
> Within that friendly old French farm!

A subaltern in 10/King's Royal Rifle Corps, and a former journalist, Lee was a poet, incidentally, who got *more* optimistic, more martial-minded as the war wended its way. He was captured near Cambrai in 1917, the year his 'Our British Dead' appeared in the *Spectator*. 'Here do we lie, dead but not discontent;/That which we found to do has had accomplishment', he versed.[11]

Relations with the French owners of billets were sometimes less than *cordiale* and, Douie thought, worsened as the war wore on. Hitchcock was convinced that the Flemish peasantry 'robbed us right and left',[12] while Geoffrey Thurlow's habit of frequent bathing irritated his French landlady; 'the French don't understand the desire to wash'. The billeting money was never enough. The men traipsed down the crops. Or milked the cows. Second Lieutenant Douglas Gillespie considered that the first job he did in France that could not be done by an NCO was arguing in French with the farmer over where his men were to sleep. On the other hand, the ability of a well-educated British officer to *parler Français* could perplex his own men, as Guy Chapman found:

> Our relief is marching in; and we are despatched by platoons to an unknown village some six miles away. There is some dispute over the pronunciation of its name. The machine-gun officer, directing the

sergeant of the reserve teams told him to go to 'oom-bare-con'. The
sergeant slapped the butt of his rifle; but, a hundred yards further on,
asked in a puzzled voice: 'Where did he say?' Whereupon from the
back of the section rose the irreverent voice of Pte. Archbold. 'He
said Oom-bare-con; but you, poor ignorant perisher, probably call it
Humbercamps.'[13]

For the British officer in a domestic billet a particular danger lurked
in the apron-clad female owner, keen on selling either her or her
daughter's flesh for francs. In a dump of miners' cottages at Herson,
Guy Chapman recalled that: 'The company was billeted in houses
presided over by grim slatterns of repellent aspect and of amorous
nature. The operation of drying one's body was fraught with embarrassment.'[14] At Arraines-sur-Somme, Edwin Campion Vaughan was
horrified when at his hotel billet a stout figure in a black torn skirt,
black bodice and red shoes appeared, and said 'I loff yoo', with evil-
smelling breath and horrid leer. 'This was madame, the keeper of the
hotel.'

Of course, such a flesh for franc arrangement could suit both ways.

Amidst all the difficulties, there were touching scenes. Billeted in
an estaminet at Agenvilliers, Graham Greenwell found the owners 'a
very cheery lot, who had some pretty little kids, who filled our laps
with tame rabbits during our dejeuner'. Children always cheered one
up; Vaughan's madame was assisted by two little girls, sisters, with
whom Vaughan 'exchanged hearts'.

Arthur Graeme West cared not a jot about the salubriousness of
his accommodation, or the niceness of his hosts. All he wanted was
to be out of the reach of the enemy. He wrote with feeling: 'For
the moment, thank God, we are back resting, and the certain
knowledge that I shan't be killed anyhow for a day or two is most
invigorating.'[15]

Unfortunately, billets were not always safe and certain sanctuary.
Billeted in a deserted house in Albert, Charles Douie stood at night
at his bedroom window 'watching the great shells bursting in the
square and illuminating in a fitful and unreal light the ruins of this
desolate and twilight city'.[16] As the war wore on, billets came more

and more to be purpose built camps, away from pleasing French domesticity, and close to the front line. On the way to rest camp at La Briqueterie – five miles from the front line – Sidney Rogerson was guided to his tent by an NCO who pointed out another tent in passing:

> 'That was your tent this afternoon, sir' he told me, 'but about two hours ago Jerry dropped an eight-inch shell there and "napoo-ed" it.'

A 'disquieting feature in a rest camp', reflected Rogerson, but he was too tired to care.[17] Robert Mackay, for his part, was shelled in Toronto camp, a whole eight miles behind the Ypres frontline. The Germans visited other horrors on the billeted; in reserve at Murrumbidgee camp, La Clytte, Guy Chapman's 13/Royal Fusiliers stared white-faced as a huge formation of German planes approached. To everyone's relief the Hun bombers dropped not bombs but 'showers of leaflets in praise of peace'.[18] The canvas 'Armstrong' huts on these mass camps became dismally familiar to both officers and men alike. On the Somme in the winter of 1916–17 Lieutenant Brian Lawrence found:

> Our huts had earth floors and were very cold and draughty, and our beds were made for us by the pioneers, out of packing cases and rabbit wire. Our chief trouble was to keep warm, as we could get only wet wood to burn, and braziers gave off such fearful fumes, it was a case of being cold in fresh air or warm in smoke and coke fumes.[19]

Soon after, Lawrence was billeted at Maurepas in the new corrugated-iron huts with a half-round roof designed by Lieutenant-Colonel Frank Nissen. Lawrence was not impressed, however, and longed to be in his snug dug-out in the line at St Pierre Vaast.[20] Clement Symons, Gloucestershire Regiment, was similarly under-whelmed by a mass pre-fab camp:

> Talk about 'rest' camp – it's ghastly – one small village which itself is never at rest (dirt and fleas) and about 6,000 men billeted there, the H_2O is bad of course and we have gone back to the ordinary Codford

Cheltenham-Sutton-Vevey-Longridge-Deverill training. Thank goodness we are going back to the trenches.[21]

A battalion's losses could be poignantly registered in its lessening accommodation needs; before marching up the line to Hooge in August 1915, Francis Hitchcock's company had needed ten huts at Vlametinghe Wood camp; returning from the line to the same camp a fortnight later they needed five.[22]

Most officers, though, thought any billet was better than a trench, a sentiment caught by Charles Scott-Moncrieff's verses:

We're in billets again, and to-night, if you please,
I shall strap myself up in a Wolseley valise.
What's that, boy? Your boots give you infinite pain?
You can chuck them away : we're in billets again.
We're in billets again now and, barring alarms,
There'll be no occasion for standing to arms,
And you'll find if you'd many night-watches to keep
That the hour before daylight's the best hour for sleep.
We're feasting on chocolate, cake, currant buns,
To a faint German-band obbligato of guns,
For I've noticed, wherever the regiment may go,
That we always end up pretty close to the foe.
But we're safe out of reach of trench mortars and snipers ...

... Here's a health to our host, Isidore Deschildre,
Himself and his wife and their plentiful childer,
And the brave aboyeur who bays our return ;
More power to his paws when he treads by the churn !
You may speak of the Ritz or the Curzon (Mayfair)
And maintain that they keep you in luxury there:
If you've lain for six weeks on a water-logged plain,
Here's the acme of comfort, in billets again.[23]

Like or loathe billets, they offered the opportunity for getting clean.

For all men coming out of the trenches, cleanliness was a priority, but for the officer who had never experienced perpetual black under his fingernails, who had never felt crabby little things walking on his flesh, washing did more than wipe away the mud, parasites and memories of trench-time: it restored his former self. Sidney Rogerson recalled: 'What joy it was to lather and feel the razor shearing off this unwelcome growth!' He then washed in a canvas bucket of water. 'Spiritually and in appearance I was a different being.'[24]

Baths could be such a joy they would merit a diary entry of their own. 'Had a bath in Albert, an event always worth chronicling!' Lieutenant Mackay wrote on 11 January 1917. Donald Kenworthy decided a bath was just the right way to celebrate his twenty-fifth: 'My birthday', he entered on 4 February 1915. 'Had a much wanted bath to celebrate.'

An officer usually bathed solitarily in a cubicle in the Divisional Bath House, lowering his body into a canvas contraption, narrow tank or wooden tub, hurricane lamps throwing some brief light through the steam-laden twilight. In the room next door his platoon, whooping half in anguish, half in pleasure, climbed into boiling communal vats; the Bath House orderlies, meanwhile, steam-cleaned everyone's uniform in a fruitless effort at de-lousing and took away underwear and shirts for washing. There were other places to bath. An officer might steal away to a hotel in Amiens, Bethune, or Poperinge if in the Ypres Salient. At a Field Ambulance, Graham Greenwell was delighted to find 'a good old English long bath' which he promptly availed himself of, his pleasure not at all spoilt by a 'whacking big shrapnel shell burst just over the house'.[25] Former medical student Hugh Munro managed to take 'a hip bath' in, of all improbable places, a convent; the nuns refused to charge him, but he left four francs as 'conscience money'. Sometimes nature provided best. Coming off the dust-ridden, sweating battlefield of the Somme, Richard Talbot Kelly decided that he could not wait for the Bath House and plunged into the river:

> The joy of endless water, clean, clear, fresh water in which we could lie and bathe and at the same time enjoy quietness and peace was a miraculous thing.[26]

Arriving in billets, the men were fed first. Officers being 'privileged beings' had to wait for their servants to unpack. This reduced the time available for the meal, so it usually had to be cold fare.[27]

The officer's mess when out of the trenches came in as wide a variety as the officer's billet. Usually in France and Flanders officers ate in a company mess, either because there was no suitably sized room for the traditional battalion mess, or simply because the battalion was so far flung over the landscape. At Citadel Camp, 'a dreary collection of bell-tents pitched insecurely on the hillside near the one-time village of Fricourt', Sidney Rogerson's B company mess was a tent that 'filled with a maximum of smoke for a minimum of warmth', while Francis Hitchcock was bemused by a company mess in a summer-house on top of the ramparts at Ypres, and Brian Lawrence ended up in a greenhouse.[28] This was doubtless irksome for a regiment like the Grenadier Guards, which sought to uphold the regimental tradition of a decent mess wherever and whenever. He would have doubtless wished to swap with Charles Douie's altogether more humble 1/Dorsets, whose mess at Frenchencourt was fit for a Grenadier: it was the chateau. 'These quarters were considered luxurious', recalled Douie, 'by those who had long been accustomed to regard themselves as fortunate if they found so much as the bar of an estaminet for mess purposes in the villages in vicinity of the line.'[29] Of the fourteen officers who sat down that day in 1916 Douie estimated nearly one half would give their lives, 'a body of men whose memory I shall honour so long as life lasts'. His enduring memory of messing on the Western Front was 'the line of merry faces in the glare of candles'.

The perennial problem of messing was lack of furniture, this having usually been removed by the owner for safe-keeping. In Peronne, Second Lieutenant Edwin Campion Vaughan of the Royal Warwickshires took the time-honoured soldier's solution:

Returned at 4.p.m. for tea, after which Radcliffe and I went round scrounging. We went through dozens of houses, climbing over roofs and knocking through walls, and ended up with lots of nice cutlery, salt cellars, glasses, etc. Our wallpaper was badly faded, so from another house I peeled curtains for our glassless windows and some lamps and tablecloths, so that by evening, with our Harrison Fisher girls framed upon the walls, we had a very cosy mess.[30]

A cosy company mess, like a cosy company billet, could be spoilt by the attentions of the owner. From Agenville, Graham Greenwell wrote to his mother:

> The vile old beast from whom we rent our Mess is a thoroughly Zola-like character with a bottle of rum always under his arm: I call him Dubusc. He provokes the most horrible scenes, wandering in sideways with unkempt beard, filthy old clothes and raucous voice. We all exclaim that we have most important business and must talk of 'les affaires', but he points at one officer reading the *Tatler* and another eating gooseberries and flies into a passion.[31]

Battalion messes were not unknown on the Western Front. At Laventie, Second Lieutenant Robert Graves sat down to battalion mess with 2/Royal Welch Fusiliers, having already been ignored by all and sundry, except to be told that only officers of the rank of captain or above were allowed to turn on the gramophone:

> We filed into the next room, a ball-room with mirrors and a decorated ceiling, and took our places at a long, polished table. The seniors sat at the top, the juniors competed for seats as far away from them as possible. Unluckily I got a seat at the foot of the table, facing the colonel, the adjutant, and Buzz Off. Not a word was spoken down my end, except an occasional whisper for the salt or the beer – very thin French stuff. Robertson [another new subaltern], who had not been warned, asked the mess-waiter for whisky. 'Sorry, sir,' said the mess-waiter, 'It's against orders for the young officers.' Robertson was a man of forty-two, a solicitor with a large practice, and had stood for Parliament in the Yarmouth division at the previous election.
> I saw Buzz Off glaring at us and busied myself with my meat and potatoes.[32]

Keeping his head down was no protection. To Graves' burning embarrassment, Buzz Off noticed that Graves, who had previously been attached to the Welsh Regiment, was wearing a 'wind-up tunic', with the stars on the shoulder instead of the sleeve and bawled him out.[33]

It was the presence of crusty colonels at battalion mess that meant that subalterns generally preferred the conviviality of company mess. Conversely, colonels liked the opportunity of a battalion mess to keep a gimlet-eye on their officers and maintained company messes could breed demoralization after bloody losses.

A jolly good dinner, be it by battalion or by company, was a guaranteed raiser of morale, an opportunity for drinks and hi-jinx. Edwin Campion Vaughan:

> The dinner was very loud. The food was excellent and the champagne flowed very freely. Nearly everybody got tight, Thomas being the first to succumb. While the CO was making a serious speech, recalling the history of the Battalion and toasting the memory of the fellows who had gone west, Tommy burst into maniacal laughter and collapsed on the floor. He was swept up and Radcliffe took to the piano to accompany the various singers.
>
> After a long singsong, a violent rag was started in which the enormous and disgusting padre offered to fight six subalterns. He knocked them about for a long time before he was debagged and spanked.[34]

The award of medals was always an excuse for a party. From his billet on 16 January 1916 Graham Greenwell, company commander and epicurean, wrote to his mother:

> I am frightfully busy arranging a grand dinner-party for to-night to celebrate the Military Crosses. We have evolved the following menu:
> Oysters
> Consomme Courcelles
> Roti de veau de Sailly: Moet et Chandon, 1906
> Poulet Conybeare
> Asperge des tranchees
> Rum omelette a la Q.M. et Macedoine
> Welsh Rarebit
> Coffee. Liquers. Cigars.[35]

Courcelles was the village in which Greenwell's 4/Ox and Bucks Light Infantry were billeted; Conybeare was an officer in the regiment.

For quiet souls in the 13/Royal Fusiliers, Guy Chapman recommended No.4 mess, where Arthur Bliss obliged with Elgar and

Schubert on his gramophone. At C company mess of the 1/Royal Welch Fusiliers, Robert Graves noticed the essays of Lionel Johnson lying on the table; 'It was the first book I had seen in France (except my own Keats and Blake) that was neither a military text-book nor a rubbishy novel.' Graves looked at the fly-leaf and saw the name 'Siegfried Sassoon'. Looking around the mess to see who might be called Sassoon and bring Lionel Johnson to war: 'The answer was obvious.'[36] They talked poetry. Sassoon wrote in his diary: 'Walked into Bethune for tea with Robert Graves, a young poet, captain in Third Battalion and very much disliked. An interesting creature, over strung and self-conscious, a defier of convention.'[37]

Graves later celebrated the friendship in the poem 'Two Fusiliers':

Show me the two so closely bound
As we, by the wet bond of blood ...

The generation of officers who fought on the Western Front were the warrior poets.

Poetry mattered to the boy of late Victorian England and Edwardian Britain in a way it never did before or has since; Palgrave's *Golden Treasury* and William Ernest Henley's *Lyra Heroica* were staples in the library of almost every boy and every school. If verse was appreciated for its own sake, it was also understood that appreciation of the muse was the sign of a civilized man. A gentleman. All those interminable lessons in the Classics left their mark too; the poetry of Robert Graves, who went straight into the army from school, was moulded by and peppered with Classical devices and allusions, a case in point being 'Escape', which by line three is running a Greek riot:

That Cerberus Guards, half-way along the road
To Lethe, as an old Greek signpost showed ...

The allusions to Classical gods and beasts might be overdone, the form a little too Virgilian, but generally the middle class and upper class schoolboy found poetry an obvious, familiar, and easy, means of self-expression when he grew to become an officer in time of war. The list of First World War officers whose poetry was published, either in their lifetimes or posthumously, is tellingly long.[38]

The 'greatest bane of the life of the soldier', decided Guy Chapman, was 'boredom, cafard, or whatever you will call it'.[39]

Writing poetry was one way of killing the monotony of billet life. Some pastimes in billets were the same as those of trenches – reading, cards (Chapman's company played 'eternal bridge'), listening to the gramophone, the 'Charlie Chaplin Walk' and 'We've only Been Married for a Year' being the turntable favourites.

Larking about was always a good stand-by. In August 1915 Graham Greenwell told his mother:

> I have just been having a tremendous fight against Conny and Freddie Grisewood, armed with long sticks and apples. It is much more fun than real war.[40]

The melancholy note of regret for lost youth in so selfless a teenage soldier is particularly poignant. When the weather broke into snow in the winter of 1915, Frechencourt was transformed from squalor into 'a village of dreams'. Charles Douie wrote:

> Kestell-Cornish, the padre and I indulged in tobogganing in the battalion Dixie carriers in a disused chalk-pit at the foot of the village and inveigled other and senior officers into the pastime, to their great discomfort.[41]

Twitchy officers were always fun to 'wind-up' with the boy subaltern's best jape; Robert Graves recalled when Captain Furber ('whose nerves are in pieces') received a rolling bomb – defused – in his billet, which was 'thought a wonderful joke'.[42] Furber, incidentally, laid a bet in June 1915 with the adjutant that the front line would be no more than a mile different two years hence. He won the bet.

Playing with guns, that was fun too. When in billets at Vermelles in June 1915 Robert Graves recalled:

> We officers spend a lot of time revolver-shooting. Jenkins brought out
> a beautiful target from the only undistorted living-room in our billet-
> area: a glass case full of artificial fruit and flowers.[43]

The case was put on a post at 50 yards. Everybody missed. It was
put on a post at 20 yards, and everybody missed, though one shot hit
the post causing the glass case to fall. Finally, someone walked up to
the case and applied the *coup de grace* from close quarters. Edwin
Campion Vaughan and his pals also went joy-shooting:

> in the afternoon a crowd of us turned out and potted at bottles. Of
> course we had money on it, and I was glad to find my hand was steady
> enough to rake in a few francs, though the CO carried off most.[44]

In more constructive mood, Vaughan determined to make a garden,
by clearing out the waist-high rubbish behind his billet in Peronne
and planting it with flowers:

> Sunday. No work today so I finished off the garden. Really finished it!
> Every bit of rubbish burnt, paths swept, rose trees cleared and beds
> weeded. I was planting flowers scrounged from other gardens when
> Ewing came out and I stood pointing at my handiwork with pride. He
> stood for a bit sneering slightly then said, 'Well, Vaughan, you know
> it's labour in vain don't you?' 'Why?' I asked. 'Because we're moving
> north tomorrow.' And with that he left me.
>
> Gazing round at the result of my many hours of hard work, I felt
> inclined to cry, but consoled myself with the thought that someone
> would get the benefit of them . . .'[45]

It is certain that they did. Two years before, the sight and smell of
such a garden prompted Edward Tennant into the touching rapture
of his 'Home Thoughts in Laventie':

> Green gardens in Laventie!
> Soldiers only know the street
> Where the mud is churned and splashed about
> By battle-wending feet;
> And yet beside one stricken house there is a glimpse of grass.
> Look for it when you pass.

Beyond the church whose pitted spire
Seems balanced on a strand
Of swaying stone and tottering brick
Two roofless ruins stand,
And here behind the wreckage where the back wall should have been
We found a garden green.

The grass was never trodden on,
The little path of gravel
Was overgrown with celandine,
No other folk did travel
Along its weedy surface, but the nimble-footed mouse
Running from house to house.

So all among the vivid blades
Of soft and tender grass
We lay, nor heard the limber wheels
That pass and ever pass,
In noisy continuity until their stony rattle
Seems in itself a battle.

At length we rose up from this ease
Of tranquil happy mind,
And searched the garden's little length
A fresh pleasaunce to find;
And there, some yellow daffodils and jasmine hanging high
Did rest the tired eye.

The fairest and most fragrant
Of the many sweets we found,
Was a little bush of Daphne flower
Upon a grassy mound,
And so thick were the blossoms set and so divine the scent
That we were well content.

Hungry for spring, I bent my head,
The perfume fanned my face,
And all my soul was dancing
In that little lovely place,
Dancing with a measured step from wrecked and shattered towns
Away . . . upon the Downs.

I saw green banks of daffodil,
Slim poplars in the breeze,
Great tan-brown hares in gusty March
A-courting on the leas;
And meadows with their glittering streams, and silver scurrying dace,
Home what a perfect place![46]

In those far-off days, people really did make their own entertainments. An impromptu concert-party was always popular. Harold
Macmillan:

The concert which we had in our company was a great success. Imagine
an old draughty barn, about 100 ft. long and 30 wide – with straw on
the brick floor of it, and for all illumination 3 oil lamps, hung round
the wall, burning rather gloomily, moody, ill-omened.

Into this barn (where 3 platoons would ordinarily be asleep) 5 strong
men introduce a cottage piano. This is gala night. On the piano 5
bottles stand, a candle in each. Then a sturdy corporal, with more
bottles and more candles – and soon the place is (to our eyes) as well
lit as any West End theatre.

So the evening begins. A recitation, very pathetic this, about the
poor lad who slept at his post, and how the colonel sentenced him to
death, and how his widowed mother pleaded for him, her only son,
and how his pal, a hero of some 17 years, did so noble a deed in battle
as to win the Victoria Cross – and the 'pal' chooses to refuse his
decoration and asks instead a favour of the colonel. 'And what my lad
is this, I pray?' 'Pardon Bill Williams, Sir' the hero said (Bill is the
delinquent.) 'he is but young. Give him his head! So Bill's alive whom
all gave up for dead!'

And then a wild and vociferous applause – almost tears in some
eyes. Quite wonderful. Then a 'sketch' by an erstwhile music-hall
comedian, now enlisted. A few rousing choruses follow, and then the
Sergeant-Major (by request) gives 'Old King Cole' (a great favourite,
which appears at every sing-song):

'What's the next command?'
     said the Major-
'I want six months' leave-'
     said the Captain-

'We do all the work,'
   said the subalterns-
'Put him in the book,'
   said the sergeant-major
(i.e. take his name and report him)
'Move to the right in fours'
   said the sergeant
'Left, right, left, right, left'
   said the corporal
'We want jam for tea,'
   said the privates.
'Tum-riddle-um, tiddle-um'
   said the drummers-
   For there's no one here
   That can compare
   With the men of the Grenadier Guards.

Then more songs and recitations and the like, till at last bed-time comes. But before we go, 'The British Grenadiers' and 'God save the King' worthily finish a not unenjoyable evening. And not unimpressive either. For in a barn like this 250 voices make a fine 'Grenadierly' noise.[47]

Guy Chapman remembered:

There was a concert held at Bully-Grenay, one of the unforgettable nights. The small hall was crowded. Beer and rum punch – one wondered whether the quartermaster distilled the spirit or merely pinched it – were sufficient. We applauded the sentimental tenor and sang the chorus with a wealth of feeling which we should deny in the morning. We cheered Sergeant Hyams of the Lewis Guns in *O-O-O, I'm an Eskimo*, a song of suitable simplicity. Fairburn sang *Mandalay*, and later, under pressure, *Little Pigs Make the Best of Pork*, with vehement gesticulation. But these only led up to our adjutant. He will never again have such an audience. *Winters' Nights* is a ragtime melody, the words negligible; but it will make an exile dream. Cutherbertson sang it so quietly that the dreams were undisturbed. In the end we were crooning the tune, would have sung it until we rocked asleep. In a moment's pause Boche shells could be heard tearing the night outside

and dropping with subdued crashes in the square. But no small strafe
could have disturbed us: we lay back and sang.[48]

One of the perks of being an officer was that he was more able and
likely to get a pass to the nearest town, or just away from camp. Sidney
Rogerson and a gaggle of fellow officers 'lorry-jumped' a lift to Amiens:

We looked about us goggle-eyed. There was not one of us who did not
feel a flutter of excitement. Civilization! A city with shops, restaurants,
and civilian women![49]

The women, though, were disappointing; 'Young or old, they were
almost all garbed in black – how thorough the French are in their
mourning, and how they appear to rejoice in it!' Rogerson mused that
women reminded soldiers not only of their celibacy, but the hardness
of their lives. To compensate, Rogerson and his fellows rushed to buy
the finer, softer things of life, 'silk pyjamas, scented soaps, and other
minor luxuries'.[50] At Cambridge he had never used bath crystals; he
bought them in Bethune after his first tour of the trenches. His
shopping in Amiens took him a long time. The pleasures of shopping
and girl-watching also captured John Glubb: 'The blasé inhabitants
of England can form no idea of the childish joy of a day of festivity in
a real town with shops and women.' And this was little Corbie.[51]

After shopping, next on the menu of the officer out on the French
town was eating and drink.

The Globe, a café in Bethune Square reserved for British officers and
French civilians, was one of the favourite rendezvous of the Prince of
Wales, then a lieutenant in the Fortieth Siege battery. The Globe had a
billiard table and an apparently inexhaustible supply of beer, although
when Alexander Stewart sipped the expensive champagne cocktails he
found they 'generally made one ill'.[52] War was the last topic of conversation. In the Salient, La Poupee on the square in Poperinge was an
officers-only café, often called 'Ginger's' after the owner's precocious
13-year-old daughter who walked to school amid falling shells.

What to do in the evening on the town or village? Roland Leighton
wrote excitedly to Vera Brittain on 5 December 1915:

You would never guess where I was yesterday evening. In a cinema, of all places. The ASC run one in this village – in a barn with seats, electric light, two performances nightly and a change of programme every day. It is quite civilised for a village only 4 miles from the trenches – n'est-ce pas?'[53]

After a 'priceless bath' Geoffrey Thurlow, in December 1916, was sent off to see a Divisional concert party; unlike the concerts 'got up' by officers and men, these featured semi or wholly professional 'artistes'. To Thurlow's disappointment the 'lady' in the show (a man in drag) was 'always mincing about and very gawky, grinning inanely the while'. More convincing a female impersonator was witnessed by Graham Greenwell at a concert organized by the Scottish Division: '. . . there was the most perfect girl. A sort of gasp went up when she came on – it was difficult to believe that she was a wolf in sheep's clothing.' Luckier still was Francis Hitchcock, when he attended the 6th Divs 'The Fancies' in 'Pop', which had the real thing:

It was a top-hole show, Murray and I enjoyed it immensely. The concert troupe consisted of nine artistes and two French girls. The latter were known as 'Glycerine' and 'Vaseline'. One was a refugee from Lille, and the other was the daughter of an estaminet keeper at Armentieres. The most priceless tune in the show was the singing of 'I'm Gilbert the Filbert' by one of these wenches who could not speak English![54]

A celebrity visit from the Scottish entertainer Harry Lauder enlivened the rest period of Robert Mackay and the 11/Argyll & Sutherland Highlanders. Lauder, who led successful fund-raising efforts for war charities as well as entertaining troops in France, was knighted for his service during the war. But this was cold compensation for the loss of his only son, John (born 1891), a captain in the 8/Argyll and Sutherland Highlanders, killed in action on 28 December 1916. Lauder wrote the song 'Keep Right on to the End of the Road' in the aftermath of John's death.

There were free and simple entertainments to be had. Never have the cathedrals and churches of northern France been so visited as they were in the Great War, as subaltern after lieutenant after captain wandered around them, tourists for an empty hour. A sort of rapture came over Bernard Adams as he gazed at Amiens cathedral: 'For down in the mud I had forgotten, in the obsessions of the present, man's dreams and aspirations for the future.' One studious 19-year-old subaltern in the 13/Royal Fusiliers filled his leisure hours in the second Army area, copying down the Latin inscriptions in the area's plentiful and cavernous churches; Guy Chapman thought him charming and the 'most delightful companion in a library' but with his incessant learned chatter likely to be maddening in a pill-box.[55] Alexander Stewart was far from being alone in, having escaped a show with his scalp and his body intact, using a French place of worship for its original purpose. 'I went to church because I felt that I should, in a seemly manner, offer up some word of thanks to the Almighty for being allowed to still live, when so many better men had been killed.'[56] Bim Tennant accompanied his French billet hosts to 'La Grande Masse'.

In the Salient, the religiously minded with time on their hands gravitated towards Talbot House in Poperinge, named by its founder Reverend Neville Talbot for his brother Gilbert, killed at Hooge, but always known as 'Toc-H', the signallers' parlance for 'T' and 'H'. It was run by the Reverend Philip 'Tubby' Clayton, who seemed to be the incarnation of Chesterton's Father Brown. As the sign said, Toc-H was 'Everyman's Club'. For those slow on the uptake there was another prominent sign, this one placed over the door of the chaplain's room: 'All rank abandon ye who enter here.' Burgon Bickersteth had a meal there with Julian, his padre brother, Clayton and three private soldiers: 'The first time I had ever sat down to eat out here in uniform with soldiers.'[57]

Toc-H, with its garden, library and attic chapel, was a spiritual and philosophical refuge, with its beauty on the inside as well as its perfectly proportioned outside. The altar in the chapel was an abandoned carpenter's bench, the appropriateness of which Clayton always rather enjoyed. Reverend Julian Bickersteth took a 'party of our lads' to be confirmed at Toc-H. 'The whole service', Bickersteth wrote,

with its beautiful setting and with the knowledge that many of those

confirmed had come straight from the battle and were to return again that night, could not fail to move the least impressionable.[58]

One of the candidates for confirmation had been killed that very morning.

Lord Cavan, after a miserable day, went to Toc-H to pray in the Upper Room. His intense prayer revived him, and he publicly declared that he owed the entire of his subsequent career to that one visit. Widely regarded as one of the best Corps commanders on the Western Front, Cavan later became Chief of the Imperial General Staff.

One of the joys of *La belle France*, Captain Arthur Adam, Cambridgeshire Regiment, considered, was its sheer size, which meant that a soldier could walk – a cheap enough pastime – and 'get far enough away from his kind to be able to unbutton his coat and look untidy'. On a rolling hill near Etaples, with Homer and bathing shorts, he then discovered the downside of walking amidst beauty: 'At times I almost wish this spot were not so good – it gives me a fierce feeling of hatred of the present bondage that is hardly to be borne – there are times on parade when it seems impossible to do what one is told.'[59]

Those who followed country sports and hobbies in Britain found opportunities in France. Julian Grenfell took his hunting dogs with him, Now, Dawn, Dusk, Hammer, Tongs, Toby; they were looked after by a French farmer's wife when he was in action. He also engaged in another noble sport; at a boxing exhibition in the local town hall, Grenfell issued a challenge to all comers. The challenge was accepted by 'a *very* large private' in the Army Service Corps, who was a professional pugilist. He closed Grenfell's left eye in the first round but Grenfell triumphed with a second round right hander that 'caught him a beauty and they had to carry him out to hospital'.[60] A swirling sea of the sensitive and the sensual, Grenfell wrote a book of philosophy and politics; one of the essays, appropriately, attacked Conventionalism.

On duty at an observation post near Blairville Wood on 16 February 1917, Edward Thomas saw: 'A mad Captain with several men driving partridges over the open and whistling and crying "Mark over"'. This, at least, was shooting, a technological advance on the partridge-killing methods of Eden and his friends in the King's Royal Rifle Corps; they pursued coveys of partridges on horseback, and when a bird tired, they slipped from the saddle and hit it over the head with a stick. 'By this unorthodox and dubious method we would occasionally add a brace or two of partridges to our fare.'[61] At billets in Airaines, Major Poore of 2/Royal Welch Fusiliers was invited by the local notary to shoot *le sanglier* (wild boar). All that Poore bagged, though, was a rabbit and a squirrel.[62] Brian Lawrence's battalion of the Grenadier Guards, meanwhile, got up a shooting party at Clary that potted some snipe (and discovered some moorhen eggs) on the Somme marshes. Issued with a shotgun to shoot German carrier pigeons, the officers of Hugh Munro's company of the 8/Argyll and Sutherland Highlanders used the gun 'surreptitiously for shooting more innocent pigeons, which lent variety to our commissariat'.

Captain John W. Jeffries, an officer with the Durham Light Infantry, was pleased to be invited to lunch with General Chetwode and his brigade major. He was surprised that the post-lunch entertainment was a bird nesting expedition, and more surprised still, when the area to be explored was a shell-strewn wilderness a mere three-quarters of a mile from the front line. The birders found a nightingale's nest with six eggs, along with the nests of a chaffinch, blackbird and missel thrush.[63]

Subalterns could be coy. In Bethune, Alexander Stewart recalled, crowds of young officers would go to a boot shop, simply to be served by the 'very smart looking girl' who worked there.[64] Attending a course at Amiens, Vaughan enjoyed a little flirtation, but no more than that; 'I have made friends with a dear little girl in a jewellery and gramophone shop in the arcade; we call in and hear a few records, taking her a little gift of sweets.'

There were young soldiers who did not want to die virgins, and Stuart Cloete, his own celibacy aside, recognized:

> When a boy has been forced into manhood by special circumstances such as war, then because there has been so much destruction of life, nature (which we usually try to deny as if we stood above it) increases sexual pressure.[65]

To the happy surprise of the amorous, French girls were more 'easy going'. Julian Grenfell wrote in his diary: 'Very hot day for me in Ypres. All these people take Free Love as a matter of course and habit. The daughter says – ask mother if she will give us a bed.' In billets at Bethune, two officers in Graves' company explained how they had tossed a coin for a mother and daughter, the loser getting the daughter who was a 'yellow-looking scaly little thing like a lizard'.[66]

Sex could be bought. No sooner had Chapman set foot in France than he was joined by a stray dog, and a small boy 'offering the services of his sister – jig-a-jig. I cuffed his head.'[67] The brothels of Le Havre were concentrated in the Rue des Galions, first class for officers, second class for other ranks. Lieutenant Dennis Wheatley of the Royal Field Artillery estimated that 'hundreds of French women plied the most ancient of all trades' in the port from midday onward.[68] In Amiens, Wheatley considered Madame Prudhomme's to be the best brothel, which is likely where Sassoon's dinner companions went 'to look for a harlot' while he stayed in his hotel room reading.[69] The notorious Skindles, meanwhile, was the place in 'Pop' for officers in search of a hot meal and a hotter woman in the Salient. A draft of young Welsh officers escorted by Robert Graves disappeared into Le Drapeau Blanc brothel in Rouen; the boys, strictly brought up sons of the professional classes, were incredibly naive and knew nothing of prophylactics. When Graves demanded of one whether he had washed himself after sex at the brothel, the boy responded indignantly that he had washed his face and hands.[70] Graves estimated that three of the ten officers contracted Venereal Disease. The consequences of catching VD were serious in more than a medical sense. Anyone who reported sick with VD had his leave to England stopped; some preferred to hide the symptoms, with disastrous results. Army medical services treated 153,531 cases of VD on the Western Front. Under General Routine Orders, Part 1, Adjutant General's Branch GRO 2785, 1 January 1918 it was announced that warrant officers and NCOs infected with VD should be considered for a reduction in rank; officers might be required to resign their commissions.

Married officers were able to get leave to meet their wives in Paris.

Of course, they might not bother about a wife. Captain Cyril Dennys, 212 Siege battery, Royal Garrison Artillery:

> I remember there was one case where a captain who was getting on in age applied for special leave ... On his leave chit he was asked for his reason. He put quite boldly, sexual starvation. And to everyone's surprise and delight he got his leave. He went off and we hoped he satisfied his needs in Paris.[71]

According to Charles Carrington soldiers alternated between feeling starved of female company (so famished indeed that Carrington, years after the war, could clearly picture 'the beautiful female impersonator who sang and danced in the "Red Roses" concert party') and having the sex instinct sublimated by the hardships and fears of the trenches.[72]

He was not aware of homosexual conduct, but clearly it existed. As a young subaltern in England, Cloete shared quarters at the Rose and Crown public house with a senior officer:

> He was homosexual and made a pass at me. I opened my new [army-issue] jack-knife, put it under my pillow and said: 'If you try to get in my bed again I'll stick it into you.' He did not try again but had no love for me after that and, owing to his influence, I was left behind as being too young and incompetent to go with the battalion. He may even have been right. He certainly saved my life.[73]

During the trial of Lieutenant Wilfrid Marsden of the Royal Flying Corps for 'gross indecency' in January 1916, a letter found among his effects was read out in court. It was from F.R. West, a 20-year-old subaltern in the King's Royal Rifle Corps:

> I had unusual luck after I left you. I strolled passed the Union Jack Club but saw only drunkards etc, so rushed with all possible speed to the old beat where I soon picked up a charming girl very fair with blue eyes and slightly wavy hair who was in the Red Cross show, uniform very becoming, stationed at Yarmouth of all places. He was up on four days leave and was perfectly charming and very affectionate. He gave me his photo. His legs my dear, were too wonderful and I am feeling very tired to-day.[74]

The letter was handed over to the military authorities, and West was brought back from the trenches of France. He was court-martialled and cashiered.

In total 17 officers were court-martialled for 'indecency' between the 4 August 1914 and 30 September 1918. By no means all of them were New Army officers. Frederic Llewellyn had served in the Boer War, rejoined the Army in 1914, and at the time of his arrest he was second in command of 8/Oxford and Buckingham Light Infantry. Too young to serve in South Africa, Alfred C. Boyd joined the Territorials in 1907, and was tried on nine separate counts of indecency at the Guildhall. Llewellyn was tried in the same series of trials, suggesting the wholesale arrest of a clique.[75]

Leafing through his diary from 1916, Charles Carrington found that he had spent 120 days in reserve and rest.

Rest, however, was relative.

'The Battalion had by this time', wrote Francis Hitchcock in his diary on 30 October 1915, 'discovered that rest in Reninhelst consisted of continual fatigues.' The 'navvying' done by Hitchcock's Leinsters included digging a sump pit on a flooded Communications Trench near Hill 60, only reachable 'after a terrible trek'.[76] His Brigade HQ tried to supplant the word 'fatigue' with 'working party' due to the former's unsavoury tone; the fatigue was still there, however, as an old sweat in Hitchcock's company pointed out. Some of the fatigues incensed because of their sheer pointlessness; Brian Lawrence's battalion of the Grenadier Guards built a road through a swamp, which turned out to be 'about as useful as making sandcastles at the seaside!'[77] Some of the fatigues were plain distressing, such as the burying of horses and people.

There were officers who wished all horses, alive as well as dead, buried. Edwin Campion Vaughan discovered to his horror that his mess was expected to ride over en bloc to watch a football match. Being one of those officers who had escaped riding lessons in Blighty, he had never been on a horse before. For half an hour of agony he 'bumped up and down at an alarming rate'. The Royal Welch Fusiliers, meanwhile, made all subalterns unable to ride a horse attend riding school every afternoon when in billets. 'At Laventie', recalled Robert Graves, 'I used to look forward to our spells in the trenches. Billet life spelt battalion mess, also riding school, which turned out to be rather worse than the Surrey-man had described.'

At Barly, Guy Chapman had his 'first experience of that admirable fountain of justice, the court-martial':

The accused was the elderly pioneer sergeant of the 60th; the charge, 'drunk in trenches'. He was duly found guilty. As he was marched out, I hurriedly turned the pages of the Manual of Military Law, and found to my horror that the punishment was death, *tout court*. So when Major the Hon. George Keppel turned to me as junior member of the court and demanded my sentence, I replied, 'Oh, death, sir, I suppose.' Major Keppel blenched and turned to my opposite number, Gwinnell. Gwinnell, who was as young and unlearned in expedience as myself, answered, as I had, 'Death, I suppose.' Our good president looked at us from the top of his six feet and groaned: 'But, my boys, my boys, you can't do it.'

It was only after a moving appeal by the president that we allowed ourselves to be overborne and to punish the old ruffian by reduction to rank of corporal in the place of executing him; but we both felt that Major Keppel had somehow failed in his duty.[78]

Francis Hitchcock was less impressed with military justice, because it once again involved 'red tape' with documents to be rendered in triplicate. The word 'Rest', he complained bitterly, was a 'camouflage' name for 'a continual fatigue'.

The everyday 'house keeping' chores of the company in billets, as in the trenches, swallowed time. As a temporary adjutant Robert Mackay worked: '19 hours a day. Remaining 5 were spent sleeping, and they were interrupted. It is the unnecessary correspondence which keeps one busy.' Graham Greenwell, never one to complain much about mud, death, cold, and hunger was moved to absolute exasperation by the amount of administration he had to undertake as a company commander, aged barely twenty, telling his mother that he was: 'Off my head with work trying to supply my Company (200 strong) with everything from iron rations, wire-cutters, and bomb bags to waterproof sheets and Balaclava helmets.[79]

Whosoever was orderly officer that day had to turn out the guard, and deal with defaulters. Edwin Campion Vaughan, meanwhile, was made mess president: 'I am quite at sea with regard to my task', he wrote. Mess president was an invidious job, because other officers became tetchy if they thought there were extravagances in the budget, and equally irritable if the provisions were not plentiful or good enough.

The men had to be paid. Novice paymaster Edwin Campion Vaughan cycled happily over to Hollencourt to draw cash for troops; on the return he wobbled all the way back with 18,000 francs stuffed in the pockets of his British Warm. Simultaneously neophyte horse-man and pay-master Bernard Martin rode 42 kilometres to collect money for the battalion from the Army Office:

> When I came from the office with rather a heavy bag of coins I thought I should never be able to mount, the horse thought so too. At every attempt he started homewards before I was astride. Luckily a lance-corporal, watching from the Pay Office window, came out and held the horse's head and the money bag while I climbed awkwardly into the saddle.[80]

There were letters to be written to relatives of the dead, kit to be inspected and on one unforgettable occasion, Stuart Cloete found himself examining his men's penises for signs of Venereal Disease. 'An embarrassing performance for all concerned', wrote Cloete, 'but it was a divisional order.' None of the examining officers, Cloete realized, would have recognized VD unless it was in its last stages. The men called it 'the short arm inspection'.[81]

At rest after a battle or a bad spell in the trenches, good officers would increase the rate and intensity of inspections purely to take the men's minds off dark tragedies. In billets at Bailleulval, Guy Chapman remembered:

> We worried them [the men] with continual inspections. It could not be helped. Many of them were like children, moving in a haze of their

own dreams, unconnected with practical things. We made these days a refrain of socks, boots, shirts, holdalls, combs, razors, shaving brushes. 'Take that to the sergeant tailor; get it mended. Put him down for a new badge, sergeant. And see you get your hair cut – *today, mind.*[82]

Church parades were a fixed and familiar feature of billet time. Bernard Martin wrote:

I don't know who ordered the church parades when we came out on rest. During my first eight months we had ten, but only three in seven months of 1917. I liked these parades, they were simple, no rituals or theology, only hymns, a lesson from the Bible and a short address by the Chaplain ... The men were indifferent though most sang the hymns, probably to words other than those printed in the hymn books.[83]

A good sermon helped heal the psychic wounds of battle. The Reverend Victor Tanner was an acknowledged master of the art of the sermon. In his 'Thanksgiving After Action' he told the 2/Worcesters, recently mauled at Passchendaele:

We are only too conscious that our thankfulness is tinged with very real sorrow for there are big gaps in our ranks today. Comrades with whom we have stood shoulder to shoulder in billets, on the march, and in the front line are absent now. Some are in hospital, and we shall look forward to seeing them again, but many have passed through the veil which hides us from the great spiritual world. Bravely they fought and nobly they died in the greatest and most sacred cause in which men have ever taken up arms, and humanity will for ever bless their memory. For them we need not mourn. Death is like the drawing aside of a veil and passing from one room into another. A nobler activity is theirs today, greater opportunities for the development of character and a sphere of wider usefulness, as we Christians firmly believe, but when we think of some of them, lads of scarce 20 years and of the majority of young men in the prime of life and full of the vigour of manhood, there cannot but come before our mind's eye a picture of the promising future which, humanely speaking, lay before them. Why does God allow them to be cut off in the prime of life?

Prematurely cut off, did I say? Jesus died at 33 years just when his manhood's powers were at their height. No, his was not an untimely end. 'I have finished the work that thou gavest me to do' were almost his last words as he entered the final struggle. And, as for him, so for us. God has an appointed task for each man's life and if that man is called upon to lay down his life in the fulfilment of his duty we may be sure that his work on earth is finished. . . . No, for our fallen comrades we need not grieve. God has other work for them to do. But for the heartbroken mothers and wives whom they have left behind and for the little ones who have been looking forward so eagerly to Daddy's return from the war, for them our hearts bleed and we pray that they may be given grace to bear their sorrow with Christian courage and holy hope, remembering that their loved ones are for ever in the safe keeping of the Good Shepherd.

But there is one thing more I want to say. What effect should the death of our comrades have upon us? Surely in the first place:

1. It should strengthen our resolve to carry on without faltering till the object for which they died has been obtained – England's honour vindicated, liberty established and a common brotherhood. When a feeling of war weariness comes over us, as it does from time to time, let us pray for the spirit of dogged perseverance and endurance.

2. If God spares us to return home it must be our resolve to build a new England on the principles of righteousness, justice and brotherhood. Here unity is strength. Let those who love righteousness and want to see those things removed from our national life which have in the past brought dishonour on the fair name of England – social injustice, luxury on the one hand and grinding poverty on the other, bad housing, immorality, class hatred and the like – band themselves together and say 'These things need not be. These things shall not be.'

If then, God spares you to come through this World War, will you not pledge yourself to fight against sin, the world and the devil and become a member of Christ's Society and so help to make its witness an effective force in solving the great problems of reconstruction which will have to be faced in the days to come?[84]

Sport was the other guaranteed method of dispelling the nightmare of a 'bad show'. This morale raiser was not ordered from on high by French or Haig, but was done by regimental officers off, as it were, their own bats.

In the sunshine behind the lines at Arras, Reverend Julian Bickersteth recalled:

> There were races of every description, including one on bicycles for chaplains and doctors, in which I managed to pass the post first. Some of the doctors were not very proficient in the art of bicycle riding, and the races caused much amusement and enthusiasm.[85]

War correspondent Philip Gibbs was a bystander, and wrote in *The Telegraph* on 4 June 1917, about 'the long-legged Church of England padre who has been with them on many a field of battle and comforted them in body and soul in many hours of horror with a fine devotion and utter truthfulness of spirit.' It was a good time for Julian Bickersteth; he had just been Mentioned in Dispatches.

John Glubb borrowed his company's horses to organize an equine sports day at Souastre in 1917:

> A sensational mounted event was the Souastre Scurry. It consisted of a gallop of about 40 yards round a field, bounded by a hedge. On the inside, the course was marked by a rope on pickets five feet high. The course was only four yards wide and included a hairpin-bend, there being some twenty-five horses entered. Altogether a most blood-curdling event, the men all being bare backed, on great lumbering draft horses! Heavy bets had been booked between the troops. The course being so short and dangerous, a great deal of wild excitement resulted. By a miracle, no horses or men were hurt. Wrestling on horseback was another popular event.[86]

Cricket, soccer and rugby, however, were the usual sports, although Burgon Bickersteth once witnessed a hockey match between Royals and the Third Dragoon Guards; 'the general, who is 47, playing for us', he added. Officers sometimes played the men; Douglas Gillespie wrote, 'I think the men enjoy a chance of knocking over an officer for a change.'[87]

On Boxing Day 1918, with his battalion marooned in Italy, Captain Graham Greenwell wrote:

This morning I had the whole Company on parade for Physical Drill and Games. There were a lot of frowning faces and tired eyes [after singing and drinking until midnight the night before], but they got through it. In the afternoon we organized a big Sports Meeting: races, tug of war, jumping and then comic turns, of which the most amusing was the officers' and sergeants' blindfold drill. Both were blindfolded and the Sergeant-Major, also blindfolded, started drilling us: it was the most laughable performance. In two minutes everyone was all over the shop. Then we had a jockey race: each Platoon sergeant carried his Platoon Officer and the Sergeant-Major carried me: the Quartermaster-Sergeant carried my Second-in-Command, Fox. The latter won and I was second. Apples were then suspended on strings which the men had to rush at, eat with their hands behind their backs, and then race back. The Quartermaster-Sergeant's ear was bitten, which caused amusement!

Finally, I gave away the prizes. It was really a great success and I think the men have thoroughly enjoyed themselves. [88]

The good officer made flesh, Greenwell had recently fixed up a recreation room for the men ('where they can read and write in peace') and organized his mother and her friends as suppliers of cigarettes. The day before, he had entered an officers' team in the six-a-side football competition in 'order to make things go'. The officers had sportingly turned out wearing long white cotton pants, so being dubbed the 'Lily Whites' by the men.

One of the oddest cricket games of the war had Edwin Campion Vaughan batting:

This afternoon we had a cricket match, officers versus sergeants, in an enclosure between some houses out of observation from the enemy. Our front line is perhaps three-quarters of a mile. I made top score, twenty-four; the bat was a bit of rafter; the ball, a piece of rag tied round with string; and the wicket, a parrot cage with the clean, dry corpse of a parrot inside ... Machine-gun fire broke up the match. [89]

By general agreement, instructional courses served no useful purpose except to give officers and men a rest. The front line, reflected Guy

Chapman, 'was the only true school'.[90] Edmund Blunden went further:

> ... I was ordered to be ready for attending a Signalling School in the real 'back area'. This development, promising in itself a period of rest and safety, was bad news; for experience proved that to be with one's battalion, or part of it, alone nourished the infantryman's spirit. [91]

Richard Talbot Kelly would not have agreed:

> I started 1917 physically and morally on the top of my form, although only a week or two before I had left the Somme depressed, seedy and feeling anything but brave ... Perhaps my ten days at the Divisional Fighting School had produced in me exactly what our wise Divisional Commander knew it would'[92]

Neither would Second Lieutenant Stephen Hewett who wrote, on receiving orders to attend a course in May 1916:

> A very easy course with short hours, and lovely weather: a heaven-sent rest from the trenches in the first week of May, which gives time to think the thoughts of early summer, more poignant than ever before in this time and place.[93]

The problem with courses was, of course, that they were still about the war.

There were only three ways to escape the war. Leave was one of them.

Leave for officers in the BEF worked on a rota system by which one's name went up the list until departure, and for officers tended to come around every six or eight months, offensives and emergencies withstanding. The men received home leave every fourteen months. Officers travelling to Scotland or Ireland could find most of their leave used up on travelling to and from home.

As Vyvian Trevenen learned from depressing experience, it was important to get aboard the homeward bound boat asap, because any unattached officer passing through port towns was likely to find himself 'borrowed'; in Boulogne Trevenen was 'grabbed to march a party of men two miles to the camp where they were to spend the night'.

On his first home leave, Guy Chapman found England an 'intoxication':

The houses seemed of unparalleled cleanliness, the train offered cushions of down; the dull fields and hedges of Hampshire, the autumn beeches assumed new radiance; the bacon and eggs from the buffet at Basingstoke were ambrosial, Waterloo Station a palace.[94]

On his second leave, Chapman was out-of step with his homeland:

Ten days' leave came my way just then, to an England already a little foreign and queer ... London appeared a little drunk and rather vulgar.[95]

Chapman's mood was not improved by discovering that subalterns were limited to spending 3s 6d on a meal in London (the maximum for any soldier in uniform was 5s). 'The chief plat on the officer lunch at the Savoy Grill was Irish stew, without alternative.'

Robert Graves similarly found himself alienated by the land of his birth:

London seemed unreally itself. Despite the number of uniforms in the streets, the general indifference to, and ignorance about, the war surprised me. ... The universal catchword was 'Business as usual.'[96]

The 'glittering unreality' of London bewildered Eden too, who much preferred to go to the family home, Windlestone, in remote County Durham; the house was now transformed into a VAD hospital and among the wounded was one of his own company, Dent. John Reith was so jarred by the rich food, luxuriousness and blaze of lights during dinner with his brother in London that he felt resentful. There were also the crowds of young men swarming around that he thought should be in uniform. Sassoon, for his part, was appalled by the jingoism of music-hall comedians, writing in 'Blighters', 'I'd love to see a tank come down the stalls . . .'

A sense of dislocation was a common, if unexpected, occurrence on home leave. Habitually, the officer on leave found his mind drifting to his friends and comrades in France and Flanders, the dead and the alive. Walking along a Devon beach, Captain T.P.C. Wilson:

> In each unsheltered field I saw a grave,
> And through the unceasing music of the sea
> The scream of shells came back, came back to me.[97]

Lieutenant E.W. Stoneham RA:

> Even when I got to England on leave, it seemed to me that I really belonged at the Front, that the leave was only an interlude. In a way I was quite ready to get back. That was reinforced by the fact that my family didn't understand what was happening out there, and I didn't really want them to know about it . . . The real world was the one that I had to get back to, and I felt no compunction about getting away when the leave was over.[98]

Conversation with his parents dried away for Bernard Martin: 'Nothing for us to talk about, absolutely nothing', he recalled.[99]

Lieutenant Charles Carrington dressed as a private and 'escaped into the life of cockney London'. He had become 'obsessed' with the comradeship of the front line, and wanted to break down the division between officers and men. But it is not too difficult to perceive Carrington's down-dressing as a relief from the rigours of commanding a company at twenty.[100]

Most unmarried officers on leave binged. In London, the RAC was effectively an officers' club and the first port of call. By September 1918 the RAC, then as now situated at 89/91 Pall Mall, had provided 'bed, breakfast and baths' for 228,125 officers. Alexander Stewart's leave in October 1916 comprised a Turkish bath at the RAC on 12 October, then:

October 13th: See Guv [his father] and Uncle. Take Tommy to Empire: dine Piccadilly.

October 14th: Dine Stillans 8p.m. Will and Laure. Take Rita to Potash and Perl Mutter [a show]. Tea at Savoy.

October 15th: Lunch with Princes at Reigate. Supper Rita and Nora Pyrland Cottage [his brother Tommy's home].

October 16th: Lunch Faggs. See Mrs Slocombe. Dine Pyrland. Go to Gaiety Supper Savoy with Rita.

October 17th: See Guv and Uncle. Lunch Pyrland. Call Faggs: see Duke. Dine Hatchetts – Maudie, Tommy and Jessica. See High Jinks [another show]. Sleep Grosvenor.

October 18th: Leave Victoria 7.50a.m. Rita sees me off.[101]

'The greatest excitement of my life', wrote Second Lieutenant Robert Hamilton in his diary, on being granted a week's leave in London, his native city. Like Stewart he packed his precious days of leave with the high and the social life. On one day alone – 13 September 1915 – he saw his Uncle Henry, went for lunch at Petit Riche, went shopping, took tea at the Waldorf Hotel (watched 'kiddies dancing; nearly cried at the prettiness of it: it was so sweet after the trenches'); had dinner at Maxim's; went to the Gaiety theatre in the evening; took a taxi home; and jawed with his cousin till late. To his 'huge joy' he got an extra day's leave, because his train from Victoria was cancelled.

Eat, drink and be merry, for tomorrow we shall die. Such was the unofficial motto of many a young officer on leave. The motto was not baseless; a week after returning to the front at Givenchy, Hamilton was killed in action. In a last, quick note to his cousin he had written: 'This is my last until we're through, and it's just to tell you I'm ever so fit and so are my chaps, and we're all very cheerful.'

On leave, public school officers would customarily visit, as well as their biological family, their *alma mater*. Geoffrey Thurlow, 10/Sherwood Foresters, wrote to Edward Brittain on 10 March 1916:

Last Tuesday there was a memorial service to the Old Boys at School who have finished the fight and I cabbed over to it; it was jolly being back again at School.[102]

Edward Brittain also made a pilgrimage to his old school, visiting Uppingham at the beginning of October 1916. He wrote to his sister:

> I had an awfully good time at Uppingham a fortnight ago, and met several of the old people who seemed to be glad to see me. The House has got a very decent captain at present – of course he was only quite a small boy when I left – and the whole place seems to be doing well in spite of the War[103]

Some officers took no leave. Captain Cross of 2/Oxford and Bucks refused it on principle; he is reported by Robert Graves as saying:

> My father fought with the regiment in the South African war, and had no leave; my grandfather fought in the Crimea with the regiment, and had no leave. I do not regard it in the regimental tradition to take home-leave when on active service.[104]

After an anguished farewell to his wife and 'Baba' on the platform at Charing Cross station, Frank Crozier vowed 'to myself never to come on leave again'.[105] As the Chinese proverb says, one can never step into the same river twice. By the same token officers going on lengthy home leave never came back to the same regiment. When Guy Chapman arrived at the 13/Royal Fusiliers's billets at Warlencourt after a month's leave – given in recognition of his three years on foreign service – he found: 'Once more there had been too many changes.' A 'baby officer' everyone had tried to protect by sending on all available courses had been killed at Trescault. Another 'babe' had been invalided home with smashed arms. The quartermaster, with four years service done, had applied to go home. The MO had been recalled to the American army. Johns, Chapman's batman, had been wounded at Hermies. The new drafts had been of the lowest quality, so dire indeed that Lieutenant P.E. Smith had been obliged to hound one to the bomb blocks with an entrenching tool handle.[106]

Few, if any officers, complained about a few days leave in Paris. Julian Grenfell wrote:

> Paris! I can't imagine how I have lived so long without being there.

I was absolutely fascinated by the whole thing. I had four divine spring days there. Isn't it gloriously light and gay and beautiful? The view from the Arc de Triomphe down the Champs Elysees is as good as anything in the world, isn't it? ... What I liked most about Paris was the light-heartedness of it all, the complete joie-de-vivre of the place and people ... I saw a bit of everything – 'igh society, and the artists, and the racing set (not the Lord Derby's, but the real racing push), the boxers too, and the nuts, and the actresses and the mannequins, and all the differently very strictly defined classes of girls all in their own particular places ... [107]

Robert Mackay had an equally topping time in February 1917:

13th. Paris 12.45. Bolted in a bee line for the station restaurant, and remained there till they had produced the finest lunch of the week. Embarrassed temporarily after lunch by the many gratuitous offers of guides, official and otherwise. Soon learned how to deal with the whole beastly crew, and showed them we were not as green as our kilts indicated. I object to guides of any sort.

Our first move was to the Banque de France where we got about 250 francs each. I think we caused some amusement there.

Got into the Continental Hotel, the finest in Paris – this after the C.O'.s advice as to hotels. He had given us an address where we could get bed and breakfast for half a crown, or something. Guess a waiter in the Continental would hand back half a crown if he got it as a tip!

We got a bedroom fit for a King. Tea at Maxime's – disappointed with it. Of course, that's not the fashionable hour! Reported to Maurice Brett, the novelist (A.P.M. at Paris) – rather a well known character. Dinner at the Continental. We had some Melba peaches at 2/3 each!

Rationing is beginning in Paris tomorrow. Why could they not put it off for three days!

14th. Bed fairly early.

15th. Breakfast in bed! If I ever get back from this war I'm going to have breakfast in bed every day of my life. I'll have coffee and rolls to it. Notre Dame, Hotel de Ville. Lovely streets and buildings. Lunch at Ciro's. Omelettes were most expensive there. We had two each. Perhaps that was why. Our uniforms saved us from dressing for all these places. Rumplemayers for tea. Very nice. Tremendous number of monde and demi-monde there! Think a great deal of the style and dress and of the looks of the Parisiennes, but that's all. They don't compare with the Rue de la Sauchie. Felt myself becoming quite Frenchified. Alan does not know French, so I get plenty of practice. Visited the Banque de France again just in case it would be necessary. Opera House at night. Romeo and Juliet. Magnificent show. Wonderful acting. Glorious singing.

16th. Taxied round the Bois de Boulogne. Full speed along the Champs Elysees. All out round the Avenues in the Park. Had the hood of our car down. These Parisians who hate the cold must have thought us mad. We didn't have coats either. Back by Quai d'Orsay. Thought of old Monte Cristo ...

Olympia at night. Found some Gordons from the 15th. They had apparently been drinking success to the Division! We were the only Highlanders in the place. Nearly mobbed but got out with all our party. Some night! Bed fairly early, as we had to leave next day.[108]

On receiving Paris leave, Frank Mellish, Royal Artillery, rushed to the French capital to meet his 'Marraine' – his French girl pen-pal. Suzanne was every bit as beautiful as Mellish had dreamed of in the trenches, but there was a small snag; her thirteen year-old brother accompanied her everywhere as chaperone. On day six Mellish resorted to desperate measures; he bribed the boy to leave him alone with Suzanne. The bribe was a bicycle.[109]

The two other ways of leaving the war were death and invalidity.

VIII

We Are the Dead:
Wounds and Hospitalization, Burials and Grief

To whom the voice of guns
Speaks and no longer stuns
Lieutenant G.B. Smith, 19/Lancashire Fusiliers

Sometimes an officer would dream a dream of his own death. Eerily, inexplicably, he would *know* with all the certainty of the physical laws of the universe that he would not survive. Such premonitions came recurrently in October 1917 to Lieutenant Steger, 2/Coldstream Guards, who saw himself fighting a hand-to-hand struggle with a giant German soldier, and at other times felt himself among the 'spirits of the officers and men of the regiment who had been killed;' Steger died at Lys in the following Spring.

Sidney Rogerson watched Arthur Skett of the 2/West Yorkshires prepare to go out into the quags and tree stumps of the Somme in November 1916 to look for a missing officer, Second Lieutenant Pym. Skett, his first time in command of a company, was at his wits' end over losing a 'sub'. Rogerson recalled:

> He [Skett] conceived it to be his personal responsibility to leave no stone unturned to find Pym. Some premonition must have come to him, for as he collected a few reliable men together to go with him, he turned to his servant, and handing him the valuables and documents out of his pockets said, 'Here are the wages I owe you. You'd better take them when you can get them', and without more ado scrambled out of the trench.
>
> Hardly had he put a foot in No-Man's land than he fell back dead, his head split open by a random bullet. Who shall say that he did not know his fate was upon him?[1]

Edmund Blunden, also at the Somme, saw Second Lieutenant Doogan singing 'Everybody's Doing the Charlie Chaplin Walk' when, 'He broke off, and without self-pity and almost casually he said, "It's the third time they've sent me over, this is the third time. They'll get me this time."'[2]

They did. After being wounded Doogan took refuge in a dug-out – which was then penetrated by a shell. On being informed that his battalion was slated for Hooge, Denis Barnett had a presentiment he would be killed and told all his brother officers in 2/Leinsters it would be so. He suffered a mortal bullet hole in the stomach.[3] Charles Douie thought that such premonitions had a real cause, because a 'power to apprehend danger is instinct in men living under primitive conditions; our conditions were worse than primitive and that power was highly developed.'[4] Douie realized, uncomfortably, that the afflicted showed the premonitions in their eyes.

Whether such premonitions were truly manifestations of a sixth sense or a revelation of God's will, or mere nervous imaginings hardly matters; soldiers in the trenches believed that when a man was resigned to his mortal fate that fate was inevitable, and he would be led irrevocably to his end.

The sheer whimsicality of death in the trenches was fuel to fatalism. Robert Graves admitted to carefully working out a formula for risk in the hope of getting through unharmed to the end, but what confounded rational schemes was the fantastic.[5] His fellow poet Edward Thomas, a subaltern in the Royal Garrison Artillery, was killed, as he sat unconcernedly smoking a pipe, by a passing shell that compressed his lungs but left his body unmarked. No factoring of risk could encompass such a singular occurrence. Or the happenstance that befell Second Lieutenant Rupert Fellowes, who did not die of the wounds he received during the action that won him the VC but because, as he lay waiting for treatment, a bomb-carrying party passed by – and a bomb accidentally slipped off the rack, exploded, and killed him. Or the death of Batty-Smith, the young and popular subaltern with 13/Royal Fusiliers, who was lying in long grass at the head of a trench-raiding party. A British trench mortar, intended for the German lines, caught a sudden gust of wind and dropped yards short. A splinter went straight through 'Batty's' brain. Guy Chapman recalled:

> The catastrophe wrenched many of us as no previous death had been able to do. Those we had seen before had possessed an inevitable quality, had been taken as an unavoidable manifestation of war, as in nature we take the ills of the body. But this death at the hands of our own people, through a vagary of the wind, appeared some sinister and malignant stroke, an outrage involving not only the torn body of the dead boy but the whole battalion.[6]

Death could be capricious. Unfortunately, it could also be tempted. One evening at Trafalgar Square junction at Fricourt, Graves, Richardson and Thomas bumped into the adjutant of the Royal Welch Fusilier's 1st Battalion and another officer, Pritchard. The adjutant mentioned in passing that the battalion had had no officer casualties since Loos. Graves wrote:

> Then he suddenly realized that his words were unlucky.
> 'Touch Wood!' David [Thomas] shouted.
> Everybody jumped to touch wood, but it was a French trench and unrevetted. I pulled a pencil out of my pocket; that was wood enough for me.[7]

Within two days Thomas had been killed by a bullet through the neck, Richardson blown into a shell-hole full of water to die of a heart-attack and Pritchard blown to smithereens by a 'whiz bang'.[8] On another occasion, one of Graves' fellow officers, Jenkins, took a small piece of stained glass from a ruined church in France. Two Irish Catholic soldiers from the Munsters passing by warned him, 'Shouldn't do that, Sir, it will bring you no luck'. And it didn't; Jenkins was killed soon after.

But luck could work both ways. There was good luck, as well as bad luck. Sometimes the certain coming of death could be unaccountably – or was it miraculously? – avoided.

Utterly tired during the heat and fighting of the Somme battle, the boyish Richard Talbot Kelly crawled into the side of a shell-hole and pulled a piece of corrugated iron over himself for a roof:

> ... after what had been an unusually peaceful night and a particularly good sleep, I woke and wriggled out of my little burrow and was rather appalled to see that during the night a German 4.2" shell had come straight through the corrugated iron immediately above my head without exploding and had made a clean and neat hole straight into the ground within 2" of my head and I had not been aware of it at all.[9]

Almost exactly the same thing occurred to him at Arras a year later. His charmed life continued at Passchendaele in 1917, where a shell landed so close to him that he toppled in the crater caused by its explosion; the boggy ground of Passchendaele, however, consumed most of the blast leaving him with internal concussion. But with his life. He was invalided home and lived to serve again, not only in the 1914–18 war but in the world war which followed it.

Luck. There was a widespread belief that you needed luck. Within five minutes of crawling into Gird ridge frontline trench on the Somme in October 1916 Anthony Eden and his commanding officer, Foljambe, felt a terrific impact in the sandbag wall they were leaning against; when they recovered, they realized that a German 5.9" shell was protruding between them. A dud. Eden's reaction was that, if they were being shelled so closely and so soon after arrival, the situation was hopeless; Foljambe took the opposite view, 'As we have survived that one', he commented, 'we are evidently not going to be killed in this battle.' And he was right.

Lieutenant Anthony Eden had luck. A day or so later, trudging up again through the mud towards the Gird Ridge frontline Foljambe reproached Eden for wearing his revolver on the wrong side and ordered him to switch it to the right side of his Sam Browne. Eden pleaded to do this after the battle, because to do it then would mean rearranging his 'Christmas tree'. Foljambe acquiesced. Mid afternoon, Eden happened to glance down and saw that his revolver holster had been ripped into by a piece of shrapnel, which would have caused serious, maybe mortal, injury if the thick cow's hide had not been there. Afterwards, Foljambe agreed that Eden could keep his revolver on the wrong side for the rest of the war. He did. By 1917 Captain Anthony Eden MC was the only combatant officer to have served continuously with the 21/King's Royal Rifle Corps since its landing in France in 1915. Eden became Brigade-Major with the 198th Infantry Brigade in spring 1918, aged twenty-one, the youngest brigade-major on the Western Front. The luck of an officer was believed to be an extending umbrella; crossing the bridge over the La Bassée Canal in the victorious '100 Days' at the war's end, Second Lieutenant Henry Ogle was simultaneously shelled and gassed with near direct hits, but suffered only bruising to his neck and shoulder. 'The men', he wrote, 'were delighted with my luck for they liked a lucky "bloke" to command them.'

When death arrived, it could be plain cruel.

Shells were hated by the infantry, whether they were high-explosive shells, trench mortar shells or shrapnel shells (named after their inventor, Lieutenant Henry Shrapnel RA), which burst like a Brobdingnagian shotgun, propelling small metal balls thither, but mostly it seemed, hither. German shrapnel burst black, hence the Tommies' nickname for it of 'Woolly Bear'. Shells and trench mortars *could* deal a clean death. Guy Chapman recorded a subaltern in the 13/Royal Fusiliers being atomized by a direct hit from a German whiz-bang:

> A booted foot and some bloody earth were all that were recovered to be placed in a sandbag and decently interred. The adjutant inherited the ambiguous task of explaining to his relatives why it had not been possible to send home his personal effects.[10]

When Francis Hitchcock pulled back the ground sheet from the body of his dead comrade Captain P. Lynch MC (and Bar), he saw that the 'whole top of his head, from his eyes had been blown away' by the explosion of an aerial dart, a type of trench mortar. Like all of the front-line dead whose bodies could be recovered, Lynch was buried in a sewn-up brown army blanket.

It was the mutilation that shells tended to bring that caused fear and loathing amongst the mud soldiers. Lieutenant Arthur Heath spoke for the infantry officer when he wrote:

It is all very well to talk of a clean death in battle, but it is not a clean death that the artillery deals. It means arms and legs torn off and men mangled out of recognition by their great hulking bullies of guns. I would sweep them all away and settle it by the quiet and decent methods of the infantry. [11]

Sitting around at the Somme between actions, Eden recalled that he and his fellow officers commonly discussed where in the body they would prefer to be hit, and 'we had all agreed that the stomach was the one to be feared'.[12] A shrapnel piece which ripped open the belly and let the intestines slop out, leaving the bemused victim grasping around in blood and dirt trying to push them back in – just about everybody witnessed that once. When Captain Blacker saw his comrade Second Lieutenant Treffy mangled, 'with a spurting artery and his abdomen gaping open with bowels extruding', his first thought was to shoot him; instead he had him carried to the aid post. The RAMC officer tried to put Treffy to sleep with morphine, but Treffy did not die until nightfall.

At Moyenville on the Somme during the retreat of March 1918 Lieutenant Basil Willey of the West Yorkshire Regiment,

saw more horrific sights than in all the rest of my military days put together. For years afterward I was never safe from the recurring vision ... of a young officer I had known and liked, stumbling toward the dressing station with a gaping wound in his abdomen and whispering, 'Oh, Doctor, is there any hope?'[13]

There was not. No, nobody wanted to go out like that.

Eden, however, was too polite. The greatest fear was emasculation. When advancing under fire Charles Carrington always 'felt a strong genetic urge to snatch the helmet off my head and hold it in front of another part of my person'. There was a true tale whispered in company messes with a grimace – and with a silent thanks 'that it was not me' – about the captain in a Midlands regiment who woke up at a Casualty Clearing Station behind the Somme as a eunuch. Through the lazy haze of morphine he managed to scribble a farewell to his fiancée saying that, as he was no longer a man, he could not marry her, and therefore life had no meaning. He begged quietly for a revolver. Over and over, he begged. Eventually a Fusilier officer nearby pressed his Webley into the captain's hand and helped guide the barrel into his mouth. With every atom of concentration, the 26-year-old captain pulled the trigger and blew the back of his head into the stretcher.

Nobody wanted that end especially.

Very high shrapnel bursts did little but scare, especially after the advent of the steel helmet, with its brim designed to keep fragments away from the head and neck. But a shrapnel burst sixty feet or below was trouble, and even a single splinter could kill, if it hit a vital organ, or if it pushed in bacteria from the soil to cause disease, notably septicaemia and gangrene. Sometimes shrapnel wounds were so insignificant that it was impossible to believe that they could bring mortality. When Nevill Young of the 2/Leinsters received a small piece of shrapnel in his shoulder at Potijze on 11 July 1915, he went off cheerily to the dressing-station exclaiming 'Jammy one'; two weeks later he was dead. 'We were all very upset, and surprised', recorded Francis Hitchcock in his diary.[14] On 12 May 1915, as Captain Julian Grenfell made his way to the front line at Railway Hill a shell burst a few yards away; a small splinter entered his head. He was so cheerful, the wound so apparently slight, that no one thought it serious. Except Grenfell himself. He remonstrated: 'I think I shall die ... you see if I don't!'[15] The Royal Dragoons suffered great casualties that day; only three officers left out of fifteen.

To the list of the Regiment's dead was added, on the 26 May, the name of Julian Grenfell. He, like Young, had taken two weeks to die. With the notice of his death in *The Times* was published his poem 'Into Battle':

> The naked earth is warm with spring,
> And with green grass and bursting trees
> Leans to the sun's gaze glorying,
> And quivers in the sunny breeze;
> And life is colour and warmth and light,
> And a striving evermore for these;
> And he is dead who will not fight;
> And who dies fighting has increase.

The fighting man shall from the sun
Take warmth, and life from the glowing earth;
Speed with the light-foot winds to run,
And with the trees to newer birth;
And find, when fighting shall be done,
Great rest and fullness after dearth.

All the bright company of Heaven
Hold him in their high comradeship,
The Dog-Star, and the Sisters Seven,
Orion's Belt and sworded hip.

The woodland trees that stand together,
They stand to him each one a friend;
They gently speak in the windy weather;
They guide to valley and ridge's end.

The kestrel hovering by day,
And the little owls that call by night,
Bid him be swift and keen as they,
As keen of ear, as swift of sight.

The blackbird sings to him, 'Brother, brother,
If this be the last song you shall sing,
Sing well, for you may not sing another;
Brother, sing.'

In dreary, doubtful, waiting hours,
Before the brazen frenzy starts,
The horses show him nobler powers;
O patient eyes, courageous hearts!

And when the burning moment breaks,
And all things else are out of mind,
And only joy of battle takes
Him by the throat, and makes him blind,

Through joy and blindness he shall know,
Not caring much to know, that still
Nor lead nor steel shall reach him, so

That it be not the Destined Will.

The thundering line of battle stands,
And in the air death moans and sings;
But Day shall clasp him with strong hands,
And Night shall fold him in soft wings.

'Into Battle' would become almost as popular with a wartime audience as Brooke's 'The Soldier'; with a post-war pacific audience Grenfell's poem would become almost as derided as Brooke's, except with old soldiers. Charles Douie considered it a 'great poem' and when John Glubb needed a title for the published version of his war diary he chose 'Into Battle', and to make the point of what he thought about it he published it prominently on the frontispiece.

Grenfell's brother Gerald ('Billy'), a lieutenant with the Rifle Brigade, joined the family for Julian's funeral in Boulogne. The Grenfells never saw Billy again; he was killed on 30 July leading the charge at Hooge, within a mile of where Julian Grenfell had been wounded

Shellfire claimed the life of the oldest British officer to die on the Western Front, Lieutenant Henry Webber of the South Lancashires. He was sixty-eight and had three sons serving as captains. Of course he saluted them. Overall, shell and mortar fragments, the Army determined in the middle of the war, were responsible for 60 per cent of infantry wounds, and rifle and machine-gun bullets 35 per cent.

There are no specific cause of death statistics for officers, but it makes sense that an officer was marginally more likely to be killed by a firearms bullet than Other Ranks. Shelling was indiscriminate, whereas rifle and machine gun fire could and did differentiate between ranks. German snipers targeted officers; the favoured bullet of the German sniper was pointed, his favourite target the head. A 'keyhole' spot of crimson would appear on the victim's forehead where the bullet entered; medics observed exit wounds 5 inches across, with the back of the cranium effectively blown off. Under attack, German infantry concentrated their fire on the subalterns, lieutenants and captains lurching across No-Man's Land towards them. One source of information about officers' deaths is their old school magazine's obituary column; in the 4 March 1915 issue of the *Eton College Chronicle*, of the four obituaries where cause of death is given, three out of the four died of bullet wounds. Edward Nash went 'forward to take control as one of the few surviving officers and was shot instantly'; Rowland Beech 'shot through the head leading his men'; B. Tollemache 'led his men to within a few yards of the German trench, when he was shot down'. Countless other school magazines tell the same tale, and point to an officer death rate from bullets at 40–50 per cent.[16]

A bullet claimed the life of the youngest officer to be killed on the Western Front, C.A.H. Hillier, a Cheltonian commissioned straight from school into the 2/Monmouthshires in Summer 1914. He was shot in the lungs in January 1915 and died a month later. The school magazine noted: 'Even in the Crimean war there does not appear to have been any younger Cheltonian killed ... '[17] Hillier was seventeen.

Any officer wearing body-armour on his charge towards the enemy was likely to find it sadly ineffective; a 1919 Ministry of Munitions Report concluded that no steel produced during the war had achieved the lightness and resisting power that made for a suit easy to wear and efficacious against German lead. Body armour was, at best, a psychological blanket: Dennis Wheatley was one who found his Wilkinson's suit 'a considerable comfort under fire'.[18] Presumably, then, he closed his ears to the many, whirling negative stories about breast plates, such as Charles Carrington's friend who was hit by shrapnel bullet on the shoulder edge of his breast plate; the body armour diverted the shrapnel bullet into the lungs, 'thus converting what might have been a slight wound into a deadly one'.

Some bullets clearly had their victim's name on them: Bernard Martin of the North Staffs recalled a newcomer officer to the trench who glanced over the parapet – and 'he collapsed against me, his brains (and a bit more) blown out by a sniper'.

Metal was not the only element of death on the battlefields of the Western Front. At Passchendaele, Guy Chapman's battalion of the Royal Fusiliers was attacked by Germans wielding *Flammenwerfer*, which threw out hissing flames 30 feet long from hose pipes leading to petrol tanks carried on the back. Guy Chapman witnessed the charred results:

Bevan [the intelligence officer], who had been scouting in No-Man's Land was brought in, his face nigger black and his groaning lips blood-red from the fire. The doctor bound him up and gave him a shot of morphia.[19]

Chapman himself fell victim to another form of German 'frightfulness', when he carelessly failed to put on his mask when the 'Boche' dropped a half a dozen mustard gas shells round battalion headquarters. All he suffered was streaming eyes. Mustard-gas was ethylene in a solution of sodium chloride and was rarely lethal; its intention was to harass and irritate, by causing blistering and temporary blindness. But in the severest cases of contamination, men's skin would blister off, they would cough up lung membranes or die dwindlingly of pneumonia.

Mustard gas was the third of the poisonous gases introduced by the Germans into France and Flanders, after chlorine and phosgene. None of the gases was particularly efficient a killer, and alertness and use of the gas mask (constantly improved) could generally ward off what Captain Alan Hanbury-Sparrow memorably called 'the Devil's breath'. Only about 3 per cent of gas casualties died, usually from internal drowning, because the victim's lungs produced up to four litres of pus-like liquid an hour, preventing the lungs from taking in air. The real Devil was in the fear that gas brought. At the faintest suspicion of gas, men would, to borrow Wilfred Owen's phrase, go into an 'ecstasy of fumbling' as they pulled their helmets on. The helmets though were hated, because *they* seemed to suffocate. A man wearing a helmet could barely see to fight. An officer could hardly command. Alan Hanbury-Sparrow tells of the discomfort of wearing a gas mask:

We gaze at one another like goggle-eyed, imbecile frogs. The mask makes you feel only half a man. You can't think. The air you breathe has been filtered of all save a few chemical substances. A man doesn't live on what passes through the filter – he merely exists. He gets the mentality of a wide-awake vegetable.[20]

And if a man didn't put his helmet on ... the memories of helmetless men gasping like fish for air remained some of the most enduring of the combatant's war. Bernard Martin, only three days in the trenches, heard the clang-clang-clang of the Gas Alarm. After putting on his helmet:

> Duty took charge of me. I must get to my platoon.
>
> I felt my way along the side of the short communication trench ... Blast from a shrapnel shell momentarily blew a gap in the gas cloud, and I saw several men (unrecognisable of course in their masks) standing irresolute as though uncertain of purpose – all but one who made his purpose apparent. He was without a mask, his head bare, his white face expressing horror. Before the gas-cloud re-formed I saw this man lurch sideways, arms outstretched, attempting to pull off another man's mask; a third man, wielding what I judged to be a bit of broken duckboard, pressed between the two. I saw one of them fall to the ground. All over in a moment, a vivid picture in my mind for ever and ever and ever.[21]

Sassoon had a recurrent nightmare in which a brother officer failed to get his gas mask on before the cloud enveloped him.

Nobody wanted a death like that either. It was the end that befell Cheltenham College's Captain Vyvian Trevenen, fatally gassed outside Bethune in May 1918.

On 1 May 1915 the Germans mounted a chlorine gas attack against the gargantuan spoil heap from the Zillebeke railway cutting known to the British as Hill 60. As the tide of gas slid over the dump into the trench held by the 1/Dorsets, they started choking and gasping; then they heard German boots storming across No-Man's Land. It was nightmare come in daytime. The situation was saved by Second Lieutenant Robin Kestell-Cornish who seized a rifle, rallied the only four men left of his platoon of forty, and fired into the gas cloud to stop the Germans breaking through.

And succeeded. The Great War has become a war without heroism, but the stand of 20-year-old subaltern Robin Kestell-Cornish and his four Dorset rifleman was the little Thermopylae of Ypres.

Captain Robin Kestell-Cornish MC and Bar died in Wimereux hospital in June 1918 after his leg was amputated following wounding in action.

What did it feel like to be wounded? The most common impression was that one had been struck a blow by a giant hand or the kick of a cart-horse. When John Reith was hit in the head by a bullet, he likened the experience to being hit by a cricket ball from a drive.

> Blast it, I've been hit. I wonder by what? Couldn't have been a shell as there wasn't an explosion. Damnation. Look at the blood pouring on my new tunic. I've been hit in the head. Has it gone through and smashed my teeth? No. They are all there. Was the bullet in my head? If so, this was the end. Meanwhile I had better lie down. Apart from anything else, I was standing on exposed ground and if hit once, could be hit again and there was no point in that. It would be nice to have a few minutes to collect oneself. I suppose, in all, this had occupied four seconds but the processes of thought were definite and sequential. I got out my fountain pen and in a very shaky hand wrote my mother's name and address and then, 'I'm alright.' Then I thought I might write in Latin the message I really wanted to send, but I let it go.[22]

On the first day of the Somme Second Lieutenant G.D. Liveing of the 12/ London Regiment went over the top on the south-west side of the Gommecourt Salient. On reaching the German wire:

> Suddenly I cursed. I had been scalded in the left hip. A shell, I thought, had blown up in a water-logged crump-hole and sprayed me with boiling water.

Liveing had been hit by a bullet; in the First Aid Post at Cross Street he was surprised by the size of the exit wound, 'a gaping hole two inches in diameter'.[23] After the shock of impact, how much a wound hurt depended on where it was located, and how preoccupied the officer was. Adrenaline, concentration on the battle, could mean that a soldier could go minutes, even hours, not realizing he was injured. Harold Macmillan, advancing under heavy shell and rifle fire at Ginchy, recalled: 'As we were going along I was wounded, with a piece of shell in the right knee, just below the knee-cap. But I managed to continue and did not feel much inconvenience until later.'[24] The cauterizing of capillaries caused by high velocity metal produced numbness in much of the body. If metal punctured the stomach, or the hand or foot, which had large conglomerations of nerve endings, the pain would be intense. Consequently, Harold Macmillan found the machine-gun bullet he sustained in the pelvis later the same day at Ginchy less painful than the bullet through the hand he had received at Loos the previous year; the machine-gun bullet wound at Ginchy 'knocked me out, but did not hurt'.[25]

Many officers have recorded how when wounded they struggled to continue to command, but when that battle was lost they would sink into a dreamy torpor. Thus John Reith mused:

> It would be nice to have a few minutes to collect oneself ... I was tired and I wanted to look up at the sky again. The opening lines of a children's hymn came into my mind: 'Above the Clear Blue Sky, in Heaven's Abode.' Well, very soon now the supreme mystery will be solved. I was completely content and at peace.

Shot in the head during an attack in a Somme wood, Gilbert Nobbs heard a voice somewhere behind him calling, 'This is death, will you come?' Only with frantic effort did Nobbs succeed in saying, 'No, not now, I won't die.'

If an officer decided that heaven could wait, he entered a more pragmatic mental state. Minor injuries could be patched up by the injured themselves or by one of his platoon (a wounded officer might be lucky enough to find his batman nearby). Officers and men had two field dressings sewn beneath the front of their tunic. In early 1915 company commanders were issued with $\frac{1}{4}$ tablets of morphia. One tablet eased pain; two tablets caused semi-insensibility until death.

The more seriously injured – assumed to be 30 per cent of an infantry attack – would have to await the arrival of the regimental stretcher-bearers, of which there were 32 per thousand fighting men. 'SBs' were soldiers in the battalion, who carried no arms and were distinguished by their brassards.

Not all wounded officers could be rescued. Officers received no priority from Stretcher Bearers because of their rank; they took their turn in the endless queue. For a popular officer, however, the men would perform outrageous acts of gallantry to try and 'bring him in'. About 15 per cent of the Victoria Crosses awarded to Other Ranks in the Great War were awarded for gallantry in the rescue of an officer. Lance-Corporal William Fuller of 2/Welsh Regiment set the gold standard for the war at Chivy on the Aisne in September 1914, advancing 100 yards under heavy rifle and machine-gun fire to pick up Captain Mark Haggard (the nephew of Rider Haggard), and carry him back to a slight ridge, where he dressed Haggard's wounds. He then carried his captain to a First Aid Station. Unfortunately, Haggard succumbed to his wounds; his last words were, 'Stick it, the Welch', which became the regiment's unofficial motto.

Any wounded officer able to walk, by himself or with help, would make his way gingerly off the battlefield towards a dressing station in the rear as the 'walking wounded'. With the battle still raging, this was a confusing and deadly enterprise in itself. Edward Liveing wrote:

> I was now confronted by a danger from our own side. I saw a row of several men kneeling on the ground and firing. It is probable that they were trying to pick off German machine-gunners, but it seemed very much as if they would 'pot' a few of the returning wounded into the bargain . . .
>
> I crawled through them. At last I got on my feet and stumbled blindly along.
>
> I fell into a sunken road with several other wounded, and crawled up over the bank on the other side. The Germans had a machine-gun on that road, and only a few of us got across. . . . Shortly afterwards, I sighted the remains of our front line trench and fell into them.
>
> At first I could not make certain as to my whereabouts. Coupled with the fact that my notions in general were becoming somewhat hazy, the trenches themselves were entirely unrecognisable. They were filled with earth, and about half their original depth. I decided, with that quick, almost semi-conscious intuition that comes to one in moments of peril, to proceed to the left . . . As I crawled through holes and over mounds I could hear the vicious spitting of machine-gun bullets. They seemed to skim just over my helmet. The trench opening out a little, began to assume its old outline. I had reached the head of New Woman Street . . . [26]

Staggering off the battlefield at Villers-Bretonneux in March 1918, supported by his batman Blunden, Frank Warren was glad of the rain because 'to me a wounded man the rain is cooling and refreshing, for the thirst of the wounded is proverbial'.[27] Stuart Cloete received liquid help of a different sort:

I was walking through the area we had fought through this morning, still green between the shellholes, and back in the trenches we had attacked from. There was no grass here; only mud and duckboard tracks winding their way between the craters, many of them ten feet deep and filled with water. If I slipped, I should drown. I still felt no pain but I was tired. At this point I became two men. My mind left my body and went on ahead. From there I watched quite objectively and with some amusement the struggles of this body of mine staggering over the duckboards and wading through the mud where the boards were smashed. I watched it duck when a salvo of German shells came over. I saw it converse with gunners who were stripped to the waist, too busy to talk but a corporal gave my body some rum . . . I then rejoined my body.

The rum may have done it.[28]

The first call for those stretchered off, and the walking wounded, was the Regimental First Aid Post, usually in a reserve trench, where a Medical Officer (MO) would assess the injury. At the beginning of the war, there were 1,279 Regular and 1,128 Territorial officers in the Royal Army Medical Corps; by 1918, such was the demand for medical service that their numbers had risen to 10,000 Regular officers and 2,845 Territorial officers. In the First Aid Post the hastily applied field dressing was replaced. A friendly MO might dole out spirits; after a 'dose' of brandy, Brian Lawrence recalled, he began to 'feel awfully well'. He had been wounded in the head and torso from a shell which had also left 'half the parapet reposing on my chest'. With a luggage tag around his neck, specifying his injury and any drugs given, the officer was carried or escorted to the next in the chain of treatment centres, the Advanced Dressing Station. Here morphia and anti-tetanus injections were given, together with lashings of tea. In the severest cases, the MO would perform amputations on the spot. Wounds were borne heroically; one had to die well. The MO of 2/Leinsters reported approvingly that Lieutenant Denis Barnett, a bullet hole through his guts, 'stuck his wound splendidly, and that men who were only hit in the arms and legs were groaning all round him in the dressing-station'.[29]

From the Advanced Dressing Station, patients were sent on by motor ambulance to a Casualty Clearing Station, where most of the surgical work was done.

John Glubb, after receiving shrapnel wounds to his neck and face ('the floodgates in my neck seemed to burst, and the blood poured out in torrents') was operated on at the Casualty Clearing Station at Ficheux:

> Early next morning I was dressed for the slaughter in long woollen stockings and laid in a line of stretchers waiting for operating. Somebody gave me an injection of morphia, and then two orderlies came up and said, 'Come on, this one will do first.' So they picked up my stretcher and bore me out, along the duckboard walks, with a steady bobbing up and down motion. Lying on my back, I looked up at the blue sky and the white drifting clouds.
>
> Then into a hut all white inside, with a row of white operating tables down the centre and white-aproned doctors and nurses moving about. They held up my stretcher and I crawled over on to the table and lay down. One or two of them came to look at me, and then the anaesthetist came up, and told me to breathe deeply through my nose. At a word from the surgeon, he put the mask on my face and I smelt that suffocating sickly smell of gas.[30]

Ideally the CCS was situated beyond artillery range, but near road and railheads. Aside from the medical staff, chaplains congregated at the CCS, making tea, writing letters, holding hands, and acting as unofficial nurses. Padre Julian Bickersteth supervised the loading of ambulances. Those who died on the operating table, or awaiting treatment, were buried outside. These extemporized graveyards now form the basis for numerous of the Commonwealth War Graves Commission cemeteries in France and Flanders, such as Dozinghem and Mendinghem. (It takes a moment to see the Tommy wit in these names, which are not Flemish.)

At Canada Farm CCS Brian Lawrence 'experienced a great sense of relief in escaping alive and being free of all responsibility. One just felt nothing mattered and that there was no need to worry about anything.'[31] Many other officers have written of their relief at dropping the burden of command as they reached this point or further down the medical care chain; they were clearly 'out of it' for a while. From the CCS, the wounded were placed in trains to be carried to a base hospital, all of which were situated on the Channel coast. Brian Lawrence recalled:

> It was an old converted French train, that is to say, the partitions had been taken out of an old passenger coach, and racks put in place of them. One was hoisted through the window on a stretcher, and then the stretcher was lodged on a rack. We did not leave till about 6pm and it was a terribly slow journey, punctuated with tremendous shunting and prolonged halts. A stretcher is not a comfortable affair, and after about twelve hours it becomes a perfect bed of torture. Long before we arrived at Boulogne I sent for the nurse, who seeing I was very feverish and in pain gave me some sort of drug so that I was very muzzy on arrival.[32]

On being unloaded at base, John Glubb was put into an ambulance, which 'drove unconscionably slowly' over cobbles until he reached the hospital:

> I was carried into a long lofty room with a row of beds on either side; the place was very dimly lighted, and two white figures glided up and down like ghosts in the darkness. One of them came and bent over me, and said, in a tender, gentle voice, 'Are you very tired, old man? Would you like a drink of milk, or sooner go off to sleep at once?' It is extraordinary what a pleasant feeling I experienced from that gentle voice. I was exhausted and its gentle kindness made all the difference to me.[33]

It was at base hospital that the relief from command came to Stuart Cloete:

I did not pay attention to the other officers in the ward. I was too preoccupied with my change of environment. The silence. The feeling that for the next few weeks I need no longer feel afraid or act with courage.[34]

Only at the base hospital were officers treated differently to the men: officers were consigned to 'Officers' Wards', the presumption being that officers – like the men – could not keep up formal military hierarchy when ill. Inevitably, not all those who reached hospital lived. Lieutenant F.P. Roe, wounded at the well-named Shrapnel Corner at Ypres, recalled:

When I woke up again I found that I had been admitted to an officers' ward of the famous No.14 General Hospital at Wimereux which was on the French coast near Boulogne. I shall never forget my first night there. There was an officer opposite me who at intervals throughout the night repeatedly called out in a loud and agonized voice, 'Mabel, Mabel!' The cries towards morning became quieter and quieter and he died peacefully early in the morning.[35]

Around 40 per cent of patients at base hospital were discharged within a fortnight. Some returned to their units, some to convalescent hospitals on the French coast (such as Lady Michelham's in Dieppe, where Vivian de Sola Pinto nursed a cheek perforated by a German grenade splinter, 'copped' during a close-quarters night fight with a German patrol in No-Man's Land), and the more seriously injured went on to 'Blighty' by hospital boat. Robert Vernede of 3/Rifle Brigade, wrote to his wife from base hospital: 'A pleasing Blighty one at last, and almost before you get this I shall with luck be in Angleterre with you a-coming to see me.' He had been wounded attacking Tea Trench, near Delville Wood, and although only a subaltern had been in temporary charge of the company.

In Blighty, officers were forwarded to officer-only hospitals. Wounded officers mostly wished to be admitted to the small exclusive hospital at 17 Grosvenor Crescent, South West London, run by Mrs Agnes Keyser, aka 'Sister Agnes', the former mistress of King Edward VII. There were other, similar establishments set up by the philanthropic for the care of wounded officers; Dennis Wheatley, invalided home with bronchitis, was placed in Sussex Lodge, Regent's Park, the private home of Mrs Hall Walker; 'She acted as Matron and she footed the whole bill'. When Alexander Stewart was wounded (by a shell splinter in the neck) in September 1917 he was conveyed to the American Women's Hospital for Officers at Lancaster Gate, London; his fiancée lived, handily, just the other side of the park. Welsh Fusilier Bernard Adams was installed in Lady Carnarvon's hospital at 48 Bryanston Square, where there descended upon him the officer's relief from the cares of command; 'I have not got to move, or think, or decide – and I can just lie for hours, for days.' (There also descended, fellow officer and patient Francis Law recalled, 'lovely creatures [who] came to cheer us up and hasten our recovery ... our days passed in great comfort and we were thoroughly spoilt.') Stuart Cloete, meanwhile, ended up in a mental hospital at 10 Palace Green with amnesia and delayed battle fatigue. He fell instantly in love with Eileen Horsman, a VAD, whom he married two years later. He recognized:

> My nurse-wounded-soldier pattern was one with a thousand precedents. Gratitude on the part of the man, a reversion to infancy and a desire to be taken care of by a woman. On the woman's part, her sympathy for pain, an effort to make up to the soldier for what he had gone through, and a kind of almost incestuous maternal feeling for this man-baby ... All in an atmosphere of war urgency.[36]

Some of the convalescent would never fight again. Lieutenant Sivori Levey, 13/West Yorkshire Regiment, faced his disabled future with admirable stoicism in 'The Road that Brought Me to Roehampton':

> Of course, to be without a leg, as everybody knows
> Has this advantage – nobody can tread upon your toes;
> And when a Theatre, or may be, a Cinema you're in,
> There's nobody who's clumsy who can kick you on the shin.
> Again, you can't get chillblains, or trench feet when you're out.
> And so you see how safely you can always get about.

They are long trails I've tramped on;
There are lonely spots I've camped on;
There are doorsteps I have stamped on;
There are pianos I have vamped on;
But the Trail I've struck,
With the Best of Luck,
Is the Road that brought me to Roehampton.

Now when your leg is separate, there's one thing to be said,
You can be half-dressed already when you are getting out of bed;
But if you're on a muddy road, it may be just your luck
To twist your foot right round, if in the mud you get it stuck.
And then you'll keep on walking round and round upon your track,
For you won't really know if you are going on or back.

They are long trails I've tramped on, etc.

When I obtain my wooden leg, I'll hop and skip and jump;
I never may be wealthy, being always on the stump;
Yet I can always stump up, and at any time I beg
To say that like some others I can always 'Swing the leg'–
So put your best foot forward – an easy thing to do –
Though it might be hard to say which is the better of the two!

They are long trails I've tramped on, etc.[37]

After discharge from hospital, any officers who might usefully be recycled to the front were sent off for further convalescence at home, or put on light duties. A period as an instructor at an Officer Cadet Battalion was normal.

And yet, many, many clamoured to return to the front, although they could easily have avoided the fate. Lieutenant J.R. Ackerley, no 'fire-eater' by his own admission, had been grateful for his 'Blighty' wound at the Somme. 'Yet', he wrote,

> so strange are we in our inconsistencies that I was not happy in Blighty and, in a few months' time, got myself sent back to France. I was at once promoted to the rank of captain.[38]

Robert Vernede, Rifle Brigade, refused to allow a friend in the War

Office to find him safe work there, and returned to France. Vernede, poet and the author of *The Pursuit of Mr Faviel*, died of wounds on 9 April 1917 after being hit by machine-gun fire at Arras. He was forty-one.

Like Siegfried Sassoon and Wilfred Owen, Robert Graves voluntarily returned to the front; when he reached the 2nd Battalion at Bouchavesnes on the Somme he said, 'I couldn't stand England any longer'.

Charles Nye expressed it:

Furthermore the monotonous training at home is repugnant to me. Also you don't know how badly England wants trained officers and I would rather be back in the trenches than skulking at home.[39]

John Glubb recuperating in England, discovered:

I was intensely depressed at my enforced idleness, and all my thoughts were with the boys in France. I resented the superficial frivolity of London, pursued under the specious pretext of keeping up civilian morale.[40]

Glubb bombarded the authorities with requests for medical boards and postings to France; on 11 July 1918 he was given command of a draft for France.

Not all wounds were physical, not all mortalities absolute. There were injuries to the mind, as well as the body.

At first, shellshock was adamantly believed to be 'windiness'; the sufferer was as likely to be shot for desertion as treated medically. The War Office explicitly proscribed the setting up of neurological units because they would act as magnets to soldiers with 'insufficient stoutness of heart'.[41] Eventually, the sheer tide of cases caused a rethink and by the end of 1916 there were 'mental wards' in base hospitals in France. On the basis of pre-war psychiatric practice, the shellshock victim was categorized as suffering from hysteria or neurasthenia (depression and anxiety). Robert Graves considered that there were twice as many neurasthenia cases among the officers than amongst the men because 'officers had a more nervous time than the men' in the trenches.[42] As medical authorities recognized during the war, officers became anguished by their inability to show the courage expected of them. Only understood in retrospect is that officers who literally 'put on a brave face' suppressed emotions, and the effect was to corrode their mental defences over time; Charles Carrington had something approaching a mental breakdown during a night and day of heavy shellfire, brought about by his frantic attempts to repress his fear and appear nonchalant.[43]

Second Lieutenant Bernard Martin recalled:

> An officer's duties and concern for his men took the edge off his own fears; we were actors in a play, every time we listened to an approaching shell we screened our nerves by acting an entirely imaginary character – the fearless man. I'd known brave men gradually lose their nerves till they couldn't play this tragedy any longer, dared not leave a dug-out to perform duties: one chap, a captain, ended it with suicide. How long did I have to keep up the role?[44]

There was, of course, no viable alternative to a stiff upper lip under fire; no soldier wanted to be led by a visibly emotional officer.

Treatment for shellshock varied from sleeping draughts to electric shocks, but was predicated on the belief that shellshock was caused by a physical malfunction of the brain after the nearby explosion of ordnance. Only in stubborn cases was psychoanalysis used. These patients were referred to one of the twenty-one neurological centres established in Britain between 1916 and 1918 (seven for officers, fourteen for other ranks), the best known being Craiglockhart Military Hospital in Edinburgh, where the patients famously included Wilfred Owen and Siegfried Sassoon. Lieutenant Sassoon was not impressed by his fellow patients, writing to Lady Ottoline Morrell, 'My fellow patients are 160 more or less dotty officers. A great many of them are degenerate looking.' He was more impressed by the psychoanalyst Dr W.H. Rivers, who used Freudian concepts to unpack 'anxiety neuroses'. (Sassoon, of course, did not have 'neurasthenia'; he had been shunted to Craiglockhart out of quiet political expediency, following his 1917 anti-war 'Declaration'.) There was always the well-founded suspicion that inconvenient or 'windy' officers were treated with kid gloves by the authorities, who suffered a paranoia that dud officers would infect those below them. To try them at courts martial for cowardice had the disadvantage of publicity.

Lieutenant Colonel Viscount Gort told the 1922 shellshock committee set up by the War Office that shellshock was a regrettable occurrence, which could be eliminated by discipline. He had a point.

On the Somme in 1916 Anthony Eden's 21/King's Royal Rifle Corps received instructions informing them to not treat shellshock sympathetically, in case it spread like yellow peril. His commanding officer, Foljambe, took the missive to heart; during the battle Eden watched him intercept a glazed-eyed, sanctuary-seeking subaltern, recently knocked over by a blast. Foljambe talked firmly to the subaltern and directed him back to the smoking frontline of battle. Three days later the Royal Fusiliers, next-door in the trenches, brought the same subaltern to Foljambe's attention, because they had been so utterly impressed by his recent grace under fire. During the German Spring offensive of 1918 Lieutenant C.J. Arthur of the Royal West Kent Regt. lost his nerve during the German offensive: 'Luckily, the colonel ... talked to me very severely and made me pull myself together ... It was an effort, but, thank God, I succeeded.'[45]

The War Office inquiry concluded that good leadership would substantially reduce the incidence of shellshock within a unit. They might have had Foljambe and Arthur's colonel in mind.

Clearly, 'shellshock' could be a traumatic neurosis for which the medicine of a chat, the proximity of a steely superior, or a brief rest out of the lines was not enough. Many soldiers suffered long-term illness; in 1930, 32,000 victims of shellshock were receiving disability pensions.

'Yet though we all loved Batty-Smith', wrote Guy Chapman, 'our mourning was short.' Charles Scott-Moncrieff explained why soldiers did not unduly grieve for their fallen comrades:

It's a fortnight on Friday since Christopher died,
And John's at Boulogne with a hole in his side,
While poor Harry's got lost, the Lord only knows where;
May the Lord keep them all and ourselves in His care.
. . . Mustn't think we don't mind when a chap gets laid out,
They've taken the best of us, never a doubt;
But with life pretty busy and death rather near
We've no time for regret any more than for fear. [46]

Stuart Cloete added: 'There was, in our unconscious minds, the feeling "better him than me"'.[47] And the prevalence of death brought a sort of immunity to grief: there were so many to grieve, where did one start?

Sometimes, however, the grief could not be held. When Etonian Major V.P. Hoare was buried under a bright sun and blue sky two officers 'kissed his dead face', the School's *Chronicle* recorded. Captain Llewellyn Wyn Griffith of the 1/Royal Welch Fusiliers sent his brother, Watcyn, a signaller, on an errand at Mametz Wood that resulted in the latter's killing: 'So I had sent him to his death, bearing a message from my own hand, in an endeavour to save other men's lives.' These thoughts whirligigged round and round Llewelyn Wyn Griffith's mind:

in unending sequence, a wheel revolving within my brain, expanding until it touched the boundaries of knowing and feeling. They did not gain in truth from repetition, nor did they reach understanding. The swirl of mist refused to move.[48]

Although Richard Talbot Kelly became so inured to death he was able to use the body of a dead British soldier as a pillow in a chalk pit on the Somme, he suffered extreme depression when his commanding officer, Major E.L.B. Anderson DSO was killed by a shell landing at the entrance to his dug-out at Passchendaele. Talbot Kelly recalled the day as 'The most miserable day of my life'. During the funeral service of Second Lieutenant Littlewood, killed by shrapnel in the Cojeul Valley, John Glubb 'could not stop the tears, when that body so strong, so gallant, and so young, was let down by the ropes into its grave'.[49] Patrick Shaw-Stewart wrote in November 1915, 'Nowadays, we who are alive have the sense of being old, old survivors.' After the death of a slew of friends and college contemporaries – Julian Grenfell, Billy Grenfell, Raymond Asquith, Charles Lister, F.S. Kelly, Edward Horner – he sank into depression and lost the will to live. He was killed in action on 30 December 1917, at the age of twenty-nine, on the Western Front.[50] He had given up a staff job with the French Army in order to re-join the Royal Naval Division on the front line.

Naturally, the greatest grief for a dead soldier officer was felt by his family. The notification of death was a terse telegram delivered by a boy on a bicycle. Marie Leighton wrote movingly of the evening in December 1915, when she waited for Roland to return home on leave – and instead learned of his death:

> He is certainly very late. It is beginning to look as if he will not come till to-morrow morning.
>
> The weather may be bad in the Channel. Anyhow, we shall have to go on with dinner.
>
> I hear a noise of the opening and shutting of doors.
>
> I start to my feet.
>
> This is he! This must be he!
>
> But two or three moments pass and he does not come into the room. And something new and strange and heavy has come into the air of the house; or so, at least, I fancy.
>
> My husband comes along. There is something very odd about his step. And his face looks changed, somehow; sharpened in feature and greyish white.
>
> 'How true it is that electric light sometimes makes people look a dreadful colour!' I think as he comes nearer to me. I ran forward then to meet him.
>
> 'Where is Roland ? Isn't he here ? I thought I heard him come'.
>
> And then for the first time I noticed that the boy's father had a bit of pinkish paper crushed up in his hand.
>
> 'Is that a telegram ?' I cried eagerly, putting out my own hand. 'Oh, give it to me ! What does it say ? Isn't he coming to-night ?'
>
> One of my husband's arms was put quietly around me.
>
> 'No. It's no good our waiting for him any longer. He'll never come any more. He's dead. He was badly wounded on Wednesday at midnight, and he died on Thursday.'

For minutes that were like years the world became to me a shapeless horror of greyness in which there was no beginning and no end, no light and no sound. I did not know anything except that I had to put out my hand and catch at something, with an animal instinct to steady myself so that I might not fall. And then, through the rolling, blinding waves of mist, there came to me suddenly the old childish cry : 'Come and see me in bed, mother!'

And I heard myself answering aloud: 'Yes, boy of my heart, I will come. As soon as the war is over I will come and see you in bed – in your bed under French grass. And I will say good-night to you – there – kneeling by your side – as I've always done.'

Good-night!

Though Life and all take flight.

Never Good-bye![51]

These last three lines of Marie Leighton's memoir, *Boy of My Heart*, are inscribed on the gravestone of Lieutenant Roland Aubrey Leighton, Worcestershire Regiment, at Louvencourt Military Cemetery.

Officers in France and Flanders would go to extraordinary lengths to retrieve, and decently bury, the bodies of brother officers. After being informed by a soldier from another regiment of the rough whereabouts of the corpse of Lieutenant-Colonel Lord Feversham, Anthony Eden led a small search and burial party into the night. They found Feversham's body near the front line just as dawn was breaking. Shells began to fall close by:

Sadly we set about our task. I read a few lines from the burial service, which someone had lent me at headquarters. Dale set up the wooden cross, we gave our commanding officer a last salute and turned away, leaving him to Picardy and the shells.[52]

Blood brothers went to even greater lengths. When Gilbert Talbot fell at Hooge his brother Neville crawled out between the lines, under fire, a week later and brought his body back. Captain Guy Crouch ('Deedoos') wrote to his parents of his efforts to make sure that his brother Lionel was decently interred:

September 3, 1916.

DEAREST MOTHER,

I have to-day been able to see the officer who was in charge of the burial party who found dear old Lionel and buried him. He says he knew who he was by his medal-ribbon, etc., and buried him near where he lay, and the padre who was with them read a short service over him. They put up a stick with his name, regiment, rank, and the date (July 21) on it (they had no crosses left), and also left a card in a shell case with the same particulars on it, in case the stick got displaced or obliterated. The whole thing was necessarily rather hurried, as the party were being shelled and one man was hit by shrapnel. The map reference is ... If we go back to that district, I will make a point of getting a proper cross stuck up and a decent grave made. In case you want to write to the officer who found him, his address is, Captain Pickford, Oxford and Bucks L.I., B.E.F.

Best love to Dad and Do.

Your loving Son,

DEEDOOS.

November 14, 1916.

DEAREST MAS R,

I went up this morning and met a party of three men and a lance-corporal (Joiner by name, who lives in Bicester Road), and we made up dear old Lionel's grave properly. The cross is of wood and has a Bucks Battalion cap badge let into the top, and the lettering is cut into the wood to make it permanent. The grave is in a hollow made by a shell, about 8 feet across and 1 foot deep. We made up the mound, and made an edging of cast-iron shell-cases ... So the top of the mound is about level with the surrounding ground, and the 1-foot dip into the shell-hole makes a very good protection to the grave itself. We put the other cross, that was there before, at the foot.

With best love to you all,

Your loving Son,

DEEDOOS.[53]

For a bereft soldier, revenge was always an option instead of grief. On hearing of the death of his brother, Denis Barnett wrote home: 'I've got a long account to settle out here, and Kenneth is at the top of it. I think they'll find that will cost them a lot.'[54]

The death of close friend Lieutenant David Thomas of the Royal Welch Fusiliers hit Robert Graves hard, Sassoon harder still. At the time Sassoon was the battalion's acting transport officer, and every evening henceforth, wrote Graves, 'when he came up with the rations, [he] went out on patrol looking for Germans to kill'.[55] It was for these solo killing expeditions that Sassoon acquired the regimental nickname of 'Mad Jack'.

There were little deaths of the soul and heart, where something inside perished but the body carried on. Many officers – Sassoon prime among them – worried that the war brought a desensitization of the soul. A month before his death, Roland Leighton had written to Vera, by then a VAD nurse in London:

I wonder if your metamorphosis has been as complete as my own. I feel a barbarian, a wild man of the woods, stiff, narrowed, practical, an incipient martinet perhaps, not at all the kind of person who would be associated with prizes on Speech Day, or poetry, or dilettante classicism.[56]

He still had hope for himself, writing on 28 November 1915; 'I don't think that when one can still admire sunsets one has altogether lost the personality of pre-war days.'

It was not only the poets who noted the coarsening effects of war. Second Lieutenant William Ratcliffe, South Staffordshire Regiment, likewise worried that the war brought a degradation of the mind:

Everywhere one sees preparation for murder; nearly every person one sees is a dirty man with some implement of destruction about his person. The countryside and the beauties of nature, which, as you know, always have a beneficial effect on a man, are all spoilt by the dust and mud of motor lorries and by huge camps.

Everywhere the work of God is spoiled by the hand of man. One looks at a sunset and for a moment thinks that at least is unsophisticated, but an aeroplane flies across, and puff! Puff! And the whole scene is spoilt by clouds of shrapnel smoke![57]

Ratcliffe, a chemistry student before enlistment, died aged nineteen on 1 July 1916.

Returning in September 1917 to the battalion, lying in Kemmel Shelters, after a stint on the staff, Guy Chapman saw that:

> The officers were as the men. Very few of the pre-Somme vintage remained: Vanneck escaped miraculously, worn and bitter, Whitehead, with two periods in hospital, Jerome and P.E. Lewis wounded and rejoined. The rest were either very young or had served in the ranks. Many were as worn as their men, suffering in turn irritation, fear, and cafard. Our speech had grown coarser; our humour threadbare, at best cruel, met by sardonic laughter. We are in truth *grognards* ... Yet the Aidos still linger in certain hearts, and in the heart of the battalion as a whole, animating it through calamities and afflictions. We have not yet lost the saving virtues of irony and humility.[58]

During the Great War 7,335 British officers were captured and made prisoners of war, the bulk of them in the book ends of the conflict, when there was movement on the battlefields of Flanders and France. Second Lieutenant Brian Horrocks was captured at Ypres on 21 October 1914 and taken, injured, to a German military hospital at Lille:

> It was a nasty hospital. The whole time I was there, which was nearly a month, neither our shirts nor our blankets were changed, and we were still wearing the blood-soaked garments in which we had been wounded. As our wounds were suppurating we soon became unpleasant objects. The most degrading thing of all, however, was the fact that, as a refinement in beastliness, we were not allowed to use bedpans or bottles, but were forced to heave ourselves out of bed and crawl, because neither of us could walk, along the floor to the lavatory which lay at the end of a stone passage. [59]

Although barely able to walk, he was judged fit to be sent to a prisoner of war camp in Germany:

> My escort turned out to be a Feldwebel of the Imperial Guard who had been at the front since the beginning of the war, and was now on his way back to Germany to do some course or other; he spoke a little

English, and had once been to London to take part in a swimming race.

At the station I was leaning out of the carriage window when a German Red Cross girl passed along the platform carrying a large bowl of soup with an appetising smell. She stopped, and then, seeing that I was an Englishman, spat into the soup and threw it on the platform. There was a bellow of rage from my escort. He made me sit well down in the carriage while he leant out and collected food from all who passed, every bit of which was passed back to me.

On another occasion we went to the station-master's office to find out about trains. As there was no one in the room, my Feldwebel pushed forward a chair for me to sit on. Suddenly the door burst open and in came a typical fat, German railway official.

'Why is this English swine seated in my office?' he shouted 'Get up!'

The Feldwebel walked slowly over to him, bent down towards the little turkey-cock and said:

'This is a British officer who was wounded fighting, which you are never likely to be. He will remain seated.'

And I did.

Afterwards he apologised for his fellow countryman, saying:

'All front-line troops have a respect for each other, but the farther from the front you get, the more bellicose and beastly the people become.'

How right he was. I have always regarded the forward area of the battlefield as the most exclusive club in the world, inhabited by the cream of the nation's manhood, the men who actually do the fighting. Comparatively few in number, they have little feeling of hatred for the enemy, rather the reverse.[60]

Eighteen-year-old Horrocks spent the next four years in various POW camps, absconded numerous times, and twice was within sight of neutral Holland. Eventually, he was sent to Fort Zorndorf, Custrin, the bad boys' camp for persistent escapers. As far as Horrocks was concerned, the POW experience was worse for older officers, because they either worried about their families or, if they were Regulars, realized that they had lost their opportunity for rising up the professional ladder. It can be added that young Horrocks was spared another anguish; he was captured wounded. Officers captured unharmed went through their own special mental hell. Alec Waugh was taken prisoner on 28 March 1918 – without so much as a scratch – after his battery was surrounded. Waugh wrote of the unharmed officer's anxiety in the POW camp:

> He did not join the army to languish behind prison bars. Should he be here at all? Was there not something he could have done to avoid this fate? Did he fail in initiative, did he fail in courage? I suppose that every prisoner has felt as I did then.[61]

Officers in the British Army were not supposed to surrender; they were supposed to make fighting stands on the epic model of Lieutenant-Colonel Elstob at Manchester Redoubt near St. Quentin on 21 March 1918, the day the Germans launched the last-roll-of-the-dice 'Michael' Offensive. (The time and the place is that of Sherriff's *Journey's End*.) Grabbing a pistol and grenades, Wilfrith Elstob told his men, 'Here we fight; here we die.' An old boy of Christ's Hospital and a vicar's son, Elstob was as good as his gentleman's word. After leading the beating back of repeated assaults by superior numbers, Elstob died fighting. He was posthumously awarded the Victoria Cross.

It was not only captured officers themselves who had doubts about their moral fibre. At the end of the war, officer POWs were ordered by a worried War Office to make a statement explaining the circumstances of their capture. To the evident satisfaction, if not relief, of the War Office, the captured officers – be they Regulars, Territorials or 'hostilities only' citizens – had maintained the Army's highest traditions of bravery and duty. In nearly all cases, their capture was the result of utter confusion, plain bad luck or the material impossibility of continuing fighting. When Lieutenant N.E. Tyndale-Biscoe RA was captured ('Up to the present the blackest day of my life') near Ribemont he had recced a village alone, fired thirty shots at the enemy with his revolver and then found himself cut off with no ammunition. He had no means to carry on the fight. In words that applied to a thousand other officers, Second Lieutenant Harry Rutherford of the Durham Light Infantry anxiously informed the War Office, that he had been captured because of 'the dense fog, the fact that we did not know the country and the fact of the company being isolated ...'[62]

In Germany, British Officer POWs were segregated from Other Ranks POWs, being either wired into separate compounds or placed in exclusively officer-only camps. Alec Waugh was confined in an *Offizier-Kriegsgefangenenlager* in walled barracks above Mainz, which had a view of the Rhine and the cathedral. 'We were crowded but not overcrowded,' he recalled, 'ten of us to a room; about 600 in the camp.'[63]

Unlike Other Ranks, officers in POW camps did not work, though whether this was a blessing or not was debatable. Behind the wire, the battle for the officer was the battle against boredom. Alec Waugh read copiously (Maupassant, Flaubert, Balzac, Chekhov, Turgenev, Dostoevsky), Gilbert Nobbs learned French and Russian, and at Lahr, in the Black Forest, Tyndale-Biscoe was allowed 'parole' to walk around the town. There were theatricals, boxing competitions and 'escape clubs'. Even so time dragged; in an odd echo of the trenches, food once again came to be the marker of the day. There was little food. 'Our red-letter days,' Waugh wrote, 'were those when we had potatoes twice.' The coffee was ersatz, made with acorns; the immovable feast on the menu was sauerkraut, which few liked. Officers paid for their food with special POW *Kriegsgefangenenlager* marks, given them by the German government; a lieutenant received 60 marks a month, and a captain 100 marks. The German government recouped this money from the officer's pay in Britain. As a price guide, Tyndale-Biscoe paid one mark for three-quarters of a sausage.[64] Life in camp was made bearable by food parcels organized either via families, Regiments or the Red Cross. ('Waiting for, and dividing out parcels,' wrote Gilbert Nobbs, now blind from his injuries, were 'the habits of schooldays'; not for the first time in the Great War, the rigours of a public school education proved the best preparation for the war's demands on the officer.)

And officers, being gentlemen who would honour their obligations, were allowed to cash cheques once a month through either a Swiss bank or American Express. The limit for subalterns was £5. Optimistic officers, therefore, made sure they carried their Cox's cheque book into battle.

IX

Last Post: When the War was Over

> It is impossible for me to say I hated the war. I did not.
>
> Captain Stuart Cloete, Household Cavalry

On the morning of 11 November 1918, a shroud of fog lay along the Western Front. Somewhere in the landscape there was desultory shelling and small arms fire, but for the most part soldiers sat around waiting for news. Francis Hitchcock's 2/Leinsters, however, kept marching, anxious to secure a bridge-head over the Dendre at Lessines before 11 a.m., in case the Germans violated the terms of the proposed Armistice and fighting did not cease. 'We did not realize that the war was coming to an end', wrote Hitchcock.[1] There had been rumours of Armistice before, which had proved no more substantial than the morning's mist. Lieutenant Arthur Gregory of the Royal Field Artillery struck a rare note of excitement:

> BEF November 11th 1918
> 10.45 a.m.
>
> My dear Mother,
>   A quarter of an hour more War! Cumulative rumours have been crowned by an official intimation. This is my last letter ON ACTIVE SERVICE. Never again, I hope, shall I wear tin hat and box respirator.
>   We were expecting to go into action early this morning, but – didn't.
> I am 6 miles S. of MONS
> Well, that's enough for one letter.
> The church bells are ringing now.
> TE DEUM LAUDAMUS
>   Arthur[2]

At 11 o'clock on the 11th day of the 11th month, the war did end. On the historic moment Hitchcock called out 'Eleven o'clock!' but the Leinsters simply 'marched on in silence'. Like the Leinsters, Guy Chapman's battalion of Royal Fusiliers were on the march, tramping along muddy *pavé*, as they had so many times before. The band played, but there was little singing. Guy Chapman recalled:

> We were very old, very tired, and now very wise. We took over our billets and listlessly devoured a meal. In an effort to cure our apathy, the little American doctor from Vermont who had joined us a fortnight earlier broke his invincible teetotalism, drank half a bottle of whisky, and danced a cachucha. We looked at his antics with dull eyes and at last put him to bed.[3]

It wasn't only the Leinsters and Royal Fusiliers who found war's end a bewildering anti-climax. 'At present we cannot realize hostilities have ceased. It is impossible to alter one's habit of mind of four years in an hour or so', wrote Burgon Bickersteth.[4] Rowland Feilding, now CO of the Connaught Rangers, noticed 'no visible change in demeanour' in his men.

The weary road. The soldier was too tired to be elated, and losses had been despairingly deep in the last 100 days of pursuing the Germans across France and Belgium. The Roll of Honour in Monmouth School chapel shows 13 names of old boys who died in action in 1918, not far off the 17 who died in the year of the Somme. Not quite everyone, though, was exhausted on the great glad morning. There were always young officers keen to be fighting. Captain John Glubb was scouring the countryside for hay for the horses of his battery, when:

> we visited a deserted farm nearby, where there was a loft full of hay which we commandeered. As I was standing below, watching the drivers throwing the hay out of the lift window, a mounted orderly rode up, and told us that the war was over. A dreadful blow! I was just beginning to enjoy it, and this will finish my dreams of the dashing column of pursuit. Raining as usual.[5]

But finally it was all quiet on the Western Front. Captain Llewellyn Evans of 2/Royal Welch Fusiliers wrote:

To me the most remarkable feature of that day and night was the uncanny silence that pervaded. No rumbling of guns, no staccato of machine-guns, nor did the roar of exploding dumps break into the night as it had done.

The War was over.[6]

Noise, decided Charles Douie, was likely how civilians remembered the Armistice, whereas 'Most soldiers will speak of the unwonted silence, for the first time unbroken by gun or rifle fire after four long years.'[7] In London, delirious crowds streamed onto the streets, even pulling in their wake the grieving such as Vera Brittain, who had lost her brother Edward, fiancé Roland, and friends Victor Richardson and Geoffrey Thurlow. Henry Ogle was sitting in a Blackpool officer's camp for convalescents (he'd received a 'Blighty' wound to his hand, more proof of his luck), listening to a lecture on the attack and defence of strong-points when:

We heard distant cheering. In those days there was only one thing that could be worth a cheer. The lecturer faltered. Running footsteps were heard and after a very cursory knock an NCO burst in with a note for the lecturer. We knew it! We did not wait to hear what the note said but I believe the officer said, 'That of course will be all this morning, gentlemen.' We gave one yell and dashed out to join the others, and a surging throng of all ranks mingled with civilians to converge on the Town Hall Square just when the Mayor of Blackpool announced the Armistice. The town went wild with relief and joy.[8]

Other soldiers who, by the fortunes of war, were washed up in Britain in November 1918 found themselves unable to join in the celebrations. Robert Graves was at a camp in North Wales:

Armistice-night hysteria did not touch our camp much, though some of the Canadians stationed there went down to Rhyl to celebrate in true overseas style. The news sent me out walking alone along the dyke above the marshes of Rhuddlan (an ancient battlefield, the Flodden of Wales) cursing and sobbing and thinking of the dead.[9]

He heard the news of the Armistice at the same time that he heard of Wilfred Owen's death.[10]

The Armistice, like the war itself, was generally another experience that divided the civilian from the soldier, the soldier from the civilian. Lieutenant Ernest Parker stood in the epicentre of celebration, Trafalgar Square, but as a bystander. He watched the lorries carrying the screaming, dancing munitions workers:

> Alas, I could not share their high spirits, for the new life which was now beckoning had involved an enormous sacrifice . . . Surrounded by people whose experiences had been so different, I felt myself a stranger and I was lost in thoughts they could not possibly share.[11]

Siegfried Sassoon walked along the Oxfordshire water meadows at Cuddesdon, finding it 'impossible to realize' that the war had ended. In the evening he too went up to London to watch – not join – the crowds, waving flags in the wet darkness. 'It was a loathsome ending to the loathsome tragedy of the last four years', he wrote.[12]

In a *Kriegsgefangenenlager* in Germany, Basil Willey recalled:

> The red flag was hoisted over the camp, and a private soldier who had been the interpreter announced himself as president of the local soviet ('Workers' and Soldiers' Council') and commandant of the camp in place of the (deposed) Prussian general. He courteously threw open the camp gates and invited us to walk wherever we liked. However, this was wisely vetoed by our own senior officer (a brigadier), and in due time (it seemed endless to our impatience) we sailed from Danzig to Leith in a Danish ship.[13]

On seeing the white cliffs of Dover, Lieutenant Tyndale-Biscoe, also returned from POW exile, found a 'feeling of most intense joy'. He rushed to a London hotel to meet up with his parents; 'the long parting was over. Thank God,' he wrote in his diary.

As the door on the war closed, thoughts went forward. For soldiers, said Graham Seton Hutchison: 'The only life which they had ever known had come to an end; and the future opened mysteriously, offering what?'[14]

What indeed? Boys who had been pitchforked into khaki and Sam Brownes straight from school and university, had enjoyed no normal adulthood. Of the 148,000 officers in the Army the vast majority were between 18 and 25. Douie wrote:

> To me, as to a multitude of other young men, acclimatisation to the conditions of peace was not easy. Since I had left school more than four years before, I had known the world only under the conditions of war. I had no memory of a man's life as it had been before the war on which I might build up a new life for the future. I found it hard to envisage life on an ordered plan covering a period of years; I do not find it easy today. Throughout the war, in common with most of the infantry, I had lived solely for the day.[15]

To Guy Chapman, England 'was an island we did not know', as foreign as France had been to Vyvian Trevenen in the beginning of the war. The Regiment was home. After being told by a government commission for the employment of ex-service officers that, at twenty-eight, he was 'far too old' Chapman took the obvious course and stayed on in the Army. (One of Chapman's brother officers was informed, by the same commission that 'military distinction was quite a useless distinction for civil life'.)[16] Charles Carrington recalled: 'I was a little scared of it [demobilisation] and was in no hurry to be thrown out of the nest.'[17] Another who found it difficult to fly the regimental nest was Graham Greenwell; in Italy at the war's end, aged twenty-two and second in command of the battalion, he wrote to his long-suffering mother:

> But it will be very hard to leave the regiment after so many years . . . Could you ever have guessed how much I should enjoy the war?

He wondered what he should do:

> I have begun seriously to consider what I am going to do now that the war is really over. I should love to stay on in the Army, but really it is very difficult to decide, as we don't in the least know what sort of conditions will be offered us. But I can guess what you will think about it.

> I wrote to Carew Hunt the other day and asked him to find out what was the position at Oxford. Students are "Class 43" on the demobilisation list – the last but one, whereas "gentlemen" are in "Class 37". So it would seem better to be a mere gentleman.[18]

Greenwell was not alone in finding the order of demobilization bewildering, if not downright angering. The demobilization priorities were: civil servants; 'pivotal men' (men in essential services); and 'slip men' (men who could provide a form from an employer promising a job); men expected to find work quickly; and those who would need longer to do so. The system was unfair because the more recently joined – who were likely to be conscripts – were also more likely to be able to show proof of a job in the waiting.

Men who had served longest were disadvantaged.

The whole system was topsy-turvy, and grindingly slow. In August 1919 the War Office announced that 106,294 officers and 2,625,811 other ranks had been processed – which left nearly a million men in uniform. In the dissolution of battalions, Other Ranks were let go first, leaving flocks of officers with nowhere to go and nothing to do.

When finally demobbed, J.B. Priestley was among those officers who walked through the door into civilian life with relief:

> No awards for gallantry had come – or were to come – my way; but I was entitled to certain medals and ribbons. I never applied for them; I was never sent them; I have never had them. Feeling that the giant locusts that had eaten my four and a half years could have them, glad to remember that never again would anybody tell me to carry on, I shrugged the shoulders of a civvy coat that was a bad fit, and carried on.[19]

Charles Carrington was pleased to walk away with a gratuity of £226, to which was added £250 when he went up to Oxford, he being among a sizeable contingent of ex-officers who took up university places delayed by war service, or attracted by the short courses put on especially for demobbed servicemen.

A man setting out on married life needed an income, not a student grant. So, after some deliberation, Alec Waugh forwent Oxford and instead joined the publishing firm run by his father, Chapman and Hall. Others needing gainful employment were not so lucky as to be able to join the family firm. It would be trite but true to say the soldiers won the war but lost the peace. Britain had few jobs for its returning heroes and unemployment became the curse of the ex-officer and ranker; in 1920 Haig's Officers' Association appealed for £5 million to assist 25,000 unemployed officers, as well as 33,000 disabled officers, 10,000 widows and 8,000 orphans. By January 1922 there were two million unemployed in Britain – about a half-million of them were ex-servicemen. While he never repented of the rightness of the war – and thought that was the mind-set of most old soldiers – Charles Douie added a bitter addendum:

> Unemployment is another matter. Here the soldier has real excuse for bitterness. . . . The brunt has fallen, moreover, as it fell in the war, on the infantry. The man who made munitions, and the man with a trade, who found his way during the war for the most part into the Royal Engineers, Royal Army Service Corps, and other technical services, has been absorbed without difficulty into industry . . . England may well bow her head in shame at the thought of her 21,000 disabled unemployed.[20]

George Coppard, ex-NCO machine-gunner, recalled that in the 1920s:

> It was a common sight in London to see ex-officers with barrel organs, refusing to earn a living as beggars. Single men picked up twenty-one shillings a week unemployment pay as a special allowance, but there were no jobs for the 'heroes' who had won the war.[21]

The personal columns of the newspapers overflowed with pleas from officers for work. One such insert in *The Times* ran:

> Old Etonian (twenty-seven) married and suffering from neurasthenia but in no way really incapacitated in urgent need of outdoor work. Would be glad to accept post of head gamekeeper at nominal salary.

Another Old Etonian, former gunner captain Gilbert Frankau, echoed in verse the dissatisfactions of many an ex-officer:

Only an officer! Only a chap
Who carried on till the final scrap,
Only a fellow who didn't shirk-
Homeless, penniless, out of work,
Asking on a start in life,
A job that will keep himself and his wife,
'And thank the Lord we haven't a kid'
Thus men pay for the deeds men did!

Only an officer! Only a chap
Wounded and gassed in a bit of a scrap
Only a fellow who didn't shirk-
Shaky and maimed and unfit for work,
Asking only enough in life
To keep a home for himself and his wife,
'And she'll work if she can, but of course, there's the kid.'
Thus men pay for the deeds men did!

Only our officers! Only the chaps
That war-time uses and peace-time scraps,
Only the fellows a bit too proud
To beg a dole from the charity-crowd,
Carrying on – with a smile for the wife,
'But it's breaking his heart because of the kid!'
Thus men starve for the deeds men did![22]

Such high hopes of the land fit for heroes, so quickly tainted and corroded away. Of those ex-officers who came to look on the war, in Richard Aldington's acid words, as 'a blast of wind, a blather, a humbug, a newspaper stunt, a politician's ramp', many did so when the MC went to that loathsome corner shop with three brass balls over the door. Former infantry captain Alfred Pollard even tried to pawn his VC.

'Temporary Gentlemen,' promoted from the ranks in the exigencies of war lost, with the siren blast of peace, their social position. Since they were no longer officers they took, from one second to the next, a header down the class ladder. For some the drop was very steep indeed; according to the War Office's analysis of the dispersal certificates of the 144,075 officers who had been demobilised by 12 May 1920, there were departing khaki, *inter alia*, 638 former fishermen, 148 carters, 1,016 miners and 266 warehousemen and porters. (An incidental consequence of this exodus of 'TGs' from the Army was that the officer corps reverted to its *ante bellum* social exclusivity.)

So prominent was the phenomenon of the temporary gentleman adrift in the brave new Britain that he became a fixture in postwar books and plays. An early outing was H.F. Maltby's 1919 play 'A Temporary Gentlemen', in which the working class hero, a former 'TG', sets his cap at the daughter of war profiteer Sir Herbert Hudson; the hero is rebuffed and becomes a commercial traveller, marrying a former Women's Auxiliary Army girl. Maltby himself was a 'TG'. In R.F. Delderfield's *To Serve Them All My Days* ex-subaltern and Welsh miner's son David Powlett-Jones suffers from 'twitch' and aimlessness until he finds solace and purpose as a teacher in a minor public school. The most infamous example of the Temporary Gentleman is, of course, ex-Lieutenant Oliver Mellors in *Lady Chatterley's Lover*. As seen by Lady Chatterley: 'The gamekeeper Mellors is a curious kind of person. He might almost be a gentleman.' Almost indeed.

Temporary Gentlemen, blue-blooded gentlemen, ex-officers all. Even if they could find a job, the job somehow failed to fit. H.E.L. Mellersh explained:

> The trouble was that so many civilian jobs seemed by comparison with fighting for one's country, unromantic, petty, even undignified. No doubt many of us had ideas above our station: we had been somebody during the war and we expected to be somebody ... There was a nobility in being a soldier.[24]

Edwin Campion Vaughan, decorated with an MC (for capturing a bridge across the Sambre Canal on 4 November 1918) never did settle to the ordinariness of civvy street and joined the Essex Regiment, before transferring to the RAF and qualifying as a pilot. He was killed in a flying accident.

Disillusion and unemployment were not confined to ex-officers; in the years after the war Britain boiled with unrest. That the discontent stopped short of the insurrections of other European countries was, Charles Douie attributed, in 'great measure to the determination of those who fought in the war never to engage in civil strife against their late comrades'. One of the less acknowledged truths of the war is that the rubbing of shoulders together in trench-land lessened class differences. The Honourable Charles Lister (Eton and Balliol) died a subaltern in the Hood Battalion in the Middle East; a few months before his death he had written of his hope that the 'dead of the war, side by side' would fill up the deep gulf of class difference.[25] At Toc-H in Poperinge, Bernard Martin had been moved by the sight of officers, NCOs and privates together at the counter. It was:

> Unthinkable in Blighty; where since the war social distinctions were rigidly maintained by 'Officers Only' notices at the entrance to many hotels, restaurants, bars and even tea shops. What the war ought to be doing, I thought is reducing class barriers, making less difference between rich and poor – the rank is but the guinea's stamp.[26]

Reflecting that the war taught him 'a deep sympathy for the "Tommy"', John Ronald Tolkien (King Edward's School) created the character of Sam Gamgee, a meld of Tommies of Tolkien's acquaintance.[27] Meanwhile, fox-hunting squire Siegfried Sassoon joined the Labour Party, while Old Etonian Gilbert Frankau picked up the poet's pen to write:

> And this England they saved shall endure,
> She shall neither dwindle nor pass,
> Her feet shall be virile and sure;
> She shall stamp on the creed impure–
> The creed of class-against-class . . .[28]

And then there was Anthony Eden. In *Another World*, his memoir of his youth and the war, Eden wrote of his regular chats with Sergeant

Norman Carmichael on the fire-step at Plugstreet Wood: 'We did not lack opinions and aired them freely on any subject that came up ... Many of the ideas which I hold to this day stemmed from them [the fire-step chats], particularly a sense of the irrelevance and unreality of class distinction.'[29] As a Conservative politician, Eden was the quintessential 'One Nation Tory', so was his successor as Prime Minister, former Guards Lieutenant Harold Macmillan. In the same way that the junior officer had been the bond between Other Ranks and the officer corps in the war, so he was a bond between classes in the peace.

The war had also extended Macmillan's intra-class tolerance. A self-confessed intellectual, Macmillan wrote:

> Another aspect of my fellow-officers, especially of some of the Regular officers, which I gradually realised, was their breadth of view and generosity as well as their simplicity. One might at first regard a fellow-officer as of limited outlook, interested only in sport, horses, and perhaps women. It was not until after a considerable period that one might find him to be a talented organist or an expert on miniatures. I learnt, therefore, to be a little ashamed of the intolerance and impudence with which the intellectual classes (to which I belonged) were apt to sweep on one side as of no account men who had not learnt their particular jargon or been brought up with their prejudices.[30]

Macmillan was correct. It was a war of revelations. The reputation of shy Edmund Blunden in 11/Royal Sussex rocketed when his colonel read a review of Blunden's poems in the *Times Literary Supplement*. A Regular officer should never be judged by his country, brick-red face, just as a poet should not be condemned for his diffidence. Colonel George Harrison of 11/Royal Sussex Regiment, wrote about Edmund Blunden MC:

> Blunden, always known to me as 'The Rabbit', with his gentle ways and his unassuming manner, was not born to be a soldier but he became one in spite of himself. His acute brain was tuned for instant action and he performed arduous duties with conspicuous success and courage.

It was a war in which men learned tolerance and courage, in which crusty officers found interest in their New Army poets, and civilian poets and schoolboys by pure will, struggle and bravery turned themselves into soldiers. Victor Richardson, Roland Leighton's friend, wrote well and wisely in 1916:

> As regards suitability for this kind of war – very few men are suitable and I most certainly am not. But one has to strive to become suitable – and very few indeed fail entirely in this respect. One has to try therefore to convince oneself – and if possible other people – that one is, at any rate a decent imitation of a soldier.[31]

Friendships formed in the trenches were eternal bindings sealed by blood. 'The splendid fellowship which we shared', said Douie of his fellow soldiers, 'has been for most of us the greatest thing in our lives.'[32] John Glubb kept in contact with his sappers for year after year, until one by one they turned to dust and ashes. In 1977 Glubb wrote:

> The last of them was Driver Clemitt, who became post-master at Appleton-le-Moors in Yorkshire. He kept bees on the moors and every year at Christmas he used to send me a present of honey in the comb, and continued to do so until he died in 1975, nearly sixty years since we had been together in France. Such were the comradeships of the Great War.[33]

Sir John Glubb, sapper and commandant of the Arab Legion, died in 1986.

Comradeship extended to the dead. In the cemeteries created by the Imperial War Graves Commission, headstones were 'uniform' to avoid class distinctions. Officers and men were buried alongside each other, to acknowledge the brotherhood that had grown up on French and Belgian soil.

Was there a 'lost generation' of golden youth, felled by war, never to be replaced? Statistically, the answer is clear: no. Although 722,785 servicemen died in the war, of which 500,000 were under the age of 30, the influenza epidemic of 1918–19 was deadlier still.[34]

Despite both these holocausts, the population of Britain actually grew between 1911 and 1921, although there was a small dip in the male population of military age (those between the ages of 19–34).

And yet, there were so many lost generations. In the technical but efficient phrase of J.M. Winter, the British officer suffered 'surplus' deaths in the war.[35]

Around 37,500 officers perished in the war, 22,000 of these before September 1917, meaning that the vast majority were public schoolboy subalterns. Dedicating the war memorial at Malvern College – the *alma mater* of Bernard Adams – the Bishop of Malvern declared that the loss of schoolboys in the war 'can only be described as the wiping out of a generation'. Presiding over the meeting in January 1918 for the 'Scheme of Erecting a Fitting Memorial to Old Cheltonians fallen in the War', Colonel Sir Arthur Lee said:

> In contemplating these figures [statistics], we are moved equally by pride and sorrow. We think that the best blood, the best young blood, that the college has produced has been poured out like water in defence of the greatest of all causes, and certainly the noblest cause that men have ever laid down their lives for their country in pursuit of.[36]

He went on to quote Ecclesiastes: 'There be of them that have left a name behind them that their praises might be reported, and some there be that have no memorial who are perished as though they have never been.'[37] The *Eton College Chronicle*, meanwhile, announced the end of the war with a poem as leader:

> And you, our brothers, who for all our praying,
> To this dear School of ours come back no more,
> Who lie, our country's debt of honour paying–
> And not in vain – upon the Belgian shore,
> Till that great day when, at the Throne in Heaven,
> The books are opened and the Judgement set,
> Your lives for honour and for England given
> The School will not forget. [38]

As one fitting memorial to the School's lost generation of 1,157 boys a fund was set up to educate the sons of Etonians who had fallen. One Old Etonian and soldier, C.E. Chambers, told the foundation meeting in March 1917, 'I feel the sentimental point of view myself. I do wish every man who has died for Eton to have his son at Eton.' Within a year the memorial fund had raised over £100,000. At Monmouth, the blind Angus Buchanan VC unveiled a stone cross on the lawn as a memorial to the fallen, a scene played out at a hundred public schools across Britain, with old boys – old beyond their still tender years – returning for dedications commemorating the dead. On Uppingham's memorial the names of 'The Three Musketeers' were inscribed in gold on pale limestone in a chapel alcove, along with the names of 444 other old boys who gave their lives. The memorial at Winchester, *alma mater* of Bim Tennant and Douglas Gillespie, was cut with the words:

> In the day of battle they forgot not God, Who created them to do His will, nor their Country, the stronghold of freedom, nor their School, the mother of godliness and discipline. Strong in this threefold faith, they went forth from home and kindred to the battlefields of the world and, treading the path of duty and sacrifice, laid down their lives for mankind.

Under the terms of his will, Gillespie left part of his estate to fund scholarships to Winchester and New College, Oxford, for 'the benefit of boys that are not well off'. His family added the profits from the posthumously published collection of his *Letters from Flanders*.

To make statistics meaningful, one needs to go to a public school and read the names upon names of the fallen, so many that the neck aches with the looking up and down as much as the heart grieves.

One does not have to genuflect at the altar of the Tennants, Asquiths, Brookes, and Grenfells to see that Britain lost many of her best between 1914 and 1918, because those who died tended to be the brave, the bright and the selfless – the volunteers, the public spirited. If anything, this is more true of the Temporary Gentlemen who fell, the boys who pulled themselves up through the ranks by ambition and dedication, with no benefit of birth. J.B. Priestley, a former 'TG', never one given to fripperies and flamboyances in ideas, said:

> **nobody, nothing will shift me from the belief which I shall take to the grave that the generation to which I belonged, destroyed between 1914 and 1918, was a generation marvellous in its promise.**[39]

The historian A.J.P. Taylor agreed, and cited the 'lost generation' as the cause in the grave deficiency in men of political talent in the turbulent decade of the Thirties.

What the dead might have done is unknowable. What the war did to the fortunes of the aristocracy is as clear as cut-glass. 'Truly, England', said Lady Curzon of the war, 'lost the flower of her young men in those terrible days ... There was scarcely one of our friends who did not lose a son, a husband, or a brother.'[40] Debrett's struggled to keep track of the haemorrhage of blue blood; in 1915 Debrett's recorded 800 members of the peerage, baronetage, knightage killed in action or died of wounds.[41] Not since the Wars of the Roses had the aristocracy been so systematically slaughtered.[42] In the cruellest of ironies, as David Cannadine observed, the aristocracy made the supreme sacrifice selflessly and stoically 'in defence of a country that was gradually but irrevocably ceasing to be theirs'.[43] With sons and heirs dead and buried in foreign fields, country houses with broad English acres were locked up and sold at auction one after the other in the 1920s. The decline of the aristocracy had already begun with the reduction of agricultural rents, but the loss of its scions in war accelerated the historical trend. Needless to say, the young aristocrats died because they were the junior officers, first over the top, last to retire.

The 'lost generation' cannot be merely measured in corpses. There were also the invalids and the broken-minded; Angus Buchanan VC lived out his life in blindness, dying in 1944 at the age of fifty (a premature death almost certainly hastened by the head wounds he received during the war; the casualty figures never include the 'delayed' dead). He resumed his career at Oxford, rowed for his college, but it was still not the sporting life he might have imagined; he could not run, he could not play rugby. Alec Waugh wrote, in a similar vein:

Arthur Hogg, one of my best Sherborne friends, lost his leg at Pas-schendaele. He did not think himself unlucky when he lay in hospital, with friends coming to see him, knowing he was 'out of it'. But when he went up to Oxford and saw the others hurrying down to the football field after lunch, he realized all that he had lost. He wondered from what source he would draw the courage to continue living.[44]

Twenty years after the war's conclusion there were still 120,000 men receiving pensions or awards for shellshock or other psychiatric disability. Not included in the figure was the legion of survivors who, behind the appearance of normalcy, suffered mental strains and stresses. Robert Graves found that for years afterwards 'shells used to come bursting on my bed at midnight; strangers in daytime would assume the faces of friends who had been killed'.[45] Charles Carrington lived in a 'mental internment camp', whereby he could not shake off the memory of the trenches. Stuart Cloete fled to the French countryside of his childhood:

I realized that this was what I needed. Silence. Isolation. Now that I could let go, I broke down, avoided strangers, cried easily and had terrible nightmares.[46]

Thousands of officers headed for a life in rural England, the greenery and blue-steeped hills of which had been solace and inspiration during the fighting. So many used their war gratuity to set up a little chicken farm, a quiet and independent – almost gentlemanly – business that the resultant over-production guaranteed failure for nearly all of them. A number of Utopian schemes were set up for disabled officers, including one in Kenya, almost without exception ill-starred.

It was guilt that truly sapped the survivors. Richard Aldington wondered:

What right have I to live? When I meet an unmaimed man of my generation, I want to shout at him, 'How did you escape? How did you dodge it? What dirty trick did you play?'[47]

Harold Macmillan wrote:

I found afterwards that few of the survivors of my own age felt able to shake off the memory of these years. We were haunted by them. We almost began to feel a sense of guilt for not having shared the fate of our friends and comrades. We certainly felt an obligation to make some decent use of the life that had been spared us. When the war finally ended most of us were at a loss as to how to take up our lives again.[48]

In 'The Shepherd', Edmund Blunden asked: 'What mercy is it I should live and move, If haunted ever by war's agony?'[49]

The agony of guilt was not aided by an uncomprehending civilian population uneasy with the returned soldiers. Beggars make everyone uncomfortable. In a sour circle, officers themselves became reluctant to talk about the war save to those they knew would understand, who were mainly members of old comrades' associations.

Writing in 1929 Charles Douie found himself once again on a weary road: 'On one day of the year the dead at least have their meed of honour; the living are without honour even on that day.'[50] *The Weary Road* was a counter-blast to the literary cult whose depiction of the Great War as pity piled upon futility was already becoming the orthodoxy. If anything, over the next decades the road grew colder, less welcoming.

Charles Douie, H.E.L. Mellersh, Stuart Cloete, Charles Carrington, John Glubb, Guy Chapman, Alfred Pollard, Edwin Vaughan Campion, Richard Talbot Kelly, Harold Macmillan, Anthony Eden and all those junior officers who fought and endured and survived, convinced their cause was right, they too were a lost generation, because the survivors never did have their meed of honour. Now all the junior officers of the Great War are dust. And they all have a memorial if we care to think of it. The memorial is what they did and what they achieved: the liberty of nations, freedom from tyranny.

The poetry of the British officer was never in the pity; it was always in the pride, the gallantry, the willing sacrifice.

***

And if posterity should ask of me
What high, what base emotions keyed weak flesh

To face such torments, I would answer: '*You!*'
Not for themselves, O daughter, grandsons, sons,
Your tortured forebears wrought this miracle;
Not for themselves, *accomplished utterly*
This loathliest task of murderous servitude;
But just because they realised that thus,
And only thus, by sacrifice, might they
Secure a world worth living in – *for you.*

From 'The Other Side' by Captain Gilbert Frankau, Royal Field Artillery.

Acknowledgements

My most obvious acknowledgement is to every British subaltern who fought on the Western Front, 1914–18. Thank you.

There were many people who helped in the preparation of this book. I owe a particular debt to my wife, Penny, for reconnaissance, intelligence gathering and morale raising (and, yes, some necessary colonel-ish urgings to 'stand fast' in those grey despairing moments that enfilade any writing of a book). A classroom of school archivists gave willing and enthusiastic support: Pat Davitt at Monmouth School, Christine Leighton at Cheltenham College, Jerry Rudman at Uppingham, the staff of Eton College Archives, Rita Boswell at Harrow, Sue Cole at Charterhouse, Trevor Hildrey at Merchant Taylors', Crosby. I am grateful to Roderick Suddaby and his team at the Imperial War Museum, the staff of Harrods' Archive, David Fraser and the staff of Monmouthshire Libraries, and Caroline Davies, Tessa Norgrove and Helen Davy and the other Friends of Haberdashers' Monmouth School for Girls, who invited me to lecture and who were such charming guinea pigs. And they also served above and beyond the call of duty: my agent, Julian Alexander, at Lucas Alexander Whitley; Andrew Blades at Oxford University; and Keith Lowe, Alan Samson and Martha Ashby at Weidenfeld and Nicolson.

For permission to quote from material to which they control the copyright I am grateful to the following: Pen and Sword for John Bickersteth (ed.) *The Bickersteth Diaries 1914–18*; Pen and Sword for Charles Carrington's *Soldier from the Wars Returning*; Penguin UK for Edmund Blunden's *Undertones of War*; the literary estate of Guy Chapman for *A Passionate Prodigality*; Harper Collins for Stuart Cloete's *A Victorian Son*; Eton College for material from the letters of John Christie; Naval and Military Press for Charles Douie's *The Weary Road*; The Colonel of the Royal Welch Fusiliers for James Churchill

Dunn's *The War the Infantry Knew*; Penguin UK for Anthony Eden's *Another World*; Naval and Military Press for Rowland Feilding's *War Letters to a Wife*; Cassell for John Glubb's *Into Battle*; Carcanet for Robert Graves' *Goodbye to All That*; Penguin UK for Graham Greenwell's *An Infant in Arms*; Naval and Military Press for F.C. Hitchcock's *Stand To: A Diary of the Trenches*; David Leighton for material from the letters of Roland Leighton; Pan Macmillan for Harold Macmillan's *Winds of Change*; Hachette for Bernard Martin's *Poor Bloody Infantry*; Dr Steven Connors for material from *The Monmothian*; Pen and Sword for Captain Harry Ogle's *The Fateful Battle Line*; Oxford University Press for John Bell and H. Owen (eds) *Wilfred Owen: Selected Letters*; Naval and Military Press for Max Plowman's *A Subaltern on the Somme*; Naval and Military Press for A. Pollard's *Fire-Eater*; PFD for J.B. Priestley *Margin Released*; Christopher Reith for John Reith's *Wearing Spurs*; Greenhill Books/Lionel Leventhal Limited for Sidney Rogerson's *Twelve Days on the Somme*; the literary estate of George Sassoon for *Siegfried Sassoon Diaries, 1914–18*; Cameron Stewart and the literary estate of Alexander Stewart for Alexander Stewart's *A Very Unimportant Officer*; Pen and Sword for Edwin Campion Vaughan's *Some Desperate Glory*; Cassell for Alec Waugh's *The Early Years of Alec Waugh*; Random House for Dennis Wheatley's *The Time Has Come, 1914–1919: Officer and Temporary Gentleman*.

Despite endeavours I have failed to track down all copyright holders, and apologise in advance for omissions. Any queries regarding the use of material should be addressed to the author c/o Weidenfeld & Nicolson.

Bibliography

Unpublished Sources

Cheltenham College: Donald Kenworthy, Vyvian Trevenen
Eton College: John Christie
Monmouth School: C. Lowry, W. Shirley
Oxford University, Great War Archive: C.E. Carr, Hew Grieg, J. Hirst, Charles Nye
Imperial War Museum: E.H. Allen, H.F. Bowser, P.A. Brown, H.J. Chappell, H.T. Clements, R.S. Cockburn, J. Coull, F.H. Ennor, E.H. Giffard, Lionel Hall, R.P. Hamilton, P.G.Heath, E.J. Higson, H. Kindersley, A. Knight, W.W. Johnstone-Wilson, W.R. Low, C.C. May, F.W. Mellish, H.A. Munro, W.P. Nevill, H.U.S. Nisbet, F.E. Packe, N.A. Pease, H. Rutherford, C.R. Tobbitt, N.E. Tyndale-Biscoe, P.G.E. Warburton, J.W. Wintringham
National Archives: WO 161
Uppingham: R. Sterndale-Bennett

Published Sources

Books

Ackerley, J.R., *My Father and Myself* (Harmondsworth, 1971)
Adams, Bernard, *Nothing of Importance* (New York, 1918)
Agate, James, *L of C: Being the Letters of a Temporary Officer in the Army Service Corps* (London, 1917)
Aldington, Richard, *Death of a Hero* (London, 1965)
Allpass, H.B.K., *Oxford, St. Bees and the Front 1911–1916* (London, n.d.)
Anonymous (on behalf of Birmingham Public Library Reference Department), *Catalogue of the War Poetry Collection* (Birmingham, 1921)
Arthur, Max, *Forgotten Voices of the Great War* (London, 2002)
Asquith, Raymond, *Life and Letters* (London, 1980)
Barker, Stephen and Boardman, Christopher, *Lancashire's Forgotten Heroes* (Stroud, 2008)
Barnett, Denis Oliver, *In Happy Memory* (n.p.p., 1915)
Barton, Peter, *The Somme: A New Panoramic Perspective* (London, 2006)
Baynes, John, *Morale* (London, 1967)
Behrend, Arthur, *Make Me A Soldier* (London, 1961)

Bell, D.H., *A Soldier's Diary of the Great War* (London, 1929)

Bell, J., (ed), *Wilfred Owen: Selected Letters* (London, 1985)

Bickersteth, John (ed.), *The Bickersteth Diaries* (London, 1995)

Bird, Anthony (ed.), *Honour Satisfied: A Dorset Rifleman at War 1916–1918* (Swindon, 1990)

Bishop, Alan and Bostridge, Mark (eds), *Letters from a Lost Generation* (London, 1998)

Blunden, Edmund, *Undertones of War* (London, 1965)

Boyd Orr, J., *As I Recall* (London, 1962)

Brennan, Gerald, *A Life of One's Own: Childhood and Youth* (Cambridge, 1979)

Brittain, Vera, *Testament of Youth* (London, 1978)

Brooke, Rupert, *Letters from America* (New York, 1916)

Brown, Malcolm (intro.), *The Wipers Times* (London, 2006)

— *The Imperial War Museum Book of 1918* (London, 1998)

— *The Imperial War Museum Book of the Western Front* (London, 1993)

Burrage, A.M. ('Ex-Pte X'), *War is War* (London, 1930)

Campbell, P.J., *The Ebb and the Flow* (London, 1977)

Cannadine, David, *The Decline and Fall of the British Aristocracy* (London, 1992)

Carrington, Charles, *Soldier from the Wars Returning* (Barnsley, 2006)

— *A Subaltern's War* (London, 1929)

— *Kipling: His Life and Work* (London, 1955)

Carton de Wiart, Lt. Gen. Sir Adrian, *Happy Odyssey* (London 1950)

Chandler, D.G., (ed), *The Oxford Illustrated History of the British Army* (Oxford, 1994)

Chapman, Guy, *A Passionate Prodigality* (Southampton, 1993)

Clayton, Anthony, *The British Officer* (Harlow, 2007)

Cloete, Stuart, *A Victorian Son: An Autobiography* (London, 1972)

Coppard, George, *With a Machine Gun to Cambrai* (London, 1988)

Corrigan, Gordon, *Mud, Blood and Poppycock* (London, 2003)

Crouch, Lionel, *Duty and Service: Letters from the Front* (n.p.p., 1917)

Crozier, F.P., *A Brass Hat in No Man's Land* (London, 1930)

Cuddesford, D.W.J., *And All For What?* (Uckfield, 2004)

Dawson, A.J. (intro), *A 'Temporary Gentleman' in France* (New York, 1918)

Deane, H.F.W. and Evans, W.A., *Public Schools Year Book* (London, 1908)

Douie, Charles, *The Weary Road: Recollections of a Subaltern of Infantry* (Uckfield, n.d.)

Dundas, Henry, *Henry Dundas, Scots Guard: A Memoir* (London, 1921)

Dunn, J.C., *The War the Infantry Knew* (London, 1988)

Eden, Anthony, *Another World* (London, 1976)

Ewart, Wilfrid, *Way of Revelation* (Stroud, 1986)

Falls, Cyril, *The First World War* (London, 1960)

Feilding, Rowland, *War Letters to a Wife* (London, 1929)

Ferguson, Niall, *The Pity of War* (London, 2006)

Fletcher, Ian (ed.), *Letters from the Front* (Tunbridge Wells, 1993)

Fuller, J.F.C., *Memoirs of an Unconventional Soldier* (London, 1936)

Garth, John, *Tolkien and the Great War* (London, 2003)

Gibbs, Stormont, *From the Somme to the Armistice* (London 1986)

Giddings, Robert, *The War Poets* (London, 1988)

Gillespie, A.D., *Letters from Flanders* (London, 1916)

Glenconner, Pamela, *Edward Wyndham Tennant: A Memoir* (London, 1919)

Gliddon, Gerald, *The Aristocracy and the Great War* (London 2002)

Glubb, John, *Into Battle: A Soldier's Diary of the Great War* (London, 1978)

Graves, Robert, *Goodbye to All That* (London, 1969)

Greenwell, Graham H., *An Infant in Arms*, (London, 1972)

Griffith, Llewelyn Wyn, *Up to Mametz* (London, 1931)

Hamilton, Frederick, *Origins and History of the First or Grenadier Guards* (London, 1874)

Hanbury-Sparrow, Alan, *The Land-Locked Lake* (London 1932)

Hankey, Donald, *A Student in Arms* (London, 1919)

Harris, Ruth Elwin, *Billie: The Nevill Letters 1914–1916* (Uckfield, 2003)

Hart-Davis, Rupert (ed.), *Siegfried Sassoon Diaries, 1915–1918* (London, 1983)

Hay, Ian, *The First Hundred Thousand* (Edinburgh, 1917)

Hayward, James, *Myths and Legends of the First World War* (Stroud, 2003)

Herbert, A.P., *The Secret Battle* (London, 1919)

Herbert, Aubrey, *Mons, Anzac and Kut* (London, 1920)

Hesketh-Prichard, H., *Sniping in France* (London, 1920)

Hibberd, Dominic, *Wilfred Owen: A New Biography* (London, 2002)

Hitchcock, F.C., '*Stand To': A Diary of the Trenches 1915–1918* (London, 1937)

Hodgson, William Noel ('Edward Melbourne'), *Verse and Prose in Peace and War* (London, 1916)

Holmes, Richard, *Tommy* (London, 2004)

Hooper, W. (ed.) *Letters of C.S. Lewis* (London, 1988)

Horrocks, Brian, *Escape to Action* (New York, 1961)

Housman, Laurence (ed.), *War Letters of Fallen Englishmen* (London, 1930)

Hoyle, J.B., *Some Letters from a Subaltern on the Western Front* (Uckfield, 2009)

Hutchison, Graham Seton, *Footslogger: An Autobiography* (London, 1931)

— *Warrior* (London, n.d.)

James, Lawrence, *Warrior Race* (London, 2001)

Jones, Paul, *War Letters of a Public School Boy* (London, 1918)

Junger, Ernst, *The Storm of Steel* (London, 1929)

Keegan, John, *The First World War* (London, 1978)

Laffin, John (ed.), *Letters from the Front* (London, 1973)

Law, Francis, *A Man at Arms* (London, 1983)

Lawrence, D.H., *Lady Chatterley's Lover* (London, 1928)

Leighton, Marie, *Boy of My Heart* (New York, 1916)

Lieving, Edward G.D., *Attack: An Infantry Subaltern's Impressions of July 1st 1916* (London, 1918)

Lodge, Oliver, *Christopher, A Study in Human Personality* (New York, 1919)

Lucy, John, *There's a Devil in the Drum* (London, 1938)

MacArthur, Brian (ed.), *For King and Country* (London, 2008)

Macdonald, Lyn, *Voices and Images of the Great War* (London, 1988)

Mackintosh, E.A., *War, The Liberator and other Pieces* (London, 1918)

Macmillan, Harold, *The Winds of Change* (London, 1966)

Martin, Bernard, *Poor Bloody Infantry: A Subaltern on the Western Front* (London, 1987)

Mellersh, H.E.L., *Schoolboy into War* (London, 1978)

Monash, J., *War Letters* (London, 1935)

Moran, Lord, *The Anatomy of Courage* (London, 1945)

Mottram, R.H., *Journey to the Western Front* (London, 1936)

Mosley, Nicholas, *Julian Grenfell: His Life and the Times of his Death 1888–1915* (London, 1976)

Noakes, Vivien, *Voices of Silence* (Stroud, 2006)

Nichols, Robert, *Ardours and Endurances* (London, 1917)

Nobbs, Gilbert, *Englishman, Kamerad!* (London, 1918)

Ogle, Henry, *The Fateful Battle Line* (Barnsley, 1993)

Osborn, E.B., *The Muse in Arms* (London, 1917)

— *The New Elizabethans* (London, 1919)

Osburn, Arthur, *Unwilling Passenger* (London, 1932)

Page Croft, H., *Twenty-Two Months Under Fire* (London, 1917)

Panichas, George A., *Promise of Greatness* (London, 1968)

Parker, Peter, *The Old Lie: The Great War and the Public School Ethos* (London, 1987)

Parkin, George R., *Edward Thring: Life, Diary and Letters* (London, 1898)

Plowman, Max ('Mark VII'), *A Subaltern on the Somme in 1916* (London, 1927)

Pollard, Alfred, *Fire-Eater: Memoirs of a VC* (London, 1932)

Pound, Reginald, *The Lost Generation* (London, 1964)

Prendergast, J., *Prendergast's Progress* (London, 1979)

Priestman, E.Y., *With a B-P Scout in Gallipoli* (Uckfield, 2010)

Priestley, J.B., *Margin Released* (London, 1962)

Pritchard Clayton, Charles, *The Hungry One* (Llandysul, 1978)

Purdom, C.B. (ed), *Everyman at War* (London, 1930)

Reith, John, *Wearing Spurs* (London, 1966)

Ribbesdale, Lord, *Charles Lister: Letters and Recollections* (London, 1917)

Richards, Frank, *Old Soldiers Never Die* (London, 1933)

Richter, Donald C. (ed), *Lionel Sotheby's Great War* (Athens, Ohio, 1997)

Rogerson, Sidney, *Twelve Days: The Somme November 1916* (London, 2006)

Sassoon, Siegfried, *Counter-Attack and other poems* (New York, 1918)

Saunders, Anthony, *The Weapons of Trench Warfare 1914–18* (Stroud, 1999)

— *Dominating the Enemy* (Stroud, 2000)

Sherriff, R.C., *Journey's End* (London, 1983)

Sheffield, G.D. and Inglis, G.I.S. (eds), *From Vimy Ridge to the Rhine, The Great War Letters of Christopher Stone* (Ramsbury, 1989)

Sheffield, Gary, *Leadership in the Trenches* (London, 2000)

— (ed.), *War on the Western Front* (London, 2007)

Shepherd, Ernest, *A Sergeant-Major's War* (Ramsbury, 1987)

Silkin, Jon, *The Penguin Book of First World War Poetry* (Harmondsworth, 1979)

Simon, B. and Bradley, I., *The Victorian Public School* (Dublin, 1975)

Sorley, Charles Hamilton, *The Letters of Charles Sorley* (Cambridge, 1919)

Snape, Michael, *God and the British Soldier* (Abingdon, 2005)

Spears, E.L. *Prelude to Victory* (London, 1939)

Stallworthy, John, *Anthem for Doomed Youth* (London, 2002)

Stewart, Cameron (ed.), *A Very Unimportant Officer* (London, 2008)

Talbot Kelly, R.B., *A Subaltern's Odyssey* (London, 1980)

Terraine, John, *The Smoke and the Fire: Myths and Anti-Myths of War* (London, 1992)

Thomas, Edward, *The Childhood of Edward Thomas* (London, 2008)

Trappman, A.H., *Straight Tips for 'Subs'* (London, 1915)

Tyndale-Biscoe, Julian, *Gunner Subaltern* (London, 1971)

Vandiver, Elizabeth, *Stand in the Trench, Achilles* (Oxford, 2010)

Vaughan, Edwin Campion, *Some Desperate Glory* (London, 1981)

Vernede, R.K., *Letters to His Wife* (Glasgow, 1917)

— *War Poems and other Verses* (London, 1917)

Ward, C. Dudley, *Regimental Records of the Royal Welch Fusiliers – Vol III 1914–1918. France and Flanders* (London, 1929)

— *History of the Welsh Guards* (London, 1936)

Watcyn-Williams, Morgan, *From Khaki to Cloth* (Caernarvon, 1949)

Waugh, Alec, *Prisoners of Mainz* (London, 1951)

— *The Early Years of Alec Waugh* (London, 1962)

West, Arthur Graeme, *Diary of a Dead Officer* (London, 2007)

Wheatley, Dennis, *The Time Has Come: Officer and Temporary Gentleman, 1914–19* (London, 1978)

Williams, Basil, *Raising and Training the New Armies* (London, 1918)

Williams, W. Alister, *Heart of a Dragon: The VCs of Wales and the Welsh Regiments, 1914–1982* (Wrexham, 2008)

Williamson, H., *Wet Flanders Plain* (London, 1929)

— *The Golden Virgin* (London, 1985)

Winter, Dennis, *Death's Men* (London, 1978)

Winter, J.M., *The Great War and the British People* (London, 1985)

Manuals and Pamphlets

SS135 *The Training and Employment of Divisions* (1918)

Notes for Young Officers (1918)

Regulations for the Officers Training Corps (1908)

Articles

Jean Moorcroft Wilson, 'Truths Written in Blood', *The Guardian*, 13/11/2004

Otley, C.B., 'Militarism and Militarization in the Public Schools, 1900–1972', *British Journal of Sociology*, 29 (1978)

Martin Petter, "Temporary Gentlemen" in the Aftermath of the Great War: Rank, Status and the ex-Officer Problem,' *Historical Journal*, No. 37 Vol. 1 (1994)

Newspapers, Magazines, Catalogues

The Carthusian
The Cheltonian
The Eton College Chronicle
Harrods' Catalogue
The Marlburian
The Monmothian
Uppingham School Magazine

Internet

www.keystothepast.info/record office
www.firstworldwar.com/diaries/rlm.htal

Notes

Introduction

1. A.M. Burrage ('Ex-Pte.X'), *War is War*, p. 71
2. Quoted in Garth, *Tolkien and the Great War*, p. 9
3. Robert Graves, 'The Kaiser's War: A British Point of View', in Panichas, *Promise of Greatness*, p. 10
4. The percentage of British Army officers killed between 1 October 1914–30 September 1915 was 14.2, compared with 5.8 per cent of 'other ranks'. For overall officer casualties in the Great War, see p. 183. A full analysis of British casualties 1914–1918 is provided by J.M. Winter's *The Great War and the British People*, 2002.
5. John Stallworthy, *Anthem for Doomed Youth*, p. 27
6. Peter Parker, *The Old Lie*, p. 65
7. H.E.L. Mellersh, *Schoolboy Into War*, p. 17. Mellersh added that he believed the Great War 'worthwhile' and gently complained about the tendency of historians to paint the war 'in colours of too unrelieved a gloom ... Those who died in the war also experienced that intensification of living; and it is no insult to their memories to record the fact.'
8. Fritz Fischer, *Griff nach der Weltmacht: Die Kriegzielpolitik der Kaiserlichen Deutschland 1914–1918*, 1961, published in English in 1967 as Germany's *War Aims in the First World War*. Fischer's thesis has been amplified and elucidated by Imanuel Geiss in works such as *Das Deutsche Reich und die Vorgeschichte des Ersten Weltkriegs*, 1978.
9. For example, ex-Lance-Corporal S.A. Boyd of 10/Royal Welch Fusiliers: 'My lasting impression of the Somme battle is the fine young officers who led us so well. They were extremely brave but so young, many under the age of 20', quoted in G.D. Sheffield, *Leadership in the Trenches*, 2000; Captain James Churchill Dunn, the 2/Royal Welch Fusilier's veteran Medical Officer, wrote in the preface to his *The War The Infantry Knew*, 'What was achieved [in the War] is made radiant in my memory by the gay self-sacrifice of junior officers and non-commissioned officers.'
10. Bernard Adams, *Nothing of Importance*, p. 224
11. Max Plowman ('Mark VII'), *A Subaltern on the Somme*, p. 23

Chapter 1: Hello to All This

1. Quoted in *The Old Lie*, Peter Parker, p. 21
2. *The Monmothian*, December 1912. Merchant Taylors', Crosby, was another public school with a Cadet Corps in distinction to an OTC.
3. *The Cheltonian*, October 1915
4. General Sir Frederick Hamilton, *Origins and History of the First or Grenadier Guards*, p. 3
5. J.M. Winter, *The Great War and the British People*, p. 31
6. Of the nine English schools investigated by the Clarendon Commission and then regulated by the Public Schools Act of 1868 Winchester is the oldest, being founded in 1382.

The other 'Clarendon Schools' are Charterhouse, Eton, Harrow, Merchant Taylors', Rugby, Shrewsbury, St Paul's, Westminster.

7. G.R. Parkin, *Life, Diary and Letters of Edward Thring*, Vol. II, p. 196

8. Harrovian L.P. Hartley recalled: 'In any case, public school life in those days had inured us to a good deal of verbal and physical unpleasantness.
I remember how, in the Second World War, a friend of mine who was too old to fight joined the local fire brigade. The other firemen complained bitterly of their lot, their hardships of one sort and another, and they said to him, "Why don't *you* complain?" He replied, "Because I was at school at Eton, a much tougher upbringing than any of you have had." See Hartley's 'Three Wars' in Panichas, *Promise of Greatness*.

9. Stuart Cloete, *A Victorian Son*, p. 157

10. *The Eton College Chronicle*, 11 March, 1915

11. In 1951 the 7th Duke of Wellington offered to give £50 to the National Playing Fields Association if anyone could prove that his famous ancestor ever said 'The Battle of Waterloo was won on the playing fields of Eton'. His £50 remained safe in his pocket. Robert Birley, headmaster of Eton 1949–1964, tracked the source of the quote to *De l'Avenir Politique de l'Angleterre* by Count Montalembert, which claimed that the Duke, on a visit to Eton, exclaimed 'C'est ici qu'a été la bataille de Waterloo.' ('It is here that the Battle of Waterloo was won.') Not the least evidence against the 'playing fields' quotation is that Eton College had no sports fields in 1781–84, the years that Arthur Wellesley was in attendance.

12. Field Marshal Sir Douglas Haig, *A Rectorial Address Delivered to the Students in the University of St Andrews, 14th May 1919*, St Andrews, 1919

13. Alan Bishop and Mark Bostridge (eds), *Letters from a Lost Generation*, p. 241

14. Bishop and Bostridge, p. 338

15. Quoted in *For King and Country: Voices from the Great War*, ed. Brian MacArthur, 2008, pp. 141–2

16. Henry Dundas, *Henry Dundas, Scots Guards: A Memoir*, p. 129

17. William Noel Hodgson, *Verse and Prose in Peace and War*, p. 33

18. Robert Graves, *Goodbye to All That*, p. 24

19. *The Eton College Chronicle*, January 27, 1916 and January 28, 1915

20. R. Talbot Kelly, *A Subaltern's Odyssey*, p. 22

21. Despite proclaiming indifference to the Classics at Eton, Shaw-Stewart carried off the School's major academic award, the Newcastle Scholarship (in which candidates sat papers in Greek, Latin and Divinity) and did so two years early; at Balliol, he won such glories as the Ireland and Hertford. He took with him the Second Trojan War, along with the *Iliad*, Herodotus and A.E. Housman's *A Shropshire Lad*.

22. A.D. Gillespie, *Letters from Flanders*, p. 111

23. Ronald Knox, *Patrick Shaw-Stewart*, pp. 159–60. The poem, 'I saw a man this morning', was found inscribed on the back flyleaf of Shaw-Stewart's copy of *A Shropshire Lad;* Shaw-Stewart wrote no other poems in adulthood.

24. Charles Carrington, *Kipling: His Life and Work*, p. 111

25. P.C.T. Crick quoted in Michael Snape, *God and the British Soldier*, p. 25

26. John Garth, *Tolkien and the Great War*, p. 22

27. Quoted in *Lost Voices of the Great War*, Max Arthur (ed.), p. 148

28. The poem first appeared in Newbolt's collection *Admirals All and Other Verses*, 1897. Newbolt's 'Clifton Chapel' also places the school as the source of manly patriotic leadership; in the poem a father takes his son into Clifton School's chapel and tells him: 'Henceforth the School and you are

one/And what You are, the race shall be.'

29. Donald Hankey, *A Student in Arms*, p. 81

30. Richard Aldington, *Death of a Hero*, pp. 285–6

31. R.C. Sherriff, 'The English Public Schools in the War', *Promise of Greatness*, pp. 152–4. Sherriff's article is the headwater of the proposition that morale-maintenance by junior officers turned the tide of the war, and was one of the inspirations for this book. If any criticism can be levelled against Sherriff's article, it is that he underplays the military effectiveness of New Army junior officers who, on occasions during the Great War, fought small, isolated battles, without a guiding hand from superiors, to effect. In particular, rallies by junior officers helped frustrate and break up the German Offensive of 1918.

32. In comparison with the leading public schools Oxford and Cambridge Universities suffered a marginally lower death rate of 19.2 and 18.0 per cent respectively of graduates who served.

33. Estimated from the Summer 1917 figures of numbers serving and deaths reported to School.

34. Vera Brittain, *Testament of Youth*, p. 50

35. Brittain, p. 11

36. Gillespie, p. 2

37. Anthony Eden, *Another World*, p. 53

38. According to Carrington, pacifists in August 1914 were 'a shrill handful.' See Charles Carrington, *Soldier from the Wars Returning*, p. 38

39. Sheffield, p. 35

40. Anthony Eden recalled that at Eton 'we were encouraged to take an interest in public affairs.' See Eden, *Another World*, p. 50

41. E.C. Osborn, *The New Elizabethans*, pp. 87–8

42. Rupert Brooke, *Letters from America*, pp. 173–180

43. Quoted in Dominic Hibberd, *Wilfred Owen: A New Biography*, p. 147

44. Robert Vernede, 'A Petition', *War Poems and other verses*, p. 61

45. Bishop and Bostridge, p. 257

46. E.B. Osborn, *The New Elizabethans*, p. 221

47. Robert Graves, *Goodbye to All That*, p. 60

48. David Cannadine, *Decline and Fall of the British Aristocracy*, p. 73

49. Reginald Pound, *The Lost Generation*, p. 255

50. Cloete, p. 192

51. Cloete, p. 194

52. Bishop and Bostridge, p. 30

53. Quoted in Parker, pp. 39–40

54. Gerald Brennan, 'A Survivor's Story', in Panichas, *Promise of Greatness*, p. 39

55. Quoted in Holmes, *Tommy*, p. 143

56. Dennis Wheatley, *The Time Has Come: Officer and Temporary Gentleman*, p. 52

57. Sherriff, in Panichas, *Promise of Greatness*, p. 137

58. Sherriff, in Panichas, *Promise of Greatness*, p. 139

59. Paul Jones, *War Letters of a Public School Boy*, p. 221

60. Vivian de Sola Pinto, 'My First War: Memories of a Spectacled Subaltern', in Panichas, *Promise of Greatness*, p. 67

61. *Eton College Chronicle*, 11 March, 1915

62. See Pound, p. 128

63. Pound, p. 151

Chapter II: Arms and the Gentleman

1. Cloete, p. 196

2. Bishop and Bostridge, p. 35

3. Carrington, pp. 75–6

4. Bernard Martin, *Poor Bloody Infantry*, p. 8

5. Mellersh, p. 37

6. Pound, p. 147

7. J. Hirst papers, University of Oxford

8. Graham Greenwell, *An Infant in Arms*, p. 3

9. Wheatley, p. 142

10. Mellersh, p. 56

11. John Hay Beith ('Ian Hay'), *The First Hundred Thousand*,

12. Bickersteth, John (ed.) , *The Bickersteth Diaries*, p. 10

13. Cloete, p. 271

14. Charles Carrington, *Soldier from the Wars Returning*, p. 75

15. Greenwell, p. 5

16. Wheatley, p. 72

17. Sidney Rogerson, *Twelve Days on the Somme*, p. 147

18. H.B.K. Allpass, *Oxford, St Bees and the Front 1911–1916*, p. 5

19. Cloete, p. 252

20. Guy Chapman, *A Passionate Prodigality*, p. 26

21. Wheatley, p. 73

22. Graves, *Goodbye to All That*, p.63 Graves' other 'worst mistakes' included failing to recognize the colonel in mufti, walking in the street without a belt and talking shop in the mess. In his paper 'The Value of the OTC as a School Activity', Major R. Sterndale-Bennett, CO of Uppingham's OTC, wrote: 'There is no doubt that this elementary training [i.e. that provided by the School's OTC] was a real asset to those cadets who took commissions; especially was this so in the early days of the war. An officer Instructor at Sandhurst wrote to one of the Public School COs: "We here bless the OTC. Those who have served in it are, from our point of view, 3 MONTHS ahead of those who have not." And 3 months was a long time in those dark days [of the beginning of the war].'
In July 1919 the War Office, to mark the work of the Officers Training Corps at Uppingham School during the war, awarded the School a German trench mortar as a war trophy.

23. Greenwell, p. 3

24. Greenwell, p. 2

25. Chapman, p. 14

26. Eden, p. 70

27. Harold Macmillan, *The Winds of Change*, p. 63

28. Hay Beith, p. 179

29. Quoted in G.D. Sheffield (ed.), *War on the Western Front*, p. 256

30. Carrington, pp.73–74

31. Eden, p. 66

32. Cloete, p. 199

33. John Christie papers, Eton College

34. Pound, p. 13

35. The Artists' Rifles trained 10,256 officer cadets over the course of the war.

36. Quoted in *The Regimental Roll of Honour and War Record of the Artists' Rifles*, 1922, p. xii

37. J. Bell (ed), *Wilfred Owen: Selected Letters*, p. 351. In July 1918 Owen told his friend Charles Scott Manrieff that he (Owen) was keen to go out to France again. He accordingly put his name down for the draft. See Hibberd, p. 327

38. Mellersh, p. 41

39. Edmund Blunden, 'An Infantryman Passes By', in Panichas, *Promise of Greatness*, p. 179

40. Cloete, p. 201

41. Cameron Stewart (ed.), *Alexander Stewart, A Very Unimportant Officer*, p. 26

42. R. Talbot Kelly, p. 35

43. Mellersh, p. 50

44. Bishop and Bostridge, p. 298

45. Henry Ogle, *The Fateful Battle Line*, p. 141

46. Ogle, p. 152

47. L.P. Hartley, 'Three Wars', in Panichas, *Promise of Greatness*, p. 256

48. Hartley, p. 256

49. Arthur Graeme West, *Diary of a Dead Officer*, p. 68

50. Those promoted from the ranks, with impeccable upper and upper-middle class credentials included Siegfried Sassoon.

51. Ogle, p. 152

52. West, pp. 45–6

53. Anonymous officer in *A 'Temporary Gentleman' in France*, A.J. Dawson (intro.), p. xxiv

54. Pound, p. 85

55. Graves, *Goodbye to All That*, p. 203

56. Cloete, p. 267

57. PRO, Cab 45/31, Sir Morgon Crofton, 26 December 1937
58. Sheffield (ed.), p. 117
59. Carrington, p. 29
60. Sassoon quoted in *The War the Infantry Knew*, J.C. Dunn, p. 309
61. This was Alan Hanbury-Sparrow, 2/Royal Berkshires, *The Land-Locked Lake*, p. 293
62. Bishop and Bostridge, p. 55
63. Allpass, p. 4
64. Mellersh, p. 58
65. Mellersh, p. 58
66. Mellersh, p. 58
67. Bishop and Bostridge, p. 99
68. Bell, p. 186
69. Macmillan, p. 64
70. Gillespie, pp. 11–12
71. Lionel Crouch, *Duty and Service: Letters from the Front*, p. 32
72. Carrington, p. 76
73. Carrington, p. 79
74. Chapman, p. 13
75. Beith, p. 216
76. Beith, pp. 216–17

Chapter III: I Like To Hear the Allyman's Shells

1. Brian Horrocks, *Escape to Action*, p. 15
2. Ian Fletcher (ed.), *Letters from the Front*, p. 16
3. Charles Douie, *The Weary Road*, p. 38
4. Chapman, p. 16
5. Gillespie, p. 13
6. Vyvian Trevenen diary, Cheltenham College
7. Trevenen RFA, MC 49th Bty., 40th Brigade, died on 10 June 1918. He was 24.
8. Robert Mackay, www.firstworldwar.com/diaries/rlm.htal
9. Chapman, p. 16
10. Crouch, pp.74–5
11. Fletcher, p. 16
12. Macmillan, p. 68
13. Macmillan was twice wounded in action; on the second occasion he sustained a machine-gun bullet in the leg. See pp. 211.
14. Chapman, p. 16
15. Robert Mackay, www.firstworldwar.com/diaries/rlm.htal; Plowman, p.11
16. Douie, p. 39
17. Douie, p. 38–9
18. Quoted in Richard Holmes, *Tommy*, p. 344
19. Edwin Campion Vaughan, *Some Desperate Glory*, p. 5
20. Bell, p. 306
21. Quoted in Holmes, *Tommy*, p. 347
22. Vaughan, p. 4
23. Douie, p. 44
24. Douie, p. 60
25. Crouch, p. 75
26. Wheatley, p. 163
27. John Glubb, *Into Battle*, p. 24
28. Crouch, p. 66
29. Rogerson, p. 165
30. Graves, *Goodbye*, p. 105
31. Talbot Kelly, p. 37
32. Martin, p. 39
33. Bishop and Bostridge, p. 74
34. Chapman, p. 22
35. Vaughan, p. 81
36. Dunn, p. 305
37. F.C. Hitchcock, '*Stand To': A Diary of the Trenches*, p. 22
38. Douie, p. 47
39. Graves, *Goodbye*, p. 107
40. Max Plowman was similarly disappointed by his installation into the West Yorkshire Regiment. He expected 'due ceremony' but there was none; the Adjutant did not appear and Plowman was simply told to report to his company commander by a 'sallow-faced cadaverous-looking young man on a horse'. To make matters worse, on Plowman's first encounter with the C.O. the latter complained about the battalion's 'damnable' discipline. Plowman lamented: 'Why should we be cursed by a man who has never set eyes on us? We are volunteers; most of us joined in '14 and our prospects of dying for our grateful country are the brightest in the world ... I am stung

with resentment.' See Max Plowman, *A Subaltern on the Somme*, pp. 16–21. Plowman eventually sought to be relieved of his commission on grounds of conscientious objection to the war and was dismissed from the Army.

41. Rowland Feilding, *War Letters to a Wife*, p. 13. Clive Percy was killed in action on 5 April 1918, and the Hon. Henry Feilding died of wounds on 11 October 1917. Rowland and Rollo both survived the War.
42. Hitchcock, p. 37
43. Chapman, p. 65
44. J. Cohen, IWM
45. Cohen, IWM
46. Laurence Housman (ed.), *War Letters of Fallen Englishmen*, p. 60
47. Martin, p. 47
48. Quoted in Max Arthur, *Forgotten Voices of the Great War*, p. 241
49. Leslie Hill, IWM
50. Rogerson, p. 5
51. Alec Waugh, *The Early Years of Alec Waugh*, p. 103
52. Rupert Hart-Davis (ed.), *Siegfried Sassoon Diaries, 1915–1918*, p. 51
53. Gillespie, p. 306
54. Martin, p. 50
55. Donald Kenworthy diary, Cheltenham College
56. C.B. Purdom, *Everyman at War*, p. 27
57. Vaughan, p. 17
58. Stewart, p. 156
59. Stewart, p. 157
60. Fletcher, p. 56
61. Fletcher, p. 70–71
62. Cohen, IWM
63. Cloete, p. 216
64. Morgan Watcyn-Williams, *From Khaki to Cloth*, p. 22
65. Greenwell, p. 35
66. Fletcher, p. 72
67. Fletcher, p. 72
68. Martin, p. 48
69. Housman, p. 30
70. Crouch, p. 47
71. Crouch, p.105

Chapter IV: Trench World

1. Graves, *Goodbye*, p. 86
2. Kenworthy, Cheltenham College
3. Quoted in *Hot Blood and Cold Steel*, Andy Simpson (ed.), p. 36. The sheer amount of work in the trenches drove Second Lieutenant Robert Hamilton, London Regiment, to pen an ironic song, 'Toiling in the Trenches', which proved 'a great hit' with his fellow officers. The first verse ran: 'There are lots of occupations from the thoughts from which I shirk/But firing-lines in trenches are the outside edge, I think/Although I'm not the fellow who is overkeen to shirk/Still I wish some other chap would pinch my bit of work.'
4. Rogerson, p. 47
5. Douie, p. 124
6. Eden, p. 83
7. Vaughan, p. 36
8. Trevenen, Cheltenham College
9. Housman, p. 219
10. Eric Marchant, IWM
11. Bishop and Bostridge, p. 93
12. Housman, p. 186
13. Douie, p. 42
14. Macmillan, p. 100
15. Philip Brown, IWM
16. Durham County Records office, http:keystothepast.info/record office/usp.nsf
17. Housman, p. 30
18. Bell, p. 213
19. Marie Leighton, *Boy of My Heart*, p. 16
20. Quoted in Brian MacArthur (ed.), *For King and Country*, pp. 247–8
21. John Laffin (ed.), *Letters from the Front*, p. 5
22. E.B. Osborn, *The New Elizabethans*, p. 209
23. Chapman, p. 222
24. See H. Hesketh-Prichard, *Sniping in France*, passim
25. Nicholas Mosley, *Julian Grenfell: His Life and the Times of his Death 1888–1915*, pp. 241–3

26. Mosley, p. 243
27. Mosley, p. 107
28. Crouch p. 43
29. Crouch, p. 44
30. Stuart Cloete, to his pleasure, was appointed battalion sniping officer: 'I enjoyed sniping. I was on my own, which I have always liked, responsible only to the Colonel and the Brigadier.' See Cloete, pp. 220–2.
31. Brittain, p. 236
32. Blunden, *Undertones of War*, p. 79
33. Quoted in Malcolm Brown, *The Imperial War Museum Book of the Western Front*, p. 53
34. Glubb, p. 49
35. Eden, p. 76
36. Eden, p. 81
37. Fletcher, p. 32
38. Graves, *Goodbye*, p. 110
39. Graves, *Goodbye*, p. 111
40. Graves, *Goodbye*, p. 111
41. Graves, *Goodbye*, p. 112
42. Blunden, *Undertones*, p. 195
43. Stewart, p. 40
44. Gillespie, p. 252
45. Housman, p. 46
46. Vaughan, p. 141
47. Vaughan, p. 153
48. Eden, p. 77
49. Douie, p. 131
50. Eden, p. 90
51. Hart-Davis, p. 65
52. G.D. Sheffield (ed.), *War on the Western Front*, p. 233
53. Carrington, p. 94
54. Housman, p. 282
55. Laffin, p. 47
56. Stewart, p. 81
57. Hitchcock, p. 152
58. Mosley, p. 119
59. Greenwell, p. 63
60. Douie, pp. 173–4
61. Housman, p. 286
62. Housman, p. 295
63. Pamela Glenconner, *Edward Wyndham Tennant: A Memoir*, p. 147
64. West, p. 128
65. John Christie, Eton College
66. Hitchcock, p. 68
67. Graves, *Goodbye*, p. 136
68. Rogerson, p. 29
69. Rogerson, p. 88
70. Fletcher, p. 57
71. Greenwell, p. 141
72. Greenwell, p.72
73. Housman, p. 269
74. Cloete, p. 230
75. Housman, p. 310
76. Hitchcock, p. 119
77. Crouch, p. 79
78. Gillespie, p. 253
79. Cloete, pp. 250–1
80. Vaughan, p. 140
81. Graves, *Goodbye*, p. 160
82. Chapman, p. 29
83. Chapman, p. 114
84. Hitchcock, p. 197
85. Stewart, p. 61
86. Housman, p. 40
87. Talbot Kelly, p. 47
88. Durham County Records office, http:keystothepast.info/record office/usp.nsf
89. Chapman, p. 107
90. Cloete, p. 231
91. Waugh, p. 132
92. Eden, p. 80
93. Hitchcock, p. 194
94. Chapman, p. 197
95. This is the figure assembled by the School in June 1919; the accepted figure for Cheltonian dead in the war is now 675.
96. Quoted in Arthur, p. 218
97. Greenwell, p. 130
98. Dunn, p. 312
99. Rogerson, p. 65
100. Quoted in Holmes, p. 321
101. Martin, p. 79
102. Graves, p. 115
103. Greenwell, p. 157
104. Quoted in Holmes, p. 325
105. Gillespie, p. 30
106. John Reith, *Wearing Spurs*, p. 129
107. Greenwell, p. 64
108. Greenwell, p. 27
109. Greenwell, p. 82

110. Durham County Records office, http:keystothepast.info/record office/usp.nsf
111. Glubb, p. 180
112. Rogerson, p. 50
113. Graves, p. 144
114. Stewart, p. 37
115. West p. 130
116. Vaughan, p. 222
117. Mallow, the bombing-officer in Max Plowman's company, was another confirmed believer in the amber nectar; his stock phrase as he reached for the bottle – which was often – was 'This war will be won on whisky or it won't be won at all.'
118. Chapman, pp. 202–3
119. Glubb, p. 91
120. Cloete, p. 217
121. Cloete, p. 218
122. Blunden, *Undertones*, p. 136
123. Chapman, p. 89
124. Greenwell, p. 147
125. Quoted in Anne Powell (ed.), *The Fierce Light*, p. 192
126. Fletcher, p. 63
127. Rogerson, p. 27
128. Rogerson, p. 63
129. Crouch, p. 61
130. Eden, p. 125
131. Douie, p. 130
132. Hart-Davis, p. 271
133. Garth, p. 186
134. Bishop and Bostridge, p. 135
135. Eden, p. 122
136. West, p. 131
137. Bickersteth, p. 216
138. Talbot Kelly, p. 76
139. Hart-Davis, p. 77
140. Malcolm Brown (intro.), *The Wipers Times* p. 194
141. Gillespie, p.147
142. Martin, p. 73
143. Stewart, p. 45
144. Charles Carrington, 'Some Soldiers', in Panichas, *Promise of Greatness*, p. 162
145. Vaughan, p. 139
146. Gillespie, p. 81
147. Plowman, p. 45
148. Greenwell, p. 95
149. Sassoon kept an assiduous birding diary in Judea; see Hart-Davis, pp. 233–4
150. Dawson, p. 65
151. Housman, p. 296
152. Talbot Kelly, p. 74
153. Laffin, p. 70
154. Housman, p. 154
155. Mosley, p. 252
156. Gillespie, pp. 132–3
157. R.C. Sherriff, *Journey's End*, p. 38
158. E.B. Osborn, *The Muse in Arms*, p. 64
159. Vivien Noakes, *Voices of Silence*, p. 83
160. Housman, p. 263
161. Vaughan, p. 107
162. *Eton College Chronicle*, 13 May 1915

Chapter V: To Serve Them All My Days

1. Sheffield, *Leadership*, p. 81. The phenomenon of paternalism in the Army is explored throughout Sheffield's book, but see esp. pp. 1–7.
2. See Sheffield, *Leadership*, pp. 186–7
3. Chapman, p. 217
4. Crouch, p. 79
5. *Eton College Chronicle*, November 19 1914
6. Hart-Davis, p. 261
7. Housman, pp. 240–1
8. Rogerson, pp. 87–8
9. Jones, p. 86
10. *Eton College Chronicle*, October 12 1916
11. *The Cheltonian*, September 1915
12. Quoted in Trevor Royle (ed.), *In Flanders Fields: Scottish Prose and Poetry of the First World War*, p. 79
13. Housman, p. 116
14. Housman, p. 168
15. Donald Hankey, *A Student in Arms*, pp. 43–4
16. Housman, p. 56
17. Quoted in Sheffield, *Leadership*, p. 130
18. Vaughan, p. 59
19. George Coppard, *With a Machine Gun to Cambrai*, p. 27
20. Vaughan, p. 179
21. Douie, p. 196

22. Quoted in Holmes, p. 574
23. Approximately one in six VCs of the Great War were awarded to Other Ranks for their bravery in saving or attempting to save officers.
24. Hart-Davis, pp. 256–7
25. Quoted in Arthur, p. 185
26. Glubb, p. 189
27. Hitchcock, p. 56
28. Rogerson, p. 14
29. Vaughan, p. 199
30. Bickersteth, p. 29
31. Douie, p. 72
32. Hitchcock, p. 89
33. Oliver Lodge, *Christopher, A Study in Human Personality*, p. 281
34. Graves, p. 147
35. Talbot Kelly, p. 23
36. Osborn, *New Elizabethans*, p. 143
37. Blunden, *Undertones*, p. 147
38. Housman, p. 56
39. Stephen Barker and Christopher Boardman, *Lancashire's Forgotten Heroes*, p. 144
40. Denis Barnett, *In Loving Memory*, p. 43
41. Vaughan, p. 71
42. Cloete, pp. 228–9
43. Quoted in Sheffield, *Leadership*, pp. 86–87
44. Noakes, pp. 308–9
45. Greenwell, p. 162
46. Vaughan, p. 153
47. Graves, *Goodbye*, p. 146
48. Edward Thomas, *The Childhood of Edward Thomas*, p. 212
49. Glubb, p. 112
50. Glubb, p. 111
51. Greenwell, p. 144
52. Sheffield, *Leadership*, p. 99
53. Chapman, p. 39
54. Greenwell, p. 132
55. Housman, p. 67
56. Rogerson, p. 8
57. Chapman, p. 209
58. Crouch, p. 44
59. Mosley, p. 246
60. Greenwell, p. 107
61. 2007 figure derived from 'Church attendance falls for fifth year in row',

Riazat Batt, *Guardian*, 22 January 2010
62. See Michael Snape, *God and the British Soldier*, pp. 20–25
63. John Baynes, *Morale*, p. 17
64. Housman, p. 67
65. Talbot Kelly, p. 23
66. Hankey, p. 127
67. Laffin, p. 82
68. Glubb, p. 87
69. Pound, p. 38
70. See W. Alister Williams, *Heart of a Dragon*, pp. 146–9
71. Laffin, p. 35
72. The term is Snapes'. See *God and the British Soldier*, passim.
73. Vaughan, p. 91
74. Snape, p. 148
75. Quoted in Snape, p. 150
76. Hankey, pp. 60–3
77. Bickersteth, p. xi
78. Chapman, p. 117
79. Bickersteth, p. 145
80. Bickersteth, p. 225
81. Douie, pp. 54–5
82. Bickersteth, p. 169
83. Noakes, p. 427
84. Laffin, p. 67

Chapter VI: Over the Top

1. Hart-Davis, p. 261
2. Parker, p. 214
3. Dundas, p. 99
4. In total 37,484 officers killed, 635,891 other ranks; this is, 15.2 per cent serving officers, 12.8 serving men.
5. Pound, p. 205
6. Bickersteth, p. 140
7. Hitchcock, p. 258. Altogether 85 per cent of army officers survived the war (although not necessarily intact). Aside from measures taken by the army from 1916 to preserve the life – and thus the usefulness of subalterns – theatres outside Europe were decidedly less hazardous.
8. E.B Osborn, *The Muse in Arms*, p. 22
9. Macmillan, p. 70
10. Douie, p. 164
11. Eden, p. 95

12. Eden, p. 98
13. Chapman, p. 126
14. Martin, p. 85
15. Housman, p. 276
16. Macmillan, pp. 67–8
17. 'Your love for me and my love for you have made my whole life one of the happiest there has ever been.'
18. Vaughan, p. 193
19. Macmillan, p. 80
20. Housman, p. 107
21. Gillespie, pp. 311–13
22. J. Coull, IWM
23. Housman, p. 197
24. Bishop and Bostridge, p. 281
25. Bishop and Bostridge, pp. 235–6
26. Hanbury-Sparrow, *The Land-locked Lake*, p. 19
27. Charles Carrington (aka 'Charles Edmunds'), *A Subaltern's War*, p. 35
28. Chapman, p. 85
29. Vaughan, p. 193
30. Quoted in Snape, p. 34
31. Frank Warren, *Honour Satisfied*, p. 57
32. Vaughan, p. 193
33. Macmillan, p. 72
34. Macmillan, p. 74
35. Macmillan, p. 74
36. Quoted in Holmes, p. 255
37. Quoted in MacArthur, pp. 313–14
38. Housman, p. 28
39. Blunden, *Undertones*, p. 198
40. E.B. Osborn, *Muse in Arms*, pp. 59–62. The title of Nichols' poem is 'The Assault'.
41. Stewart, p. 217
42. Stewart, p. 108
43. Chapman, p. 108
44. Stewart, p. 217
45. Laffin, p. 46
46. Cloete, pp. 234–5
47. Eden, p. 138
48. Housman, p. 305
49. Housman, p. 296
50. Housman, p. 286
51. Quoted in Sheffield, *Leadership*, pp. 115–16
52. Cloete, p. 235
53. Graves, p. 152
54. See Holmes, passim
55. Eden, p. 92
56. J.R. Ackerley, *My Father and Myself*, p. 97
57. Quoted in Powell, p. 7
58. Vaughan, p. 196
59. Bell, p. 243
60. Stewart, p. 220
61. See Arthur, p. 154
62. Sheffield, *Leadership*, p. 147
63. Frank Richards, *Old Soldiers Never Die*, p. 87
64. Macmillan, p. 90
65. Housman, p. 313
66. Cloete, p. 231
67. *London Gazette*, 22 May 1918
68. Vaughan, p. 225
69. Housman, pp. 280–1
70. F. Crozier, *The Men I Killed*, pp. 71–2
71. Cloete, p. 229
72. Greenwell, pp. 172–3
73. Warren, p. 107
74. Graves, p. 133
75. Brown, *Imperial War Museum Book of the Western Front*, p. 64
76. Cloete, pp. 212–13
77. John Christie, Eton College
78. Housman, p. 315
79. Macmillan, p. 88
80. Cloete, p. 231
81. Sheffield, *Leadership*, p. 133
82. Housman, p. 317
83. Carrington, *Soldier from the Wars Returning*, p. 195
84. Housman, p. 281
85. Quoted in James Hayward, *Myths and Legends of the First World War*, p. 73
86. Vaughan, p. 229
87. Martin, p. 91
88. Greenwell, p. 175
89. Vaughan, p. 214
90. Housman, p. 171–2
91. Quoted in MacArthur, pp. 230–2
92. Dundas, p. 88
93. West, p. 110
94. West, p. 147
95. Bickersteth, p. 172
96. Dunn, p. 372
97. See Sheffield, *Leadership*, p. 181

98. Dundas, p. 177
99. Brown, *Imperial War Museum Book of the Western Front*, pp. 272–3
100. Housman, p. 271
101. Jones, p. 253
102. Chapman, p. 226
103. Housman, p. 57
104. Macmillan, p. 99
105. Bill Bland, Imperial War Museum
106. See *Fire-Eater* by A.O. Pollard, passim
107. Rogerson, p. 163
108. Gillespie, p. 138
109. Quoted in Holmes, p. 51
110. Norman Taylor, Imperial War Museum
111. Housman, p. 84
112. Quoted in MacArthur, p. 45
113. Edward Chapman, Imperial War Museum
114. Cloete, p. 250
115. Waugh, p. 92
116. Sherriff, *Journey's End*, p. 58
117. Housman, p. 283
118. Bishop and Bostridge, pp. 326–7
119. E.B. Osborn, *New Elizabethans*, p. 227
120. From 'Banishment', *Counter-Attack and Other Poems*, 1918
121. C. Nye, Oxford University, Great War Archive
122. Housman, p. 216
123. Hitchcock, p. 131
124. Ogle, pp. 202–4
125. Mellersh, p. 181
126. Quoted in Powell, p. 58

Chapter VII: It's A Long Way to Tickle Mary

1. Gillespie, pp. 214–15
2. Quoted in Holmes, p. 351
3. Eden, p. 92
4. Beith, p. 96
5. Housman, p. 269
6. Hitchcock, p. 42
7. Dunn, p. 308
8. Kenworthy, Cheltenham College
9. Gillespie, pp. 70–1
10. Douie, p. 63
11. The lines from 'The Billet' are quoted in Noakes, p. 96. For Lee's status as a spanner in the popular paradigm of the war poets as always 'progressing' from idealism to disillusionment see Elizabeth Vandiver, *Stand in the Trench, Achilles*, 2010.
12. Hitchcock, p. 87
13. Chapman, p. 45
14. Chapman, p. 110
15. Housman, p. 289
16. Douie, p. 118
17. Rogerson, p. 97
18. Chapman, p. 214
19. Fletcher, p. 68
20. Fletcher, p. 72
21. Housman, p. 271
22. Hitchcock, p. 85
23. Quoted in Noakes, pp. 94–5. Charles Scott-Moncrieff was commissioned into the King's Own Scottish Borderers in August 1914. He won an MC in 1917.
24. Rogerson, p. 103
25. Greenwell, p. 44
26. Talbot Kelly, p. 104
27. Rogerson, p. 116
28. Fletcher, p. 98
29. Douie, p. 83
30. Vaughan, p. 100
31. Greenwell, p. 121
32. Graves, pp. 108–9
33. Graves, p. 109
34. Vaughan, p. 108
35. Greenwell, p. 83
36. Graves, p. 146
37. Hart-Davis, p. 31
38. It includes: Captain Gordon Alchin, RFA; Second Lieutenant Richard Aldington, Royal Sussex Regiment; Second Lieutenant H.B.K. Allpass, Essex Regiment/Cambridgeshire Regiment, killed in action on 15 September 1916 in the Ancre valley, the author of *Oxford, St Bees and the Front*; Second Lieutenant Martin Armstrong, 8/Middlesex Regiment, first volume of poems published in 1912; Lieutenant Herbert Asquith, RFA, son of the Prime Minister and author of *The*

Volunteer and Other Poems, Sidgwick & Jackson, 1915; Lieutenant Gilbert Bain, The Gloucestershire Regiment; Second Lieutenant Harold Beckh, East Yorkshire Regiment, author of *Swallows in Storm and Sunlight*, killed in action 14 August 1916; Lieutenant-Colonel Frederick Bendall, 3/Royal Fusiliers; Lieutenant Roland Berill, RFA; Lieutenant Edmund Blunden, Royal Sussex Regiment; Lieutenant J. Bourke; Lieutenant Archibald Bowman, 13/Highland Light Infantry, sometime Professor of Logic at Princetown; Captain Francis Brett Young, RAMC; Captain Brian Brooke, Gordon Highlanders; Sub-Lieutenant Rupert Brooke, RND; Lieutenant John Brown, RGA, invalided home with neurasthenia March 1915; Second Lieutenant Sir Michael Bruce; Lieutenant-Colonel John Buchan; Lieutenant Ivar Campbell, Argyll & Sutherland Highlanders; Second Lieutenant Alec de Candole, Wiltshire Regiment/Machine Gun Corps, author of *The Faith of a Subaltern*, killed in action 4 September 1918; Lieutenant Roland Carton, Duke of Cornwall's Light Infantry; Lieutenant A. Newberry Choyce, Leicestershire Regiment, author of *Crimson Stains: Poems of Love and War*, 1917; Major John ('Jack') Churchill, younger brother of Winston Churchill; Lieutenant Reginald F. Clements, Royal Sussex Regiment; Second Lieutenant Leonard Niell Cook MC, Royal Lancers, killed in action 7 July 1917; Second Lieutenant Gerald M. Cooper, Scots Guards; Major Weric Cooper, 3/Royal Fusiliers; Captain Joseph Courtney, RAMC; Lieutenant Eliot Crawshay-Williams, RHA, later a novelist and playwright; Captain John Crombie, Gordon Highlanders; Lieutenant J. Crommelin-Brown RGA, author of *Dies Heroica*, Hodder & Stoughton, 1918; Major

Geoffrey Crump, Essex Regiment; Captain RCG Dartford; Second Lieutenant Arthur Dawson, Indian Army; Lieutenant Geoffrey Dearmer, 2/Royal Fusiliers, died 1996, the last surviving of the Great War poets; Captain Richard Dennys, Loyal North Lancashire Regiment, died of wounds July 1916; Lieutenant F. Douss, Suffolk Regiment; Second Lieutenant Clifford Druce, Gloucestershire Regiment; Lieutenant C. Du Cann, Army Cyclists Corps; Captain George Duggan, died of wounds on 16 August 1916; Lieutenant J. Dumbrell, Royal Sussex Regiment; Captain Geoffrey Elton, 4/Hampshire Regiment, later lecturer in modern history at Queen's College, Oxford; Captain Geoffrey Faber; Captain James Fairfax, RASC; Captain M.G. Field; Second Lieutenant Ivan Firth, RFA; Lieutenant Martin Fitzgerald, Machine Gun Corps; Captain Charles Foxcroft, 2/4 Somerset Regiment, later the MP for Bath; Captain Gilbert Frankau, RFA, invalided from service February 1918; Second Lieutenant Hugh Freston, 3/Royal Berkshire Regiment, whose poetry volumes were *The Quest of Beauty* and *The Quest of Truth*, published by Blackwell, killed in action on 21 January 1916; Captain Maurice Gamon, Lancashire Fusiliers, killed in action; Lieutenant Walter Garstang, West Yorkshire Regiment; Second Lieutenant Crosbie Garstin, commissioned in the field into King Edward's Horse; Lieutenant Edward John Garston, The Middlesex Regiment; Lieutenant-Colonel Rowland Gibson, Royal Fusiliers; Wilfrid Gibson, RASC; Captain Ronald Gorrell Barnes, 7/Rifle Brigade, founder of the Royal Army Education Corps; Captain H.S. Graham, RET; Captain Robert Graves, Royal Welch Fusiliers; Second Lieutenant J.D. Greenway, Rifle Brigade; Captain

Julian Grenfell, Royal Dragoons, died of wounds 30 April 1915; Captain Llewelyn Wyn Griffith, Royal Welch Fusiliers; Second Lieutenant Wilfrid Halliday, West Yorkshire Regiment; Lieutenant Clive Hamilton (aka George Lewis), Somerset Light Infantry; Lieutenant William Hamilton, Machine Gun Corps, author of *Modern Poems*; Lieutenant F.W. Harvey DCM, Gloucestershire Regiment; Lieutenant Henry Harwood; Digby Haseler, King's Shropshire Light Infantry, and author of *Verses from France to the Family*, 1918; Lieutenant Alan Herbert, RND (Hawke Battalion), later an MP and writer; Captain The Hon. Aubrey Herbert, Irish Guards, who was one of the inspirations for Buchan's *Greenmantle*; Lieutenant Raymond Heywood, Devonshire Regiment; Second Lieutenant Brian Hill; Lieutenant-Colonel Edward Hoare, The King's Own (Royal Lancaster) Regiment; Lieutenant William Noel Hodgson MC, Devonshire Regiment, author of *Verse & Prose in War*, killed on the opening day of the Somme; Captain William Kersley Holmes, RFA; Captain Cyril Morton Home, King's Own Scottish Borderers; Captain Cyril Horne, King's Own Scottish Borderers, killed in action 27 January 1916; Lieutenant Geoffrey Howard, Royal Fusiliers; Ford Maddox Hueffer, Welch Regiment, later to change his surname to Ford, and already a well-known writer when commissioned in 1915 at the age of forty-one; Second Lieutenant Dyneley Hussey, Lancashire Fusiliers; Lieutenant A.L. Jenkins, Duke of Cornwall's Light Infantry; Lieutenant Donald Johnson, The Manchester Regiment, the winner of the Chancellor's Medal for English Verse at Cambridge University, killed on 15 July 1916 at the Somme; Second

Lieutenant D.T. Jones, Machine Gun Corps; Lieutenant Wilfred Joseph, West Yorkshire Regiment; Second Lieutenant Roderick Watson Kerr MC, Tank Corps, leader writer for *The Scotsman*; Lieutenant Thomas Michael Kettle, Royal Dublin Fusiliers, Irish statesman, killed in action at Givenchy on 9 September 1916; Lieutenant Edward Knox, wounded at Passchendaele, later the editor of *Punch;* Major H.G. Lang, author of *Simple Lyrics*, 1917; Second Lieutenant Joseph Lee, King's Royal Rifle Corps (60th Rifles); Lieutenant Roland Leighton, Worcestershire Regiment, died of wounds 23 December 1915; Lieutenant Sivori Levey, 13/West Yorkshire Regiment; Lieutenant John Lodge, Bedfordshire Regiment; Lieutenant P.H.B. Lyon, Durham Light Infantry; Lieutenant Walter Lyon, Royal Scots, killed on 8 May 1916 at Potijze Wood, Ypres; Lieutenant D.O. Lumley, author of *Songs of a Subaltern*; Second Lieutenant Ian Mackenzie, Highland Light Infantry; Lieutenant Ewart Alan Mackintosh MC, Seaforth Highlanders, died of wounds 24 July 1917; Captain John Macleod, Cameron Highlanders; Second Lieutenant S.B. Macleod; Second Lieutenant Murray McClymont; Second Lieutenant Hamish Mann, 8/The Black Watch (Royal Highlanders), died on 10 April 1917 of wounds received during the Battle of Arras, whose *A Subaltern's Musings* was published posthumously by John Long in 1918; Lieutenant H.G. Mansfield, Essex Regiment; Captain John Mason, Royal Scots; John Masefield MC, North Staffordshire Regiment, the cousin of the poet laureate, died of wounds on 2 July 1915; Lieutenant Ernest Melville, Argyll & Sutherland Highlanders; Lieutenant Alan Milne, Royal Warwickshire Regiment, later author of *Winnie-the-Pooh*; Charles Montague, Royal

Fusiliers, born in 1867, and already well know as an author before the conflict; Lieutenant Francis Morris, Sherwood Foresters; Ralph Mottram; Robert Nichols, RFA, author of *Ardours and Endurances*, Chatto & Windus, 1917, invalided home with shellshock August 1916; Captain Henry Ogle MC, Royal Lancaster Regiment; Captain Wilfred Owen MC, Manchester Regiment; Lieutenant Nowell Oxland, 6/Border Regiment, killed in action 9 August 1915; Captain The Hon. Robert Palmer, died of wounds 21 January 1916; Second Lieutenant Harold Parry, King's Royal Rifle Corps, killed by shellfire at Ypres on 6 May 1917; Vivian Pemberton MC, Royal Munster Fusiliers, whose *Reflections in Verse* was published posthumously after his death on 7 October, 1918; Captain Claude Penrose, RGA; Lieutenant Victor Perowne, Scots Guards; Captain The Hon. Colwyn Philipps, Royal Horse Guards, the author of *Verse: Prose Fragments: Letters from the Front*, 1916, killed in action on 13 May 1915 during second Battle of Ypres; Second Lieutenant Max Plowman, West Yorkshire Regiment; Second Lieutenant John Boynton Priestley, Duke of Wellington's Regiment, gassed and invalided out of active service, transferred to Entertainments Section, and later a popular playwright; Lieutenant A. Victor Ratcliffe, West Yorkshire Regiment, killed in action; Herbert Read DSO MC, Yorkshire Regiment, author of *Naked Warriors*; Captain George V Robbins, East Yorkshire Regiment, killed in action May 1915; Captain J.M. Rose-Troup, Queen's Regiment; Major Owen Rutter ('Klip Klip'), Wiltshire Regiment; Francis St Vincent Mawr; Captain Siegfried Sassoon MC, Royal Welch Fusiliers; Second Lieutenant KM Scobie, RGA; Captain Charles Scott-Moncrieff MC, King's Own

Scottish Borderers, later renowned as a translator of Proust; Major William Shakespeare, RAMC; Second Lieutenant Edward Shanks, 8/South Lancashire Regiment, invalided out of the service in 1915; Lt-Commander Patrick Shaw-Stewart, RND, killed in action 30 December 1917; William Short, RFA, killed in action 21 June 1917; Lieutenant Henry Simpson, Lancashire Fusiliers, killed by a sniper's bullet on 29 August 1918 near Hazebrouck; Captain Osbert Sitwell, Grenadier Guards; Lieutenant G.B. Smith, Lancashire Fusiliers; Captain Charles Hamilton Sorley, Suffolk Regiment, shot in the head by a sniper at Loos, 13 October 1915, his poems found amongst his kit; Major Sir Edward de Stein, Machine Gun Corps/King's Royal Rifle Corps; Lieutenant Robert Sterling, Royal Scots Fusiliers, winner of the Newdigate Prize at Cambridge for 'The Burial of Sophocles', killed in action on St George's Day 1915; Captain J.E. Stewart MC, Border Regiment/South Staffordshire Regiment, killed near Kemmel, 26 April 1918, author of *Grapes of Thorns*, 1917; Lieutenant John Still, East Yorkshire Regiment, author of *Poems in Captivity*, 1919; Padre G.A. Studdert Kennedy (nicknamed 'Woodbine Willie' for his habit of handing out cigarettes to the troops), author of *Rough Rhymes of a Padre*; Captain R.B. Talbot Kelly MC, RFA; Captain Claude Templer, Gloucestershire Regiment; Captain W.F. Templeton, Royal Scots Fusiliers; Lieutenant The Hon. Edward ('Bim') Tennant, Grenadier Guards, who went to France at eighteen, despite a brigade order that no one under nineteen should serve in the trenches, and killed by a sniper on 22 September 1916; Captain E.C. Thomas; Lieutenant Edward Thomas, Royal Garrison Artillery, killed near

Arras on 9 April 1917; Chaplain Edward Thompson; Second Lieutenant J.R.R. Tolkien, Lancashire Fusiliers; Second Lieutenant Albert Tomlinson, South Staffordshire Regiment; Second Lieutenant Robert Vernede, The Rifle Brigade; Captain M.K. Wardle, Leicestershire Regiment; Second Lieutenant Gilbert Waterhouse, 2/Essex Regiment, author of *Rail-Head* and other poems, killed on opening day of the Somme; Chaplain Lauclan Watt; Lieutenant Alexander Waugh, Dorset Regiment; Lieutenant Willoughby Weaving, Royal Irish Rifles, author of *The Bubble, and other poems*, Oxford, 1917; Arthur Graeme West, Oxfordshire and Buckinghamshire Light Infantry killed 3 April 1917; Lieutenant Bernard White, Northumberland Fusiliers; Captain Eric F. Wilkinson, MC, 8/West Yorkshire Regiment, killed in action at Passchendaele on 9 October 1917; Lieutenant Walter Lightowler Wilkinson, 8/Argyll & Sutherland Highlanders; Lieutenant Llewellyn Williams, RE; Captain T.P.C. Wilson, 10/Sherwood Foresters, Staff Captain 51st Brigade, killed on 23 March 1918, author of *Magpies in Picardy*, The Poetry Bookshop, 1919; Lieutenant Cyril W. Winterbotham, Gloucestershire Regiment, killed in action 27 August 1916; Lieutenant Ernest Armine Wodehouse, author of *On Leave: Poems and Sonnets*, Elkin Mathews, 1917, brother of P.G. Wodehouse and winner of the Newdigate Prize in 1902; Second Lieutenant James Yates, Royal West Kent Regiment; Lieutenant Edward Hilton Young, RNVR, served with the naval guns in Flanders.

39. Chapman, p. 25
40. Greenwell, p. 44
41. Douie, p. 83
42. Graves, p. 101
43. Graves, p. 100
44. Vaughan, p. 90
45. Vaughan pp. 109–10
46. E.B. Osborn, *Muse in Arms*, pp. 9–11
47. Macmillan, pp. 69–70
48. Chapman, p. 120
49. Rogerson, p. 145
50. Rogerson, p. 148
51. Glubb, p. 104
52. Stewart, p. 53
53. Bishop and Bostridge, p. 196
54. Hitchcock, p. 86
55. Chapman, pp. 212–13
56. Stewart, p. 129
57. Bickersteth, p. 207
58. Bickersteth, p. 207
59. Housman, p. 22
60. Mosley, p. 246
61. Thomas, p. 198
62. Dunn, p. 365
63. Durham County Records office, http:keystothepast.info/record office/usp.nsf
64. Stewart, p. 53
65. Cloete, p. 257
66. Graves, p. 104
67. Chapman, p. 17
68. Wheatley, p. 152
69. Hart-Davis, p. 148
70. Graves, p. 195
71. Quoted in Arthur, p. 259
72. Carrington, *Soldier from the Wars Returning*, p. 162
73. Cloete, p. 200
74. 'Some queer goings on in the trenches', A.D. Harvey, *New Statesman*, 15 January 1999
75. 'Some queer goings on', Harvey, *New Statesman*
76. Hitchcock, p. 113
77. Fletcher, p. 68
78. Chapman, pp. 81–2
79. Greenwell, p. 106
80. Martin, p. 66
81. Cloete, p. 215
82. Chapman, p. 84
83. Martin, p. 131
84. Brown, *Western Front*, p. 248
85. Bickersteth, p. 180
86. Glubb, pp. 162–3

87. Gillespie, p. 154
88. Greenwell, p. 206
89. Vaughan, p. 99
90. Chapman, p. 206
91. Blunden, *Undertones*, p. 207
92. Talbot Kelly, pp. 130–1
93. Housman, p. 133
94. Chapman, p. 63
95. Chapman, p. 82
96. Graves, p. 120
97. Quoted in Noakes, p. 259; the lines are from Wilson's poem 'On leave (2)'.
98. Quoted in Arthur, p. 200
99. Martin, p. 112
100. Carrington, p. 219
101. Stewart, p. 148
102. Bishop and Bostridge, p. 243
103. Bishop and Bostridge, p. 281
104. Graves, p. 196
105. Frank Crozier, *The Men I Killed*, p. 44
106. Chapman, p. 265
107. Mosley, p. 252
108. Robert Mackay, www.firstworldwar.com/diaries/rlm.htal
109. F.W. Mellish MC, Imperial War Museum. Mellish had to be persuaded to take a commission, and felt guilty about leaving his comrades, as if he was 'letting the side down'. Still, he discovered a pleasant wind-up pleasure in being a subaltern; he outranked his elder brother, who was a mere officer cadet. Mellish took to visiting the latter in his barracks at Farnborough. Military protocol required the elder brother to stand and salute. After a decently long time, Mellish would graciously tell his brother to 'Stand at ease'. Following the War Mellish played rugby for both England and South Africa.

Chapter VIII: We Are the Dead

1. Rogerson, p. 43
2. Blunden, *Undertone*s, p. 122
3. Hitchcock, p. 77
4. Douie, p. 84
5. Graves, p. 112. To take a German's life he would run a 1 in 5 risk; to save a German's life he would take a 1 in 20 risk.
6. Chapman, p. 83
7. Graves, pp. 161–2
8. Graves, p. 164
9. Talbot Kelly, p. 103
10. Chapman, p. 108
11. Laffin, p. 47
12. Eden, p. 111
13. Basil Willey, 'A Schoolboy in the War', in Panichas, *Promise of Greatness*, p. 328
14. Hitchcock, p. 56
15. Mosley, p. 206
16. In all probability, means of death were not consistent over the course of the war. An officer was more likely to suffer a death courtesy of a bullet in 1914–15 than in 1917.
17. *The Cheltonian*, March 1915
18. Wheatley, p. 142
19. Chapman, p. 191
20. Hanbury-Sparrow, pp. 309–10
21. Martin, pp. 55–6
22. Reith, p. 189
23. Quoted in Powell, p. 11
24. Macmillan, p. 87
25. Macmillan, p. 88
26. Quoted in Powell, p. 11
27. Warren, p. 108
28. Cloete, p. 242
29. Hitchcock, p. 77
30. Glubb, p. 187
31. Fletcher, p. 114
32. Fletcher, p. 115
33. Glubb, p. 191
34. Cloete, p. 251
35. Quoted in Holmes, p. 480
36. Cloete, p. 257
37. Quoted in Noakes, pp. 225–7. The title of the poem is 'The Road That Brought Me to Roehampton'.
38. Ackerley, p. 128
39. C. Nye, Oxford University
40. Glubb, p. 195
41. Quoted in Lawrence James, *Warrior Race*, p. 489
42. Graves, p. 144
43. Carrington (as Edmunds), *A Subaltern's War*, p. 98

44. Martin, p. 141
45. C.B. Purdom, p. 180
46. Quoted in Noakes, p. 95
47. Cloete, p. 252
48. Wyn Griffith, *Up to Mametz*, p. 113
49. Glubb, p. 175
50. Pound, p. 226
51. Leighton, pp. 220–1
52. Eden, p. 177
53. Crouch, pp. 140–2
54. Housman, p. 40
55. Graves, p. 161
56. Bishop and Bostridge, pp. 182–3
57. Laffin, p. 69
58. Chapman, p. 180
59. Horrocks, pp. 17–18
60. Horrocks, pp. 18–19
61. Waugh, p. 134
62. H. Rutherford, Imperial War Museum. Rutherford was captured on 23 March 1918. Of the approximately 170,000 British servicemen taken prisoner on the Western Front, some 65,000 were captured between 21 March and 5 April 1918, the initial stage of the German 'Michael' Offensive.
63. Waugh, p. 131
64. N.E. Tyndale-Biscoe., Imperial War Museum

Chapter IX: Last Post

1. Hitchcock, p. 313
2. Brown, *Western Front*, p. 198
3. Chapman, p. 273
4. Bickersteth, p. 298
5. Glubb, p. 219. Frank Mellish, another gunner, was equally dismayed by the Armistice. He: 'felt as if I had been slapped in the face with the largest and wettest fish ever. I just could not believe that after four years ... there should be no retribution and that our cunning, fierce and ruthless enemy should be allowed to pack up his souvenirs and go back to his practically untouched and unblemished homeland.'
6. Dunn, p. 524
7. Douie, p. 16
8. Ogle, p. 202
9. Graves, p. 228
10. Owen was killed in action on 4 November 1918 during the Battle of the Sambre. His mother received the War Office telegram announcing his death as the church bells in town were pealing to celebrate the signing of the Armistice.
11. Quoted in Holmes, pp. 616–17
12. Hart-Davis, p. 268
13. Willey, p. 329
14. Graham Seton Hutchison, *Warrior*, p. 314
15. Douie, p. 219
16. Chapman, p. 280
17. Carrington, p. 243
18. Greenwell, p. 249
19. J.B Priestley, *Margin Released*, pp. 136–7
20. Douie, pp. 18–19
21. Coppard, p. 218
22. Quoted in Noakes, pp. 371–2
23. The largest occupational groups of officers were 'Commercial and clerical,' comprising 27% of the total commissioned men, followed by 'Students and teachers,' 18%, and 'professional men,' 15%. A student/teacher and a professional man were unambiguously middle class, while 'commercial and clerical' would have included men from both the middle and upper working class.
24. Mellersh, p.188. Likewise Alfred Pollard VC, MC and DCM was not enticed by an office job: 'I could of course have gone back to my stool with the Alliance Company but after four and half years of open-air life the prospect did not appeal.'
25. Pound, p. 217
26. Martin, pp. 40–1
27. Garth, pp. 94–5
28. Quoted in Noakes, p. 368
29. Eden, p. 81
30. Macmillan, pp. 98–9
31. Bishop and Bostridge, pp. 296–7
32. Douie, p. 151
33. Glubb, p. 223

34. The flu pandemic killed as much as 3 per cent of the world's population.
35. See Winter, *The Great War and the British People* passim
36. *The Cheltonian*, March 1918
37. *The Cheltonian*, March 1918
38. *Eton College Chronicle*, November 14, 1918
39. Priestley, pp. 132–3
40. Cannadine, p. 81
41. See Winter, pp. 98–9
42. Winter, pp. 98–9
43. Cannadine, p. 87
44. Waugh, p. 93
45. Quoted in Winter, p. 300
46. Cloete, p. 317
47. Aldington, p. 177
48. Macmillan, p. 98
49. Edmund Blunden, *The Shepherd, and other poems of Peace and War*, 1922
50. Douie, p. 4

Index